STANDARD CATALOG OF

SMITH & WESSON

Jim Supica and
Richard Nahas

Published by

700 E. State Street • Iola, WI 54990-0001
Telephone: 715/445-2214

Please call or write for our free catalog of firearms/knives publications.
Our toll-free number to place an order or obtain a free catalog is 800-258-0929 or please use our regular business telephone 715-445-2214 for editorial comment and further information.

Library of Congress Catalog Number: 96-75277
ISBN: 0-87341-404-7
Printed in the United States of America

DEDICATION

Krause Publications contacted me a year ago and said they were interested in putting out a book dedicated to Smith & Wessons. They asked if I would be willing to write it. I was excited that they would choose my favorite guns for this unique venture—an identification and price guide dedicated to the products of a single manufacturer. I was also flattered that they would call me, but I knew I didn't have the depth of knowledge, especially on twentieth century guns, to tackle this alone. However, I thought immediately of Rick's famous compilation.

I first saw Richard Nahas' compilation of S&W data about five years ago, and I guess my reaction was the same as nearly every other S&W enthusiast who has seen it—"Can I have a copy?" Here was an opportunity to make this gem available to other collectors and general firearms buffs.

I have added commentary, prices, and photos. Many other individuals have helped. However, the core of this book remains the data that Richard has laboriously and meticulously compiled over the past six years. For this, I thank him on behalf of collectors everywhere.

Finally, I'd like to dedicate my work on this book to the love of my life, Eve, who proved while I was working on "The Book," that not only could she run Old Town Station, but she could do it better than me; to our boys, Jamie, David, and Daniel; and to my parents for their love and encouragement, and for naming their poodles Wesson and Smith. -- Jim Supica

****

This book is dedicated to the memory of Danny Woo and to my wife, Bonnie. For her unfailing support and devotion I am more grateful than words can ever express. Thanks also for feeding me at the computer for the past six years. -- Richard Nahas

FOREWORD

Collectors, gun dealers, and gun enthusiasts have been waiting a long time for a catalog-style book that would provide an understanding of all Smith & Wesson products. The wait is over. This catalog compiled by Jim Supica and Richard Nahas offers for the first time a comprehensive pricing guide for the large quantity of S&W products. When used properly it will aid all gun buyers and sellers in receiving a fair deal.

The compilation of this data is a major project that Jim and Richard have worked very hard to complete. As historian at Smith & Wesson, I see a great need for this type of book. However, it is important to understand that in the history of firearms nothing is as cut and dry as a collector would like it to be. The serial number tables, for example, can only be used as a general reference, as the S&W factory did not produce their revolvers or pistols in chronological order by serial number. In the category of specials, many were manufactured in such small quantities that they slip by everyone's list. This book will help bring these to light.

As the collecting of S&Ws progresses, the authors will continue to add changes to this book, making it the standard pricing guide for Smith & Wesson products.

Roy G. Jinks
Smith & Wesson Historian

CONTENTS

ACKNOWLEDGMENTS

The authors have found helpful information in the books and publications listed on pages 34 and 35. In addition, we are especially grateful to the following individuals without whom this book would not exist:

John Demuth

Deborah Faupel, editor, Krause Publications

Roy Jinks, S&W factory historian and author, for his historical and technical writings of Smith & Wesson

Jon Maxwell, collector and tireless notetaker, for his contribution of collector information on the automatic pistols

Don Mundell

Robert Neal, author, for his original research and words of encouragement to continue

Col. Charles W. Pate, author, for his contribution on military handguns and original research at the National Archives

Gary Skeet

Martha Skeet

Danny Woo, armorer (deceased), for his comments and assistance in the first proofreading

We would like to offer our sincere thanks to the following individuals for their willingness to share their expertise with fellow enthusiasts by providing invaluable information, advice, and assistance for this book:

Bill Anderson
John Appleton, Appleton Assoc.
Steven Beatty
M/Sgt C.H. Benjamin, USAF Ret.
Roger Bishop
Jerry Boss
Ray Brazille
Ray Cheely
Terry Clokey
Ed Cornett
John C. Cox
Bob Coyle, Lew Horton Distributing Co., Inc.
Diamond B Guns
Cort Flint
Jerry Fountain
John Gangel
Gary Garbrecht
Blair Gluba
Larry Geartner
Joe Green
Wayne Hazelrigg
Lloyd Jackson
Ken Jorgensen, S&W
Dick Kolesar
Karl Leonhardt
Bob Lockett, The 2nd Amendment Gun Shop
George Luttrell
Ernie Lyles, Gilbert Small Arms Range, Inc.
William Maier
J. B. Mazsk
John McCabe
Harrison McConnell
Don McTiernan
Bill Molnar, The Gun Room
Bill Orr
Paul Piquette, S&W Master Engraver
W.R. Powell, Firearms Consultant
Bob Radaker
Clarence Rinke
Walter V. Roberts
Jim Sebring
Mike Stuckslager
Bruce Thompson
John Wallace
Robert Webb

Our sincere thanks to the following firms, organizations, and institutions:

Smith & Wesson, Springfield, MA

Smithsonian Museum of American History, Washington, DC

The Springfield Armory Museum, Springfield, MA, especially Steven Beatty, John McCabe, and Don McTiernan, for their contributions on military handguns

The National Archives, Washington, DC

The Connecticut Valley Historical Museum, Springfield, MA

The Smith & Wesson Collectors Association

Virginia Gun Collectors Association, for their collective comments and continued support among the vast sea of varied arms and arms collectors

Missouri Valley Arms Collectors Association

Lew Horton Distributing Co., Inc., Westboro, MA

Clark Brothers, Warrenton, VA

Professional Armaments, Inc., Murray, UT

SAFETY

Safety must be the first word in any firearms-related discourse.

There are many good safety rules for firearms. If the following are religiously adhered to, they will eliminate ninety-nine percent of tragic firearms accidents:

1. **Treat every firearm as if it were loaded.**
2. **Never allow the muzzle to point at anything you are not willing to see destroyed.**
3. **Be sure of your target and know what lies behind it.**
4. **Keep your finger off the trigger until your sights are aligned on target.**
5. **Be sure your guns are never accessible to unauthorized or untrained individuals.**

Collector Courtesy and Safety

There are special concerns for us who are gun collectors, dealers, and enthusiasts.

Primarily, we must guard against a tendency to ignore rules #1 and #2. We handle a large number of guns in situations where it is assumed the guns are unloaded—gun shops, gun shows, displays, auctions, and so on. In these instances, we consider guns as merchandise or collectibles rather than weapons. Being around hundreds or thousands of guns that are all "presumed" to be unloaded can result in mental laxness and unacceptably sloppy gun safety.

One of the authors recently liquidated at auction a five-hundred-gun collection from the estate of a knowledgeable and safety-oriented collector/dealer. Since the owner's death, the collection had been inspected and moved twice by two different gun-savvy individuals who had supposedly checked the guns to be sure they were unloaded. In the final safety check before auction, we found five loaded guns. We have also had the unsettling experience of finding loaded guns at other auction previews or gun shows.

In a field or range situation, it is an accepted and expected practice to check any gun you receive to be sure whether or not it is loaded. However, in a collector setting, this may not always be possible. On some very valuable mint condition or highly decorated arms, working the mechanism to check the loaded status runs the risk of marring the finish and significantly reducing the dollar value assigned to "new in the box, unfired, unturned" condition. This makes adherence to rules #1 and #2 even more vital.

There are some additional rules in collector situations, whether it be the world's largest gun show or a friend's gun room, that are a combination of safety and courtesy. Violation of these rules is the quickest way to prove yourself a lout and gun amateur, and to wear out your welcome:

1. **Never handle a gun without asking the owner's permission.**
2. **Never open the mechanism, dry fire, or otherwise manipulate a collectible gun without asking the owner's permission.**
3. **If you are showing your guns, triple check to be sure they are unloaded. It is a good practice to tie the guns with plastic cable ties so they are inoperative, and to be sure not to display any loose, unsealed ammunition. Well-run gun shows will require this.**
4. **Control your children. Strictly enforce the "no touch" rule.**

A Word About Semiautomatics

Most individuals who are familiar with guns know that the firing chamber of a semiautomatic pistol can be loaded even if the magazine has been removed from the gun. However, if you are only familiar with the S&W first, second, and third generation double action semiautos, you need to pay special attention when handling a new Sigma. The metal frame S&W double action semiauto pistols generally have a "magazine disconnect safety" intended to prevent the gun from being fired when the magazine has been removed. The Sigma line does not include this feature, and is designed so that the round in the chamber can be fired when the trigger is pulled even if the magazine has been removed. A basic rule is never to trust a mechanical safety device to compensate for unsafe gun handling.

Safety and Older Guns

Finally, there are additional safety concerns in dealing with older guns. It is important to remember that a lot can happen to a gun over decades of use and abuse, and it's always a good idea to have a competent professional gunsmith check out an older gun for safe functioning before even thinking about shooting it. Always be certain that you are using the correct ammunition for a gun, and that the gun hasn't been converted to another caliber without being properly marked (uncommon, but it does happen). Never shoot modern high-pressure smokeless powder ammunition in a gun that was originally designed and manufactured for lower pressure black powder cartridges. On older revolvers, the gun should never be carried with a live cartridge under the hammer. They can fire accidentally if dropped or struck on the hammer spur with the firing pin over the primer of a live cartridge.

Above all, enjoy yourself! Safely!

HOW TO USE THIS BOOK

We have tried to make this book easy to use so that even someone who knows nothing about guns can identify a particular model and look up its value. We have also tried to include a level of detail in the listings that will be useful to the most advanced collector, dealer, or enthusiast.

Accordingly, the gun catalog portion of this book is divided into nine sections, based on the type of gun.

1. Tip-Up Revolvers

Barrel tips up to load, hinged at top rear of barrel. Empty cases must be punched out individually. They are listed by frame size, from smallest to largest. Manufactured ("mfd.") 1857-1881.

2. Top-Break Revolvers

Barrel tips down to load, hinged at bottom rear of barrel. Empty cases are automatically ejected when the gun is opened. They are listed by frame size, from smallest to largest. Mfd. 1870-1940.

3. Single-Shot Pistols

Self-explanatory. Only possible confusion is the "Straight Line" model, which looks like a semiauto at first glance. Mfd. 1893-1936.

Major types of S&W handguns, top to bottom: tip-up, top-break, hand ejector revolver, and semiautomatic pistol

Location of model number in yoke cut of modern S&W revolver

4. Early Hand Ejectors (Named Model Revolvers, 1896-1957)

A hand ejector (abbreviated "HE") is the typical modern revolver with a solid frame and a cylinder that swings out to the left side to load. Listed by caliber, from smallest to largest.

Empty cases are ejected by manually pushing on the end of the rod extending from the front of the cylinder—hence the name "Hand Ejector." From 1896 to 1957, these guns were known primarily by a model name, often including the caliber, and sometimes the frame size, such as "K-.22." See next listing below.

5. Numbered Model Revolvers (Modern Hand Ejectors, 1957-date)

Beginning in 1957, S&W assigned a specific number to each different named model. These revolvers are listed in numerical order.

> To check if your gun is a named or numbered model, open the cylinder and look at the front frame strap where the cylinder yoke rests when the cylinder is closed. If there is a model number (for example "MOD 442"), your gun will generally be listed in this section. If not, refer to the previous section.

Please note that the model number may be stamped on some revolver frames without the "MOD" abbreviation in front of it.

6. Semiautomatic Pistols

Semiautomatic or "self-loading" pistols reload the chamber automatically after each shot, from a detachable magazine in the grip. Nearly all S&W semiautos have a model number stamped on them, and this section is listed in numerical order.

7. Long Guns

Rifles and shotguns, along with the curious "revolving rifle," light rifle, and machine pistol.

8. Commemoratives and Specials

Club guns, commemoratives, first editions, Twelve Revolvers series, and Lew Horton Specials.

9. Miscellaneous - Non-gun S&W Products

Air guns, gas guns, flare guns, police items, ammunition, knives, catalogs, gimcracks, and geegaws.

Not a complete listing, but at least a beginning on cataloging the many miscellaneous items produced or marketed by Smith & Wesson—from neckties to washing machines!

A NOTE ON THESE GROUPINGS: In most previously published works, S&Ws have usually been listed either by caliber, chronologically, or seemingly at random. The first two types of listings can be very instructive when studying the entire S&W product line, and can be very useful to the knowledgeable collector who is looking up a specific gun. However, they can be confusing to the neophyte who may not be sure exactly what model he is looking up, much less the caliber or when it was made.

After careful consideration, we decided that listing by the above nine types would be the easiest and quickest method, allowing all users to find the specific gun they seek.

Using our system, the area most likely to create confusion is the division of the hand ejectors into "named" and "numbered" groupings. We considered using the caliber or chronological order, or grouping them all together, or breaking them down along other divisions, such as:

- Prewar vs. postwar
- Carbon steel vs. stainless
- Frame size (M, I, J, K, L, and N)
- Related model (Model 629 listed with Model 29)

Heck, we even considered listing by the number of screws in the frame!

However, we always came back to the fact that a model number stamped on the frame is a quick and sure identification, and should be used in numerical order to allow speedy location of the desired information whenever possible.

The major weakness of this system is that it creates something of an artificial break in the 1950s era hand ejectors. The reader must remember that the last .38 M&P produced in 1957 is no different than the first Model 10 produced the same year, other than the model number stamped on the latter. This is recognized by collectors in their terminology. For example, a .44 Magnum without a model number marking will often be referred to as a "Pre-Model 29." In researching 1950s era hand ejectors, you would do well to check the information under both the named and numbered HE sections. These 1950s models have been cross-referenced between the two sections for your convenience.

Using the Nine Sections

When you have determined in which section you're most likely to find your gun, turn to the beginning of that section and review the listing of all guns in that section.

The sections on tip-ups, single-shots, long guns, commemoratives, and miscellaneous guns are relatively brief, due to the limited number of models of these types.

Most sections have additional information at the beginning explaining a little more about that type of gun, including special safety and legal concerns. Also explained in more detail is how to find the specific gun you are looking for within that section.

A grouping of related models within one of the nine sections may be preceded by a narrative "background information" section providing historical context and other information pertaining to that group of guns.

Using the Listing for the Individual Model

The listing for each individual gun will include most of the following:

- **Model name**, along with other names and collector nicknames.
- **Description** of the model, including physical description, various options, historical background, etc.
- **Historic notes** pointing out historic usage of a gun or ownership of that model by famous or infamous individuals.
- **Serial number range, number produced, years produced.**
- **ID key**, included primarily on the early models, is the briefest possible list of characteristics that identify that SPECIFIC model. If all these characteristics are present, the gun must be the model indicated.
- **Value ranges**, which list the retail value of the gun based on condition. It is vital to study the introductory chapter on evaluating condition to be able to effectively use the value ranges listed. The condition ratings have specific meanings, and without a thorough understanding of these, the values are meaningless.
- **Variations** are the reported variations of a specific model that may be of special interest to collectors, including both variations created by the factory and variations interesting because of their historical usage.
- **Chronology of changes**, included primarily on the numbered models, indicating changes during production, sometimes noted by adding a dashed suffix to the model (i.e., Model 29 was followed by Model 29-1, which in turn was followed by Model 29-2, etc.). When a chronology

of changes is listed, it will include the model, the year the change was instituted, and the change that was made. For example:

11-3 1962 Eliminate triggerguard screw

• **Product codes** are found only on listings for items produced since 1984. These are the numbers used by S&W to identify specific configurations or variations of the model, and may be found on the gun's box. They can be used to absolutely specify a particular model and configuration. Sometimes called the "SKU" (Stock Keeping Unit). Product codes include the code, configuration, year, and sometimes additional comments. For example:

102502 2" SRB 84-95 28 oz.

Using the Illustrated Glossary

The Illustrated Glossary and Index following the catalog sections provides explanations and photo illustrations of terms used by S&W collectors. The terms are indexed to the catalog section where appropriate.

About the Value Ranges

The values in this book are not cast in stone. We have tried to reflect the actual marketplace—prices at which items exchange hands between a buyer and seller, both of whom are willing and motivated to close a deal in a gun show type setting. We sought the input of many knowledgeable dealers and collectors.

The retail price is listed on models in current production. Buyers at commercial retail gun shops should expect to pay anywhere from eighty-eight to ninety-six percent of retail. Price should reflect the service you receive and the dealer's reputation for standing behind his merchandise. The NIB price listed for current production models is the price at which such items are being sold in gun show or trade paper contexts, and the prospective buyer should understand that he will be investing his time instead of his money in locating the particular model he wants at this price.

Pricing is not an exact art by any means. Sometimes, especially on rare items, any two of the most advanced authorities in the nation may not be within fifty percent of each other's value estimates. On common items, a professional dealer will of course be able to buy slightly below many of the values listed. He may also ask slightly above the values listed—this is how he feeds his family. In return, the individual who buys at the professional dealer's gun shop or through his catalog should expect to receive knowledgeable guidance and someone who will stand behind the merchandise long after the gun show hobby dealer has packed his tablecloth and gone home.

Where we did not have a sense of the value of a particular variation, we tended to withhold comment, leaving it to the reader's discretion to determine how much rarity is worth in that particular situation. Bear in mind that rarity does not always equal a high premium. There may be only ten examples known of a given item, but there may be only two people who care about that variation.

Also, it may take some time to sell a scarce variation at full value. There is a ready market for common models that are in current vogue as "shooters." However, it may take a specialist dealer six months or more to find the right buyer for a particular obscure variation. The collector who wishes to sell such an item quickly will usually have to settle for some fraction of the potential value.

Commemoratives and related guns have often been priced in NIB (new in box) condition only. Once such an item has been fired, its value tends to drop toward that of a similar non-decorated gun used as a shooter. This would probably be true to a lesser degree on individually engraved guns, where the premium paid is more for the artistic quality of the decoration, although individually engraved guns that have been used will bring less than those that are pristine.

The collector should be ever vigilant about the purchase of rare handguns. As more information becomes available to the trading public (such as through this book), counterfeit handguns also become more available. Certainly every collector, including the authors, has made a costly purchase with insufficient information and regretted it later.

For the high dollar rarities, there is a very small but very enthusiastic market. However, tapping into that market may be difficult. It is not uncommon for one of these items to begin its trip up the buying chain at a fraction of its ultimate price, going to successively more sophisticated buyers, each of whom makes a profit on the item until it finds its way to one of maybe a half dozen or so collectors who both want and can afford it for their collections. Some dealers with these connections will pay nearly any price for an exceptional piece on the "next greater fool" marketing theory, which states that for the best known example, there is always someone out there who has to have it and will pay more.

The authors must confess that we have not yet found the key to exploiting this approach, probably more through our parsimonious reflexes when confronted with the prices of these items than the lack of greed. The few times we have tried to cash in, we have found ourselves seemingly perched precariously at the top of the pyramid. At such moments, we can only take solace in the Collector's Consolation Corollary: "You can't pay too much for a fine gun; you can only pay too soon."

The beginning collector is encouraged to find a mentor for advice and guidance in this fascinating (and sometimes costly) avocation. Attend lots of shows and ask lots of questions. Collectors agree that the best educated collector is one who keeps extensive notes on his personal observations for future reference.

COLLECTING SMITH & WESSON:
Special Concerns and Tricks of the Trade

Smith & Wesson may legitimately be characterized as the premier handgun manufacturer of the United States and the world. Its rich history and wide range of products make it a fascinating study for historians and a treasure trove for collectors. It was the first American maker of repeating handguns that fire self-contained metallic cartridges, and continues as the leader in the police, civilian, military, and sporting handgun market today.

In light of this, perhaps the only thing surprising about S&W collecting is that there are not more gun collectors specializing in this field. While interest is growing rapidly, the S&W collecting community is still small enough that the liquidation of a significant collection or the decision of a few serious and well-heeled individuals to enter the field can still cause a ripple in the values of the scarcer items.

Another result of this is that there are still major areas of collecting to be explored. A relatively new collector could develop a significant collection with less outlay of funds than in several other specialties, and without having to plod through tired, overworked fields. The new S&W collector is in the happy position of entering a hobby where the basic guidelines are known, but there are still discoveries to be made.

Although there may be fewer S&W specialists than one would expect, the interest in S&W products among the general gun owning population is overwhelming. Odds are good that any shooting sportsman or general gun enthusiast will have at least one Smith & Wesson around. It would be difficult to find a gun shop anywhere that didn't have a few S&Ws in the handgun display case. Anytime a double action revolver or semiauto pistol

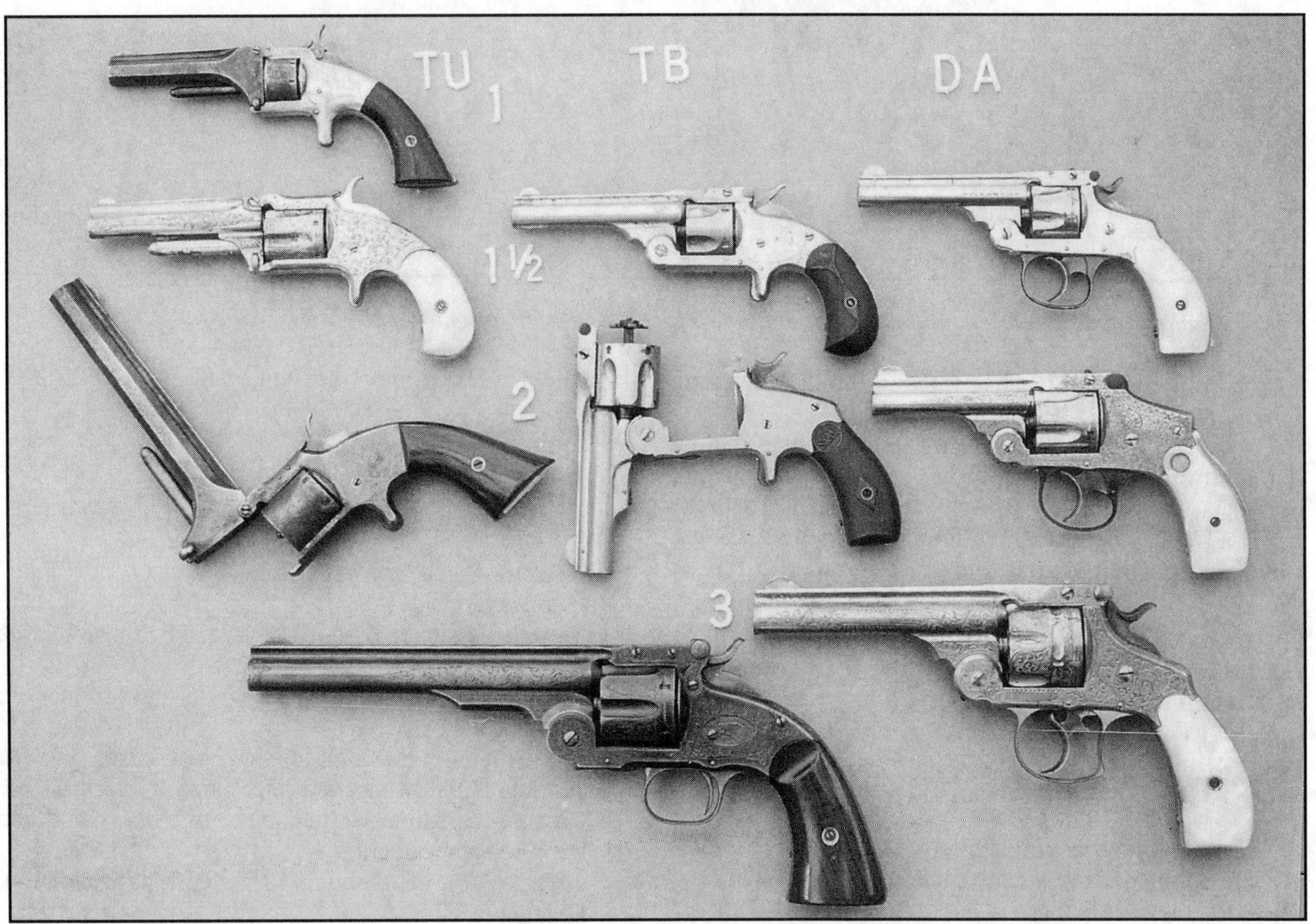

Tip-up and top-break frame sizes. Left column: tip-up; Center column: top-break single action; Right column: top-break double action. Top to bottom: Model 1 (TU only); Model 1-1/2 (TU and TB); Model 2 (TU and TB); Model 3 (TB only).

Hand ejector frame sizes. Left column, top to bottom: M, I, J, K; Right column: L, N.

purchase is planned, it's likely that a Smith & Wesson product will at least be considered.

Accordingly, we've tried to make a book that will be straightforward and useful to the general dealer or gun enthusiast, as well as contain a level of detail useful to the most advanced collector. We'll start out by discussing a few concepts that you need to grasp in order to "speak S&W."

(Hint: Check out the Illustrated Glossary and Index at the end of the book when you run into other confusing terminology.)

Frame Sizes of Revolvers

S&W revolvers are often referred to by "frame sizes." On the tip-ups and top-breaks, these are numbers. On hand ejectors, they are letters.

Tip-Up and Top-Break

Model 1 frame -- smallest; 7-shot .22 tip-up only

Model 1-1/2 frame -- medium small; 5-shot .32 tip-up or top-break

Model 2 frame -- medium; 6-shot .32 tip-up or 5-shot .38 top-break

Model 3 frame -- large; 6-shot .44 top-break

Hand Ejectors

M frame -- smallest; 7-shot .22 old model "LadySmith" only; no longer made

I frame -- small; 6-shot .32 size; no longer made; replaced by J frame

J frame -- small; 5-shot .38 size; current production; "Chiefs Special" size

K frame -- medium; 6-shot .38 size; current production; ".38 Military & Police" size

L frame -- medium-large; compromise between K and N size; current production

N frame -- large; 6-shot .44 size; current production; ".44 Magnum" size

Once the collector has these straight, he should avoid the temptation to get cocky. There are such niceties as the

Location of five screws on hand ejector

"Improved I-frame" to consider. It appears there is also a little known separate letter system for the stainless steel frames. A stainless J-sized frame is an E frame, K is F, L is H, and N is G. How about the newly lengthened J (or is it E?) frame necessary to accommodate the new Model 640-1's chambering of .357 Magnum? If it has not yet been named, the authors would like to respectfully suggest "J and a half." It could happen.

Screws—3, 4, or 5

S&W collectors often refer to hand ejector (HE) revolvers by the number of screws in the frame. From about 1905 to 1955 most hand ejectors had five screws—four sideplate screws and a screw in the front of the triggerguard. About 1955, the top sideplate screw was eliminated on most models, and these are referred to as "four-screw" guns. Around 1961, the triggerguard screw was eliminated, and all subsequent production is known as "three-screw." When counting screws, remember that the rear sideplate screw is covered by some types of grips, and don't overlook the triggerguard screw that enters from the front of the triggerguard.

To confuse things further, the earliest hand ejectors, 1896-1905, had only four screws (pre-five-screw four-screws?), and some models had a "sixth" screw, a bug screw that held in place the top sideplate screw, found in early alloy frame revolvers.

Pinned and Recessed

This refers to hand ejectors made prior to about 1982. Prior to that time, all hand ejectors had the barrel fixed to the frame by a pin through the rear, and magnum revolvers had recessed chambers to enclose the heads of cartridges. See further comments and photos in the glossary at the end of this book.

Generations of Semiautos

The centerfire double action style semiautos are sometimes referred to by their generation:

First Generation: Made 1954-1982. Examples have two-digit model designations, most notably Model 39 and Model 59.

Second Generation: Made 1980-1988. Many improvements, some oriented to ensure reliable function with new styles of ammunition developed since introduction of first generation. Examples have three-digit model designations.

Third Generation: Made 1988-date. Many improvements, most obvious on casual inspection are improved ergonomics of a more rounded comfortable grip. Examples usually have four-digit model designation.

Note: *Not all S&W semiautos fit into the "generation" designations. Examples include the early .32 and .35 pocket semiautos, all .22 semiautos, and the polymer framed "Sigma" series introduced in 1994.*

Type of Finish

Generally, but not always, a blued top-break revolver will bring a bit more than a nickel gun in comparable condition. There are at least three reasons: First, for most of the nineteenth century nickel was a more popular finish and in most, but not all, models was a more common finish than blue. Secondly, nickel finish is more durable than blue, so a higher proportion of surviving nickel guns will show more finish than their blued counterparts. Finally, a nickel gun that has lost a good portion of its finish can have a dark and bright mottled appearance that many collectors dislike, while a blue gun tends to have a more blended appearance to its color as it loses its finish.

As we move into the hand ejectors, single-shots, and semiautomatics, the situation tends to be reversed. In most, but not all, of the later models, blue was much more common than nickel and there was an additional charge for nickel plating.

In recent years, stainless steel has become the overwhelming choice of handgun buyers, and on a S&W purchased for actual use, stainless models nearly always bring more than their blued or nickeled counterparts.

Where a substantial premium is paid for a particular finish, we have tried to note it in the listing of the individual model.

Refinished Guns

Identifying a refinished gun is very much an inexact art, but can be vitally important when considering paying a hefty premium for an antique or rare variation gun that has a high percentage of original finish. Some things to look for include:

• Markings should be crisp. Edges of letters should not show drag marks or blurring.

• Metal edges should be sharp, not rounded.

• Check the heads of studs and pins that protrude through the frame to see if they have been polished flat or are rounded as originally made. This is an obvious clue. For example, the stud that receives the center sideplate screw on top-break revolvers is difficult to remove and is often left in the frame and polished flat when the gun is refinished. On a gun with original finish, or on most factory refinished guns, the end of this stud will be rounded and protrude slightly above the surface of the frame. Likewise, the pin that holds the front sight is sometimes left in place and polished flat during a non-factory refinish.

• Inspect the finish carefully for pits or scratches under the finish that were too deep to polish out during refinishing. Don't rush—spend some time in strong light with a magnifying glass.

• Compare the color of the finish to known original examples.

• Look at the finish of parts that originally had a finish contrasting with the rest of the gun. For example, most pre-stainless guns had a color case hardened trigger and hammer. Nickel top-breaks were usually made with a blued or color case hardened triggerguard and a blued latch. A gun with all these parts nickeled (aka a "bumper job") should generally be considered refinished.

• On most blued top-breaks, it is commonly believed that the muzzle and the tops of the frame posts on either side of the latch should be polished white, and bluing on these areas suggests reblue.

• Never say never. It is believed there are exceptions to nearly all "rules."

A Contrarian Caveat on High Condition Guns: Most experts recommend buying the highest condition guns one can afford, and certainly "mint" guns are those that tend to bring the record prices. (Coincidentally, many of the "experts" are in the business of selling guns. Hmmmmm ....) It is our opinion that there are "restoration" artists who can "restore" a gun so as to fool even the most expert observer. As the dollar amount realized for the highest condition guns continues to outstrip the cost of such "restoration," you can't help but wonder if at some point the market for the highest condition items will sound a retreat due to concern over this practice.

Factory rework star

We like guns that show honest use consistent with their history. We are not entirely comfortable paying double price on an antique gun for those last few percentages of original finish. We are quite possibly in the minority in these opinions.

Factory Refinish

Any refinishing will generally diminish the value of a gun as compared to one with comparable original finish. However, among S&W collectors, a gun that has been refinished at the factory will bring a price somewhere between original finish and a non-factory refinish. The factory no longer refinishes older guns. Most factory refinished guns are marked in some manner to indicate the rework. Check for markings on the butt, on the rear face of the cylinder, including under the ejector star, and on the grip frame under the grip panels. Markings believed to suggest a possible factory refinish include:

• Five-pointed star on the butt: Probably the best known rework marking, this indicates the gun was returned to the factory for rework. However, the work may have been a repair other than refinishing. Use of the star declined in the late 1950s and early 1960s.

• Date on grip frame under grip panels: A three- or four-digit number indicating month and year of refinish (for example "954" would be September 1954); often found in conjunction with other markings.

• A diamond with the letter "B" or "N" (blue or nickel) or "S" (standard -- i.e., blue): Sometimes seen as a star with an "N". Sometimes marked on the rear face of the cylinder. Usage of this marking believed to have followed the star on the butt. It has been suggested that a diamond refinish mark usually indicates a major part replacement, such as barrel, cylinder, or frame.

• "B", "N" or "S" inside of a rectangle: Usage believed to have followed diamond marking. Sometimes noted as "R-S" or "R-N" (for "refinish - standard" or "refinish - nickel"?) on the grip frame under the grip panel.

Rare Barrel Lengths

Cataloged barrel lengths are nominal measurements only. Actual barrel measurement may vary as much as 1/8" from that listed. Revolver barrel length is measured from the front of the cylinder to the tip of the muzzle. Semiauto barrel length is measured from the breech face to the tip of the muzzle.

Before paying a substantial premium for an unusual barrel length, inspect it carefully for signs of being cut, stretched, or replaced.

In most cases, markings on a barrel, such as S&W name and address and patent dates, are centered on the barrel in relationship to the barrel length. For example, the markings on the top of an original rare 6" American barrel will end closer to the breech end than they would on a standard 8" barrel. Some shorter than standard barrels will have special markings in special locations, such as on the side of the barrel rather than on the top of the rib, due to lack of space for the full standard markings in the usual location.

Check to see that the barrel is both original to the gun in question (see section on matching serial numbers) and of the correct model. Many models will interchange barrels. For example, one of the authors has purchased on two different occasions what he thought was a rare 4" barreled New Model #3 only to discover the barrel was actually a common 4" barrel for the .44 DA. These would have been easy enough to detect by the lack of serial number or by the different patent dates, if only he had been a little smarter and a little slower to reach for his wallet. It is certainly possible that the factory used interchangeable model barrels rather than discard excess parts, but incorrect barrel markings will raise a red flag of caution for the careful buyer.

Look at the muzzle to see if it's properly crowned, including the slight recess usually found on a barrel rib. Check the attachment and configuration of the front sight to be sure it's factory type. Look at the finish of the barrel to see if it is consistent with the rest of the gun.

There is a "restoration" practice called "stretching" the barrel that has been used to "restore" cut barrels to their original length. Tip-offs for older stretched barrels include failure of rifling groves inside the barrel to line up perfectly, and missing barrel markings. However, newer procedures consisting of relining the barrel interior and remarking the exterior are reportedly virtually undetectable to the naked eye.

Check for cracked or split forcing cones.

Other Modifications and Unusual Configurations

The general rule is that any modifications from the original configuration of the gun will adversely affect value. However, this is less true in some areas than in others.

Post-factory markings that confirm a known particular historical usage of a gun have always been an exception, and in many cases add to the value.

While "condition" collectors may have no interest in such items, collectors interested in the Old West may not object as strongly today as in the past to "period of use" modifications such as bobbed barrels or removed triggerguard spurs. In fact, the new sport of "cowboy action shooting," where participants assume Old West personas and compete with period firearms, has had the effect of increasing the value of the S&W top-breaks in medium condition grades and has provided a ready market for period altered guns that are otherwise mechanically sound. Perhaps regrettable is that many of the guns used in cowboy action shooting are refinished by their owners, which should further boost the value of original finish remaining on old S&Ws in the future.

Factory errors do occur, and will bring a premium from interested collectors. However, they can also be the product of after-factory gunsmithing or fakery. The buyer should proceed with caution.

Matching Serial Numbers

To bring full price, serial numbers and assembly numbers on a S&W should match.

Early production revolvers used assembly numbers to designate which parts went with which gun. On these, the serial number was marked on the butt and the right grip panel, but a separate assembly number, usually one to four characters (both numbers and letters) was marked on the grip frame under the grip panels and on the various major parts—usually cylinder and barrel on tip-ups and cylinder, barrel, and latch on top-breaks.

In the 1870s the assembly number system was replaced by using the gun's serial number on the major component parts.

On hand ejectors through the late 1950s, the serial number is stamped on the frame, barrel, cylinder, crane, extractor star, and right grip panel, in addition to on the butt.

After about 1960, revolvers had assembly numbers stamped on the frame, sideplate, yoke, and sometimes on the cylinder under the extractor and on some small parts. After about 1988, only the frame and sideplate are marked with assembly numbers.

The effect of a mismatched number on price is variable. Probably of least concern are situations where it appears there is a transposition error in numbers. An example would be where all parts but the cylinder are marked 4567 but the cylinder is marked 4576, although admittedly this is not common. Mismatched grips are not usually a major concern unless the grips are incorrect for the model, such as the occurrence of civilian grips on a military model that should have cartouches. On top-breaks, generally a mismatched latch is of less concern than other major parts. A mismatched top-break cylinder may be somewhat acceptable, especially if it is from a close serial number or from another gun in the same known usage (for example, many Japanese military New Model #3s are found with mismatched cylinders from other Japanese military guns).

However, where a barrel and frame don't match, or none of the parts match, there will generally be a major impact on collector value. This is especially true when guns appear to be partially a rare model or configuration and partially a common type.

Stocks (Grips)

S&W tends to call them stocks. Most of the rest of the world calls them grips. On early models, the gun's serial number is stamped or penciled inside the right grip panel and should match the s/n on the gun's butt.

Original S&W grips were invariably fitted closely to the metal of the gun. Gaps and undersized or oversized grips should be a clue to check if the grips have been replaced. Ivory grips are reported to "shrink" with age, and may be correct to the gun even if slightly undersized. Wear patterns on grips should be consistent with the wear on the gun.

In removing grips, never pry them off the gun since the grip may be marred or even broken by this stress. Original grips may cling tightly to the gun. The best way to remove tight grips is to unscrew the grip screw part way, then gently tap on the screw head with the screwdriver handle. This should loosen the off side (right) grip. Then remove the grip screw and the right grip. The left grip may now be loosened by tapping on the inside surface of the grip from the right side of the grip frame.

Replaced grips that are correct for the model and variation will have only a slight impact on the collector value. Replaced grips that are incorrect for the gun will reduce the collector value, but may not affect or even enhance the value as a shooter.

Fancy Grips: Fancy grips of pearl, ivory, stag, exotic wood, or other material were available both from the factory and from non-factory aftermarket suppliers. Beginning about 1893, factory-produced pearl or ivory grips had small round S&W medallions inlaid, to distinguish them from non-factory grips. Boxes from this era may be found with a flyer glued in the bottom urging buyers to insist on genuine S&W grips with the medallion.

Period pearl or ivory grips will nearly always bring a premium. The only exceptions would be rare variations that had a unique grip, such as military guns with inspector cartouches on the wooden grips. In the 1800s, pearl was considered the more deluxe grip. Contemporary collectors seem to pay more for ivory, however. Fancy grips by S&W are generally worth more than aftermarket grips.

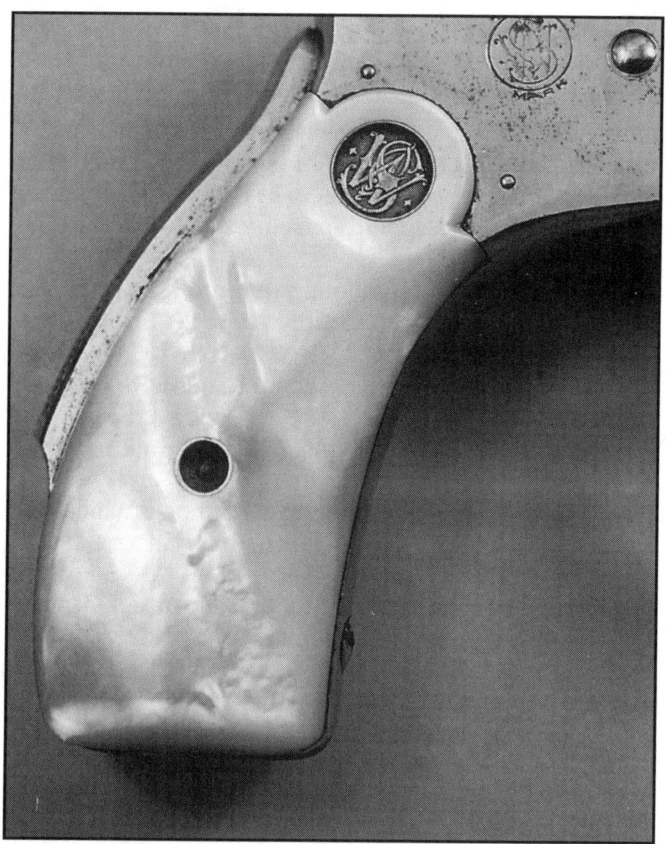

Smith & Wesson medallion pearl grips

Pearl and ivory grips may be found decorated by checkering, inscription, or relief carving. Pearl grips were especially difficult to work for this type of decoration, due to their brittleness and the toxicity of the dust created. Pearl grips were reportedly worked underwater to minimize these hazards. Decorated exotic grips tend to bring an additional premium. An excellent set of old ivory grips with high relief carving for a large frame single action may be worth $1000 or more by themselves off of a gun.

Aftermarket ivories will usually bring a premium, especially if solid ivory and not a modern synthetic (sometimes made with ivory dust). It is said that grips appearing to be ivory can be tested by applying a heated needle to the back surface of the grip to see if it melts. The same test may be applied to pearl grips. Contrary to what one might think, it is also claimed that genuine pearl grips tend to become less slippery when wet than synthetic pearl grips.

Ivory grips will tend to yellow with age, the grain of the ivory may become more pronounced, and slight cracking or crazing may appear. (It is sometimes difficult to distinguish ivory from bone—ivory tends to show growth rings or grain more than bone.) Pearl may also tend to yellow slightly. Such appearance will generally not detract from the value if consistent with the gun, and may actually slightly enhance the value by giving some reassurance that the grips are of the same vintage as the iron.

On wooden grips, custom designs by noted makers or designers such as Roper or Herrett may bring a premium, or be collectible on their own. Again, whether such grips enhance or detract from a gun's value will depend on whether the replacements are correct for the period, and whether the standard grips that should have been on the gun are common or scarce.

Tip-Ups: Standard grips on all tip-up models were smooth rosewood.

Top-Breaks: Smooth walnut grips were standard on the American, Russian, and Schofield models.

Hard rubber grips were introduced in the late 1870s and eventually became standard for the top-break revolvers. Checkered wooden grips are rather common on the New Model #3, and smooth wood grips have been observed. The Baby Russian was made with hard rubber grips in nickel, and wood grips in blue (scarce).

Hard rubber (abbreviated HR) is a synthetic-looking molded material. It is usually black in appearance, although it may turn brown with age, especially if continuously exposed to sunlight. They tend to be rather fragile and subject to breakage if abused. A common flaw is a chip out of the bottom at the grip pin. A rubber band wrapped around a hard rubber grip will leave a permanent light brown stain where it seems to leech out the dark color.

Most hard rubber grips had molded checkering with the familiar intertwined S&W logo in a circle at the top of the grip. Exceptions were the early single action .32 centerfire, which had first a no logo grip, followed by a block letter logo grip, and finally the intertwined logo grip, and the Baby Russian, which was made with a block letter logo grip.

Unusual hard rubber grip variations, worth a premium, include the rather striking mottled red grips. This type of material was standard only on the revolving rifle, but examples may be found in all sizes. The revolving rifle also has a red mottled hard rubber forend, and for some reason, the grips seem to always be darker and more muted than the forend. Blue mottled grips have been reported, but the authors are not sure whether Ed is pulling their legs on this one. An entirely different molded pattern, quite scarce, will be found on some second model .32 DAs. Called the "floral," "peacock," or "wild turkey" grips, these have a floral pattern rather than checkering, with some type of bird lurking in the design.

Reproductions of hard rubber grips are currently being made out of modern synthetic material by companies such as NC Ordnance. These are accurate reproductions, and seem more durable than the originals. Tip-offs to a repro grip may include checkering that seems too sharp for the age and a darker, shinier black color to the grip. Also, a repro may have tiny bubbles in the casting and may not fit the gun perfectly. Reproduction mottled HR grips and forends for the revolving rifle have also been reported.

Early Hand Ejectors: Hard rubber continued to be the standard grip material on early small and medium frame hand ejectors, but was soon replaced by walnut. The large N frames began with walnut as standard in 1907.

The use of gold-colored S&W logo medallions inset into walnut grips began about 1910 and continued through 1917. From about 1917 to 1929, standard walnut grips had no medallions.

About 1929, chrome- or silver-colored medallions were reintroduced as standard on wooden grips. Two sizes of medallions exist, with the large size used on second and third Model 44 Hand Ejectors, among others. The small size was used on most guns.

Magna style grips were introduced as an option with the .357 Magnum in 1935. Magna grips come up higher alongside the backstrap, providing a larger surface to spread recoil at the web of the thumb, while still leaving the front and rear strap of the grip frame exposed. They came to be the common style, and in later years were considered the "service" grip.

Grip adapters are metallic pieces that fit on the front strap of a grip frame, filling the space there and providing a more comfortable grip for most shooters. They were made by S&W as well as others. They were commonly used on many, if not most, police revolvers prior to the popularity of replacement rubber grips such as Pachmayrs.

So-called "diamond" grips have a diamond of uncheckered wood around the grip screw and escutcheon. They were introduced as early as 1880 and were standard up through about 1968. "Coke bottle grips" refer to diamond grips used on some guns around the 1950s that had a slight coke bottle or "girlish figure" shape to them.

Modern Hand Ejectors: Goncalo Alves, a figured South American wood, was offered as an exotic option as early as the 1950s. It eventually came to replace walnut as the standard material for oversize target grips.

These massive "target stocks" have been offered on many recent hand ejectors, and became standard on many large frame guns. These entirely enclose the grip front grip strap, adding substantial bulk to the grip.

Modern wood grips, left to right: checkered target, service (or Magna), smooth target, round butt combat, square butt combat. Bottom: custom Spegel boot grips.

In the last few decades rubber grips have become more and more popular on revolvers. The first thing many police departments did with issue S&Ws was to toss the wood grips in the trash and slap on a set of "Pachmayrs" (the best known maker of replacement rubber grips). Recognizing this trend, S&W has moved toward eliminating wood grips on all production models and instead using rubber or synthetic grips by such manufacturers as Pachmayr, Michael's of Oregon (Uncle Mike's), and Hogue (maker of the pebble-textured one-piece "monogrip"). However, wooden grips continue to be manufactured by S&Ws Ace Grip Company.

Rubber grips can be found in a wide variety of types to fit any hand or preference. Some options include square or round butt, enclosed or exposed backstrap, and with or without finger grooves. Different variations will be seen on the same model from the factory.

The J frame revolvers have been offered with tiny wood grips so as not to increase the size; these are sometimes called "splinter" or "sliver" grips. The grips for the Centennial models come up higher on the grip frame, and are called "high-horn" grips. Spegel boot grips were initially a custom grip designed to provide a larger, more secure gripping surface without substantially increasing the bulk of the gun. A rubber version of this boot grip as manufactured by Michael's of Oregon is now standard on many J frame short barrel revolvers.

The round butt configuration for revolvers has proven more popular since it is easier to find custom grips to make a small grip frame feel large than to make a large grip frame fit an average or small hand. Accordingly, present plans are to phase out square butt guns in favor of a line featuring all round butt revolvers. (There is an interesting cycle here: All the earliest tip-ups and some early big Model 3 top-breaks had square butt configuration. The round butt was introduced on the tip-ups in 1868 and by 1878 was standard on all S&Ws. However, in the early twentieth century, the square butt began to make a comeback, and by WWII, the round butt configuration was somewhat scarce on all but the smaller revolvers.)

Most recent semiautos will be found with synthetic grips. Wood grip panels were tried on some second generation guns, but it was found that the very thin wood required tended to split. Third generation centerfire semiautos are made exclusively with one-piece wraparound synthetic Xenoy grips, which play a large part in their improved handling characteristics. For most third generation models, replacement Xenoy grips can be had from S&W with either straight or curved backstraps to fit the shooter's preference.

Boxes

This topic is worthy of a book unto itself, and will be touched upon only briefly here, mainly because the authors are bewildered by the whole concept and appalled by the prices musty old cardboard brings.

The cardboard boxes used to ship guns, and the accompanying paperwork, can be considered "ephemera"; the survival rate of such material is much lower than for the guns themselves. Rare boxes for the earliest models can sell for well in excess of $1000. A collector with a "minty" gun will usually pay $20 or so for a correct box to display with it, even for a relatively common model. As with guns, the price of boxes tends to increase with age and rarity.

As factory historian Roy Jinks often points out, Smith & Wesson was in business to make a profit, and not to provide a neat and consistent set of tracks for future collectors. It should be remembered that an efficient manufacturer would not throw out perfectly good boxes to make a neat and sudden change in their packaging, and many inconsistencies will be found in this field.

Special permanent cases for the storage of sidearms, especially for fancy or presentation arms, were popular during the 1850s through 1870s. Model 1s will be found with gutta-percha cases. Wooden cases will be found for most tip-up and single action top-break revolvers. The only wooden case of that period that was actually manufactured by S&W was for the Model 1-1/2 Single Action Centerfire. However, standard wooden cases were offered by the larger distributors such as MW Robinson, and have come to be considered "factory casings" by collectors. Cleverly made reproductions of period casings have been in circulation for many years, and differentiating between original and reproduction cases is an arcane art mastered by relatively few collectors.

Wooden cases for special individual guns or for special models have remained available, both through S&W and aftermarket suppliers up through the present day.

It is believed that the earliest S&Ws were shipped in mottled blue, green, or black two-piece boxes. These were followed by a deep red or maroon for .32s and a light green for .38s and .44s up to about the 1880s.

Beginning about 1880, a wide variety of colors were used, including black, brown, maroon, mustard, blue, and red. The use of "end labels" containing specific information on the gun in the box began about 1880, with the DA models. A green label generally designated a blued gun, with nickel guns packed in boxes with orange or white end labels. The only known "picture box" from this era (a box with a picture of the gun on the top) is one made for the Baby Russian.

Some twentieth century guns (ca. 1920s?) will be found in a box with an attached lid and beveled edges on the inside front corners.

About 1935, a blue lift cover type box with an embossed picture of the gun was utilized. A plain red two-piece box was introduced prior to WWII, and some guns were shipped in these into the 1950s.

Postwar, in the late '40s and early '50s, K and N frame revolvers were shipped in two-piece gold picture boxes. Some of the many variations are shown in the Summer 1987 edition of the *S&W Journal.*

These were followed by two-piece blue boxes with metal reinforced corners, which continued up into the 1980s. A large number of variations are encountered, including solid or broken border, "sun burst," and various methods of wording in the Smith & Wesson marking (Smith & Wesson, Smith & Wesson Inc., Bangor Punta, etc.). For at least part of this period, blued guns were shipped in blue boxes, and nickel guns were shipped in gray or silver boxes. Early stainless guns were in blue boxes with "Stainless" marked directly on the box (not a label).

In the late 1980s, a new type of one-piece blue cardboard box was introduced, with a lid that folded over the top and wings that tucked into the corners.

In 1994, the Performance Center began shipping guns in a plastic case, with the gun in a plastic bag inside. Current plans are to discontinue cardboard boxes, and ship all future products in the plastic cases.

Screwdrivers, etc.

Collectors also avidly seek the original manuals, paperwork, and accessories such as "wipers" (cleaning rods) and screwdrivers that were originally packaged with the guns.

One of the early included tools was a screwdriver with a hollow brass handle that contained three or four interchangeable blades, used from about 1880 to about 1920. Late production had a knurled nut added to hold the blade in place.

Prewar target revolvers were shipped with a small knurled steel handle screwdriver. WWII through the late 1950s production included a larger similar screwdriver to accommodate the 1940 change to micrometer click sights.

In the late 1950s the handle was changed to knurled aluminum. This was followed by a fluted aluminum handle, first with a long blade tip and then a short blade tip.

Beginning about 1988, the standard configuration screwdriver was replaced with a flat steel two-blade key ring type tool, or a flat steel four-blade circular tool.

Wipers from the 1800s usually consisted of a brass or steel rod with a flat slotted tip on one end, while the other end curved into a circular handle. In the 1900s the working end was changed to a threaded hole to accept a screw-in mop, brush, or cleaning jag. Prewar was generally steel, while postwar was aluminum.

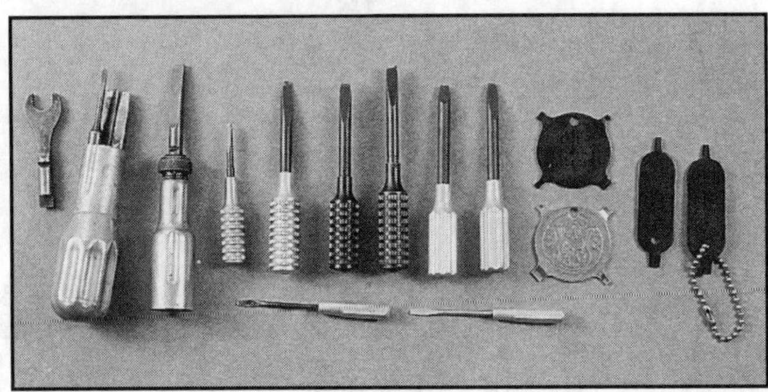

S&W screwdrivers (two small screwdrivers at bottom may not be S&W)

For several decades, the screwdriver was packaged in a sealed plastic bag with a "wiper" and other small items. Collectors will want this sealed bag in NIB condition guns. One interesting variation is the tapered swab packaged with the Model 53 Jet made specifically to fit that gun's unique bottlenecked chambers.

Sights

The earliest sights were rather simple affairs. The front sight was composed of a pinned semicircular blade and the rear sight consisted of a notch in the cylinder stop of tip-ups and a raised portion of the latch on top-breaks.

Hand ejector "fixed" or "service" or "M&P" sights generally consist of a notch rear sight in the topstrap of the frame and either a half round or ramped front sight. Fixed front sights will be found either pinned or otherwise attached in place or forged integral to the barrel. Integral forged front sights are an identifying characteristic of some models.

The first standard production target sights were offered on the New Model #3 Target Model, beginning in 1887.

Forged (integral) vs. pinned front sight

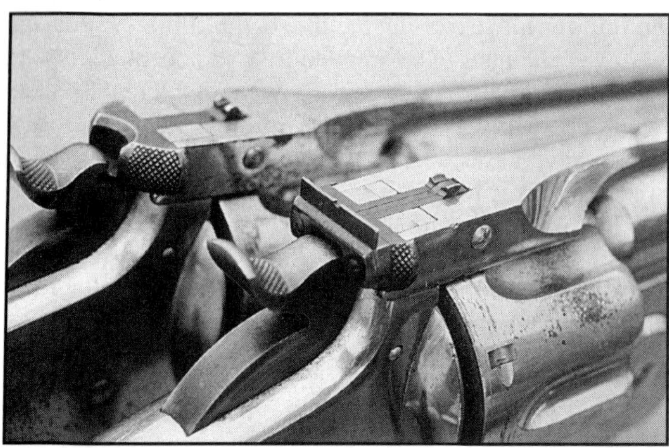

Above and right: Target sights and standard sights on New Model #3s

King custom reflector front sight

Several configurations were available, the most common being a rear sight holding a separate sight blade that could be adjusted by loosening and retightening the screws, and a "Paine" type front sight consisting of a long "bead" on top of a thin flat-topped blade. Another popular front sight was the "Winans" style, consisting of a rounded blade with an inset bead. An alternate rear sight consisted of a thicker drift adjustable rear sight, with more of a triangular than blade profile when viewed from the side.

Adjustable target sights were an option on most models, with some models introduced specifically as target models with adjustable sights standard. As handgun target shooting grew in popularity as a sport, a wide range of special sights became available. Some of these could be ordered installed at the factory, and others were installed by gunsmiths.

The Patridge sight was a popular front sight. It provided a tall thin rectangle for the sight picture, with the rear face of the sight blade vertical or undercut to eliminate glare. Perhaps the opposite approach was exhibited by the King reflector front sight, which incorporated a tiny mirror to throw additional light onto the rear face of the front sight blade. Bar inserts into the front sight were popular with some shooters, as were gold, silver, or ivory beads. A flat circle "bead" insert was a "Call bead," and a hemisphere was a "McGivern bead."

The front sight configuration that proved most popular and eventually became standard configuration for most revolvers is the ramp style, developed by Frank Baughman for the FBI as the "Baughman quick-draw ramp." Like the Patridge, this provides a square-topped thin rectangular post front sight picture, but has a vertical front face with the rear face consisting of a ramp rising towards the muzzle, usually serrated to reduce glare. The result is a quick positive sight picture with a front sight that won't snag on the holster during the draw. A red rectangular insert is sometimes used, and this "red ramp" (RR) front sight is possibly the most common.

The biggest advancement in rear sights was the development of the "micrometer click adjustable" rear sight, first introduced on the K22 Masterpiece in 1940. An improved version of this sight is still the standard adjustable or "target" rear sight today. It is possibly most commonly found with a white outline (WO) on three sides of the blade to increase visibility.

The past decade has brought the increasing popularity of scopes and electronic sights for hunting and competition

Modern revolver front sights, clockwise from top right: red ramp, pinned ramp, Patridge w/gold McGivern bead, Patridge w/red post

applications, along with experimentation with laser sights. Provisions for mounting a scope were initially made on some special runs, and now most adjustable sight models are drilled and tapped for scope as standard production. Other recent sight options include interchangeable front sight blades (as on the Classic and Classic DX models), a four-position adjustable front sight, and a Bomar silhouette rear sight.

On autopistols, current production includes the acclaimed Novak Lo-Mount rear sight with its melted snag-resistant triangular profile on many fixed sight models, and protective wings on most adjustable sights. The "three dot" sighting system is also popular, with a white dot inlaid in the front sight and in each side of the rear sight.

Night sights are offered on some models. These usually consist of glow in the dark tritium inserts in front and rear sights, usually three dot or dot and bar configurations.

Simple and least expensive factory style engraving

Engraving

In many cases, engraved guns are valued more as art than as collectible guns. As in art, an authentic "old master" is worth a lot of money, while you may have trouble giving away the firearm equivalent of a sofa-sized "starving artist parking lot sale" rendition of Elvis at the Last Supper on black velvet.

Factors to consider when evaluating an engraved gun:

1. **Factory engraved:** Factory engraving will always enhance the value of the gun. To be worth full value, a factory engraved gun should be confirmed by a factory letter.

2. **Extent of coverage:** For many years the factory has offered three levels of coverage, price varying with size and type of gun. With approximate current prices, these are:

"A" - full coverage	$1400 - $1900
"B" - 2/3 coverage	$1300 - $1500
"C" - 1/3 coverage	$800 - $1250

3. **Period of engraving:** Is the period of the engraving the same as the period of usage of the gun? This is especially important on non-factory engraved guns. Almost any period engraving can add some interest to an older gun, even if relatively crudely done. This seems particularly true on guns from the 1800s, where a "pawnshop engraving job" can add a colorful air to an old shooting iron. Modern engraving on an old gun is very much a matter of taste. Even if beautifully done, it tends to turn off many collectors. Some individuals may want to own a showy older gun without shelling out the big bucks a high condition period engraved piece would bring, and may well pay a premium for a tarted-up old gun. Mediocre or poor modern engraving, or worse yet, modern engraving fraudulently passed off as older engraving, will nearly always diminish the value of an antique gun.

4. **Hand cut, rotograved, or laser etched:** Hand cut generally requires the most skill and time, and brings the greatest premium. Beautiful engraving can also be done with modern electric engraving tools, but may suffer in detail and will not bring as much. Laser etched designs are valued more as a standard variation of a particular model than as an individual piece of art.

5. **Artistic quality of the engraving:** Two factors to consider here are the overall artistic quality of the layout and the skill with which it has been executed, all of which brings us to…

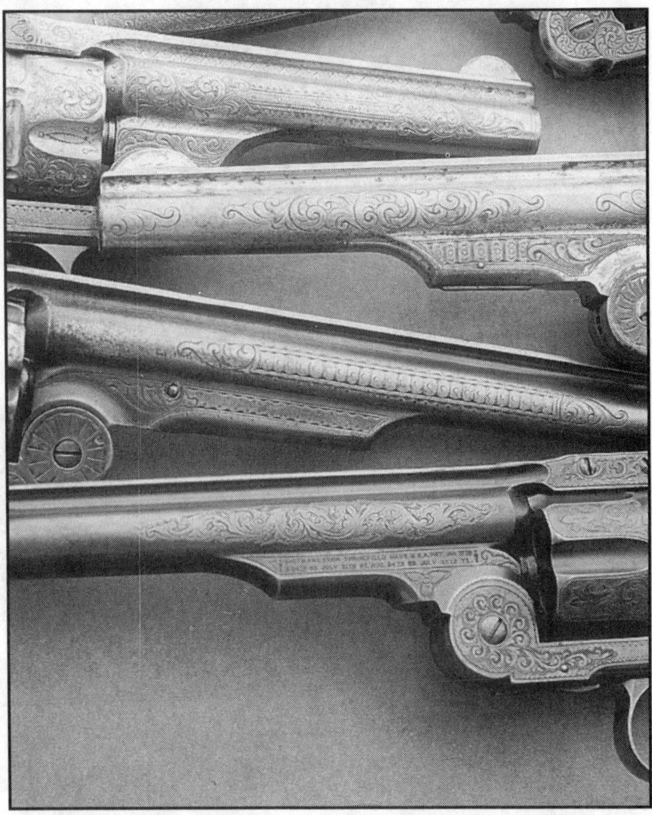

Examples of nineteenth century barrel treatments

Examples of nineteenth century scroll engraving. New Model #3 (third from the top) is Young style; top and two bottom guns are New York or Nimschke style.

Above and below: examples of mediocre engraving. Note choppy background shading, uneven layout, and overrun cuts.

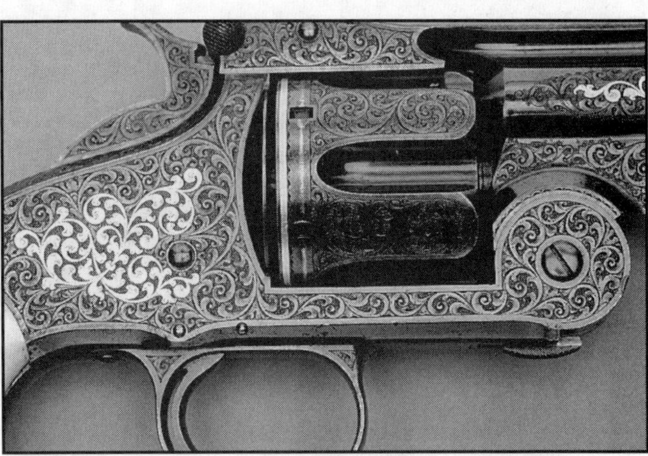

Gustave Young engraved and gold inlaid Second Model American (Photo courtesy Diamond B Guns and John Gangel)

6. **The engraver and style of engraving:** Pieces that can be definitively attributed to one of the great master engravers will always bring a premium price. However, this is regrettably seldom a sure thing, as engravers seldom signed their work, and the specific engraver is not always reflected in the factory records. There are a handful of individuals who MAY be qualified to tentatively identify an engraver by inspecting his work. Sometimes a specific piece may be identified from the rubbings done by the original engraver and kept in his "pattern book."

Lacking one of these types of confirmation, it is usually safest to refer to engraving as being "in the style of" a particular engraver rather than making specific attribution. Also remember that most highly skilled engravers could carve in a number of different styles, if the customer wished.

Neither of the authors profess to be anything resembling an expert on firearms engraving. However, if the reader will promise to take it with a grain of salt, we will offer the following comments on engravers and styles of special note, in order to give the prospective student of gun art a starting place:

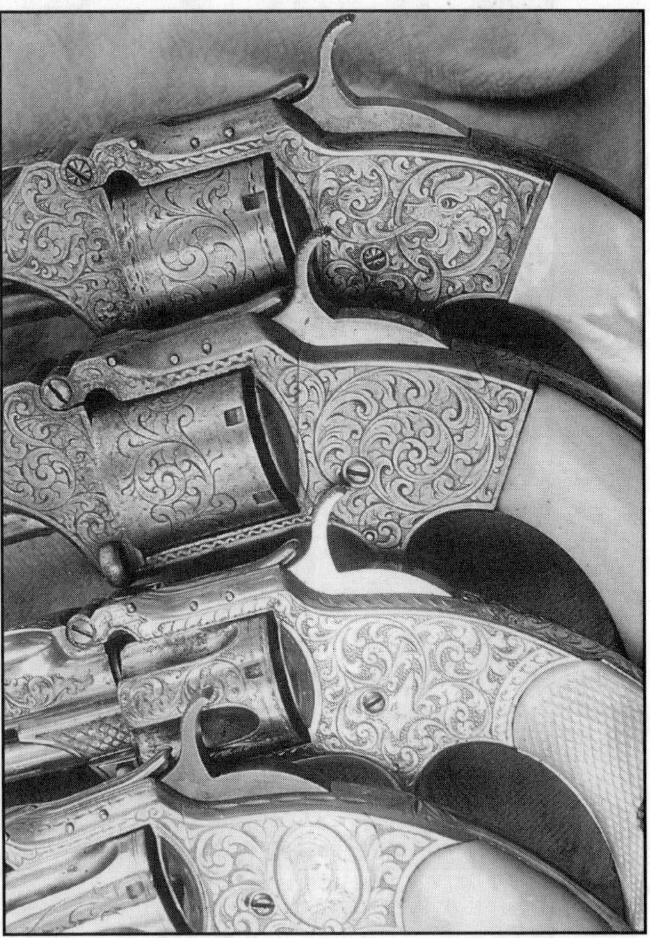

Examples of nineteenth century engraved tip-ups. Top and third down show "inhabited scroll." Bottom includes a lady's portrait.

Nimschke: L. D. Nimschke is probably the best known of the great engravers. He is most commonly associated with a large profuse floral scroll style, also sometimes called "New York style" engraving. Whether Nimschke's

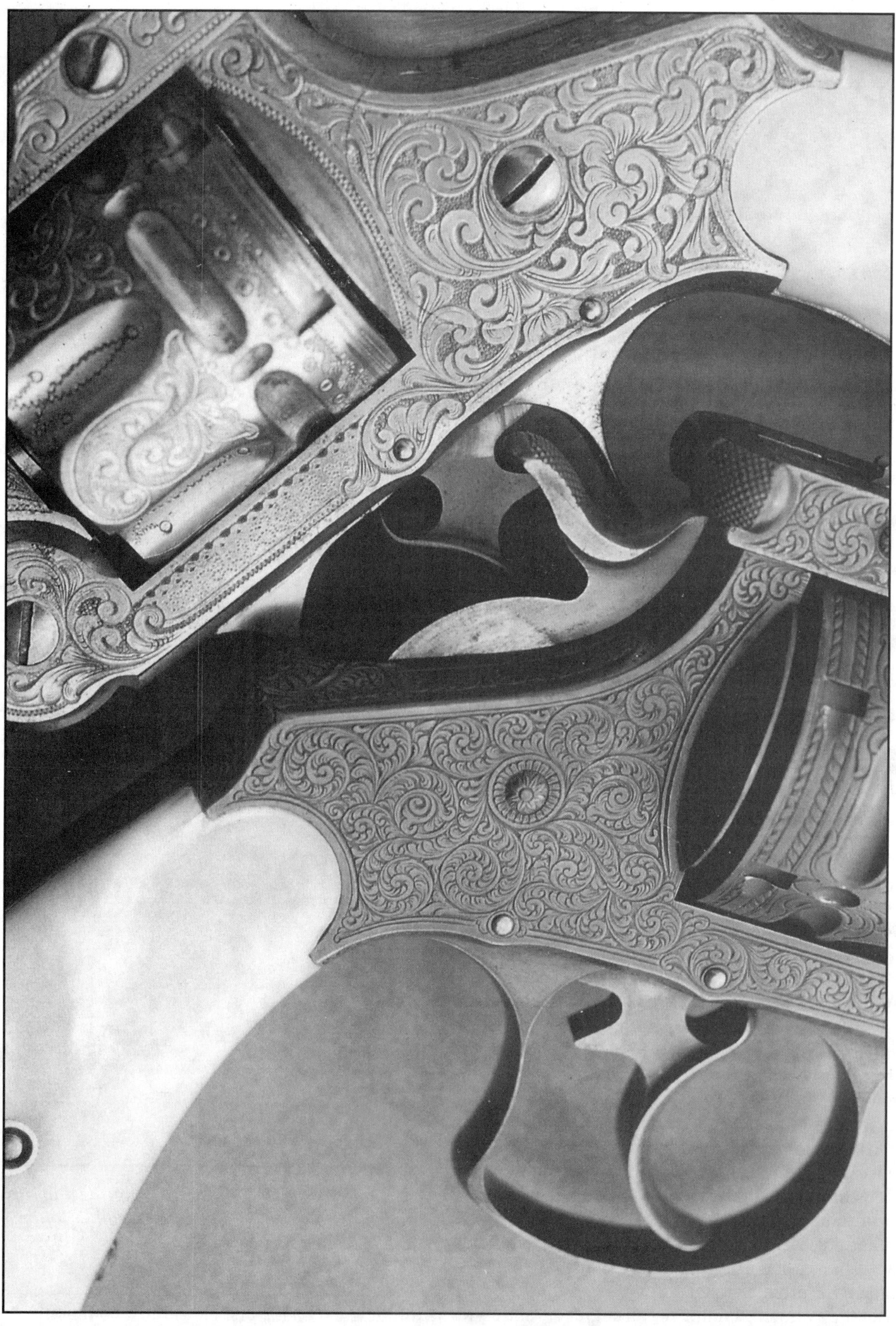

Nimschke style engraving. Top: large floral pattern thought typical of Nimschke; Bottom: profuse English scroll, less typical but attributed to Nimschke by R. L. Wilson.

style was widely imitated or he was the master of this particular popular style is open to debate. Probably a little of both. Nimschke was an independent artist rather than a factory employee, and worked on many makes of guns. Often he would engrave for a distributor rather than the manufacturer. His pattern book has been published in R. L. Wilson's *L. D. Nimschke, Firearms Engraver*.

Gustave Young: Young was a master engraver for Colt before he was hired as in-house factory engraver for S&W in 1867. His hand created some of the most exquisitely decorated Smith & Wessons ever made. His style is typically thought of as utilizing smaller vine scroll patterns than most New York style engraving, with his scrolls often having nearly perfectly circular endings.

Oscar, Eugene, and Robert Young: Gustave's sons, they worked with and succeeded him as S&W factory engravers. Their skill approached that of their father, and their styles were similar. Oscar was with the factory full-time until 1916.

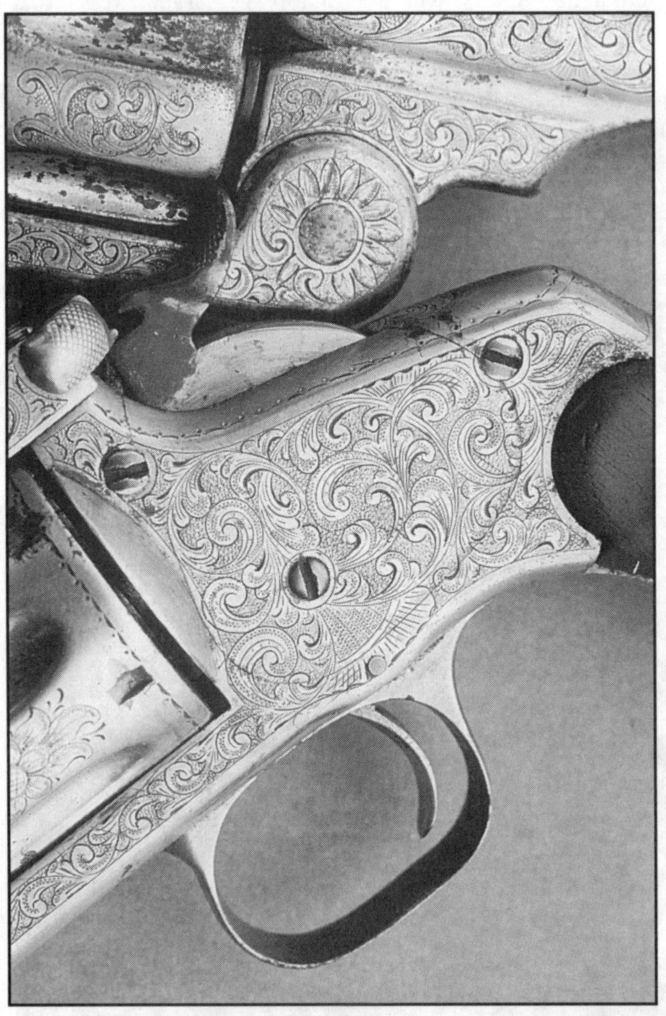

Non-factory engraving. This lightly cut style has been observed on several Model 3s. Note that the design is defined nearly entirely by lines and dots, with no "sculpting" effect.

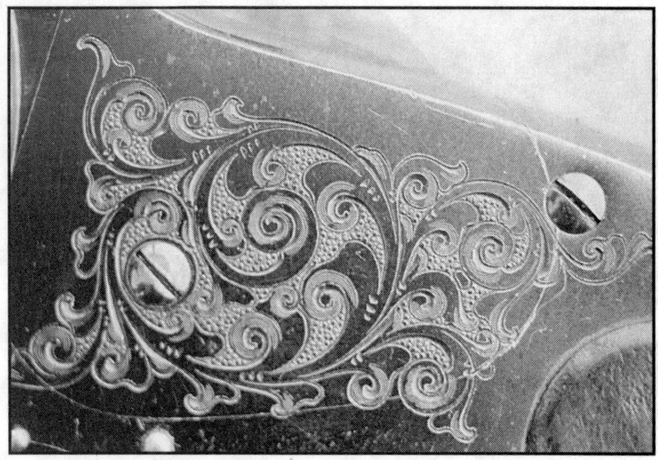

Young family factory engraving

Floral style Young (Oscar?) factory engraving

Paul Piquette: The current S&W master engraver is turning out some beautiful work.

Germanic vine scroll: An open vine style of engraving.

Rose pattern: Rose and other floral patterns; usually more literal than other scroll styles.

English scroll: Tight, almost circular scroll patterns.

Inhabited scroll: Sometimes, small fanciful creatures unlike any found in nature will be found "inhabiting" the scroll work. This has been attributed by some to the Mideastern origins of many engraving patterns, and the ancient Moslem proscription of making images of actual creatures as created by Allah.

Panel scenes: In general, representational art is rather scarce in firearms engraving, especially older engraving. A few old S&Ws will be found with panel scenes on them, however.

Tiffany: Noted New York jewelers Tiffany created a very few beautifully decorated firearms by an etching process rather than engraving. These have a distinctive appearance, and are sometimes combined with striking

Factory engraved Young (Oscar?) panel scene

ornate Tiffany grips. Modern replicas of this century-old process have been reported, and a buyer contemplating paying a large sum for a Tiffany etched piece would do well to get an expert's opinion.

Punch dot engraving: A style of engraving done by punching dots into the metal rather than cutting the metal with chisels. Not a S&W factory style, but sometimes found as aftermarket engraving on nineteenth century revolvers. Generally brings less than quality cut engraving, but can be colorful and evocative of the era.

Gold: Gold wash (a very thin gold layer sometimes used for broad highlights, such as cylinder flutes), gold plate (a thicker layer of gold, generally applied to the entire gun or a major component, such as the cylinder), and gold inlay (gold wire, figures, or other decoration added on to the engraved pattern) will add value to engraving.

Lasersmith: A process introduced in 1989 for laser etching images on metal.

Current S&W Master Engraver Paul Piquette took time from his busy engraving schedule to provide the following comments and list of S&W factory engravers. The authors' additions to Mr. Piquette's comments are in parentheses:

"This list includes some outside vendors—the list of actual individuals would probably be larger except that

Engraving by current S&W Master Engraver, Paul Piquette

Non-factory period engraved panel

Punch dot (top) non-factory engraving compared to cut engraving

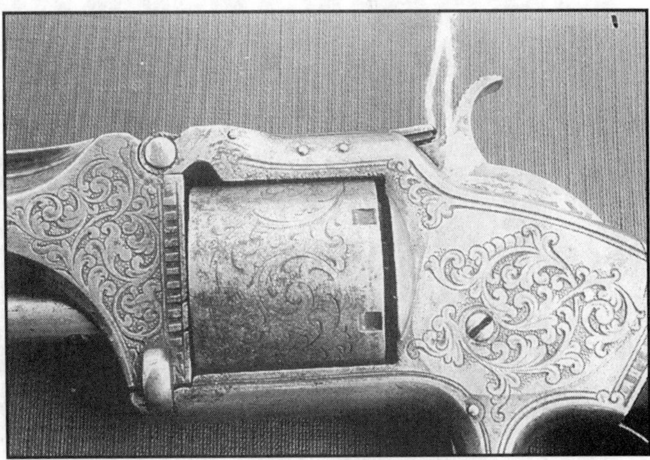

Germanic vine scroll type engraving

records from the vendors such as Tiffany, American Engravers, and L. D. Nimschke didn't indicate the actual engraver's name. However, this is still a comprehensive list.

"Several of these fine artisans worked both as factory and as commissioned engravers, especially in the 1850s. The Youngs were the first actual factory engravers. The period from 1960-1974 saw many engravers come and go. They worked either as apprentices under Russell Smith or

Examples of what are probably non-period and non-factory engraving. Top is "Mexican style," possibly from 1900-1940 era; bottom may be more recent.

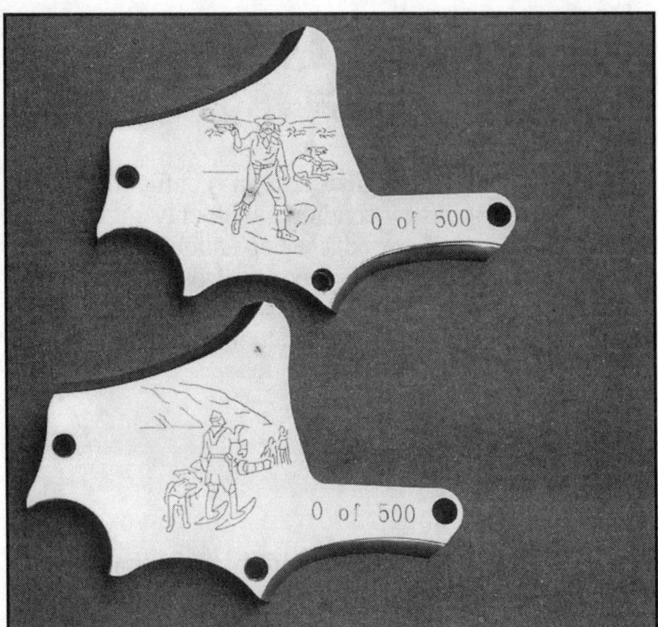

Lasersmith engraving: sideplates from "Twelve Revolvers" series

Lovely Kornbrath engraved registered Magnum (Photo courtesy of Gary Garbrecht)

had some experience as engravers. At least thirteen came and went, some to continue their engraving work independently or for other firms.

"At present, John Pease is an engraving vendor working exclusively for S&W at the moment. He studied under Domingos Joaquin and more formally under Thomas Freyburger. John is an excellent scroll cutter and does good gold borderwork. I'm working alone in-house at the Smith & Wesson Academy, and I have had an apprentice, although it is not a formal S&W program. I've elected to help a fourteen-year-old young lady named Stefanie McKinney, who shows great artistic ability. It is my hope that in a few years she'll be mature enough to handle real creative pressure and quite possibly be ready for a formal career as an engraver. I've also got four young sons who may want to fill my shoes someday."

S&W Engravers:

Richard Bates Inshaw
F. W. Martin* (his work found especially on Model One First and Second Issues)
S. T. Merritt
E. A. Timme
P. S. Yendell
L. D. Nimschke**
Gustave Young**
Oscar Young*
Eugene Young*
Tiffany Jewelers**
Harry Jarvis* (ca 1903-1953)
Leon Goodyear* (ca 1920s and 1930s)
R. J. Kornbrath*
Alvin White*
Russell Smith*
Virginia LeBlanc (first woman S&W engraver)
Siefried Rentszchke
John Anderson
Gregg Duplaise
Dave Klemper (Worked at S&W twice—late 1960s and early 1980s)
Mike Kapinos
Bryson Gwinnell (Later engraved for Colt)
Bob Burt (First African American S&W engraver)
Steve Kamyk (Currently engraving for Colt)
Mike Grovronwich
Tom Freyburger
Dominqos Joaquin*
Denise Thirion (of American Engravers, R. L. Wilson)
John Pease
Paul Piquette*

Authors' note: It appears that this list may be in very general chronological order. The authors have included an asterisk (*) after those names that seem to be most well-known among S&W collectors.

EVALUATING CONDITION

Condition Ratings in This Book

Generally, this book uses condition grades based on those established by the NRA, with slight modifications and expansion to fit the subject matter of this book. If you are familiar with those ratings, you may generally use them with confidence. However, for a full understanding of how the terms are used here, please see the discussion following these definitions.

NIB - "NEW IN BOX": In the same condition as when the gun left the factory, with accompanying box, literature, and accessories. This is important to note, as older boxes may have substantial value in themselves. The gun must be unfired and unused. Comparable terms expressing the same gun condition might include "mint" or "100%." Generally this condition is not found in antique guns, but a gun that is "antique NIB" will bring substantial premium over "antique excellent."

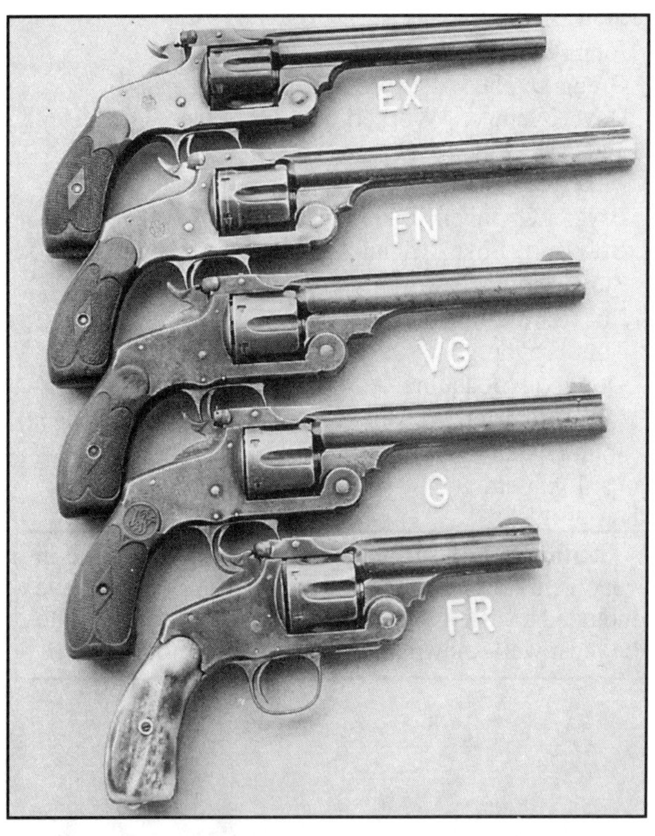

Antique conditions, top to bottom: excellent, fine, very good, good, fair (fair has barrel from another model)

EXCELLENT: All original parts and configuration. For modern guns, nearly new condition, with only slight finish wear at muzzle or sharp edges. For antique guns, sharp markings, unmarred grips, fine bore. Also, excellent guns should generally exhibit at least the following percentages of original finish, depending on production era:

Post 1945:	98%
1920-1945:	95%
1890-1920:	90%
1865-1890:	85%
Pre 1865:	80%

Stainless steel: Due to the durability of the finish, most used stainless steel guns are found in excellent to very good condition so long as they are unmodified and in perfect working order.

FINE: All original parts and configuration, or possibly a very minor alteration from original configuration that was made during the period of use (fancy grips added, sight configuration changed slightly, etc.). This condition rating applies primarily to older and antique firearms. Sharp markings, only minor grip blemishes, good bore. Also, at least the following percentage of original finish by production era:

1920-1945:	90%
1890-1920:	70%
1865-1890:	50%
Pre 1865:	30%

Factory refinish: A factory refinished antique S&W with 98% of the refinish remaining, which was in excellent condition before refinishing (i.e., sharp markings, no pitting remaining under refinish) may approach "fine" in value.

VERY GOOD: All original parts. For modern guns, must be in perfect working order, no corrosion or pitting, minor scratches only. For antique guns, smooth metal and sharp edges, clear markings. Also, at least the following percentage of original finish by production era:

Post 1945:	85%
1920-1945:	60%
1890-1920:	40%
1865-1890:	10%
Pre 1865:	less than 10%

Factory refinish: A modern S&W with 98% of factory refinish or an antique S&W with 85% of factory refinish remaining may bring "very good" values.

Modern professional refinish: Antique guns with 98% of a non-factory high quality refinish or restoration may bring "very good" values.

Older professional refinish: Antique guns with 85% of a professional non-factory refinish from the period of original use may bring "very good" values.

Modified configuration: Older or antique guns with major modifications that were clearly made during the period of use may bring "very good" value if otherwise in fine to excellent condition. This is probably most often noted where Old West hog legs have had their barrels bobbed.

GOOD: Good working order. Markings are legible. There may be minor repairs and light pitting. May be refinished. Grips may be worn or cracked, but should be serviceable. Configuration may have been modified. Bores should be "shootable" on modern guns, but are disregarded on antique guns. Antique guns may lack any original finish, but modern guns in "good" condition will probably show at least the following percentages base on production era:

Post 1945:	75%
1920-1945:	60%
1890-1920:	30%

FAIR: Modern guns must be in safe working condition, but can be well worn, showing visible repair or replacement parts, or needing adjustment or minor repair. May be pitted so long as pitting does not affect function or safety. Antique guns may have major parts replaced and minor parts missing, may be rusted, pitted, heavily buffed or refinished, may have rounded edges, illegible markings, cracked or broken grips, and should be working or easily repaired.

POOR: Broken, poorly refinished, heavily rusted and pitted, or otherwise generally undesirable. Most often valued only as "project guns" for amateur gunsmiths, curiosities for display, or parts guns.

> *Note:* Most recent production guns are found in "good" or better condition, since it seems to take decades of heavy use and/or substantial abuse to reduce a quality modern firearm to "fair" or "poor"

The above condition definitions were approached with some trepidation. Our intent is not to change or replace the NRA definitions, but to refine them as applied specifically to Smith & Wessons.

NRA has established two different sets of condition standards for antique and modern firearms. They are as follows:

NRA Modern Firearms Condition Ratings

NEW: Not previously sold at retail; in same condition as current factory production.

NEW, DISCONTINUED: Same as "new," but discontinued model.

PERFECT: In new condition in every respect.

EXCELLENT: New condition; used but little; no noticeable marring of wood or metal; bluing perfect (except at muzzle or sharp edges).

VERY GOOD: In perfect working condition; no appreciable wear on working surfaces; no corrosion or pitting; only minor surface dents or scratches.

GOOD: In safe working condition; minor wear on working surfaces; no broken parts; no corrosion or pitting that will interfere with proper functioning.

FAIR: In safe working condition, but well worn; perhaps requiring replacement of minor parts or adjustments, which should be indicated in advertisement; no rust, but may have corrosion pits that do not render the article unsafe or inoperable.

NRA Antique Firearms Condition Ratings

FACTORY NEW: All original parts; 100% original finish; in perfect condition in every respect, inside and out.

EXCELLENT: All original parts; over 80% original finish; sharp lettering, numerals, and design on metal and wood; unmarred wood; fine bore.

FINE: All original parts; over 30% original finish; sharp lettering, numerals, and design on metal and wood; minor marks in wood; good bore.

VERY GOOD: All original parts; zero to 30% original finish; original metal surfaces smooth with all edges sharp; clear lettering, numerals and design on metal; wood slightly scratched or bruised; bore disregarded for collector firearms.

GOOD: Some minor replacement parts; metal smoothly rusted or lightly pitted in places, cleaned, or reblued; principal lettering, numerals, and design on metal legible; wood refinished, scratched, bruised, or minor cracks repaired; in good working order.

FAIR: Some major parts replaced; minor replacement parts may be required; metal rusted, may be lightly pitted all over, vigorously cleaned, or reblued; rounded edges of metal and wood; principal lettering, numerals, and design on metal partly obliterated; wood scratched, bruised, cracked, or repaired when broken; in fair working order or can be easily repaired and placed in working order.

POOR: Major and minor parts replaced; major replacement parts required and extensive restoration needed; metal deeply pitted; principal lettering, numerals, and design obliterated; wood badly scratched, bruised, cracked, or broken; mechanically inoperative; generally undesirable as a collector's firearm.

As you can see, these definitions are rather concise and elegant, and designed to apply to a wide range of firearms in a wide range of conditions. What we have tried to do is to focus them on S&Ws, particularly addressing the following concerns:

Disparity Between Antique and Modern Definitions: The widely differing standards for antique and modern guns make a great deal of sense when you consider that they must cover both a seventeenth century flintlock and a 1995 production polymer framed semiauto. However, they can cause a problem in S&Ws when the products span both sides of the modern/antique line.

Legally, the cutoff date between modern and antique firearms is 1898—those made in or before that year are antique, with more recent production being modern. Hence, if you take two top-break revolvers, both in "80% original finish" condition, but one made in 1898 and the other in 1899, the "antique" gun would be rated "excellent" while the "modern" gun would be closer to "good."

You will notice that in this book, we have tended to apply "antique" condition terminology to tip-up and top-break revolvers, even though some top-breaks were produced as late as 1940, and that we've applied "modern" condition terminology to hand ejectors even though some were produced as early as 1896. This was done primarily to avoid artificial breaks in condition ratings based on an arbitrary cutoff date.

Disparity Between Guns Produced Decades Apart: In real life, the more recently the gun was produced, the better the condition it is likely to be found in. It would create an unrealistic picture of the marketplace to insist that an 1858 First First would have to have the same objective amount of condition to be considered "antique excellent" as an 1898 .32 HE 1st model. The same rationale would apply to an 1899 New Departure compared to a Sigma under the modern ratings.

Disparity of Original Finish Remaining within a Definition: This is probably most apparent in the NRA "antique fine" definition, which includes guns with 30% to 80% original finish. In practice, an antique gun with 80% original finish may bring a price double or more than one with 30% original finish.

In our experience, collectors and dealers tend to make unconscious mental adjustments in their rating and pricing to adapt to these "disparities." To reflect this we have tried to build a sliding scale of condition relative to era into the book's definitions, without going outside of the accepted ranges of the NRA definitions.

The Real World of Modified and Refinished Guns: There is little allowance in the NRA definitions for otherwise high condition guns that have been refinished or modified during their period of use. Our experience is that these guns find ready buyers at higher prices than their strict NRA condition rating would warrant, so we have tried to include these in the scope of the book's definitions. Particularly, factory refinished guns and Western era modified guns are of special interest to S&W collectors, as discussed earlier.

RESOURCES AND BIBLIOGRAPHY

S&W Factory Records

S&W collectors are very fortunate to be able to access original factory records on many individual Smith & Wesson firearms. This should be the starting place for researching special features on a gun or special history attributed to a gun. It will also often be the most dependable and definitive information available on a specific gun.

Through the foresight and generosity of the Smith & Wesson company and Factory Historian Roy Jinks, the factory records and gun collection are being donated to the Connecticut Valley Historical Museum in Springfield, Massachusetts. Here, they are being professionally archived, preserved, and indexed, with funding provided in part by the S&W Collectors Association (SWCA). The information contained in the records will be made available to qualified researchers and interested collectors on a fee basis. It is anticipated there will be no charge to members of SWCA.

Factory Letters

Meanwhile, a "factory letter" on a specific gun is available from S&W for a research fee of $20. When requesting a factory letter, include as much information as possible on the gun, starting with the basics—model and serial number. Since even experienced collectors and dealers can make a mistake in identifying a model, it's best to include all possible information including barrel address, patent dates, all other markings, caliber, barrel length, and finish. A photo, photocopy, or even pencil and paper tracing of the outline of the gun may be helpful. Be sure to specifically ask about any special features or history about which you have a question. It may give the researcher a clue that he would not know to follow otherwise.

The factory letter will generally include background information on the model in general, the date the specific gun was shipped, its destination, and any special or unusual features on the gun as shown in factory records. Sometimes, a portion of this information will be unavailable. For example, records are missing for many of the earliest tip-ups, and it's difficult to find accurate information on a New or Old Russian due to the numerous duplicate serial number ranges of the multiple Russian contracts.

Of course, the vast majority of S&Ws were shipped in standard configuration to large distributors. The chances of getting a "hit" (i.e., especially unusual or interesting information) on a standard configuration gun with no known history are slim, but it does happen. Even on a standard model, however, a factory letter can make an interesting part of a display for the piece.

Where factory letters are especially important are situations where a premium is being asked for special features or history. At a minimum, the letter should not flatly contradict the feature claimed. For example, a gun offered as a rare 2" barrel variation should not "letter" as shipped with a 4" barrel, and a gun attributed to an individual who died in 1922 should not "letter" as being shipped in 1925. At best, the letter may confirm the specific features or history attributed to the gun.

To order a factory letter, send the complete description and $20 to Smith & Wesson, Attn.: Mr. Roy Jinks, PO Box 2208, Springfield, MA 01102.

Smith & Wesson Collectors Association

Membership in SWCA is a worthwhile investment for any S&W enthusiast. The quarterly *S&W Journal* is worth the price of membership by itself. The association has an annual meeting held each year in a different part of the country. This "members-only" get-together includes a S&W-only gun show featuring both trade tables and competitively judged display exhibits, as well as lectures, social functions, awards, and a fundraising auction. Here you will see S&Ws that you will see nowhere else, and most importantly, meet other enthusiasts and future friends. Membership applications are available from SWCA, PO Box 444, Afton, NY 13730. Sponsorship by a current member or reference from a collectible gun dealer are required. Current dues are $25 U.S., $35 international.

National Rifle Association

The NRA is far and away the most effective advocate protecting your endangered right to own firearms. Any collector who is not a member is simply not pulling his/her own weight. Not every collector agrees with every position that the NRA takes. This is fine, and appropriate; work to redress your concern within the organization. Meanwhile, present a united front protecting gun owners' rights.

Contact the NRA at: NRA, 11250 Waples Mill Rd., Fairfax, VA 22030. Dues are $35 annually, $90 for three years, $140 for five years, with the prestigious life membership available for $750 ($375 for individuals over the age of 65 or disabled veterans) on a lump sum or installment plan basis. Telephone number for membership inquiries only is 800-672-3888.

Springfield Research Service (SRS)

They will research specific military-issued handguns for a fee. SRS, P.O. Box 4181, Silver Spring, MD 20904.

Books

There are but a few outstanding reference books on Smith & Wesson, and some of these have acquired a collectible status of their own. They include:

The History of Smith & Wesson by Roy Jinks. Still in print, this concise and readable reference by the S&W factory historian is indispensable to anyone interested in these guns and their history. Well-illustrated, it covers all S&W guns from the beginnings of the firm through 1975, along with the history of the company and related topics. A must for serious and casual collectors. 290 pages, about $28. Beinfield Publishing Co., Los Angeles.

Smith & Wesson, 1857-1945 by Robert Neal and Roy Jinks. Out of print, this 434 page large format book is the "Bible" of S&W collecting. Well-illustrated, it lists all Smith & Wesson guns by caliber through the end of WWII. It also includes invaluable information on experimental models, factory engraving, catalogs, and patents. Originally published in 1966 by A. S. Barnes & Co., it was revised and expanded in 1975. The serious S&W collector will need to purchase a copy eventually, unless he/she is only interested in postwar models. The bad news is, when copies can be found, they usually exchange hands in the $350 range. In the meantime, try interlibrary loan—you might get lucky.

S & W books, top to bottom: two versions of Neal and Jinks, Parsons, Jinks, McHenry and Roper

Smith & Wesson Revolvers - The Pioneer Single Action Models by J. E. Parsons. Out of print, 227 pages, some illustrations, published in 1957 by William Morrow & Company, New York. Fascinating and authoritative account of the early S&W revolvers, especially in relationship to the American West. An extensive appendix is dedicated to reprinting the correspondence between Col. Schofield and S&W. Usually sells for around $50. Individuals interested in this era may also want to check out another book by the same author, *The Peacemaker and Its Rivals,* which concerns primarily the Colt Single Action Army, but has a chapter dedicated to S&W products of the era and interesting reports of the army ordnance trials.

Smith & Wesson Handguns by R. C. McHenry and W. F. Roper, originally published in 1945 by Standard Publications, Inc. This book was the first to try to sort out S&Ws for collectors. Recently reprinted, original copies sell as collectibles for around $60.

S&W Collectors Association 25th Anniversary Journal reprints the first eleven years of *The S&W Journal,* official publication of the S&W Collectors Association. Contains important and detailed information found nowhere else, with an index. Current plans are to continue compiling and reprinting back issues through the first twenty-five years (SWCA founded in 1970). Price $20 to members.

The Knives of Smith & Wesson by C. E. Rinke, illustrates many standard models as well as prototypes and one-of-a-kind S&W knives.

While not focused primarily on S&Ws, individuals interested in firearms engraving would do well to check out *Firearms Engraving As Decorative Art* by Frederic A. Harris, and *L. D. Nimschke, Firearms Engraver* by R. L. Wilson. Another book by Wilson not yet available as this goes to print should also be of considerable interest, titled *Steel Canvas.*

Magazines

The S&W Journal, published quarterly by the SWCA, again contains information found nowhere else. It is a necessity for the advanced collector and well worth the price of membership for any S&W enthusiast. The *Journal* tends to be the cutting edge of S&W research. Membership details noted above.

Gun Report (monthly, $29.95 subscription, PO Box 38, Aledo, IL 61231) and ***Man At Arms*** (bimonthly, $24 subscription, PO Box 460, Lincoln, RI 02865) are two professionally produced magazines for gun collectors in general that often run information on S&Ws. The MAA May 1988 issue was devoted entirely to S&W, with an article on S&W rarities by David Burghoff and an article by Charles Pate on the Australian Colonial Police model.

American Rifleman, membership magazine of the NRA, 11250 Waples Mill Road, Fairfax, VA, often has articles of interest to S&W collectors.

Gun List, 26 issues a year, $27.95 subscription, Krause Publications, 700 E. State St., Iola, WI 54945, is an indexed firearms paper featuring classified ads broken down by brand name for individual guns for sale. A recent issue had 60 listings in its "S&W Early Models Pre-1940 For Sale" class, and nearly 500 listings in its "S&W For Sale" class.

Cada Gun Journal, 12 issues a year, $29.95 subscription, One Appletree Square, Minneapolis, MN 55425, has classified ads broken down by brand name for individual guns and articles of interest to gun collectors. Recent issues have had from 30 to 150 listings in its S&W classifications.

Shotgun News, 36 issues a year, $58 subscription, PO Box 669, Hastings, NE 68902 is an advertising paper for "anything that shoots." Dealer oriented with more display ads than classified, can be useful for dealer prices for current production models and police trade-in or military surplus guns.

Old Town Station Dispatch, quarterly, $20 subscription, Jim Supica, Pres., PO Box 15351, Lenexa, KS 66285, is a catalog and journal of antique arms with articles and individual guns for sale; emphasis on antique S&W and the Old West. Recent issue had 140 S&W tip-ups and top-breaks for sale.

There are a number of excellent newsstand gun magazines that publish information on S&W production models, and, seemingly with more frequency lately, articles on out of production collectible and historic firearms. They include *Guns & Ammo*, *Shooting Times*, *Guns*, *Gun World*, *Handguns*, *Combat Handguns*, *Handgunning*, and *American Handgunner*, among others.

Price Guides

There are a number of general firearms price guides on the market. While all are useful, the authors have found the following three to be of special merit.

Standard Catalog of Firearms by Schwing, Houze, and Madaus, Krause Publications, updated annually. Utilizes the NRA condition rating system (excellent through poor). Photo illustrated.

Blue Book of Gun Values by Steve Fjestad, updated annually. Utilizes the percentage condition rating system, based on percent of original finish remaining on the gun (10% through 100%).

Flayderman's Guide to Antique American Firearms and Their Values by Norman Flayderman, updated every few years. Illustrated, contains background information, uses NRA condition rating system, limited to antique American guns.

Corrections and Additions

We have tried our best to assure the accuracy and completeness of the information in this book. Where there was a question, we tried to err on the side of including too much information instead of too little. No doubt we have made some errors and included obscure variations while overlooking more significant material. There are probably a few prices listed that will bring more amusement than enlightenment to experienced collectors.

We welcome corrections, additions, and comments. Please include any documentation that might allow us to substantiate changes in future editions.

Richard Nahas
SMX Systems
PO Box 66
Manassas, VA 20110

Jim Supica
Old Town Station, Ltd.
PO Box 15351
Lenexa, KS 66285
Phone 913-492-3000
Fax 913-492-3022
E-mail "OldTownSta@aol.com"

TIP-UP REVOLVERS

Contents

This section covers "tip-up" or "bottom-break" revolvers. They are listed by "model number." Model number indicates frame size from smallest to largest:

Model 1: Small frame .22 cal., 7-shot
Model 1-1/2 ("One and a half"): Medium-small frame .32 RF cal., 5-shot
Model 2: Medium frame .32 RF cal., 6-shot

Within each model, variations are listed in general chronological order.

Basic characteristics:

- Barrel tips up to remove cylinder for loading and unloading
- Chambered for .22 or .32 rimfire cartridges (Also .41 rimfire, very rare)
- First type of revolver made by S&W
- "Spur trigger" - no triggerguard

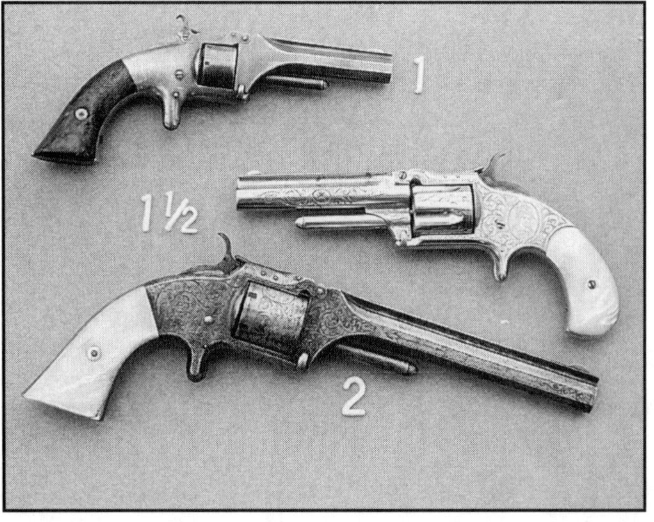

The three tip-up frame sizes: One, One and a Half, and Two

Operation: Gun is opened for loading by lifting latch at bottom front of frame, below barrel. Barrel tips up and cylinder slips out. Empty cases are manually punched out of the cylinder using the ejector stud, which is parallel to and below the barrel. Cartridges are then loaded into the cylinder before it is replaced in the gun. Latch catches automatically when the barrel is lowered to closed position.

> COLLECTOR'S TIPS:
> **1) Do not fire modern ammunition in these guns.**
> **2) Never carry an old single action revolver with a live round under the hammer.**

Serial numbers and assembly numbers: Serial number identifies the specific gun, and appears stamped in the metal of the grip butt (visible without removing grips), and is usually stamped in the wood on the inside of the right grip. These numbers should be the same.

An assembly number, consisting of one to three characters (numbers, letters, or both) appears stamped in three places on the gun: the rear of the barrel under the bore (gun must be open to find it), the front or rear of the cylinder (sometimes obscured by corrosion), and the grip frame under the grips (grips must be removed to find it). These numbers should all match. See comments in opening chapters on the effect of mismatched numbers on value.

Legal Status: All S&W tip-up revolvers are antiques since they were all manufactured prior to 1899.

Model Number One Background Information

The Model Number One was introduced in 1857 and was manufactured in various forms through 1881. This minuscule weapon marked both the beginning of the era of the self-contained cartridge and the beginning of the firm of Smith & Wesson. Both legacies continue to this day.

Samuel Colt's revolver, introduced in the late 1830s, revolutionized firearms technology by providing a reliable repeating mechanism. Like other guns of the era, the Colts had to be loaded by packing each of the chambers with loose black powder and a lead ball, followed by placing a percussion cap on the nipple of each chamber. Six shots in rapid succession was a great leap forward, but the reloading process was cumbersome and time consuming. Pre-loading the ball and powder into fragile paper cartridges would speed things up somewhat, but not much. What was needed was a repeating gun that would chamber a self-contained cartridge that would stand up to the rigors of weather and rough handling and could be quickly loaded and unloaded.

The first Smith & Wesson partnership, 1854-1855, took a preliminary stab at the problem with a hollow based lead projectile containing primer and propellant in its base, which was fired from a lever action pistol with a tubular magazine mounted under the barrel. The gun was soon nicknamed "The Volcanic," and in the mid-1850s both Horace Smith and Daniel Wesson left the enterprise to the ministrations and ownership of a shirt manufacturer. You may have heard of him and his lever action rifles that evolved from the first Smith & Wessons. His name was Oliver Winchester.

Meanwhile, in Europe progress was being made toward developing self-contained cartridges using a metal case to hold the powder and/or primer. Both pinfire cartridges (wherein a firing pin protruded from each cartridge) and flobert cartridges (an underpowered early rimfire type concept) showed some promise.

Slowing development in the U.S. was that Colt held an exclusive patent for the revolving mechanism necessary to make an effective revolver. When that patent expired, D. B. Wesson invented the .22 rimfire cartridge and a small 7-shot spur trigger revolver to fire it. Smith & Wesson teamed up again to manufacture the new type of gun.

One impediment proved to be that the concept of a revolver cylinder bored through from one end to the other had been previously patented by one Rollin White. White had patented the bored through cylinder incidental to a plan to improve Colt's revolver. Colt had not been interested in White's concept.

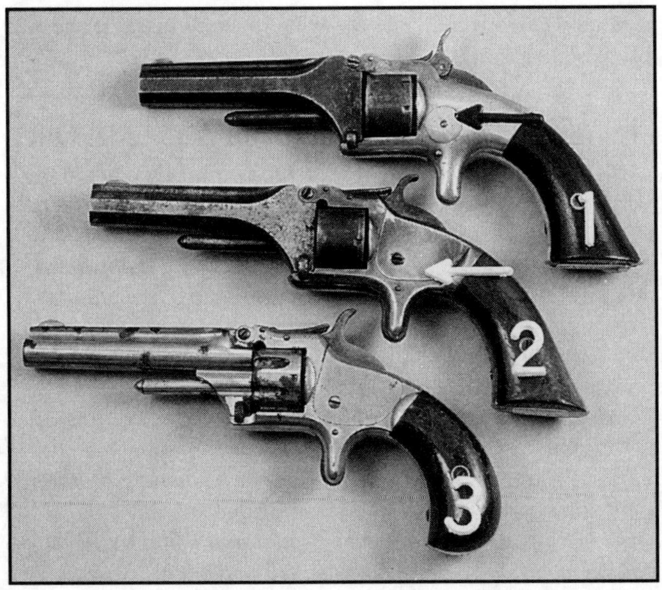

Model One: (1) 1st Issue (note small circular sideplate); (2) 2nd Issue; (3) 3rd Issue (note birdshead butt)

S&W soon purchased the right to use the Rollin White patent and began manufacture. The White patent provided S&W with a virtual monopoly on the manufacture of effective cartridge revolvers through 1872.

S&W called their little .22 rimfire cartridge the Number One cartridge—a name that came to be applied to the gun that fired it. The cartridge was essentially the same as the .22 short that is still sold today. However, modern smokeless ammunition should NEVER be fired in these little old .22s.

The Model Number One is the gun that started it all.

MODEL NO. 1 1ST ISSUE REVOLVER:

Cal-.22 Rimfire Short, single action, 7-shot non-fluted cylinder with a 3-3/16" octagonal barrel, and spur trigger. Normally a silver plated brass frame, blue barrel and cylinder, square butt with smooth rosewood grips or pearl or ivory on special order, round blade front sight. This frame has rounded sides with no triggerguard. Collectors recognize six different "types." This model has special collector appeal as the first revolver produced by S&W, and the first production American revolver for a metallic cased cartridge. Small circular sideplate. Collector's shorthand: Sometimes called the "First first," or followed by type, thus: "First first third."

See below for serial number range

11,671 mfd. total of all six types 1857-1860

ID Key: .22 tip-up w/square/flared butt, round-sided frame (cross section of frame behind hammer would be oval); small round sideplate

Types by approximate serial number ranges, listing change or variation:

First Type, s/n 1-213: Barrel latch is a spur projecting from the bottom front of the frame; recoil plate revolved with cylinder

Exc	Fine	VG	Good	Fair	Poor
12000	8000	5000	4000	3000	1500

Second Type, s/n 213-1130: Projecting spur barrel latch continues; recoil plate made part of the frame

Exc	Fine	VG	Good	Fair	Poor
5000	4000	2500	1700	1200	800

Third Type, s/n 1130-3000: Bottom catch with side projections

Exc	Fine	VG	Good	Fair	Poor
3000	2400	1900	1300	750	500

Fourth Type, s/n 3000-4200: Recoil plate altered

Exc	Fine	VG	Good	Fair	Poor
2500	2000	1700	1000	650	500

Fifth Type, s/n 4200-5500: Rifling changed from 3LH to 5RH grooves

Exc	Fine	VG	Good	Fair	Poor
2500	2000	1700	1000	650	500

Sixth Type, s/n 5500-11671: Rotating plate eliminated

Exc	Fine	VG	Good	Fair	Poor
2000	1700	1500	900	600	400

MODEL NO. 1 2ND ISSUE:

Cal-.22 Rimfire Short, similar to the 1st Issue, except with a flat-sided frame and larger irregularly shaped sideplate; 7-shot non-fluted cylinder, 3-3/16" octagonal barrel, blued barrel and cylinder, with silver plated brass frame, or full plating in nickel. No triggerguard, patent dates on the cylinder, round blade front sight, single action tip-up with spur trigger. Approximately 4,402 had slight casting flaws, and were marked "2D QUAL'TY."

Serial number range continued from 1st Issue:
11672-126361 117,000 mfd. 1860-1868

ID Key : 22 tip-up w/square/flared butt w/flat-sided frame; large irregular sideplate

Exc	Fine	VG	Good	Fair	Poor
600	450	285	200	150	90

Variations:

- "2D QUAL'TY": Double to triple above values.
- Straight sideplate: Early production has a straight line rather than curved at rear of sideplate. Worth 25% to 100% premium.
- First 20,000 have two patent dates on cylinder. Third patent date added later and is more common.

Gutta-Percha Cases for Model Ones:

It is estimated that 5,000 gutta-percha cases were made for the Model Number One 1st Issue and 2nd Issue by a company called "Littlefield and Parsons." Gutta-percha may be considered an early type of plastic, and looks and feels similar to the "hard rubber" material commonly used for nineteenth century pistol grips, but with less luster.

Two types of cases are commonly recognized and are identified by the images molded in relief on their lids. The "Pistol" type case has a Model One 1st Issue on the lid and the "Stand of Flags" case has a cluster of flags on poles as the central decoration. The interior is velvet lined and includes an irregularly shaped holder for about fifty-six cartridges.

Old gutta-percha is a rather fragile material, and cracks and chips are not uncommon. The hinge connection is especially delicate. Surviving cases are highly sought after by collectors, and will bring $700 to $3,000 depending on variation and condition.

Gutta-percha cases were made by the same manufacturer for other small handguns, as well as for playing cards and other purposes. Model Ones are sometimes found paired with these other types of cases. While valuable, they don't bring the premium paid for those originally made for the guns.

Wooden cases were sold by M. W. Robinson, and doubtless others, and are worth $250 to $500.

MODEL NO. 1 3RD ISSUE:

Cal-.22 Rimfire Short, similar to the 2nd Issue, except with a fluted cylinder, round butt frame with a birdshead grip with smooth rosewood finish stocks, blue or nickel finish or nickel frame with blue barrel and cylinder ("half-plate"). Round barrel with top rib, round blade front sight, seven marked "2D QUAL'TY". The 2-11/16" barrel is much scarcer and has "S&W" and patent markings on the left side of the barrel. The 3-3/16" barrel has markings on the top rib with "Smith & Wesson Springfield Mass" and patent dates of April 3, 55-July 5, 59-Dec 18, 60.

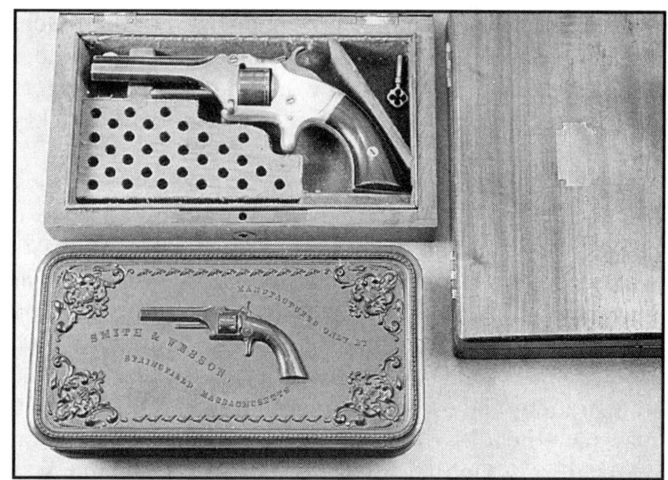

Model One casings, top to bottom: MW Robinson wood, gutta-percha.

Serial number range 1-131163 131,163 mfd. 1868-1881

ID Key: .22 tip-up w/birdshead butt

Exc	Fine	VG	Good	Fair	Poor
400	325	225	150	100	75

Variations:

- Short barrel (may actually measure between 2-5/8" to 2-3/4")

Exc	Fine	VG	Good	Fair	Poor
650	500	425	275	200	150

- "2D QUAL'TY": Very rare - value would be in range of 10X the standard model or more, beware of fakes
- Topstrap of frame changed about s/n 10000
- Blue or half-plate less common than nickel

Wood cases were made for Model One 3rd Issues, and will bring $250 to $500.

Contemporary Commentary on the Model One:

"I was armed to the teeth with a pitiful little Smith & Wesson's seven-shooter, which carried a ball like a homeopathic pill, and it took the whole seven to make a dose for an adult. But I thought it was grand. It appeared to me to be a dangerous weapon. It had only one fault -- you could not hit anything with it. One of our conductors practiced a while on a cow with it, and as long as she stood still and behaved herself she was safe; but as soon as she went to moving about, and he got to shooting at other things, she came to grief." - Mark Twain

"Yep, I've seen that kind, but never handled 'em. I was afeared I'd break it." - Jim Bridger

"Boy, if you shoot me with dat and I find out, I put you acrost my knee and spank hell outen you."
- Old Nick Janis on examining Alson B. Orstrander's S&W Model One

Model One and a Half, left to right: New Model (rare short barrel), rare Transitional, Old Model

Model Number One and a Half and Model Number Two Background Information

As may be apparent from the quotes above, a more powerful cartridge was soon found to be desirable. Make no mistake about it however—no one wanted to be shot by the greasy dirty little .22 projectile from a Model Number One in the days before antibiotics. This is readily proven by its popularity into the 1880s and its plethora of imitators. Furthermore, the concept of a revolver firing a self-contained weatherproof metallic cartridge was an immediate success that continues today.

However, S&W readily recognized that a round with more immediate authority was desirable, especially for military usage. This led to the development, on the eve of the Civil War, of the Number Two .32 rimfire cartridge and the 6-shot Model Number Two to shoot it.

While hardly a powerhouse, the .32 rimfire was a considerable improvement over the .22, so much so that the Model Number Two became a tremendous favorite as a sidearm among Civil War officers. While the gun was never officially adopted by any military, this popularity gave rise to its common nickname among collectors—**"The Model Two Old Army."**

With the slackened demand for all guns following the Civil War, S&W wanted to introduce a more civilian oriented pocket version of the popular Model Two, while retaining the more powerful .32 cartridge. They did this by slightly shrinking the overall design, and going from a 6-shot to a 5-shot cylinder.

What with already producing a Model Number One and a Model Number Two, S&W was faced with the dilemma of what to call their new gun that fell in between the two previous sizes. They came up with the logical, if somewhat ungainly moniker of "Model Number One and a Half."

Thus the foundation was laid for the S&W practice of numbering frame sizes, which was carried over into their top-break models.

COLLECTOR'S TIP: It is easy to become confused by the nearly identical model names of the tip-up .32s and the top-break .32 and .38 single actions. See background information at the beginning of the top-break section for clarification.

MODEL NO. 1-1/2 "OLD MODEL" (aka "Model 1-1/2 1st Issue"):

Cal-.32 Rimfire, single action tip-up, 3-1/2" standard or 4" (rare) octagonal barrel, 5-shot non-fluted cylinder, spur trigger with no guard, blue or nickel finish or silver plating on special order, square butt with rosewood grips, round blade front sight, six marked "2D QUAL'TY" due to small casting flaws.

Serial number range 1~26300 ~26,300 mfd. 1865-1868

ID Key: 5-shot, square butt, unfluted cylinder, octagonal barrel

Exc	Fine	VG	Good	Fair	Poor
500	350	250	200	150	100

Variations:

- 4" barrel (est. 200 made): Double or triple the above values
- "2D QUAL'TY": Around 2X to 4X the above values, beware of fakes
- "Half-plate" (blue barrel and cylinder, nickel frame): Rare, worth premium

MODEL NO. 1-1/2 TRANSITION MODEL:

Possibly around 650 produced with Old Model unfluted cylinder and octagonal barrels with New Model birdshead grip frame.

Serial number range 27200-28800

ID Key: 5-shot, birdshead butt, unfluted cylinder, octagonal barrel

Exc	Fine	VG	Good	Fair	Poor
2500	1500	1000	850	600	400

MODEL NO. 1-1/2 NEW MODEL (Model 1-1/2, 2nd issue):

Cal-.32 Rimfire long, similar to 1st Issue with birdshead grip and round butt with rosewood grips, 5-shot fluted cylinder, blue or nickel finish, spur trigger with no guard, 3-1/2" standard round barrel, round blade front sight, 2-1/2" round barrel rare with markings on the side (standard length barrel has markings on top of barrel rib). Forty-one marked "2D QUAL'TY" due to slight flaws.

Serial number range 26301-127100
100,700 mfd. 1868-1875

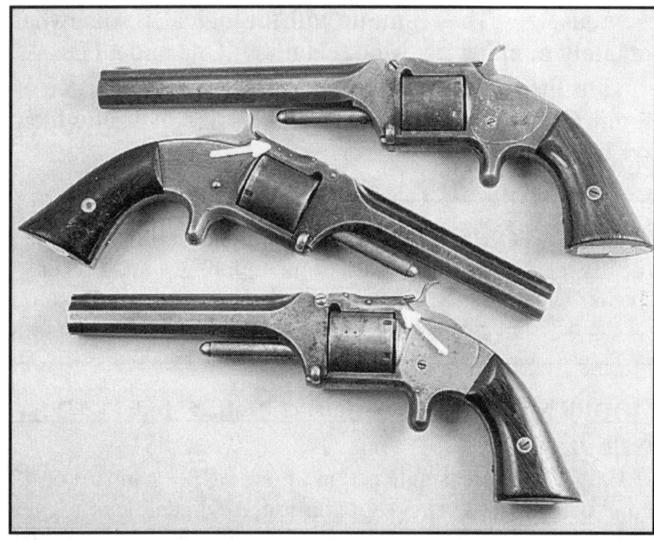

Model Two "Old Army," top to bottom: 3-pin 6-inch, 3-pin 5-inch, early 2-pin 5-inch

Historic Note: Serial number 41993 owned by Ulysses S. Grant

ID Key: 5-shot, birdshead butt, fluted cylinder, round barrel

Exc	Fine	VG	Good	Fair	Poor
350	250	200	150	120	100

Variations:

- Short barrel: Double to triple above values
- "2D QUAL'TY": Maybe 5X above values

MODEL NO. 2 OLD MODEL REVOLVER (No. 2 Old Army):

Cal-.32 Rimfire Long, 6-shot non-fluted cylinder, 5" and 6" barrels standard, 4" rare, 8" extremely rare. Octagonal barrels. Smooth rosewood grips on a square butt, bottom break action (tip-up), no triggerguard (spur trigger). Round blade front sight. A popular Civil War sidearm, but never purchased by the army. Single action on a forged wrought iron frame. Many look-alike copies were produced abroad. Finish- Estimated that 80% were blue, 10% nickel, remainder half-plate, silver, engraved, or other special. Advanced collectors recognize as many as nine different types of the Model Two. Thirty-five marked "2D QUAL'TY" due to slight casting imperfections.

5" or 6" Early Model: Two pins in topstrap, serial number range 1~3000.

5" or 6" Standard Model: Three pins in topstrap, remainder of the serial number range. A 4" barrel, 3-pin, made 1864-67 is quite rare, 10 mfd. with 8" barrel.

Another extremely rare variation consists of guns with sideplate mounted safeties, origin unknown. The few known examples are in the 57000 s/n range.

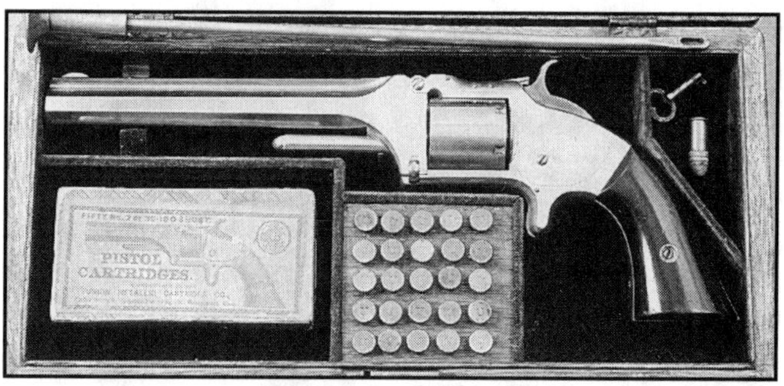

Scarce nickel Model Two in period case

Serial number range 1-77155 77,155 mfd. 1861-1874

Historic Notes: S/n 22592 owned by Rutherford B. Hayes. S/n 20615 and 20757 by Gen. George A. Custer. S/n 30619 attributed to Wild Bill Hickok, reportedly on his person the day he was killed. The first S&W to be officially adopted by a police department, the Kingston Ontario Canada Police Department, 42000 s/n range, no known markings. About 2600 were made marked "Kittridge & Co. Cincinnati Ohio" on the left side of the barrel for that famous distributor; s/n's are under 10000.

Probability of Civil War usage may be estimated by knowing that the serial number cutoff for 1864 production is 29359, and for 1865 is 48475.

ID Key: 6-shot tip-up .32

	Exc	Fine	VG	Good	Fair	Poor
Std. 3-pin	1200	800	500	375	275	175

Variations:

- Early 2-pin: Add up to 50%
- 4" barrel: 2 to 4X standard values
- 8" barrel: 5 to 10X standard values
- "2ND QUAL'TY": 5X or more standard values
- Factory wood case worth substantial premium
- At least one example reported as expertly modified to fire rimfire or centerfire ammunition

Model Number Three Tip-Up (Very Rare)

MODEL NO. 3 POCKET PISTOL:

Cal-.41 Rimfire S&W, this model was produced in 1867 on a limited basis and fashioned after the Model 1-1/2 New Model on a slightly larger scale. It was made to hold only four cartridges. Serial number 38, nickel, is known to exist. No other examples are yet known, although an unfinished specimen has been reported.

Estimated value in the $25,000 to $75,000 range.

TOP-BREAK REVOLVERS

Contents

The guns in this section are listed by frame size/model number:

MODEL 1-1/2 frame: .32 cal. 5-shot
MODEL 2 frame: .38 cal. 5-shot
MODEL 3 frame: .44 cal. 6-shot (includes other calibers on this frame)

Within each frame size, single actions are listed first, then double actions, then hammerless (lemon squeezers). Within action type, they are listed chronologically.

The Model 3 was made in several calibers besides .44. They are all listed in the Model 3 section.

Basic characteristics:

- They are hinged at the bottom front of the frame and "break open" with the barrel and cylinder tipping down from the frame for loading and unloading.
- Cartridges and empties are automatically ejected when the gun is opened.

Operation: A latch is located just ahead of the hammer, in most cases mounted on the topstrap extending from the rear of the barrel. (Usually the rear sight is mounted on this latch.) On most, but not all models, the latch is opened by lifting the latch. On some of the single action models, the hammer may need to be eased back to the first notch (NOT full cock) before opening the latch.

After lifting the latch, the barrel and cylinder tip forward and down, ejecting any shells in the cylinder. To open the gun without ejecting the shells, press on a small projection, stud, or lever located at the bottom of the hinge.

Removal of the cylinder, if desired, may be accomplished on most models by opening the gun, holding the latch up from the barrel, and unscrewing the cylinder in a counterclockwise direction while pulling gently. In some of the big single action Model 3s, a screw and cylinder retaining device must be removed or loosened before the cylinder can be removed.

COLLECTOR'S TIP: Be certain that no part of the latch or cylinder retainer is dragging on the cylinder while it is being removed or reinserted. This can result in a serious scratch in the gun's finish, which will adversely affect the value.

Safety Notes: Shooting modern high pressure smokeless powder ammunition in antique guns designed for black powder cartridges can be extremely hazardous to both gun and shooter! Many older revolver designs must be carried with an empty chamber under the firing pin to avoid accidental discharge.

Serial numbers and assembly numbers: Most of the top-breaks will have the serial number in the following locations:

1. Butt of the grip frame, visible without removing grips.
2. Rear face of cylinder.
3. Barrel—somewhat hard to find. Locate the latch serial number and then look to its right on the rear of the barrel in most cases.
4. Bottom of the latch.
5. Scratched, penciled, or stamped on the inside of the right grip panel.

These serial numbers should all match. See comments on how mismatched serial numbers affect value in the opening chapters.

Some of the American and Russian Model 3s have the serial number only on butt and grip, and will have assembly numbers consisting of one to three characters stamped on the barrel, cylinder, and latch in the locations noted above, and on the frame under the right grip panel (grips must be removed). Assembly number in all four locations should match.

Legal Status: Top-breaks span both sides of the 1898 antique/modern cutoff date. The following top-break revolvers are all antiques, with the frames manufactured prior to 1899:

All single action top-break revolvers, regardless of frame size or caliber
All Model 3 large frame size double action revolvers
All .32 DA models below s/n 209301
All .32 Safety Hammerless models below s/n 91400
All .38 DA models below s/n 382022
All .38 Safety Hammerless models below s/n 119900

The .38 Perfected and all other top-break revolvers not listed above are modern.

Top-Break Background Information

In 1870 the top-break mechanism was introduced on S&Ws with the large frame Model 3 American and was a significant leap forward in revolver design. The American was also the first "big bore" cartridge revolver produced in the U.S. In 1876, S&W debuted their first .38 caliber revolver with the top-break version of the medium Model 2 frame size, followed in 1878 by a .32 centerfire top-break on the medium-small Model 1-1/2 frame size.

Top-breaks were significantly sturdier designs than tip-ups, and were much faster to load and unload. Their chambering was primarily for the then-new centerfire calibers, which provided more reliable ignition, reloadability, and more powerful rounds with less fear of tearing the rim.

The introduction of the top-breaks coincides with the expiration of the Rollin White patent in 1872, which ended S&Ws protected monopoly on the production of effective cartridge revolvers. Archrival Colt introduced their famous solid frame Single Action Army, or Peacemaker, in 1873, a few years after the S&W Model 3. Throughout the remainder of the nineteenth century, the repeating handgun market was dominated by two types of revolvers: the top-breaks as produced by Smith & Wesson; and the solid frames manufactured by Colt, and in much smaller quantity, Remington. Despite a few other interesting designs, most notably the Merwin Hulbert twist-open revolver, most other gun makers followed one or both of these patterns, with the top-breaks probably becoming more predominant after 1880. Tip-ups and open-tops retained some popularity for .22 revolvers.

While double action revolvers had been popular in Europe for some time, the double action mechanism was first used on S&Ws in 1880 in .32 and .38 caliber, followed in 1881 in .44. Colt had introduced their solid frame double action a few years earlier in 1877. S&W took the concept a step further by creating a concealed hammer revolver, their "Safety Hammerless," in 1887.

Advocates of the solid frame style claimed superior durability, although this was more true of the single action models than the rather delicate double action solid frames. Top-break enthusiasts pointed to the difficulty and slowness of single ejection and individual chamber loading of the solid frames compared to the simultaneous ejection and exposed cylinder face reload of the top-breaks.

The introduction of the swing-out cylinder solid frame revolver (the "Hand Ejector") by S&W in 1896 and Colt earlier in 1889, marked the beginning of the decline of both top-break and solid-frame styles of revolver. The hand ejector offered nearly as much frame strength as the solid frames and nearly as convenient reloading accessibility and speed as the top-breaks. However, top-breaks remained in the S&W line nearly until World War II and were offered by other manufacturers after the war.

In determining what types of handguns were actually in use from 1870 to 1900, it's interesting to compare the production figures of the two major players. In looking at the big-framed, single action cartridge revolvers so entrenched in our collective imagination as the symbol of the Old West, S&W produced around 195,000 Model 3s in their first decade of production (1870-1879) compared to around 85,000 first decade Colt Single Action Armies (1873-1882). In fact, we find that Colt's numbers did not catch up with S&W until the early 1900s. By that time, both firms had made about a quarter million "hog legs." It's important to note, however, that about two-thirds of S&Ws total production of Model 3s went to overseas military contracts.

In looking at total production of centerfire revolvers, 1870 to 1900, we find slightly over half a million Colt solid frames compared to over one and a quarter million S&W top-breaks. If we add open-top, tip-up, and hand ejector types to these numbers, we come up with about 800,000 Colts compared to about 1,400,000 S&Ws.

It's readily apparent that Smith & Wesson top-break revolvers played a dominant role in the firearms market during the last third of the colorful nineteenth century.

Model Name Confusion: Model 1-1/2 and Model 2, Tip-Up and Top-Break

When they introduced the improved top-break configuration, S&W continued the practice of identifying frame size by number. This nomenclature has been carried forward by collectors, and can result in substantial confusion when trying to differentiate between tip-up and top-break revolvers. That's all you need to be aware of, and you may wish to stop reading here, because the rest of this commentary will probably make your head hurt.

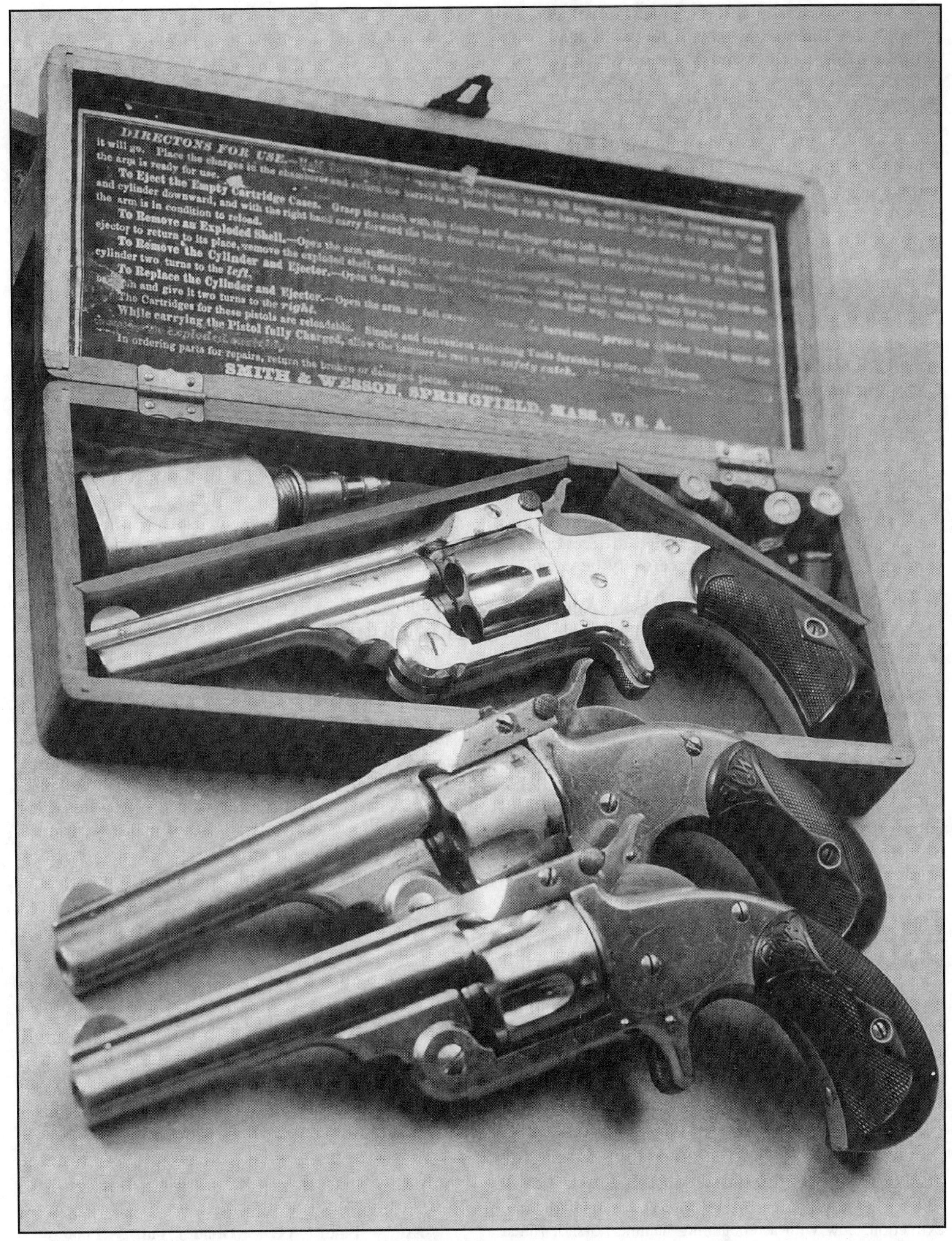

Model 1-1/2 Single Action. Note three different types of grips and factory made wood case.

There's no problem with the small Model One and large Model Three guns—the former were made only in tip-up configurations and the latter, for all practical purposes, only in top-break. Also, the double action revolvers avoid the confusion somewhat, since they are seldom referred to by frame size. Instead, they are usually referred to by caliber followed by the words "Double Action" (often abbreviated, both in writing and verbally, as "DA," i.e. ".38 DA").

However, when it comes to the single action medium-small framed Model One and a Half and the medium framed Model Two, it's a different story. I've seen two S&W collectors have a fifteen-minute conversation with neither realizing the other was talking about a different model. (Okay, Okay, I've *participated* in such a discussion. More than once.)

Let's consider the top-breaks, using the common names for the .32 single action top-break as examples. "The .32 Single Action" listed as first preference in the Neal and Jinks and Jinks books differentiates it from the DA models, but the tip-up 1-1/2 is also a single action. "The Model 1-1/2 Single Action" listed as first preference in Flayderman is no better, and perhaps even more confusing. You sometimes hear it referred to as the "Model 1-1/2 Centerfire," which differentiates it from the tip-ups, but could conceivably be confused with the .32 frame DA.

To be totally precise, you would have to call it either the ".32 Centerfire Single Action" or the "Model 1-1/2 Single Action Centerfire." We have gone with ".32 Single Action" for simplicity's sake, but the matter is far from settled.

The situation is a little less difficult with the Model Two frame .38 single action top-break, since the tip-up Model Two was in .32 caliber. Thus the name ".38 Single Action" tells us exactly which gun we're talking about. However, be aware that many collectors will still call it, properly, a Model Two (usually followed by 1st Model, 2nd Model, or 3rd Model).

This is probably a partial explanation for the common usage of "Model Two Old Army" when referring to the Model Two tip-up rimfire. It avoids confusion with the Model Two top-break centerfires. (Of course, this assumes that you find no confusion in calling a gun that was never officially adopted by any branch of the armed service an "army" model.) Did I mention the terminology here is somewhat cloudy?

.32 Frame - Model Number 1-1/2

MODEL NO. 1-1/2 SINGLE ACTION (.32 Single Action):

Cal-.32 S&W Centerfire, top-break action with auto extraction, now with a rebounding hammer, 5-shot fluted cylinder, 3", 3-1/2" (standard), 6" (scarce), 8" or 10" (both very rare) round barrel, blue (scarce) or nickel finish, grips of checkered hard rubber in black, brown, or mottled red, or plain wood on a birdshead grip. Three styles of hard rubber grips, earliest plain checkering w/no S&W logo s/n 1-15000, then checkered w/plain block letter S&W logo about 15000-29000, then checkered w/fancy intertwined S&W logo about s/n 29000-97500. Pinned round blade front sight, spur trigger with no guard, half cock notches with the hammer action. Approx. 500 factory wooden cases are reported to have been made. Matching serial found on the cylinder, barrel, frame, top latch, and grips. Early Model: with eccentric strain screw for mainspring tension under the grips in a serial range of 1-6500. May be quickly identified by absence of strain screw on front strap of grip. Later Model: with an outside strain screw for mainspring tension. Patent dates on barrel: Jan 17 and 24, 1865-July 11, 1865; Aug 24, 1869-Feb 20, 1877; reissue July 25, 1871.

Serial number range 1-97574 97,574 mfd. 1878-1892

ID Key: 5-shot .32 single action top-break

Exc	Fine	VG	Good	Fair	Poor
350	275	225	165	125	75

Variations:

- Early production without strain screw, add 25 to 50%
- 6" barrel, add 50%
- 8" or 10" barrel, 5X to 10X standard price
- 10% to 20% premium for blue

.32 Double Action

.32 DOUBLE ACTION FIRST MODEL REVOLVER:

Cal-.32 S&W, 5-shot fluted cylinder, 3" round barrel with top-break action and auto-ejection on pivoting down the barrel, plain hard rubber black grips, blue or nickel finish, straight cut sideplate, round blade front sight pinned into the barrel, triggerguard with a reverse curve that is separate from the frame. One of the rarest S&W production models. (Not pictured, but see photo of .38 DA 1st, which has a similar straight cut sideplate).

Serial number range 1-30 30 mfd. 1880

ID Key: Serial number below 31, front and rear edge of sideplate are straight lines, not curved

Exc	Fine	VG	Good	Fair	Poor
12000	9000	6000	4000	3000	2000

.32 DOUBLE ACTION SECOND MODEL:

Cal-.32 S&W, similar to First Model except with a curved sideplate, 3" ribbed barrel, pinned round blade front sight, black hard rubber stocks with S&W monogram, with one groove around the cylinder, blue or nickel finish, 5-shot cylinder with short flutes, triggerguard still with a reverse curve, top-break action.

Serial number range 31-22172 22,142 mfd. 1880-1882

ID Key: S/n range, curved sideplate edges, recurve triggerguard back, cyl. grooved w/double stop notches

Exc	Fine	VG	Good	Fair	Poor
275	225	190	160	100	70

.32 DA: (2) 2nd Model w/box and spare floral grips; (3) 3rd Model; (4) 4th Model

Variations:

- Floral/Wild Turkey grips: A few will be found with unusual hard rubber grips bearing the S&W logo, but with a floral pattern rather than checkering and pictures of wild turkeys in the floral pattern. Worth 50%-100% premium.

.32 DOUBLE ACTION THIRD MODEL:

Cal-.32 S&W, 3", 3-1/2", or 6" barrel, no groove around the cylinder and with longer flutes, black hard rubber stocks with S&W monogram, pinned round blade front sight, blue or nickel finish, 5-shot, triggerguard still with a reverse curve

Serial number range 22173-43405 22,232 mfd. 1882-1883

ID Key: S/n range, no cyl. grove, single set cyl. stops, recurve triggerguard

Exc	Fine	VG	Good	Fair	Poor
275	225	190	160	100	70

Variations:

- Slight premium for 6" barrel

.32 DOUBLE ACTION FOURTH MODEL:

Cal-.32 S&W, 3", 3-1/2", 6", 8", or 10" barrel, rounded triggerguard, blue or nickel finish, black hard rubber stocks with S&W monogram, pinned round blade front sight, top-break action, 5-shot.

Serial number range 43406~282999
~239,600 mfd. 1883-1909

ID Key: S/n range, rounded triggerguard, pinned front sight

Exc	Fine	VG	Good	Fair	Poor
200	175	150	125	75	40

Variations:

- Small premium for pre s/n 209301 antiques
- Add 25% for 6" barrel
- 5X to 10X standard price for 8" or 10" barrel

.32 DOUBLE ACTION FIFTH MODEL:

Cal-.32 S&W, 3", 3-1/2", or 6" barrel, blue or nickel finish, round blade front sight integral with the barrel, black hard rubber stocks with S&W monogram, 5-shot, rounded triggerguard.

Serial number range ~283000-327641
44,641 mfd. 1909-1919

ID Key: S/n range, rounded triggerguard, forged front sight integral to barrel (usually)

Exc	Fine	VG	Good	Fair	Poor
350	250	200	150	85	40

Variations:

- Add 25% for 6" barrel

.32 Safety: (1) 1st Model; (2) 2nd Model; (3) 3rd Model

.32 Safety Hammerless

(aka "Safety," "New Departure," or "Lemon Squeezer")

.32 SAFETY HAMMERLESS FIRST MODEL:

Cal-.32 S&W, 5-shot fluted cylinder, 2" (rare - known as "bicycle gun"), 3", or 3-1/2" (most common) barrel, with a rear grip safety on the backstrap, top-break action, blue(scarce) or nickel finish, checkered black hard rubber grips with S&W monogram, double action only, with triggerguard, fully enclosed hammer, round blade front sight. Designed by D.B. Wesson. Serial number found on the butt, cylinder, and top latch.

Serial number range 1-91417 91,417 mfd. 1888-1902

ID Key: Barrel release latch in back center of topstrap pushes down to open

Exc	Fine	VG	Good	Fair	Poor
325	260	210	175	125	75

Variations:

- Bicycle gun: 2" barrel with markings on side of barrel, double to triple standard value

COLLECTOR'S TIP: Early bicycle guns with the markings on top of barrel and extending back onto frame topstrap above the cylinder will bring 5X to 10X standard price. These were special order—the bicycle gun was not catalogued until the late 1890s.

.32 SAFETY HAMMERLESS SECOND MODEL:

Cal-.32 S&W, 5-shot fluted cylinder, 2", 3", 3-1/2", or 6" ribbed barrel, blue or nickel finish, checkered hard rubber grips with S&W monograms, pinned front sight, has T-shaped barrel latch with knurling on each side, top-break action, double action only, with triggerguard.

Serial number range 91418~170000
~78,500 mfd. 1902-1909

ID Key: S/n range, T-shape barrel latch lifts to open, patent dates on barrel, pinned sight

Exc	Fine	VG	Good	Fair	Poor
300	235	170	135	100	65

Variations:

- Bicycle gun: 2" barrel with markings on side, double standard value
- Add 25% for 6" barrel
- 1-1/2" barrel very rare, worth substantial premium if original
- 1" barrel reported, but not confirmed

.32 SAFETY HAMMERLESS THIRD MODEL:

Cal-.32 S&W, 5-shot fluted cylinder, 2", 3", or 3-1/2" barrel, blue or nickel finish, round blade front sight forged into the barrel on 3" and 3-1/2" versions, on 2" it may be pinned or forged, black rubber grips with S&W monogram, top-break action, double action only, with triggerguard.

Serial number range ~170000-242981
~73,000 mfd. 1909-1937

.32 Safety "Bicycle Gun"

ID Key: S/n range, T-shaped latch lifts to open, no patent dates, forged front sight (usually)

Exc	Fine	VG	Good	Fair	Poor
300	235	170	135	100	65

Variations:

- Bicycle gun: 2" barrel with markings on side, double standard value

Note: *New Model #3 Target Model .32-44 listed in Model #3 section, .320 Revolving Rifle listed in Long Gun section*

.38 Frame - Model Number 2

.38 Single Action

.38 SINGLE ACTION 1ST ISSUE ("Baby Russian," Model No. 2 First Model):

Cal-.38 S&W, 5-shot fluted cylinder, 3-1/4" (standard) or 4" round barrel, blue(scarcer - about 6500 made) or nickel finish, top-break action, spur trigger, no triggerguard, pinned round blade front sight, round butt, checkered hard rubber stocks w/S&W monograms. Wood grips on most blue guns.

"Baby Russian" nickname derived from appearance similar to Model 3 Russians. Although sometimes applied to both First and Second Model .38 Single Actions, the term really designates only the first model with its longer under-barrel ejector housing.

The first 138 or so Baby Russians have an added safety device of dubious utility called the Aldritch .38 hammer lock. When this was discontinued early in production, frames had already been manufactured for it with an extra screw hole on the right side of the frame just behind the recoil shield. These 1000 or so guns were completed with a filler screw in this hole. Subsequent production lacked the hole.

Serial number range 1-25548 25,548 mfd. 1876-1877

Historic Note: Used by Baltimore City Police 1876-1917 (they switched to .38 DAs and Perfecteds). Examples are very rare, fall in serial number range of 4600-6949, are marked "Balto City Police" on backstrap (three different styles of engraving known), 4" nickel guns, known examples were shipped to Trimble & Kleibacker in Baltimore in the summer of 1876.

ID Key: .38 spur trigger w/long ejector housing under barrel

Exc	Fine	VG	Good	Fair	Poor
500	325	275	225	175	125

Variations:

- Baltimore City Police: 5X to 10X standard value
- Aldritch .38 hammer lock (1st 100 or so): Maybe double value
- Slight premium for early guns with filler screws on right side of frame
- Blue w/wood grips, add 50%

.38 SINGLE ACTION SECOND MODEL (Model 2 2nd Issue):

Cal-.38 S&W, 5-shot fluted cylinder, 3-1/4",4", 5", 6", 8", or 10" round barrel, blue or nickel finish, shorter extractor housing under the barrel from the 1st Issue, no triggerguard, top-break action, a strain screw for the leaf type spring is now found on the frame's inside strap to tension the hammer spring.

Serial number range 1-108255 108,255 mfd. 1877-1891

ID Key: Spur trigger .38, w/sides of spur triggerguard integral to frame, stubby ejector housing

Exc	Fine	VG	Good	Fair	Poor
325	275	225	175	125	75

Variations:

- 5X to 10X premium for 8" or 10" barrel
- 10-25% premium for 6" barrel
- Red mottled hard rubber grips worth 10% premium

.38 SINGLE ACTION THIRD MODEL (Model of 1891 Single Action):

Cal-.38 S&W, 5-shot fluted cylinder, 3-1/4", 4", 5", or 6" barrel, checkered hard rubber grips with S&W monograms or plain pearl w/gold plated S&W monograms, blue or nickel finish, has a separate triggerguard, rebounding hammer, may be found with single-shot barrels in .22, .32, or .38 caliber as combination sets, top-break action, numbered concurrently with the First Model Single-Shot and the Mexican Model.

This is a very attractive gun, looking like a 2/3 scale New Model Number 3, and is highly sought after. However, unfortunately, there has always seemed to be a discrepancy between the number of guns supposedly manufactured and the availability of this model on the collector's market. By manufacturing records, this model should be about as common as the Baby Russian .38 SA 1st, and maybe twenty times more common than the Model of 1891 Single-Shot, with which it shares a common frame. However, our subjective impression is that one sees ten .38 SA 1sts for every .38 SA 3rd, and that the Model of 1891 Revolver is, if anything, scarcer than the Model of 1891 Single-Shot.

The shared serial number range of the interchangeable 1891 Models may have given rise to some of the confusion. The First Model Single-Shot in .22, .32, and .38; the .38 SA "Mexican Model"; and the combination revolver/single-shot sets all share the same Model of 1891 frame and the same serial number range

.38 Single Action: (1) 1st Model (Baby Russian) w/picture box; (2) 2nd Model; (3) 3rd Model (Model of 1891)

with the .38 SA 3rd. What's more, this gun can be more or less changed from one of these configurations to another by substituting the single-shot barrel for the revolver barrel and cylinder (or vice versa). Plus the "Mexican Model" configuration can be approximated by installation of a factory spur trigger conversion kit or perhaps more commonly by chicanery and fraud.

Whatever the cause, this model is unaccountably difficult to find.

Serial number range 1-28107 26,850 mfd. 1891-1911

ID Key: .38 single action w/triggerguard, barrel usually marked "Model of 1891"

Exc	Fine	VG	Good	Fair	Poor
1200	800	650	500	300	185

.38 SINGLE ACTION MEXICAN MODEL (Model 1880"):

Cal-.38 S&W, 5-shot fluted cylinder, 3-1/4", 4", 5", or 6" barrel, checkered hard rubber grips with S&W monograms or walnut, blue or nickel finish, flat sided hammer, removable spur trigger, no half cock notch on the hammer, will also accept a single-shot barrel, top-break action. Numbered concurrently with .38 Single Action 3rd Model. Wide and narrow trigger variations known. Most of these were shipped to Mexico.

A rare model that brings a substantial premium, there are probably more fakes in circulation than authentic examples. S&W marketed as an option for the standard Model of 1891 a kit that would convert it to spur trigger configuration. They also reportedly offered a kit to convert the Mexican model back to standard configuration.

Serial number range 1-28107 2,000 mfd. 1891-1911

ID Key: .38 single action spur trigger w/sides of spur triggerguard not integral to frame, and flat sided hammer, and no half cock notch, and barrel marked "Model of 1891" and still be careful!

Exc	Fine	VG	Good	Fair	Poor
3500	2000	1200	950	750	500

.38 DA: (1) 1st Model; (2) 2nd Model; (3) 3rd Model; (4) 4th Model

.38 Double Action

.38 DOUBLE ACTION FIRST MODEL:

Cal-.38 S&W, 5-shot fluted cylinder, 3-1/4" or 4" round barrel, groove around the cylinder, with two sets of stop notches, top-break action, squareback recurve triggerguard, blue (scarce) or nickel finish, hard rubber grips with S&W monogram, round blade front sight. Straight cut sideplate cut extends across the frame.

Serial number range 1~4000 ~4,000 mfd. 1880

ID Key: Straight cut sideplate edges, cylinder grooves, two sets cyl. stops, recurve rear triggerguard

Exc	Fine	VG	Good	Fair	Poor
650	500	400	300	200	150

.38 DOUBLE ACTION SECOND MODEL:

Cal-.38 S&W, 5-shot fluted cylinder, 3-1/4", 4", 5", or 6" barrel, similar in appearance to first model except with curved sideplate edges, black or red mottled hard rubber grips with S&W monogram, blue or nickel finish, top-break action.

Serial number range ~4001-119000
~115,000 mfd. 1880-1884

ID Key: .38 DA, curved sideplate edges, grooved cyl., two sets cyl. stops, recurve triggerguard

Exc	Fine	VG	Good	Fair	Poor
275	225	200	160	100	60

Variations:

- Slight premium for 6" barrel
- Slight premium for red mottled grips

.38 DOUBLE ACTION THIRD MODEL:

Cal-.38 S&W, 5-shot fluted cylinder, 3-1/4" 4", 5", 6", 8", 10" barrel, checkered black hard rubber grips with S&W monograms, longer cylinder flutes and solid trigger back, blue or nickel finish, top-break action.

Historic Notes: 300 or more 3rd and 4th Model DAs to Cleveland Police Dept., marked on backstrap "No. XXX, C.P.D." Sgt. and higher marked with rank. Also, 800 sold to Boston Police Dept. *may* be marked "BPD" on backstrap, serial numbers in range of 141000 and 145000.

Over 1000 were sold to American Railway Express Co., both 3rd and 4th models, between 1892 and 1905, shipped first through Hartley & Graham, and then purchased direct from S&W. The earliest known s/n is 264116, and s/n's are found

.38 DA American Express marking

scattered, w/small clusters in the following ranges: 288000s, 408000s, 443000s, 444000s, 461000s, 472000s, 476000s, 477000s, and 486000s. They are marked "AM. EX. CO. (#)" on backstrap. Highest known backstrap number is 934.

Serial number range 119001-322700

203,700 mfd. 1884-1895

ID Key: .38 DA, no cyl. groove, 1 set cyl. stops, recurve triggerguard, pinned front sight, s/n range

Exc	Fine	VG	Good	Fair	Poor
275	225	200	160	100	60

Variations:

- Premium for authentic CPD or BPD marked guns.
- 8" or 10" barrels worth maybe 5X standard.
- Premium for American Railway Express guns.
- Any .38 DA with an original 2" barrel would be worth a substantial premium. However, watch out for .38 DAs with 2" barrels from Safety .38s or Perfecteds. These were usually spare factory barrels lacking a serial number.

.38 DOUBLE ACTION FOURTH MODEL:

Cal-.38 S&W, 5-shot fluted cylinder, 3-1/4", 4", 5", or 6" barrel, checkered hard rubber grips with S&W monograms, blue or nickel finish, similar to 3rd model, top-break action, service or target sights available.

Serial number range 322701-539000

216,300 mfd. 1895-1909

ID Key: Similar to 3rd model, except for internal changes and s/n range

Exc	Fine	VG	Good	Fair	Poor
225	190	150	125	100	75

Variations:

- Slight premium for pre-1898 antiques, before s/n 382022
- 1000 shipped to Peru in 1908, 5", blue, marked with seal of Peru, in s/n ranges of 535553-536052 and 536553-537052, worth premium
- Group of 125 shipped to Lovell, Boston, marked "FRP"; significance unknown, s/n ranges of 381896-382020
- See "Historic Notes" and police and American Express variations listed under 3rd model
- Target sights rare, worth premium

.38 DOUBLE ACTION FIFTH MODEL:

Cal-.38 S&W, 5-shot fluted cylinder, 3-1/4", 4", 5", or 6" barrel, hard rubber grips with S&W monograms, blue or nickel finish similar to 3rd and 4th models, top-break action, service or target sights available.

Serial number range 539001-554077

15,000 mfd. 1909-1911

ID Key: Similar to 3rd and 4th model except s/n range and usually w/forged front sight integral to barrel

Exc	Fine	VG	Good	Fair	Poor
225	190	150	125	90	60

.38 DOUBLE ACTION PERFECTED MODEL:

Cal-.38 S&W, 5-shot fluted cylinder, 3-1/4", 4", 5", or 6" barrel, checkered hard rubber grips with S&W monograms or walnut, has both a topstrap release and a side thumb release on the left side (apparently for the belt and suspenders kinda guy), blue or nickel finish, S&W monogram stamped on the frame's left side, top-break action. The only top-break with an integral triggerguard. *See photo at "Perfected" in Illustrated Glossary.*

Serial number range 1-59400 59,400 mfd. 1909-1920

ID Key: Both a top-break cylinder latch and a cyl. release on frame. Top-break with sideplate on right side of frame.

Exc	Fine	VG	Good	Fair	Poor
400	325	250	200	160	125

Variations:

- A few Perfecteds were made *without* thumbpiece cyl. release on frame, ID by sideplate on right side of gun

.38 DA Peruvian seal

.38 Safety: (1) 1st Model; (2) 2nd Model; (3) 3rd Model; (4) 4th Model; (5) 5th Model

(rather than on left side as with all other DA top-break S&Ws) and integral triggerguard combined with relatively low serial number, worth 50-100% premium.

.38 Safety Hammerless Revolvers

(aka "Safety," "New Departure" or "Lemon Squeezer")

.38 SAFETY HAMMERLESS FIRST MODEL:

Cal-.38 S&W, 5-shot fluted cylinder, 3-1/4" 4", 5", or 6" barrel, checkered hard rubber grips with S&W monograms or plain pearl w/gold plated S&W monograms, blue or nickel finish, concealed hammer, safety bar in the backstrap, top-break action, double action only, top latch must be pushed sideways, round blade front sight pinned in the barrel.

Serial number range 1-5250 5,250 mfd. 1887

ID Key: "Z-bar" latch - must be pushed sideways to open revolver

Exc	Fine	VG	Good	Fair	Poor
550	375	300	225	160	100

Variations:

- 50% premium for 6" barrel

.38 SAFETY HAMMERLESS SECOND MODEL:

Cal-.38 S&W, 5-shot fluted cylinder, 3-1/4", 4", or 5" barrel, checkered hard rubber grips with S&W monograms, blue or nickel finish, differs from 1st model with a knurled thumbpiece on the top latch, top-break action.

Serial number range 5251-42483 37,350 mfd. 1887-1890

ID Key: Latch pushes down to open and is fitted to frame contour; s/n range

Exc	Fine	VG	Good	Fair	Poor
325	260	210	175	125	75

Variations:

- .38 Safety Army Test Revolver: See .38 Safety 3rd Model

.38 SAFETY HAMMERLESS THIRD MODEL:

Cal-.38 S&W, 5-shot fluted cylinder, 3-1/4", 4", 5", or 6" barrel, checkered hard rubber grips with S&W monograms, blue or nickel finish, top-break action. Major changes were that the barrel catch now protruded over the frame area with a small cutout, and there was a pin in the triggerguard.

Serial number range 42484-116002
73,500 mfd. 1890-1898

ID Key: Latch pushes down to open and protrudes above frame; s/n range

Exc	Fine	VG	Good	Fair	Poor
315	250	200	165	125	75

Variations:

- 25% premium for 6" barrel.
- U.S. Express Company: Sixty-six guns engraved "USX" on side of revolver in s/n range 89249-89717, double or triple value.
- .38 Safety Hammerless Army Test Revolver: 100 sold to U.S. government in 1890, marked "U.S." on the left side barrel lug. These guns are 3rd Models, although they are in the 2nd Model serial range 41333-41470. Blue w/ 6" barrel.

Exc	Fine	VG	Good	Fair	Poor
7000	5000	4000	3500	2500	1500

.38 SAFETY HAMMERLESS FOURTH MODEL:

Cal-.38 S&W, 5-shot fluted cylinder, 3-1/4", 4", 5", or 6" barrel, checkered hard rubber grips with S&W monograms, blue or nickel finish, has a "T"-type barrel latch with two knurled side knobs, barrel is marked "38 S&W CTG," top-break action.

Serial number range 116003-~220000
104,000 mfd. 1898-1907

ID Key: T-shaped barrel latch lifts to open, pinned front sight

Exc	Fine	VG	Good	Fair	Poor
270	215	165	135	90	60

Variations:

- 5" and 6" barrels worth premium

.38 SAFETY HAMMERLESS FIFTH MODEL:

Cal-.38 S&W, 5-shot fluted cylinder, 2", 3-1/4", 4", 5", or 6" barrel, checkered hard rubber grips with S&W monograms, blue or nickel finish, "SMITH & WESSON" on the right and "38 S&W CTG" on the left side of the barrel, top-break action.

Serial number range 220000-261493
41,500 mfd. 1907-1940

ID Key: T-shaped barrel latch lifts to open, usually w/forged front sight integral to barrel

Exc	Fine	VG	Good	Fair	Poor
280	225	165	135	90	60

Variations:

- 5" and 6" barrels worth premium
- Checkered walnut grips scarce, worth premium if original to gun
- Last few of the serial numbered frames were reportedly not finished, but rather given away in the white to employees, friends, and so on as souvenirs

Note: *New Mod #3 .38 Winchester, New Mod. #3 .38-44 Target Model, and .38 Winchester DA are listed in Model 3 section.*

.44 Frame - Model Number 3 Background Information

"Model Number 3" was the S&W factory designation for its line of large frame top-break revolvers. The Model Number 3s seem to be perhaps the most sought after group of antique S&Ws, for a number of reasons.

In many ways, it was the first full-sized metallic cartridge handgun utilizing an indisputably effective defensive round. It was an international favorite, and in its later configurations provided a level of accuracy that made it the choice of champion target shootists of the era. There are a seemingly endless number of variations to be sought.

Perhaps most accounting for this model's popularity with collectors, however, is the romantic era it represents.

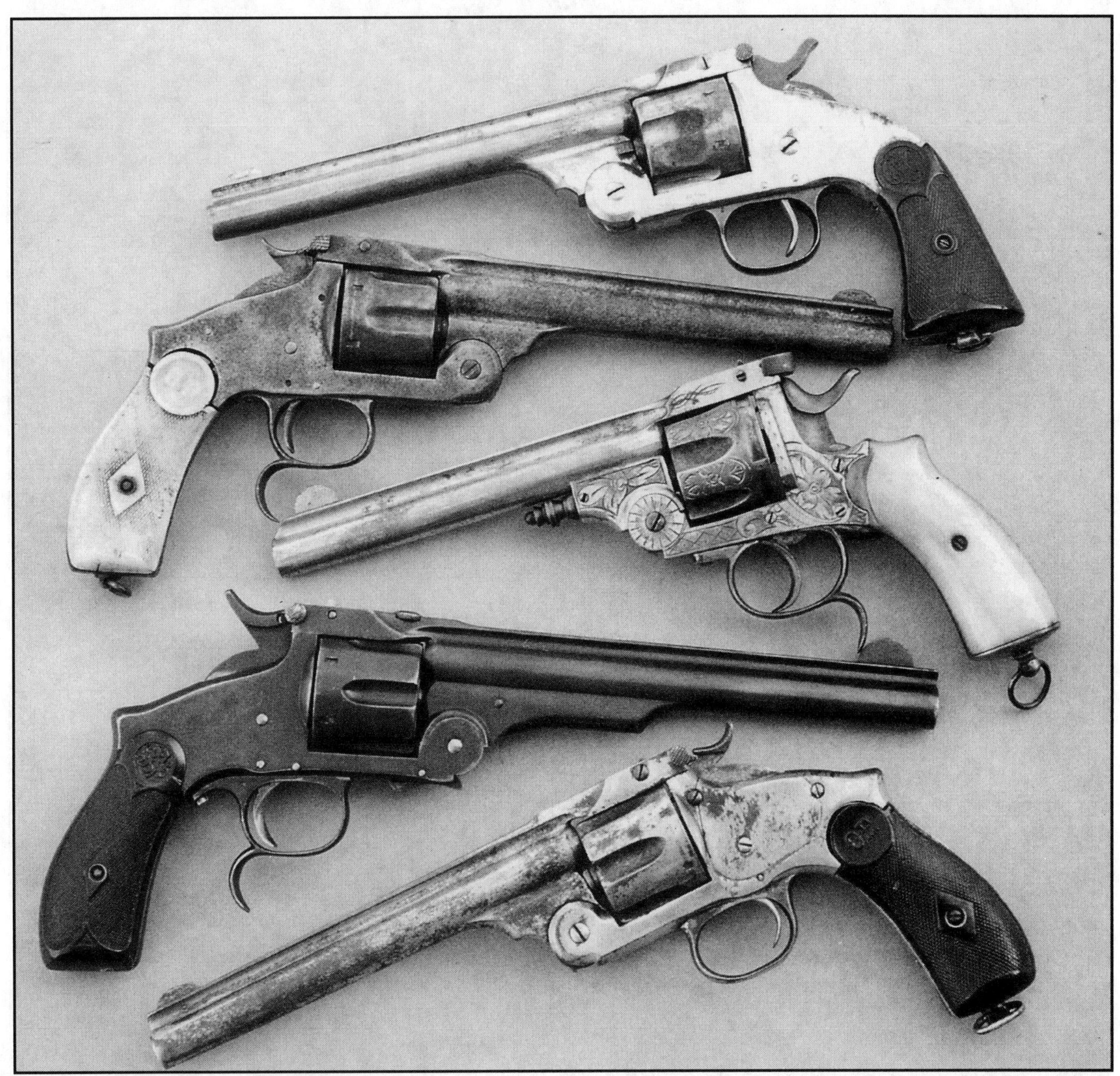

Imitation—the sincerest form of flattery. Foreign copies of the Model Three.

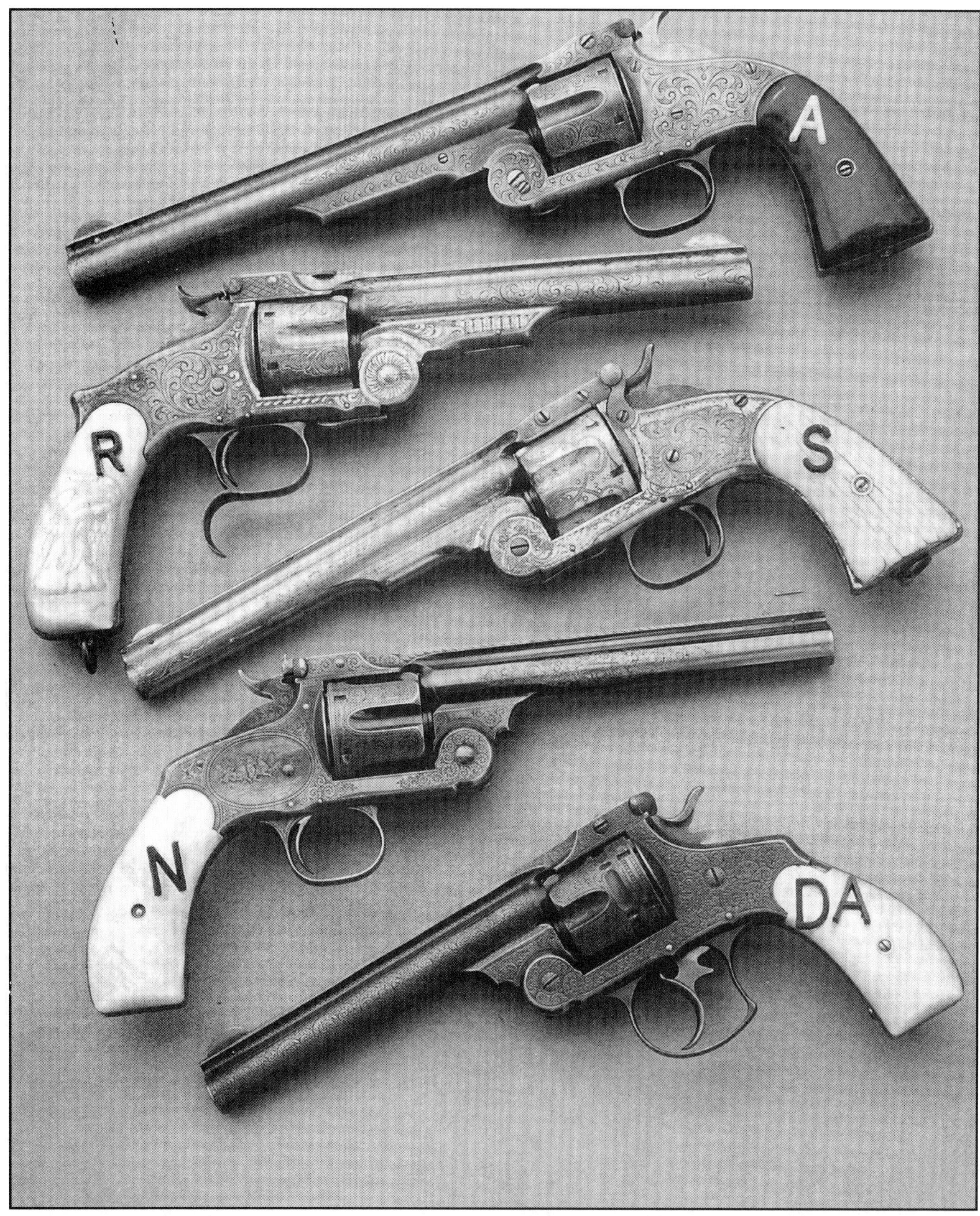

Model Three "families": (A) American; (R) Russian; (S) Schofield; (N) New Model #3; (DA) 44 Double Action

Big single action six-guns are undeniably evocative of the Old West of the late nineteenth century. Elsewhere around the globe, it was a time of empire and military adventurism. The S&W Model 3 was a vital part of this era.

However, there is also an understandable tendency among general gun enthusiasts to be confused by the different variations of the Model 3. While nearly everyone who is halfway gun-savvy immediately recognizes the familiar lines of a Colt Single Action Army, there are many otherwise knowledgeable dealers and collectors who can't tell the difference between an American and a New Model #3 without referring to a book. It's really not difficult, if you give it a moment's thought.

There are basically four groups or "families" of single action Model 3s, with the double actions forming a fifth group. A quick glance at the shape of the grip and the location of the latch will allow you to immediately place a big S&W single action into one of the four major groups, and a check of a few other features will confirm your identification. There is only one exception, listed last:

AMERICANS: Made 1870-1874

- Square butt, no knuckle on backstrap
- Latch mounted on barrel
- .44 caliber, long ejector housing, 8" barrel standard

RUSSIANS: Made 1873-1878

- Round butt, extreme knuckle on backstrap
- Latch mounted on barrel
- .44 caliber, long or medium ejector housing, 6-1/2" or 7" barrel standard
- Originally all made with triggerguard spur, but these were sometimes cut off later

SCHOFIELDS: Made 1875-1877

- Square butt, no knuckle on backstrap
- Latch mounted on frame
- .45 caliber, medium length ejector housing, 7" barrel

NEW MODEL NUMBER THREES and related models: Made 1878-1912

- Round butt, moderate knuckle on backstrap
- Latch mounted on barrel
- Variety of calibers and barrel lengths with .44 and 6-1/2" standard, short ejector housing
- Could be special ordered with triggerguard spur (but scarce)

THE EXCEPTION: The so-called "First Model Russian" or "Old Old Model Russian" 1871-1874

It looks like an American. It is collected by American collectors. It quacks like an American. However, it is chambered for the .44 Russian cartridge, has "Russian Model" marked on the barrel, and is officially known as a Russian. Go figure.

COLLECTOR'S TIP: *To distinguish .44 American from .44 Russian cylinders,* remember that American cylinders will be bored straight through while Russian cylinders will have a sharp shoulder where the case mouth rests.

DOUBLE ACTIONS: Made 1881-1913

As with nearly all other handguns, double actions may be identified at a glance by the fact that their trigger hangs in the middle of the triggerguard rather than at the rear of the triggerguard.

American Background Information

"The history of the S&W Model 3 American is one of service. Neither toy nor ornament, few were tucked away in bureau drawers to be discovered in pristine condition a century later. This was a work gun; a big, heavy-caliber holster gun worn openly and ready to hand; a timely gun indigenous to America on the move and a part of America's greatest adventures." - Roy Double

The American was the first big bore cartridge revolver and has traditionally been associated with the American West. It was the first cartridge revolver adopted by the U.S. military, and saw usage in the Indian Wars. In this sense, the "U.S. American" may be considered the "Walker" of cartridge revolvers.

Many subtle changes were made throughout production. Roy Double's outstanding monograph on this model, printed in *The S&W Journal*, divides production into three issues of American, four models of rimfire, two Russian Army issues, and two transitional periods. This classification system has not caught on with collectors however, and most continue to think primarily in terms of First Model Americans and Second Model Americans.

<u>FIRST MODEL AMERICAN (Model No. 3 First Model Single Action):</u>

Cal-.44 Rimfire Henry (rare), and .44 American (.44 S&W) -- this model commonly called "American" regardless of whether RF or CF. Single action, 6-shot fluted cylinder, 8" barrel with a rib, some mfd. of 6" and 7", blue or nickel finish, square butt frame, smooth walnut grips, full and half cock notches, top-break action, cylinder is 1.450" long.

Historic Notes: S/n 20029 has been attributed to Wyatt Earp as the gun used by him in the "gunfight at the OK Corral," although there is some question on this. Texas Jack Omohundro owned s/n 2008, and presented s/n 4868 to the Earl of Dunraven. S/n's 7052 and 7056 attributed to Dallas Stoudenmire. S/n 25274 attributed to John Wesley Hardin. Recent studies have shown that some Americans were used at the Battle of the Little Big Horn.

ID Key: Square butt w/barrel mounted latch, flat frame bottom, hammer and latch don't interlock

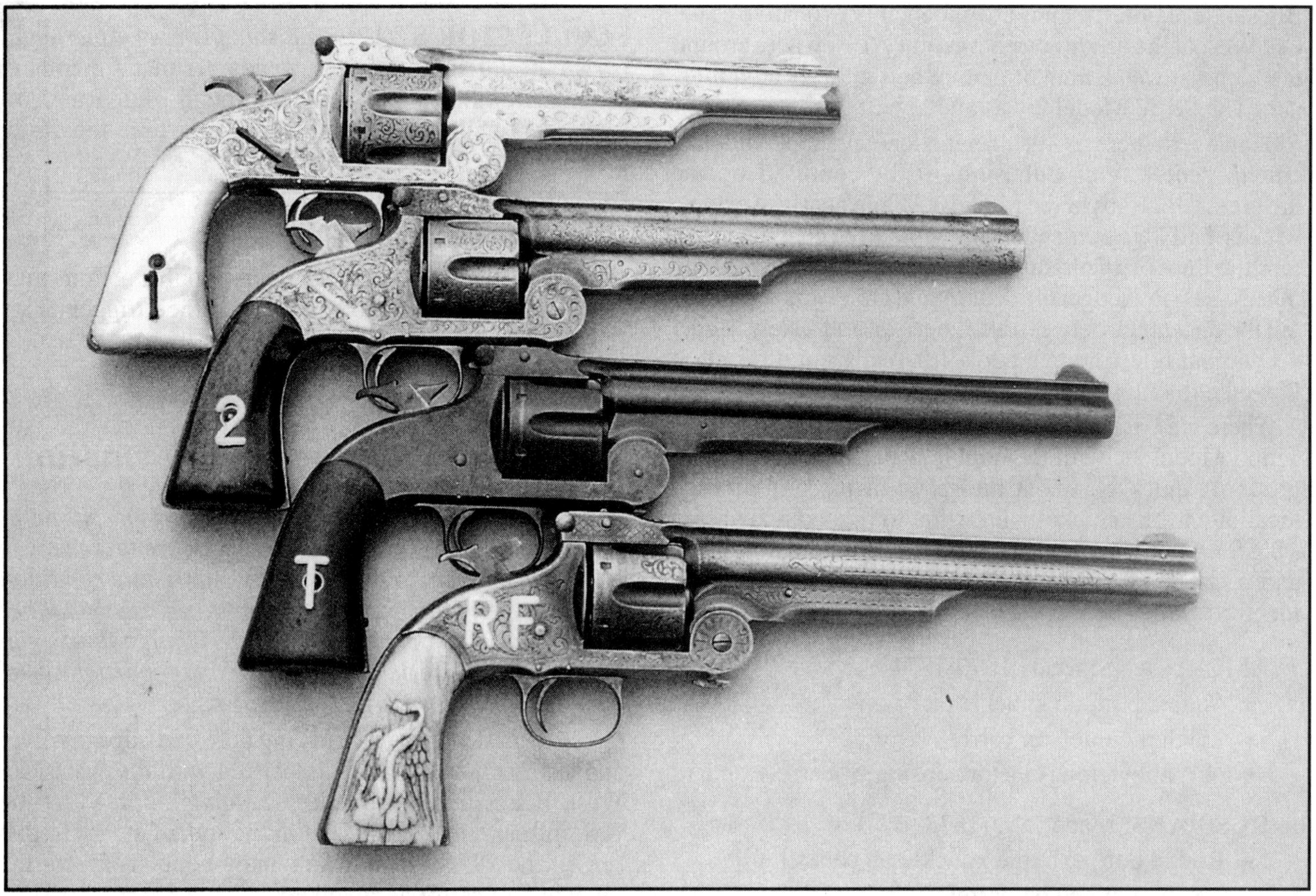

American Model types: (1) 1st Model, note flat bottom frame and non-latching hammer, scarce short barrel; (2) 2nd Model, note bump bottom frame and latching hammer; (T) Transitional Model; (RF) Rimfire Model

Exc	Fine	VG	Good	Fair	Poor
5000	3250	2000	1600	1250	800

Variations:

- Vent hole ("oil hole") in rear extractor housing under barrel, first 1500 guns or so, add 25% premium.
- 6" or 7" barrel, add 50% if original.
- **.44 Rimfire Henry Cal.:** About 200 mfd. in this caliber. Identified by triangular shaped firing pin and slot in frame. Serial number 1 was an Army test gun in this configuration, now located in the Springfield Armory N.H.S. All others believed to have nickel finish and in s/n range 4000-4200.

Exc	Fine	VG	Good	Fair	Poor
15000	8000	4000	3000	2000	1500

- **"Nashville Police":** Thirty-two mfd. with 6" barrel, marked "Nashville Police" on backstrap, extremely rare, verify by serial number. Values run 25% to 50% above U.S. Army order values listed above.
- **Transitional American:** As mentioned above, there are several variations that may be considered "transitional." Most collectors consider a combination of a 2nd American interlocking hammer and latch with a 1st American flat bottom frame to be a Transitional American. Another criteria is the shorter cylinder of

U.S. Purchase 1st Model American marking

1.423". Transitions are found in two serial number ranges, 3200-3700 and 6800-8000.

Exc	Fine	VG	Good	Fair	Poor
5000	3250	2000	1600	1250	800

- **U.S. Army order of 1000:** Cal-.44 S&W, 800 blue and 200 nickel, with "U.S." marked on the barrel rib, "OWA" inspectors mark on the left grip. Barrel, cylinder, and frame have "A" and "P" marks (nickel has "A"s only). Serial range 125-2199. To bring full price, gun must be on list of known s/n's. Specific serial numbers are listed in the Parsons' book *S&W Revolvers* and in the reprint of Charles Pate's article found at the end of the 20th Anniversary compilation of *The S&W Journal.*

Historical Note: Used 1872 through 1876 by the First through Seventh Cavalry, along with other sidearms, including Colt SAA after 1873.

Exc	Fine	VG	Good	Fair	Poor
10000	7000	4000	3000	2000	1500

- **U.S. Variation:** NICKEL - Note: Unlike many Model 3 nickel guns, it is correct for a U.S. American nickel gun to have nickel plated latch and triggerguard. Nickel plated U.S. Americans will have the "A"s and "U.S." markings, but no "P"s. Add 10-25%.

1000 "U.S. American" Serial Numbers

The following is the list of the U.S. purchased American Model 3 serial numbers. This is taken from an old handwritten list, and some serial numbers are unclear. Twenty serial numbers are listed twice on the original list, and it seems likely that some of these were old errors.

All guns below serial number 1895 were blue except for serial numbers 1722, 1729, 1863, and 1868, which were nickel. All guns from s/n 1895 through 2199 were nickel, except for serial numbers 1951,1958, 1967, 1998, and 2053, which were blue.

125	412	492	581	676	762	837	939
164	413	493	585	683	763	839	956
192	415	495	586	696	764	840	958
211	418	496	587	699	769	841	962
225	419	498	588	700	770	844	985
242	420	508	590	702	771	845	991
249	423	513	596	705	774	846	994
257	425	516	599	707	776	847	1000
277	427	519	601	708	777	848	1003
282	428	521	602	711	779	849	1005
292	431	522	605	712	780	853	1010
293	436	523	607	713	783	855	1014
308	439	524	609	714	784	856	1017
330	447	527	610	715	785	857	1018
331	448	529	611	716	791	858	1021
334	451	531	615	718	796	861	1022
340	452	533	616	723	797	864	1024
352	457	536	619	724	798	865	1025
355	458	539	625	725	801	870	1026
358	459	542	628	728	802	873	1029
362	462	544	630	729	803	876	1030
364	464	545	631	730	804	881	1031
365	465	548	633	732	806	882	1036
367	466	549	636	734	808	883	1038
370	467	550	637	739	810	891	1040
371	469	554	641	740	811	892	1042
375	471	555	642	744	812	894	1044
382	474	556	643	749	814	896	1046
385	475	562	646	750	822	899	1047
386	483	564	654	753	823	906	1050
388	484	570	660	754	824	907	1051
390	486	571	664	756	825	908	1056
393	487	575	665	757	828	911	1059
397	488	576	666	758	829	914	1061
406	490	577	667	760	830	926	1062
408	491	580	671	761	835	929	1067

1068
1069
1070
1071
1077
1079
1082
1083
1086
1089
1090
1091
1092
1093
1095
1097
1098
1099
1102
1108
1122
1123
1124
1125
1128
1132
1137
1144
1146
1149
1155
1157
1165
1170
1171
1175
1184
1187
1189
1192
1193
1196
1197
1198
1199
1212
1224
1227
1230
1231
1232
1234
1248
1249
1252
1256
1258
1259
1259
1261
1262
1266
1267
1268
1269
1270
1271
1272
1273
1274
1275
1277
1278
1279
1280
1282
1283
1284
1285
1287
1288
1289
1290
1292
1293
1295
1296
1297
1300
1301
1303
1304
1306
1308
1309
1311
1312
1313
1314
1315
1316
1317
1318
1319
1320
1321
1324
1325
1326
1328
1329
1330
1331
1332
1333
1334
1335
1336
1337
1338
1340
1341
1342
1343
1344
1345
1346
1347
1348
1350
1351
1352
1353
1354
1355
1356
1357
1358
1359
1360
1361
1362
1363
1364
1365
1366
1367
1368
1369
1370
1371
1372
1374
1375
1376
1377
1378
1379
1380
1381
1383
1384
1387
1388
1389
1390
1391
1392
1393
1394
1395
1396
1397
1400
1401
1402
1404
1405
1406
1407
1408
1409
1410
1411
1412
1413
1414
1415
1416
1417
1418
1419
1420
1421
1422
1424
1425
1426
1427
1428
1429
1430
1431
1432
1433
1434
1435
1436
1437
1439
1440
1441
1442
1443
1444
1445
1446
1447
1448
1449
1450
1451
1452
1453
1454
1455
1456
1457
1458
1460
1461
1462
1463
1465
1467
1468
1469
1470
1471
1472
1473
1474
1475
1476
1477
1478
1479
1480
1482
1483
1484
1485
1486
1487
1488
1489
1490
1491
1493
1494
1495
1496
1497
1499
1500
1501
1502
1504
1505
1506
1507
1508
1509
1510
1511
1512
1513
1514
1515
1516
1517
1518
1519
1520
1521
1522
1523
1524
1525
1527
1528
1529
1530
1531
1532
1533
1534
1535
1536
1538
1539
1541
1542
1543
1544
1545
1546
1547
1548
1549
1550
1551
1552
1553
1554
1555
1556
1557
1559
1560
1561
1562
1563
1566
1567
1568
1569
1570
1571
1572
1573
1575
1576
1577
1578
1579
1580
1581
1583
1584
1586
1587
1588
1589
1590
1591
1593
1594
1596
1597
1598
1599
1600
1601
1602
1604
1605
1606
1607
1608
1609
1611
1612
1614
1615
1616
1618
1619
1620
1621
1622
1623
1624
1625
1626
1627
1628
1629
1630
1634
1635
1637
1638
1641
1643
1649
1651
1654
1655
1656
1657
1658
1660
1661
1662
1664
1665
1667
1671
1673
1674
1675
1676
1677
1678
1679
1681
1682
1685
1686
1688
1689
1692
1693
1694
1695
1696
1697
1698
1699
1720
1721
1722
1729
1732
1733
1735
1737
1738
1742
1745
1759
1761
1767
1768
1770
1775
1778
1781
1782
1784
1787
1788
1790
1791
1795
1798
1802
1803
1807
1814
1816
1820
1821
1825
1826
1829
1830
1831
1832
1833
1834
1835
1836
1837
1838
1839
1842
1843
1844
1846
1847

1848	1901	1935	1981	2011	2038	2072	2104
1849	1902	1936	1982	2012	2039	2073	2105
1851	1903	1937	1983	2013	2040	2074	2106
1852	1904	1938	1984	2014	2041	2076	2107
1857	1905	1939	1985	2015	2042	2077	2109
1859	1906	1941	1989	2016	2043	2078	2110
1863	1907	1943	1990	2017	2044	2079	2111
1867	1908	1944	1991	2018	2045	2080	2112
1868	1909	1945	1992	2019	2048	2081	2114
1870	1910	1947	1993	2020	2049	2083	2115
1871	1911	1949	1994	2021	2050	2085	2116
1872	1912	1950	1995	2022	2051	2086	2118
1874	1914	1951	1996	2023	2052	2087	2121
1875	1915	1955	1997	2024	2053	2089	2122
1877	1916	1956	1998	2025	2054	2090	2124
1880	1918	1958	1999	2026	2055	2091	2126
1882	1920	1961	2000	2027	2057	2092	2128
1884	1921	1962	2001	2028	2058	2093	2130
1885	1922	1967	2002	2029	2059	2094	2139
1886	1923	1970	2003	2030	2060	2095	2152
1887	1924	1972	2004	2031	2062	2096	2153
1888	1925	1973	2005	2032	2063	2098	2154
1890	1926	1974	2006	2033	2064	2099	2169
1891	1927	1975	2007	2034	2065	2100	2170
1893	1928	1976	2008	2035	2069	2101	2176
1895	1930	1978	2009	2036	2070	2102	2177
1900	1931	1979	2010	2037	2071	2103	2192
							2199

SECOND MODEL AMERICAN (Model No. 3 2nd Model Single Action):

Cal-.44 American (.44 S&W) or .44 Rimfire Henry (scarce), similar to First Model, except with a larger trigger pin, which necessitates a "bump" in the formerly straight line of the bottom of the frame, an interlocking hammer and latch (notch at top of hammer face and small flat teat sticking out of rear of latch) and a steel front sight. 8" barrel was standard length but is also found in 5", 5-1/2", 6", 6 -1/4", 6-1/2", and 7", blue or nickel finish, smooth walnut stocks, round blade front sight inserted and pinned in the barrel, rear sight is a notch cut in the top lug of the barrel catch, top-break action, square butt. 604 mfd. with a shoulder stock. The Russian contract is also numbered within this series. Also mfd. in cal-.44 Rimfire Henry, approx. 3,014 mfd.

Serial number range 8000-32800 20,735 mfd. 1872-1874

ID Key: Square butt w/barrel mounted latch, bump on bottom of frame, interlocking hammer and latch

Exc	Fine	VG	Good	Fair	Poor
4500	2750	1700	1250	1000	675

Variations:

- Short barrel: 25 to 50% premium for barrel lengths other than 8" if original.
- Handle deviations: 25 to 50% premium for guns with unusual grip frame with a more extreme bend in the grip angle.
- Rimfire: 25 to 50% premium, identify by triangular firing pin and slotted frame, some known with first model style hammer and latch. Many rimfires went to Mexico through distributor Wexell & Degress.
- Stocked: Add 25% for a gun originally cut for stock by factory, s/n's over 20000 (if cut through numbers, may have been adapted at later date). A correct gun and stock together will bring triple to quadruple what a gun alone will bring.

The bottom American shows scarce short barrel and grip angle deviation.

- Stock (604 mfd.) alone worth $2000 to $5000 depending on condition and buyer.
- Argentinean Army: 500 shipped to Argentina 10/10/1873, .44 American cal, marked "Ejercito Argentino" on left side extractor, or, more probably, on bottom of frame in front of triggerguard (sources vary). S/n range is 28300 to 28950. Hard usage, very rare, double to triple standard values.
- Spanish colonial Cuba: 111 sent to Spanish Cuba, no known examples, worth premium.
- U.S. Navy purchase reported, no known examples.

Russian Model Background Information

In the 1870s, S&W obtained from the Russian government for military usage a series of orders for Model 3s that would eventually total around 150,000 guns. The Russians required various changes to the design, which S&W accommodated and incorporated into much of their commercial production. In fact, some of the changes between the first and second model Americans can be traced to Russian requirements.

Perhaps the most significant change was the cartridge. The .44 American (as it later came to be known) used an outside lubricated "heeled" bullet in which the diameter of the rear portion of the bullet was reduced to fit into a brass case that was the same diameter as the forward part of the bullet (a similar system may still be observed today in the ubiquitous .22 rimfire cartridges). The Russians wanted a round where the bullet fit into a case of larger diameter, and hence the .44 Russian round was born. This would eventually become S&Ws big bore cartridge of choice for the remainder of the century, one of the most accurate target cartridges ever designed, and the parent cartridge of the .44 Special and .44 Magnum rounds.

With the new cartridge and the initial minor changes, the First Model Russian is essentially the same gun as the American models, except for the chambering. Soon the Russians were requesting more radical changes, especially to the grip, resulting in the classic Russian Model profile: round butt, extreme knuckle or "prawl" at top of the backstrap, and triggerguard spur.

Many collectors feel that this gives the 2nd and 3rd Model Russians a distinctly Victorian or European look. It certainly makes the gun very difficult to cock without changing the hand's position on the grips, unless the shooter is endowed with orangutan thumbs.

There are several hypotheses about the utility of the triggerguard spur. Some contend that it was simply a rest for the middle finger of the shooting hand. Others have reported that it was utilized as a hanger, to secure the pistol when tucked through a waist sash. Bill Powell reports a theory that it was originally called a "Parry guard," intended to allow a revolver-wielding Cossack to deflect a saber slash with his sidearm and still retain all his fingers. My personal favorite, at least in terms of creativity, is the theory that military tactics of the time called for the cavalry to charge with revolvers already cocked, and the spur provided a gripping surface for the trigger finger in such a situation (don't try this at home!). Be that as it may, the spur was often considered cumbersome by American users, and specimens are not infrequently found with this enhancement lopped off.

Serial number information for the Russian models tends to be rather confusing, as each of several Russian contracts was believed to have had its own s/n range starting with 1.

Commercial guns initially included "RUSSIAN MODEL" at the end of the barrel address. Some foreign government buyers objected to this wording, and an alternate marking ending in a "REISSUE" patent date was made.

FIRST MODEL RUSSIAN (Old Old Model Russian) (Model No. 3 Russian First Model):

Identical to American Models *except* chambered for .44 Russian cartridge instead of .44 American, and civilian commercial guns are marked "Russian Model" on barrel. Cal-.44 S&W Russian, 6-shot fluted cylinder, smooth walnut grips, blue or nickel finish, 6", 7", or 8" barrel, round blade front sight, top-break action, with butt swivel. They are found with either features of the Transitional American or the Second Model American.

Commercial guns numbered with the American models in s/n range 6000-32800 1871-1874

Russian contract guns s/n 1-20000

ID Key: Same as American models, but w/stepped chambers and marked "Russian Model"

Exc	Fine	VG	Good	Fair	Poor
4750	3000	1900	1450	1200	800

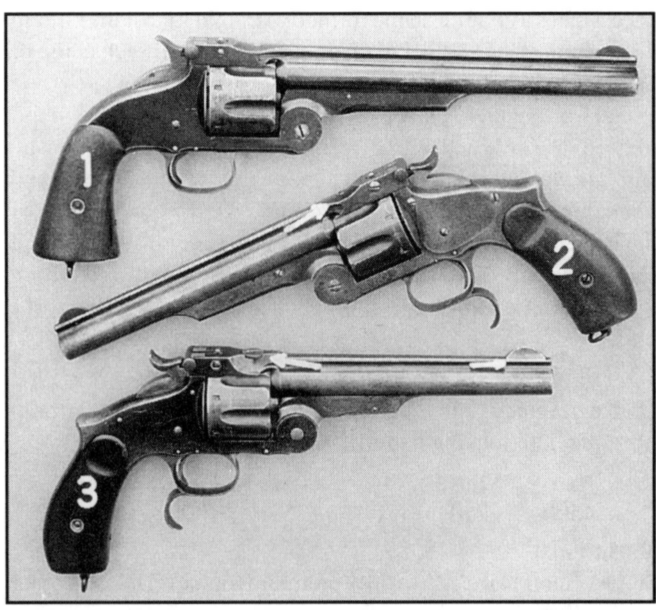

Russian Models: (1) 1st Model or Old Old Model Russian; (2) 2nd Model or Old Model Russian; (3) 3rd Model or New Model Russian

Variations:

- Russian Contract Version: 20,000 made for Russian government, in their own serial number range, barrel markings are in Cyrillic, w/double headed Russian eagle at breach. Subjected to hard usage, few found their way back to the U.S. and are very scarce today. Worth 50% to 100% premium.
- Reject Version: Approx. 500 mfd. for Russian government, but rejected and sold commercially, these guns will have serial numbers on all parts (as opposed to assembly numbers on most commercial guns). Most had the Cyrillic markings removed and were re-marked with the English markings, and are worth about the same as standard commercial guns, perhaps with a slight premium. The few that were sold commercially in the U.S. with Cyrillic markings still intact lack the Russian eagle at the end of the barrel address, and are closer in value to the Russian Contract guns.
- Shoulder stocks: See comments under Second Model American.

SECOND MODEL RUSSIAN (Old Model Russian) (Model No. 3 Russian Second Model):

Cal-.44 S&W Russian and .44 Rimfire Henry (rare), 6-shot fluted cylinder, 7" barrel length standard, walnut grips, blue or nickel finish, spurred triggerguard, round butt, humpback gripstrap (extreme knuckle or "prawl" at top of grip where the web of the thumb contacts the grip when holding the gun), altered hammer, a detachable buttstock was available, top-break action, with butt swivel. Russian contract models have Cyrillic markings and the Russian Double Eagle.

Each of three Russian contracts believed to have had their own serial number range starting with 1. Commercial guns were continued in the American s/n range, about 32800-39000. Yet another s/n range of 1-9000 included commercial guns along with the Japanese and Turkish contracts, with the barrel address ending in the "REISSUE" patent date instead of the words "RUSSIAN MODEL" (both Old and New Model Russians were made in this s/n range).

85,200 mfd. for all variations 1873-1878
6,200 mfd. for Std. Commercial Model:
Cal .44 S&W Russian

ID Key: Round butt, extreme knuckle, triggerguard spur, long ejector housing, 7" barrel, pinned front sight, small screw on topstrap.

Exc	Fine	VG	Good	Fair	Poor
3000	2200	1500	1000	750	500

Variations:

- Unusual barrel lengths of 5-1/2", 6", 6-1/2", and 8" will command 25-50% premium.
- Russian Contract Model: Cal- .44 S&W Russian, Cyrillic markings, the Russians called this Old Model Russian the "Infantry Model" or "1873" model, found with or without serial numbers at end of barrel marking, 70,000 mfd., 25-50% premium.
- Japanese government variation: 5,000 mfd. in the s/n range 1-9000, shipped through distributor Ahrens, barrel marking ends with "REISSUE July 25, 1871" instead of "Russian Model." Found both in blue and nickel, and 7" or 6-1/2" (worth additional premium) barrel. Usually found with Japanese navy anchor with two wavy lines on butt or army marking of Japanese character in circle at breech end of barrel, 25% premium.
- Cal-.44 Rimfire Henry commercial: 500 mfd., 25-75% premium.
- Special Turkish Model: Cal-.44 Rimfire Henry, 1,000 mfd. in 1-9000 s/n range, double to triple standard model value.
- Second Turkish order: Cal-.44 Rimfire made by altering standard commercial guns, and in same s/n range as commercial, 2,000 mfd., 75-100% premium.
- Schuyler Hartley Graham: 2nd and 3rd Model commercial Russians will not infrequently be found with the mark of this distributor—the letters "SH" in a diamond stamped on the butt.
- Shoulder stocks very rare, few known. On a gun alone that is factory cut for stock, add 50%. Gun with stock worth at least triple what gun alone would bring.

Japanese purchase markings on (2) 2nd Model, and (3) 3rd Model. Note also differences in cylinder retaining screw on Old and New Model Russians.

THIRD MODEL RUSSIAN (New Model Russian) (Model No. 3 Russian Third Model):

Cal-.44 S&W Russian or .44 Rimfire Henry, 6-shot fluted cylinder, 6-1/2" barrel, walnut grips, blue or nickel finish, shorter extractor housing than its predecessor and integral front sight, top-break action, with butt swivel. Total production approx. 60,638 mfd. for all contracts.

Each Russian contract for the 3rd Model is believed to have started over with s/n 1. Commercial guns are usually in a continuation of the American and Russian model s/n range 39000-53500. Yet another serial number range of 1-9000 was made with the "REISSUE" patent date at the end of the barrel marking instead of the words "Russian Model," and included both Old and New Model Russians.

Standard Commercial Production: .44 S&W Russian
13,500 mfd. 1874-1878

Historic Note: S/n 1096 owned by Pat Garrett, s/n 40369 attributed to outlaw Sam Wells, aka "Charlie Pitts."

ID Key: Round butt, extreme knuckle, triggerguard spur, medium ejector housing, 6-1/2" barrel, front sight forged integral with barrel, large thumb screw on topstrap.

Exc	Fine	VG	Good	Fair	Poor
2500	1900	1400	950	700	500

Variations:

- Short barrel: A very few made with 5-1/2" barrel, pinned front sight, 50-100% premium.
- Stocked guns: 1586 guns cut for shoulder stocks, 25% premium. A correct gun and stock together will bring triple to quadruple what a gun alone will bring. Seven were factory engraved, and will bring substantial premium.
- Stock alone worth $2500 to $5000 depending on condition and buyer.
- Schuyler Hartley Graham: Old and New Model Russians often found with a "SH" in a diamond marked on the butt. This marking by distributor Schuyler Hartley & Graham is interesting, but does not add substantially to the value of the gun.
- Russian Contract - "Cyrillic": .44 S&W Russian w/"KO" or "HK" inspectors, Cyrillic barrel markings. Russians called it the "Cavalry Model" or "1874" model, found with or without serial numbers at end of barrel marking, and w/ or w/o a boxed "1874" on the left side of the knuckle. 41,138 mfd., 25-50% premium.
- Japanese Model: 1,000 mfd. w/same markings as 2nd model, 25% premium.
- 44 Rimfire commercial: 25-50% premium.
- Turkish Model: .44 Rimfire Henry w/"W" inspector's mark, 5,000 mfd. in s/n range of 39100-52500 by converting standard .44 Russian models, triangular firing pin and plugged firing pin hole recut to slot configuration, may have Arabic numerals under grips, 75-100% premium.
- **Ludwig Loewe copies:** Not made by S&W, a copy of the 3rd Model Russian made by the German firm of Ludwig Loewe for the Russian government, Cyrillic barrel markings, will bring almost as much as a S&W Cyrillic Russian contract gun. Commercial Ludwig Loewe revolvers with the markings in "English" are more scarce, and may bring a bit more. It is also known that Ludwig Loewe made copies in .44 rimfire, and .44-40 chambered models have been reported (although the design would have to be modified considerably to accept the latter cartridge). Either of these would bring a premium.
- **Russian Tula Arsenal copies:** The Russian government also produced their own copies at their Tula arsenal, again Cyrillic marked. Very rare in the U.S., and reportedly quite scarce in Russia as well. Can bring 3X to 5X standard value. However, of course this premium would be reduced if a large number of Tula guns were discovered and imported from Russia.
- Other copies: Other European copies of S&W Russian models tend to bring about half or less of what an original S&W would bring.

Cyrillic barrel markings on Russian models, top to bottom: S&W contract, Tula Arsenal, Ludwig Loewe, and Ludwig Loewe English commercial marking

Schofield Background Information

The S&W Schofield (usually pronounced "SKO-field" rather than "SHOW-field") revolver is probably the best known by the general public of any of the Model Threes, and the one most associated with the Old West in the collective American imagination. Such is its popularity that some gun enthusiasts who are not familiar with the older S&Ws will tend to call any large frame S&W top-break a "Schofield." It has received some exposure in movie and TV westerns, most notably and recently in Clint Eastwood's "Unforgiven," but also in earlier efforts such as "Nevada Smith," "Trackdown," and "Alias Smith & Jones."

The Schofield originated with the efforts of Col. George Schofield to improve the American Model Three for military usage. As noted earlier, the American was the first cartridge revolver adopted by the military in 1870, with a purchase of 1000. However, in 1874 the Army purchased 8000 Colt Single Action Army models, noting a preference for their strength and simplicity. In Army tests of this era, S&W Americans and Russians passed the firing and functioning criteria, but were criticized for their complexity and number of parts. The greater ease and speed of reloading was noted, but was not given much credence as a tactical advantage. The Russian model was criticized for the awkwardness of its grip, hammer, and triggerguard spur.

As early as 1871, Schofield had been working on improvements to the S&W American that he felt would render it more suitable for military usage. The most obvious of these consisted of changing the latch from barrel mounted to frame mounted. The Schofield model was tested and met with military approval. They requested that it be produced for the .45 Colt cartridge. S&W demurred, noting that the rim of the .45 Colt was inadequate for positive extraction in the S&W design, and no doubt considering that the cylinder and frame of the Model 3 would have to be lengthened to accommodate the long round. Instead, S&W offered to redesign the military cartridge to a .45 caliber round that would function in both types of revolvers. This was found acceptable, and 3000 S&W Schofields were initially ordered in 1875. Further minor modifications were made, and an additional 5000 in the "Second Model" configuration were delivered in 1877. By the end of 1877, the Army had purchased around 8000 S&W Schofields, and around 15,000 Colt SAAs. A few guns were made for the civilian market, but the vast majority of Schofields were military guns.

Markings: Patent dates are found on either side of the ejector housing lying under the barrel. The left side reads "Smith & Wesson Springfield Mass. U.S.A. Pat. Jan. 17th / and 24th 65. July 11th 65. Aug. 24th 69. July 25th 71"; the right side "Schofield's Pat. Apr. 22d 1873" with a "June 20th 71" patent date added to later guns.

On government purchase guns, a large "U.S." is marked on the butt. This appears on the toe of First Models, was moved to the heel on the early Second Models (up to about serial number 6000), and back to the toe on subsequent Second Models. Small military inspection and acceptance marks are found in the metal in three places on each gun: the top of the frame bottom strap, the rear face of the cylinder, and the bottom rear of the barrel. They consist of the letters "P" and "L" on First Models and "P" with either "E," "C," or "W" on Second Models. Mixed inspector initials are often found on Second Models, and should not be considered incorrect. The smooth wood grips bear a cartouche on the left grip only for First Models, either "JFEC" or "SBL." A wider variety of cartouches appear on Second Models, with the right grip either plain or marked "CW" and the left either "JRJr" with a date, "CW" with a date, or "DAL 1877." The scarcer civilian guns made for commercial sale lacked these military markings, with the possible exception of the "P" on the frame.

The government contract called only for blued guns, but there are reports of nickel-plated guns prepared for individual officers as well as nickel civilian revolvers.

All guns were serial numbered in their own range beginning with "1." The serial number appears on the butt, rear face of the cylinder, both latch pieces, latch screw, barrel under the latch, and inside of the right grip.

Military Usage: Many Schofields were issued to active units, reportedly including the 4th, 9th, and 10th Cavalry. The 4th was involved in the Geronimo campaign. The 9th and 10th comprised the famous "Buffalo Soldiers," African-American troops stationed in the American Southwest. There they fought in the Indian Wars, including campaigns against the Apaches, and served in civil disturbances such as the Lincoln County War.

Other Schofields went to state militias. New York received 2000 in 1877; Michigan 536 in 1878 and 1879; Indiana 300 in 1878 and 1879; Territory of Washington 180 in 1882 and 1891; California at least 100 and possibly 300 in 1880; Kansas 100 in 1879; West Virginia 79 in 1878; with lesser quantities going to Arkansas, Colorado, Georgia, Illinois, and Tennessee. Florida, Maine, Nevada, North Carolina, Oklahoma, and Pennsylvania received fewer than seven guns each. It's probable that some of the guns sold to state militias had been previously issued to regular army units.

A Schofield believed to have been used at the Battle of the Little Big Horn is owned by the Smithsonian Institution, although it has never been clear which side its owner was fighting on. After the annihilation of Custer and his men, there was some argument in print that the outcome might have been different had the troops been armed with Winchester repeaters and the fast loading Schofields instead of single-shot Trap-doors and slow reloading Peacemakers.

Col. Charles Pate, noted authority on S&W military revolvers, writes that the big S&W was still in use by regular army units as of 1887. Springfield Research Service reports that some Schofields were apparently still in service with volunteer units in 1898 during the Spanish American War. However, many had been retired earlier. As noted above, the .45 Schofield round would function in either the army issue Colt or S&W. However, one can imagine the disconcerting effect of trying to chamber a Colt cartridge in a Schofield and finding the nose of the bullet poking out the front end of the cylinder. Bad for morale, especially in the heat of battle. This rather complicated ammunition supply problem supposedly was a major reason that many Schofields were withdrawn from service and sold as surplus during the 1880s.

The story of the long cartridges and the short cylinders may be more folklore than truth, however. Pate reports that the Army was trying to order more Schofields in 1878, but that Smith & Wesson was not interested in producing any more. It should be noted that 1878 was the year that S&W introduced its New Model Number Three, replacing the American, Russian, and Schofield, and perhaps the factory wanted to focus its large frame single action revolver production on its new and improved model.

Western Usage: Many of the surplus Schofields were purchased by dealers such as Bannerman and Schuyler, Hartley & Graham. They were then offered for sale, often with the barrel cut to a handier 5" length and the gun nickel plated to withstand the rigors of Western usage. The combination of quick reloadability and big .45 caliber power made them popular with lawmen, outlaws, and others who were serious about their sidearms. Schofields were reportedly used by Frank James (s/n 3444 and 5476), Jesse James (s/n 366), Cole Younger (s/n 2341), Bill Tilghman, and Frank McLowery among others.

Wells Fargo: It's estimated that several hundred Schofields with the cut-down 5" barrels were purchased by Wells Fargo to arm its messengers. The guns were marked by the company on the left side of the under-barrel ejector housing by stamping over the Schofield patent.

Wells Fargo Schofields showing both types of company name marking and all three sizes of numeral markings

The marking reads "W.F. & CO'S EX" along with a restamping of the gun's serial number. The "'S" was dropped from the company name in 1898, and guns are found marked both ways, suggesting the period of use. It's believed that all authentic Wells Fargo Schofields known to date have serial numbers under 6000.

Three different sizes of numerals have been reported in the Wells Fargo serial number markings. Most common is the small size, about the same size as the company name abbreviation. A medium size was reportedly marked by the Chicago office, with a large size numeral being the scarcest.

Unfortunately, whenever a relatively simple marking adds interest and value to a gun, there is a temptation to forgery. This is the case with Wells Fargo Schofields, with faked markings not uncommon. A quick tip-off to some fakes is the stamping of the company name. It is believed that on all authentic WF guns a "line-stamp" was used. "W.F. & CO EX" stamped in uneven individual letters should raise immediate suspicion. The numerals in the stamping, on the other hand, were individually stamped, and their spacing may be uneven.

San Francisco Police: Schofields are sometimes found with a large two- or three-digit number, usually under 300, stamped on the backstrap. These have been called "San Francisco Police" Schofields. Although concrete verification is lacking, the story is that these guns were shipped to San Francisco at the time of the Sandlot Riots, and eventually wound up with the California militia.

Reproductions: At date, the Schofield is the only S&W top-break that has had a modern replica reproduction made. The reproduction is offered by Navy Arms and is so marked. It can also be easily distinguished by the longer cylinder and frame on the repro, necessary to handle the longer .45 Colt and .44-40 cartridges for which it is chambered. It has been reported that Cimmarron Arms will also offer a Schofield reproduction, and that other S&W top-break model reproductions may follow.

COLLECTOR'S TIP: Fakery - While replicas are great fun to shoot, and increase general interest in the originals, experience has shown that when a reproduction is offered, it is not long before some unscrupulous individuals may be tempted to use them as the basis for altered and artificially aged fakes of the originals. While it does not seem likely that the current reproductions could be passed off as originals, the beginning collector may want to get a second opinion on a potential purchase. Fraudulently aged repros seem to be more common at flea markets, poorly supervised gun shows, "as is, where is" auctions, and other "cash 'n' carry" semi-anonymous type forums. Avoiding such situations is one of the advantages of dealing with an established reputable dealer with specific product knowledge who will stand behind the authenticity of the items he sells.

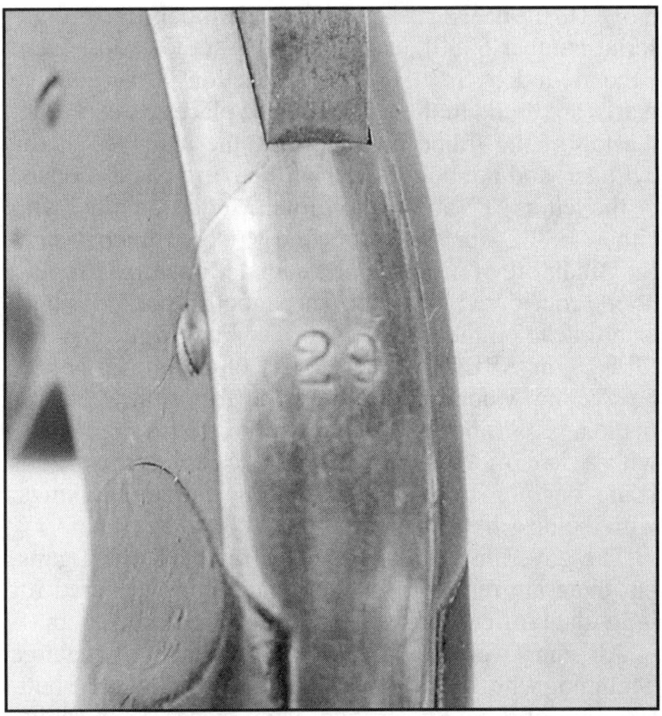

Schofield "San Francisco Police" backstrap marking

FIRST MODEL SCHOFIELD:

Cal-.45 S&W, named after Col. George Schofield; single action, 7" barrel, 6-shot fluted cylinder, blue finish, barrel catch attached to the frame, plain walnut stocks on a square butt, round blade front sight with a notch cut in the rear barrel latch, top-break action, with an iron frame patterned after the Model No. 3 American. Military markings include "U.S." on butt, cartouche on grips, and "L" and "P" on barrel and cylinder, and frame marked "L."

Serial number range 1-3035 3,035 mfd. 1875

ID Key: Square butt, frame mounted latch, groove down top of barrel, Schofield markings on right ejector housing, latch shape—viewed from side has a circle around the screw head at the bottom of the latch and comes to a point at the top.

Exc	Fine	VG	Good	Fair	Poor
7000	4000	3000	2000	1500	1000

Variations:

- Civilian version: Very rare, only 35 made, lack military markings. 200% premium.
- Wells Fargo marked: Barrel cut to about 5". Marked "W.F. & CO (or CO'S) EX" followed by s/n on right side extractor housing. Many fakes. If authentic, may bring more than a Schofield with an uncut barrel and comparable finish.
- Cut barrel Schofields: Will bring about 1/2 in the higher grades and 2/3 in the lower grades of what an uncut example would bring.
- San Francisco Police: Large two- or three-digit number on backstrap. Worth slight premium.

SECOND MODEL SCHOFIELD:

Cal-.45 S&W, improved version of First Model with a steel frame, blue finish, original nickel finish rare, 7" barrel, top of barrel catch is knurled. Square butt with plain walnut stocks, with cartouches on both grips of army issue guns, left grip dated 1876 or 1877.

U.S. Army Issue: "U.S." on butt, 5,005 mfd.

ID Key: Square butt w/frame mounted latch; similar to first model, most obvious difference is serial number range and shape of latch -- viewed from side, it has a rounded circle at the top of the latch.

Exc	Fine	VG	Good	Fair	Poor
6500	3500	2500	1750	1400	900

Variations:

- Civilian version: Scarce, only 650 made, worth 25-50% premium. Lack military markings, except possibly "P" on frame.
- Wells Fargo marked: Barrel cut to about 5". Marked "W.F. & CO (or CO'S) EX" followed by s/n on right side extractor housing. Many fakes. If authentic, will bring about the same as an original Schofield with an uncut barrel. A very small number believed to exist with original uncut 7" barrel and authentic Wells Fargo markings.
- Cut barrel Schofields: Will bring about 2/3 of what an uncut example would bring.
- San Francisco Police: Large two- or three-digit number on backstrap. Worth slight premium.
- Kelton Thumb safety: A very few known to have been fitted by the factory with an experimental manual safety. Very rare, worth substantial premium.

New Model Number Three Background Information

Cataloged from 1878 to 1908, the NM #3 was the pinnacle of S&W large frame single action revolver design.

Standard configuration is .44 Russian caliber, 6-1/2" barrel, fixed sights, wood or hard rubber grips, nickel or blue finish. Barrel lengths from 3-1/2" to 8", target sites, fancy grips, fancy finish, detachable shoulder stock, engraving, and chambering for other cartridges were available on special order.

It spawned related models, based on the same configuration and frame, including the NM #3 Target Model in .32-44 and .38-44 caliber, the NM #3 Frontier in .44-40, the NM #3 .38 Winchester, the Turkish Model in .44 Rimfire, and the .320 cal. Revolving Rifle.

In 1878, the S&W New Model #3 followed hard on the heels of its popular Model 3 predecessors, the American, Russian, and Schofield models. Its improved handling characteristics and mechanical improvements made it an instant success, and arguably the finest single action revolver design of the nineteenth century. It dominated target competition in the late 1800s, and was purchased for military or police usage by Japan, the U.S., Turkey, Australia, Argentina, and Spanish colonial Cuba. Guns went to England, France, Germany, Italy, China, Switzerland, and elsewhere.

A Family of Related Models: It's important to note that there are several models based on the basic New Mod. #3

(1) 1st Model Schofield, (2) 2nd Model Schofield. Note differences in latch profile.

New Model #3 in scarce 8-inch and 4-inch barrel configuration (standard is 6-1/2-inch)

frame and configuration. Where a model of gun has its own serial number range, we have listed it as a separate model. In several cases, the primary difference between these models and the standard New Model #3 is that the related model was made for a different cartridge. A quick check to see whether you may have a related model rather than a standard NM#3, is to compare the serial number to the features of the gun. A gun with a relatively low serial number (under 5500) and any of the late production features, such as short ejector housing, no teeth on extractor gear visible at hinge, single line barrel marking, and/or long cylinder, indicate the gun is one of the related models rather than a standard NM#3. A rimfire gun with early features should be looked at as a probable Turkish Model.

NEW MODEL NO. 3 SINGLE ACTION:

Cal-.44 S&W Russian std., also chambered: .32 S&W, .32-44 S&W, .320 S&W Revolving Rifle, .38 S&W, .38 Colt, .38-40, .38-44 S&W, .41 S&W, .44 Rimfire Henry, .44 S&W American, .44-40, .45 S&W Schofield, .450 Revolver, .45 Webley, .455 Mark I, and .455 Mark II. All calibers other than .44 Russian scarce to rare in the original NM#3 serial number series (most NM#3 type guns in a caliber other than .44 Russ are one of the related models—see "Family of Related Models" comments under "New Mod.#3 Background Information" above). 6-shot fluted cylinder, barrel lengths of 3-1/2", 4", 5", 6", 6-1/2", 7", 7-1/2", and 8"; 6-1/2" is standard, hard rubber or walnut grips, blue or nickel finish, top-break action, many variations found. Early production has a slightly longer ejector housing and a toothed gear extraction cam. Middle to later production has a shorter ejector housing and a circular extractor cam with a single finger. Later production variations include longer topstrap and cylinder (lengthened from 1-7/16" to 1-9/16") and single line barrel address (lacking patent dates included on earlier production).

Serial number range 1-35796 35,796 mfd. 1878-1912

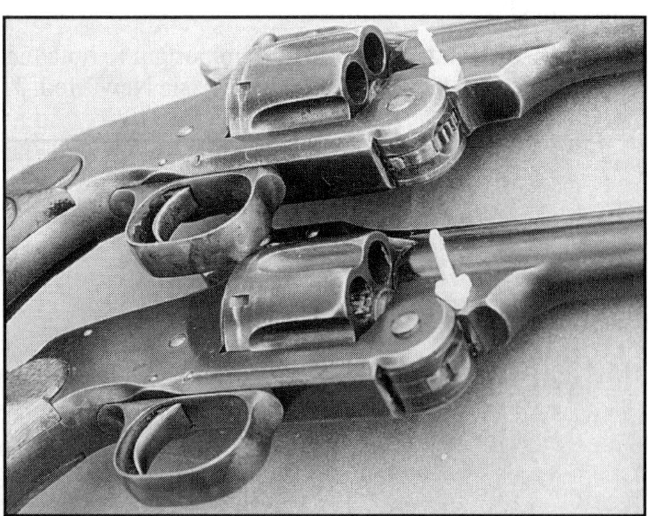

New Mod. #3, top to bottom: early type longer ejector housing w/toothed extractor cam, later and more common shorter ejector housing w/finger extractor cam

Note: Although the NM#3 was cataloged into the early 1900s, all frames were manufactured by 1898, making the gun an antique.

Historic Notes: Factory records show shipment to the following interesting destinations: Greek Minister of War, Athens; six guns to champion target shot F.E. Bennett; twenty-two guns to champion target shot W. Winans; one to three guns to Annie Oakley along with two to her husband, exhibition shooter Frank E. Butler; two to Union Metallic Cartridge Co.; two to Am E Powder Co.; S&W Revolver Club; s/n 13303 to W.F. "Buffalo Bill" Cody; nine guns to champion target shot Ira Paine; five guns to champion target shot Oscar Olson; Chafin & Co. for Russian Patent; Creedmore Ctg. Co.; two to champion target shot W.E. Petty; Leonard Smokeless Powder Co; DB Wesson; A.S. Jones, secy., NRA; writer and target shot A.S.A. Himmelwright; and s/n 32661 to Col. Theodore Roosevelt. Specific serial numbers of these guns can be verified through the factory records.

Furthermore, a NM#3 is reported as the gun used by Bob Ford to kill Jesse James (s/n 3766), and one was carried by Virgil Earp.

ID Key: Single action, round butt, moderate knuckle on backstrap, short ejector housing. See related models below for their distinguishing characteristics.

Exc	Fine	VG	Good	Fair	Poor
3500	2000	1200	1000	700	450

Variations:

- Russian Model style finger guard spur available on special order, worth slight premium.
- Unusual barrel lengths: 6", 7", add 10%. 5", 8", add 25%. 7-1/2", add 25-50%. 4", add 50-100%. 3-1/2" very rare and worth 3X to 5X standard value, possibly more.
- Unusual calibers: Will bring premium, depending on rarity, when found in the main NM#3 s/n range. (For example, a NM#3 chambered for .44-40 and showing late production features such as a short ejector housing, with a s/n under 2000 would be a Frontier Model, and priced as such rather than as a NM#3 in a rare caliber. The same gun with a s/n in the 30000 range would be considered a standard NM#3 in a rare caliber.) Anything other than .44 Russian is at least scarce in the main production series, and will bring a premium. Among those that are found, .32-44 and .38-44 seem to be the most often encountered, possibly followed by some of the .45 caliber British rounds. Among the rarest would probably be .38 S&W, .38 Colt, and .41 S&W. It is believed that guns with s/n's 27942 through 28017 are all chambered in .32-44 and .38-44 calibers, and other unusual chamberings have shown up around that s/n range. Premium value depends on rarity and could range from 20% to 5X.
- Target sights will bring 10-20% premium, slightly more for unusual configurations.
- **State of Maryland:** U.S. military purchase, reportedly for the Maryland militia. 280 mfd. in nickel in .44 Russian, purchased by the U.S. Govt. 6-1/2" barrel, marked "U.S." on butt, "HN" on cyl., frame, bbl, and right grip; and "DAL 1878" on left grip. Includes all s/n's 7126-7405. 1878. Will bring 3X to 4X standard value.

- **Japanese Navy:** Nearly a third of all NM#3s produced were exported to Japan, most for military usage. The first two shipments totaling around 800 guns went through distributor Ahrens in 1879. Many Ahrens Japanese guns will be found with 7" barrels, triggerguard spurs, and factory installed lanyard rings. Subsequently, Takata & Co. handled a number of shipments through the 1880s and 1890s totaling 8,754 more guns. The Takata guns were supposedly standardized as 6-1/2" blue, wood grips.

A variety of Japanese military markings are found on many of these guns. Perhaps most often seen is one of two types of anchors—either a plain anchor or one with two wavy lines through it, denoting navy usage. The location is most commonly on the bottom of the frame in front of the triggerguard, followed by the butt, and occasionally on the knuckle of the grip backstrap. A Japanese character inside

Above and below: NM#3 U.S. purchase "State of Maryland" model markings

Above and below: Two types of anchor markings found on Japanese navy NM#3s

a circle is seen at the rear of the barrel address on some guns, and this is reportedly a Japanese army marking. Perhaps scarcest is the so-called "artillery" configuration, consisting of a series of Japanese characters on the left extractor housing, non-factory swivel, and an added three-digit number. The addition of non-factory swivels is common on Japanese military NM#3s.

Mismatched serial numbers, especially mismatched cylinders, are fairly common on Japanese military NM#3s, and will not diminish the value much so long as the mismatched part is from another Japanese shipped gun. Some collectors feel that a lighter color bluing combined with a lighter orangish shade of refinished grips indicate a Japanese arsenal refinish.

Japanese guns are found scattered throughout the serial number range, but clusters may be expected in the following ranges:

Many of s/n 5426-5702, first Ahrens shipment, about 230 guns, 1879

All of 9001-9600, second Ahrens shipment, 1879

Some of 15105-15198, 15304-15397, 15490-15599, 15901-15993, 16106-16256, and most of 16301-16401, first Takata shipment, 4/17/1884

Nearly all of 16901-16999, various Takata shipments, mostly 1887

Most of 21701-23856, including all of 21987-22107, Takata

Many of 23301-23698, Takata

Many of 24315-25000, Takata, 2/6/1889

All of 26467-26566 and 26718-27107, Takata, 10/4/1890

All of 27018-27300 and 27380-27475 and most of 27480-27575, Takata, 1/31/1891

All of 28111-29668, 29869-29950, 30001-30100, and 30151-30232, Takata, 1896 and 1897

Nearly all 30263-30392, Takata, 1896

Many of 32243-32540, Takata 8/7/1899

All of 32668-33197, Takata 9/1/1898

Many of 33501-33642, Takata 5/16/1904

Most of 34181-35079, 35320-35500, and 35657-35791, Takata, from 1904 to 1908

Japanese marked guns will bring a 10-20% premium, depending on the scarcity of the marking, with an "artillery" variation perhaps bringing as much as 50%. Unmarked Japanese shipped guns do not tend to bring a premium.

- **Australian Model:** About 310 total (250 in first shipment) mfd. in nickel w/7" barrel and extension stocks, 30 mfd. in nickel w/o extension stocks in a 6-1/2" barrel for the Australian Colonial Police in .44 S&W Russian. A broad arrow proof mark is found on the butt. The stocks were marked with a broad arrow and the matching gun's serial number by the Australians. However, gun and stock were not kept together, and rarely will match when found today. Guns and stocks used in western Australia may lack broad arrow markings. Australian stocks usually, but not always, differ from standard production NM#3 stocks in that the screws enter the wood from the right side of the stock rather than the left. They were used with an unusual double flap holster that allowed the gun to be holstered with the stock attached, and a matching rectangular leather pouch for the stock alone when not attached to the gun. Serial numbers are mostly between 12202-13188 with a few in the 23000 range. Serial numbers and much more information may be found in Charles Pate's article in the May 1988 *Man at Arms* magazine. Gun alone worth 20% premium. Stock brings $700 to $1200. Gun and stock together, with both holsters, will bring 3X to 4X standard value.

  Fifteen guns were sent to the Australian Exhibition in 1880 prior to this purchase, and probably resulted in the government purchase.

NM#3 Argentine army marking

- Other stocked NM#3s: Similar in value to Australian, possibly a little less. Look for them especially in the 12000 serial number range and from s/n 25132-25732.
- **Argentine Model:** 2,000 mfd. Stamped "EJERCITO ARGENTINO" on the bottom of the grip frame just forward of the triggerguard. Shipped through Hartley & Graham 1/10/1881. Nickel, subjected to hard usage, very rare in the U.S. today. S/n range 50-3400. 3X to 4X standard value.
- **U.S. Government: Revenue Cutter Service ("Coast Guard Model"):** Apparently standard issue to the U.S. Revenue Cutter Service, predecessor of the U.S. Coast Guard. No markings, found with 5", 6", and 6-1/2" barrels. Known serial numbers include 17548, 18555, 18623, 18677, 18681, 18690, 18695, 18696, 18746, 18752, 18755, 18770, 18774, 18801, 19147, 19236, 19253, 19301, 19319, 19331, 19412, 19424,19914, 19921, 19929, 19932, 19936, 19939, 20095, 20096, 20762, 23754, 23795, 23810, 23876, 23878, 23880, 23881, 23884-23887, 23889, 23891, 23893, 23895, 23909, 25744, 25745, 25748, 25749, 25753, 25758, 25761, 25772, 25775, 25777, 25781, 25788, 25789, 25791, 25796-25800, 25833, 25836, 25842-25845, 25847, 25905, 25921, 26139-26146, 26162, 26163, 26166-26168, 26171-26175, 26177, 26178, 26180-26182, 26184-26189, 26192-26210, 26248, 26272, 26651, 26655, 26662, 26670, 26676, 26681, 26688, 26691-26693, 26698, 26699. 27302, 27305, 27328-27330, 27332, 27333, 27339. 27352, 27353, 27355-27357, 27359, 27360, 27362-27370, 27865, 27866.

  Col. Charles Pate is in the process of additional research that will no doubt shed further light on this interesting military variation.

  Worth 3X to 4X standard value.

- Spanish Colonial Cuba: A very large shipment of guns was made to Don Jose Vallero of Cuba on 9/22/1880. These are believed to have seen military usage, possibly during the Spanish American War, and many of them were returned to the U.S. after that war through such surplus dealers as Bannermans. Most known examples show hard usage, many have non-factory lanyard rings, and some are known to have large unusual characters marked on the butt. Serial numbers are scattered, but include *some* of the guns in ranges 5-99, 9705-9775, 9900s, 10103-10189, 10308-10400, 10502-10600, 10702-10800, 12355-12390; and *most* of the guns in ranges 10901-11000, 11102-11199, 11301-11399, 11701-11798, 12701-12797. Worth small premium.
- Thumb safety: S/n's 24512-24517 equipped with a manual safety, very rare, worth at least 5X to 10X standard value.

New Model No. 3 Target Model Background Information

"No. 3 Target revolvers dominate(d) the Bisley target shooting scene until the advent of smokeless cartridges."
- David Penn, Imperial War Museum

The Target Model version of the NM#3 was introduced for competitive shooting to allow a smaller caliber, lower recoiling alternative to the remarkably accurate .44 Russian cartridge. Special .32 and .38 caliber rounds were designed for this gun, and both were long brass cases with the bullet seated completely within the case.

While significantly less common than the New Model #3, the Target Model does not bring a premium, probably due to the romance of the big-bore .44 and the fact that many target models received better care than holster guns, and a larger number are found in excellent condition.

Confusing terminology: This probably marks the beginning of S&Ws hyphenated caliber cartridge or model designations (".32-44," ".38-44," etc.). It is most often used to indicate a model in a caliber smaller or larger than what is usually standard on that frame size. Here, for example, it denotes a .32 or .38 caliber gun on a .44 caliber sized frame.

The .38-44 can be especially confusing since a totally different .38-44 cartridge and revolver were introduced in the 1930s. The .38-44 target round for the NM#3 Target was a low powered black powder round in a long brass case with the bullet seated entirely inside the brass case. The .38-44 round, also called the .38 Super Police, introduced in 1930 for the .38-44 Heavy Duty hand ejector model, was a souped up .38 Special round and the predecessor of the .357 Magnum. Its case was of a slightly smaller diameter than the old NM#3 .38-44 Target round. Hence the following:

> **WARNING:** The modern .38-44 Heavy Duty round was not designed for this gun and would be extremely hazardous to shoot in it.

NEW MODEL NO. 3 TARGET SINGLE ACTION:

Cal-.32-44 S&W target or .38-44 target, similar to New Model No. 3 w/6-1/2" round barrel, checkered walnut grips, blue or nickel, extension stocks available, top-break action, target sights. Later production variations include longer topstrap and cylinder (lengthened from 1-7/16" to 1-9/16") and single line barrel address (lacking patent dates included on earlier production).

Serial number range 1-4333 4,333 mfd. 1887-1910

Historic Note: S/n 3653 shipped to Annie Oakley

ID Key: NM#3 configuration in .32 or .38 caliber, target sites, s/n below 4334

Exc	Fine	VG	Good	Fair	Poor
3000	1500	1000	800	600	350

Variations:

- Add 10% for .38-44.
- Slight premium for late long topstrap.
- Stocked guns: See comment on standard model NM#3.
- Conversions to .22 rimfire: Such conversions of bot standard and target model NM#3 are known, including revolver conversions by Harry Pope, and single-shot conversions by A. Niedner and others.

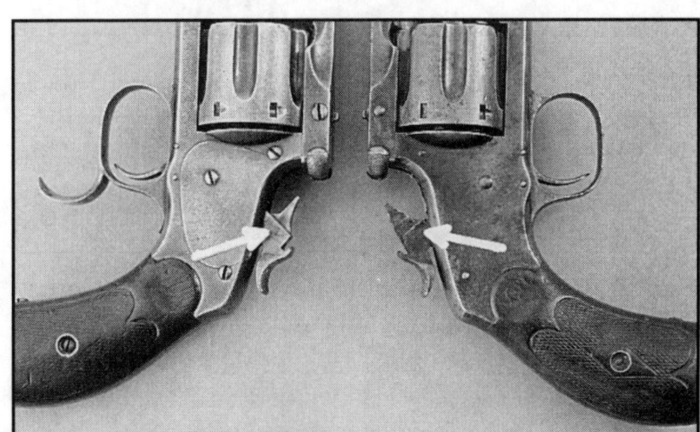

Firing pins on standard NM#3 (left) and Turkish Model Rimfire NM#3 (right). Note also special order triggerguard spur on standard model.

NEW MODEL NO. 3 TURKISH:

Cal-.44 Rimfire Henry, 6-shot fluted cylinder, 6-1/2" barrel, blue finish, top-break action, with butt swivel, checkered walnut grips, round blade front sight, similar to New Model No. 3, with a rectangular hammer nose. Inspectors mark "AFC" on left grip.

Serial number range 1-5461 5,461 mfd. 1879-1883

ID Key: NM#3 configuration with large triangular firing pin and corresponding slot in frame

Exc	Fine	VG	Good	Fair	Poor
6000	4000	3000	2000	1200	750

NEW MODEL NO. 3 FRONTIER SINGLE ACTION:

Cal-.44-40 Winchester, 6-shot fluted cylinder, 4", 5", or 6-1/2" barrel, blue or nickel finish, checkered hard rubber grips or checkered walnut, normally with fixed sights, adjustable

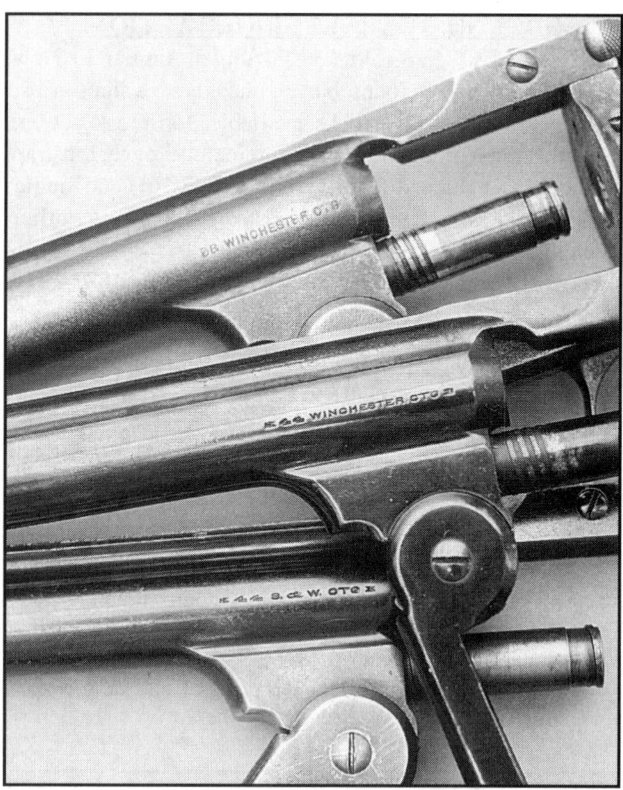

Barrel caliber markings on very rare .38-40 New Model #3 (top), scarce Frontier Model (center), and standard .44 Russian New Mod. #3 (bottom). Only later production was so marked.

target sights by order, 1-9/16" length cylinder, top-break, many marked "44 Winchester Ctg" on barrel.

Serial number range 1-2072 2,072 mfd. 1885-1908

Note: 786 converted to .44 S&W Russian, for shipment to Japan, usually not found w/Japanese markings.

Historic Note: S/n 711 shipped to Walter Winans. S/n 1653 and 1654 to Ira Paine.

ID Key: NM#3 configuration w/long 1-9/16" cylinder in .44 cal. with s/n below 2073

QUICK ID TIP—All guns: In differentiating .44-40 from .44 Russian, look in the chambers of the cylinder. .44 Russian chambers will have a distinct line circling the chamber where the cartridge mouth rests. .44-40 cartridges are slightly bottlenecked and will either have no distinct circles in the chamber or two milder subtler steps to accommodate the bottleneck. (You can feel the ridge in a .44 Russian chamber with a pencil or probe, whereas a .44-40 chamber will feel smooth.)

Exc	Fine	VG	Good	Fair	Poor
4500	2500	1700	1250	800	600

Variations:

- Unusual barrel lengths: See comments under NM#3 standard model
- Deduct 25% if converted back to .44 Russian

NEW MODEL NO. 3 .38 WINCHESTER:

Cal-.38-40 Winchester, 4" or 6-1/2" barrel, 5" also known, blue or nickel finish, black hard rubber grips on a round butt, service or target sights, top-break action with auto shell extractor, round blade front sight, because of the cartridge used, this model has a longer topstrap with a 1-9/16" cylinder. Most marked "38 Winchester Ctg." One of the rarest production models.

Serial number range 1-74 74 mfd. 1900-1907

ID Key: NM#3 configuration w/long 1-9/16" cylinder, .40 cal bore, with s/n below 75

Exc	Fine	VG	Good	Fair	Poor
8000	6000	5000	3000	2500	1750

.44 Double Action

.44 DOUBLE ACTION FIRST MODEL ("44 DA") (New Model Navy No. 3 Revolver):

Cal-.44 S&W Russian, 6-shot fluted cylinder 4", 5", 6", or 6-1/2" barrel, top-break action, blue or nickel finish, ribbed barrel, double action, target or service sights, red or black hard rubber stocks on a round butt frame, the Wesson favorite is also numbered in this series.

Serial number range 1-54668 53,590 mfd. 1881-1913

Historic Note: S/n 352 attributed to John Wesley Hardin

Note: Although cataloged into the twentieth century, all frames were manufactured prior to 1899, making this gun an antique.

ID Key: Large frame DA, .44, either 1-7/16" cylinder with any s/n, or 1-9/16" cyl. with s/n above 15340

Exc	Fine	VG	Good	Fair	Poor
1000	700	500	350	250	200

DA Model 3s. Front: .44 DA First Model w/scarce target sights; Rear: Frontier DA. Note longer cylinder to accommodate .44-40 cartridge; long cylinder also is found on late production .44 DA 1st.

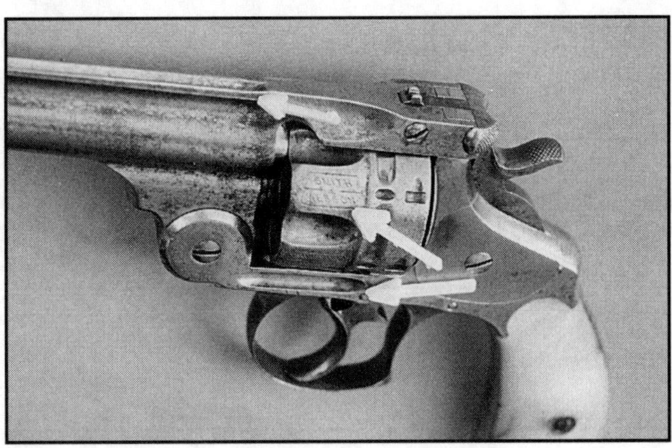

Rare Wesson Favorite Model. Note barrel rib groove, patent markings on cylinder, and lightening cut in frame.

Variations:

- At least one reported in .45 caliber, believed to be government service test gun
- A very few reported made in .38 Colt

.44 DOUBLE ACTION WESSON FAVORITE:

Cal-.44 S&W Russian, 6-shot fluted cylinder, 5" barrel, nickel finish with blue finish rare, designed like the Model 44 Double Action First Model with numerous changes. Pinned round blade front sight with a notch cut rear sight over the barrel catch, top-break action, designed lighter in weight than previous models. Numbered in the same series with the First Model Revolver. Highly sought variation, not much known, suspected that many were shipped to foreign destinations. Very rare in the U.S., many of the few known examples have been renickeled.

Serial number range 8900-10100
Estimated about 1,000 mfd. 1882-1883

ID Key: .44 DA configuration w/groove down top of barrel, patent dates on cylinder, groove on bottom sides of frame, lightweight barrel, interior of frame cut to reduce weight, s/n range

Exc	Fine	VG	Good	Fair	Poor
10000	7500	6000	4000	2500	1500

.44 DOUBLE ACTION FRONTIER:

Cal-.44-40 Winchester, 6-shot fluted cylinder, 4", 5", 6", or 6-1/2" barrel, blue or nickel finish, top-break action, walnut or black hard rubber grips with S&W monogram, service or target sights, 1-9/16" cylinder to accommodate the longer cartridge. Often marked "44 Winchester Ctg." About 1900 barrel markings changed from two line with patent dates to single line without.

Serial number range 1-15340 15,340 mfd. 1886-1913

Note: Although cataloged until 1913, all frames were manufactured prior to 1899, making this gun an antique.

ID Key: .44 DA config. w/long 1-9/16" cylinder, s/n below 15341, .44 caliber barrel

Exc	Fine	VG	Good	Fair	Poor
1400	900	650	475	325	250

.38 WINCHESTER DOUBLE ACTION:

Cal-.38-40 Winchester, 4", 5", or 6-1/2" barrel, blue or nickel finish, round butt with walnut or black rubber grips, target or service sights, top-break action with auto shell extractor, designed identical to the .44 Double Action Frontier except for caliber. Most marked "38 Winchester Ctg" on barrel.

Serial number range 1-276 276 mfd. 1900-1910

ID Key: .44 DA config. w/long 1-9/16" cylinder, s/n below 277, .40 caliber barrel

Exc	Fine	VG	Good	Fair	Poor
4000	3000	2000	1500	1000	750

Note: *The .320 Revolving Rifle was based on the NM#3 frame with an extended barrel and detachable stock, and is listed in the "Long Guns" section.*

Scarce .38/40 Double Action. Note caliber marking.

Model Number Three Barrel Markings

American Model, U.S. purchase. *Except for the "U.S." at the rear, this is how all First and Second Model Americans were marked. The "U.S." appears only on the one thousand purchased by the U.S. military.*

First Model Russian, commercial model. *Externally, the gun is identical to the American except for this barrel marking and the chambering. Second and Third Model Russian barrels are found with the same wording, but the appearance of the Second and Third Models is very different from the First Model. See Third Model Russian, commercial model below.*

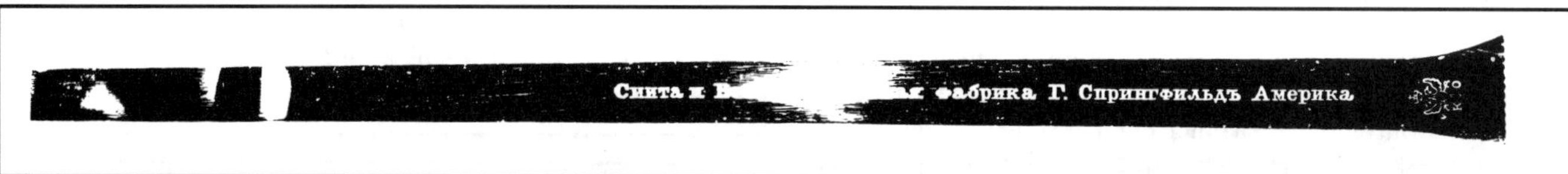

First Model Russian, Russian contract, S&W made. *Cyrillic lettering.*

Second Model Russian, Japanese contract, reissue marking. *Except for the Japanese character in a circle at the rear of the barrel, many commercial guns were also marked this way. Others ended in the words "Russian Model" rather than the reissue date.*

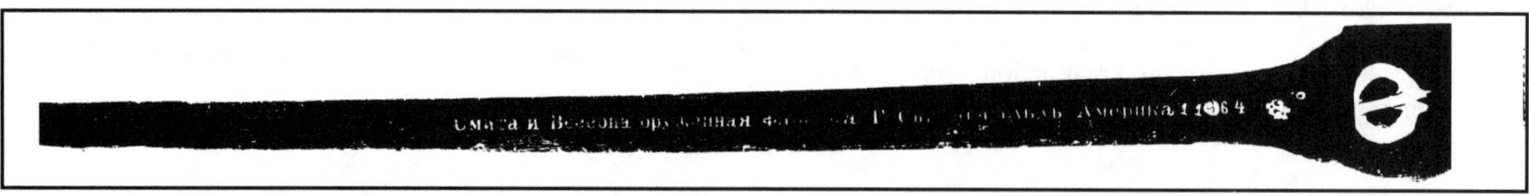

Second Model Russian, Russian contract, S&W made. *The same wording and Cyrillic letters appear on the Third Model Russian, Russian contract.*

Third Model Russian, Japanese contract, reissue marking. *Except for the Japanese character in a circle at the rear of the barrel, many commercial guns were also marked this way. Others ended in the words "Russian Model" rather than the reissue date.*

Third Model Russian, commercial, *"Russian Model" marking.*

Third Model Russian pattern, Russian made, Tula Arsenal. *Not made by S&W.*

Third Model Russian pattern, Russian contract, Ludwig & Loewe made. *Not made by S&W.*

Third Model Russian pattern, Ludwig & Loewe commercial production. *Not made by S&W.*

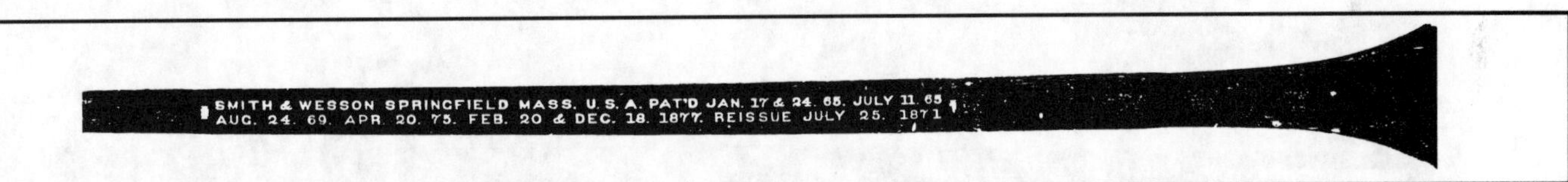

New Model Number Three, *earlier two-line barrel marking. This and/or the next marking was used on all models based on the New Model Number Three.*

New Model Number Three, *later one-line barrel marking.*

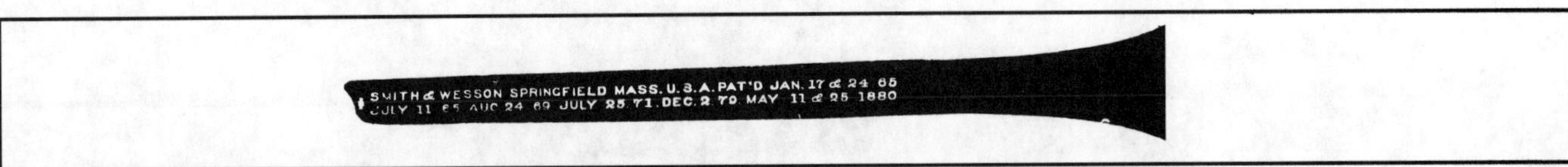

.44 Double Action First Model. *Typical of the large frame DA top-break models.*

SINGLE-SHOT PISTOLS

Contents

FIRST MODEL (Single-Shot Model of 1891):

Cal-.22 Long Rifle, .32 S&W or .38 S&W, 6", 8", or 10" barrel, top-break action, with a revolver recoil shield, black hard rubber grips, smooth or checkered walnut and ivory, front sight-Paine Target Blade pinned in the barrel rib, target sights mounted in the barrel catch are adj. for windage and elevation. Blue or nickel finish, also sold as combination sets with the .38 single action frame, (approx. 92 sets made), cylinder, and barrel with a presentation case. Serial number located on front strap of the grip with matching number on the latch. Serial number range 1-28107 in the .38 Single Action 3rd Model series. See also comments under that model. 1893-1905

.22 Long Rifle	862 mfd.
.32 S&W	229 mfd.
.38 S&W	160 mfd.

Exc	Fine	VG	Good	Fair	Poor
750	600	475	400	325	250

Variations:

- HM POPE marked barrel worth premium.
- .32 and .38 caliber worth 50-75% premium.
- Cased set w/1891 revolver barrel and cylinder and one or more single-shot barrels on 1891 frame worth 4X to 8X above values, if original. Beware of sets put together after the fact—look for matching s/n's on single-shot and revolver components. Expert opinion recommended.

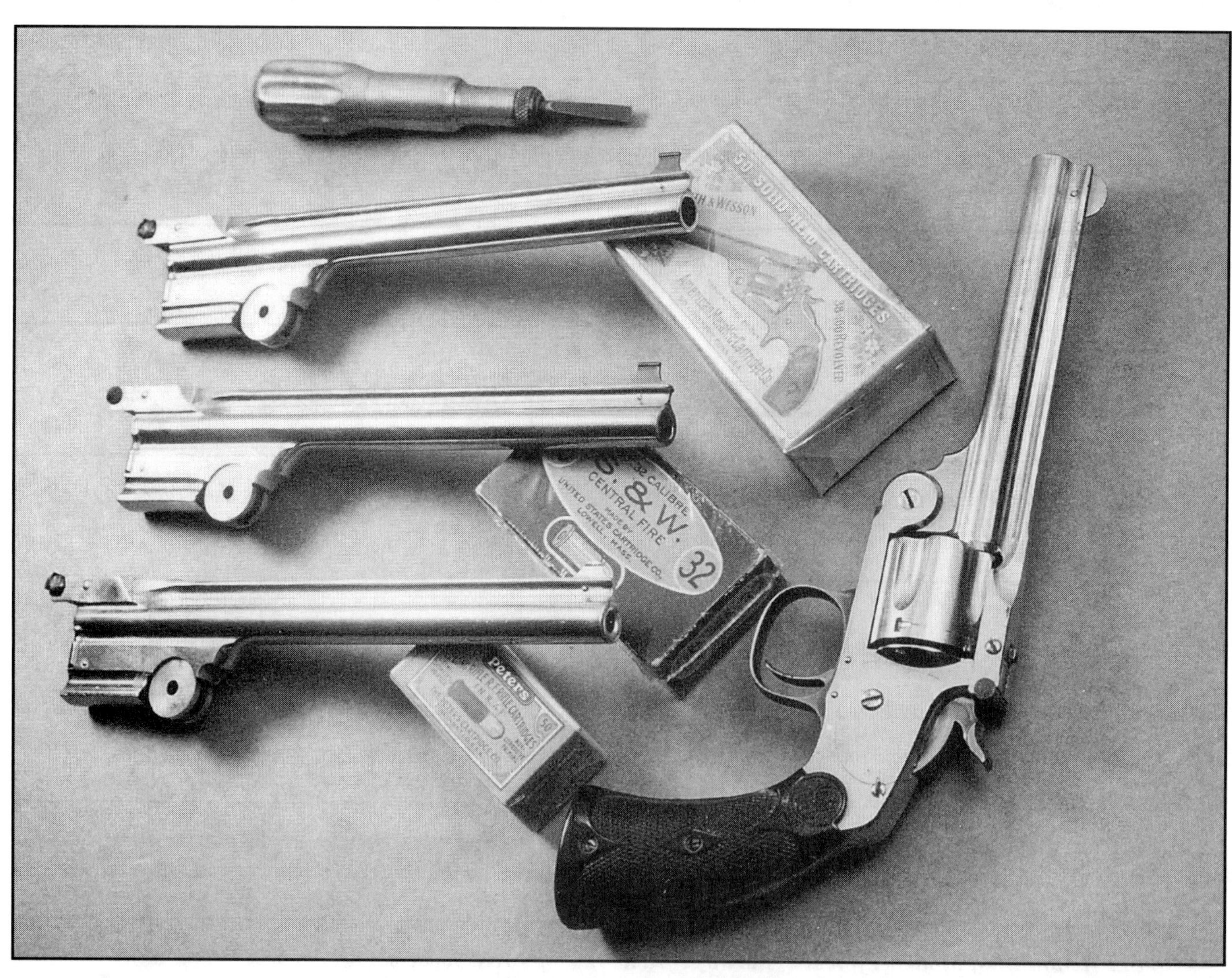

Model of 1891 .38 SA 3rd Model, with 1st Model single-shot barrels in .38, .32, and .22

H. M. Pope marking on barrel of First Model Single-Shot Pistol

SECOND MODEL:

Cal-.22 Long Rifle, has top-break action, now without the recoil shield, hand and stop slots are not present, relief grooves cut in sides of the frame, 10" barrels, 6" are rare, blue or nickel finish, may have First Model barrels on Second Model frames, black hard rubber grips of the extension type with S&W monograms, the triggerguard is still a separate piece from the frame.

Serial number range 1-4617 in an original series
4,615 mfd. 1905-1909

Exc	Fine	VG	Good	Fair	Poor
700	575	475	400	325	250

THIRD MODEL (Perfected Target Pistol):

Cal-.22 Long Rifle, 10" barrel standard, 6" or 8" scarce, blue finish, has trigger centered in the triggerguard, the triggerguard is now part of the frame, this will fire double action as well as single action, walnut extension type grips with or without S&W monograms. Modeled from the .38 Perfected Model using 32 HE parts. Barrels from the 1st and 2nd Model will not fit the 3rd model.

Serial number range 4618 -11641 continued from 2nd model 6,949 mfd. 1909-1923

Exc	Fine	VG	Good	Fair	Poor
700	575	475	400	325	250

Variations:

- Some versions found with Olympic Barrels, these engage the bullet nose into the grooves and lands and require to be pushed in the last 1/8". Worth premium.

FOURTH MODEL (Straight Line Target):

Cal-.22 Long Rifle, single-shot, has a 10" sideswing barrel, blue finish, adjustable target sights, smooth walnut grips, This model is shaped like an autoloader, originally supplied with a felt lined metal case, tools, and a test target. Patridge front sight, with rear adj. for windage and elevation, four production changes made in 1928.

Serial number range 1-1870 1,870 mfd. 1925-1936

Exc	Fine	VG	Good	Fair	Poor
1250	1000	700	600	500	400

Variations:

- Cased set with accessories worth double above values. Most cases blue metal. Nickel cases very rare.

Single-shot target models: (1) 1st "Model of 1891," note intact recoil shield; (2) 2nd Model; (3) 3rd Model "Perfected"; (4) 4th Model "Straight Line"

EARLY HAND EJECTORS
(Named Model Revolvers, 1896-1957)

Contents

Note: Many are continued after 1957 as Numbered Models—continued in next section

The early hand ejectors are listed in order of caliber: .22, .32, .357, .38, .44, .45, .455. Where the same model was made in more than one caliber, it is listed under the caliber most commonly encountered. Many of these guns were continued as numbered models (see next section).

Basic characteristics:

- Solid framed revolvers with swing out cylinders
- No model number designated on frame under crane (open cylinder and look at left side of frame under rear of barrel)
- Made prior to 1957, when S&W began giving each model a number

Early Hand Ejector Background Information

The hand ejector is the style of gun that epitomizes S&W to the world.

Just as the concept of revolvers firing self-contained metallic cartridges had a rather anemic beginning with the Model One, the S&W Hand Ejector (HE) line was launched with the slightly awkward 1896 First Model .32 HE. By 1899, however, the first K frame .38 caliber Smith & Wesson HE was made—the revolver that would define "police handgun" for the next one hundred years.

Another nineteenth century S&W pattern that would be repeated in the twentieth was that of developing new cartridges that would dramatically expand handgun capabilities. Early S&W developed cartridges such as the .32 S&W, .38 S&W and .44 Russian were eventually eclipsed by the cartridges developed for the hand ejectors: .38 Special, .44 Special, .357 Magnum, and .44 Magnum.

Collectors of hand ejectors will be alternately delighted and frustrated by the many variations. While there is a brisk and sometimes pricey market for the largest and smallest, the big N frames and tiny LadySmiths, a collector

LadySmith .22 Hand Ejectors: (1) 1st Model, (2) 2nd Model, (3) 3rd Model

who wishes to enjoy the hobby without mortgaging the house may find the opportunity in the early .32 and .38 I, J, and K frames. Please note that many of the various "changes" in these models are differentiated only by fairly subtle internal modifications and s/n range.

As you use this section, please remember that many of these models were continued after 1957 when S&W began assigning model numbers to all its products. To get the complete picture on a particular variation, it may be helpful to check the information on its numbered model successor listed in the next section.

.22 Caliber

M Frame .22s (the original "LadySmiths") Background Information

The smallest hand ejectors ever made by S&W, these tiny guns are loved by collectors. The "LadySmith" is the only gun made on the smallest frame, designated the "M" frame. These seven-shot .22s should not be fired with modern ammunition.

An old story that has circulated for many decades concerns the discontinuance of the model. It seems that Mr. Wesson was shocked to learn that this was the gun of choice for ladies of the evening. Being of a stern Yankee puritanical bent, he ordered the production ended. True story? Probably not. But it's good enough that if it isn't, it should be.

COLLECTOR'S TIP: Do not confuse these with the "LadySmith" line of modern firearms currently manufactured by S&W. "LadySmith" was just too good a name to let die, and has been applied to selected current models along with subtle design modifications to reach the women's handgun buying market.

Three models are listed below: 26,152 mfd., 1902-1921

.22 (LADYSMITH) FIRST MODEL:

Cal-.22 Long, 2-1/4", 3", or 3-1/2" barrel, checkered hard rubber grips on a round butt, frame mounted cylinder release on the left side, blue or nickel finish, pinned barrel, 7-shot, round blade front sight, double action.

Serial number range 1-4575 4,575 mfd. 1902-1906

ID Key: Tiny M frame, round butt, cylinder release button on side of frame

Exc	Fine	VG	Good	Fair	Poor
1500	1200	900	700	500	400

.22 (LADYSMITH) SECOND MODEL:

Cal-.22 Long, 3" or 3-1/2" barrel, cylinder locking device was placed on the barrel bottom with a knurled knob and removed from the frame's left side. Blue or nickel finish, round butt, pinned barrel, fixed sights and few with target sights, black hard rubber grips, also found with pearl or ivory grips. No cylinder release button on side of frame; cylinder opens by pulling on front end of ejector rod under the barrel.

Serial number range 4576-13950 9,374 mfd. 1906-1910

ID Key: Tiny M frame, round butt, no cylinder release button

Exc	Fine	VG	Good	Fair	Poor
1400	1100	800	600	500	350

.22 (LADYSMITH) THIRD MODEL (.22 Perfected):

Cal-.22 Long, 2-1/2", 3", 3-1/2", or 6" barrel, plain smooth walnut grips with gold S&W medallions, square butt design, blue or nickel finish, rebounding hammer, pinned barrel, fluted cylinder. Target versions have 6" barrels with a pinned Paine Front sight and adj. rear sight. Matching serial numbers are found on the butt, cylinder, and barrel bottom. Patent dates of Aug 4, 1896; Nov 10, 1903; and Sept 14,1909 marked on top rib.

Serial number range 13951-26154 12,203 mfd. 1911-1921

ID Key: Tiny M frame, square butt

Exc	Fine	VG	Good	Fair	Poor
1350	1050	850	650	450	350

Variations:

- 6" barrel w/target sights: Add 50-150%
- 6" barrel w/fixed sights: Add 75-150%

I and J Frame .22s Background Information

S&W distributor Phil Bekeart is credited with originating the concept of a .22 caliber revolver on a .32 hand ejector frame. Probably the best known and loved member of this family is the "kit gun," so named as an ideal size and caliber to pack along on a fishing or camping trip in the tackle kit.

.22/32 (.22/32 Bekeart Model or .22/32 Heavy Frame Target):

Cal-.22 Long Rifle, mfd. on the .32 hand ejector "I" frame, with a 6-shot fluted cylinder, 6" round barrel, blue finish, adjustable rear sights, round butt frame with checkered walnut extension type grips. Front sight is a thin blade with bead top pinned in a raised boss, pinned barrel, double action, 5-screw, flat faced hammer, knurled round end extractor rod. Named after San Francisco dealer Phillip Bekeart who originally contracted S&W to manufacture this revolver. The first 292 are considered the "True Bekeart" Models (his original delivery) while about 3000 were mfd. and were stamped with a separate serial number on the bottom of the wooden grips. Several hundred thousand of regular mfd. were produced with a different rear sight from 1912 to 1953. The Bekeart Model has the rear

.22/32 HE "Bekeart" Model

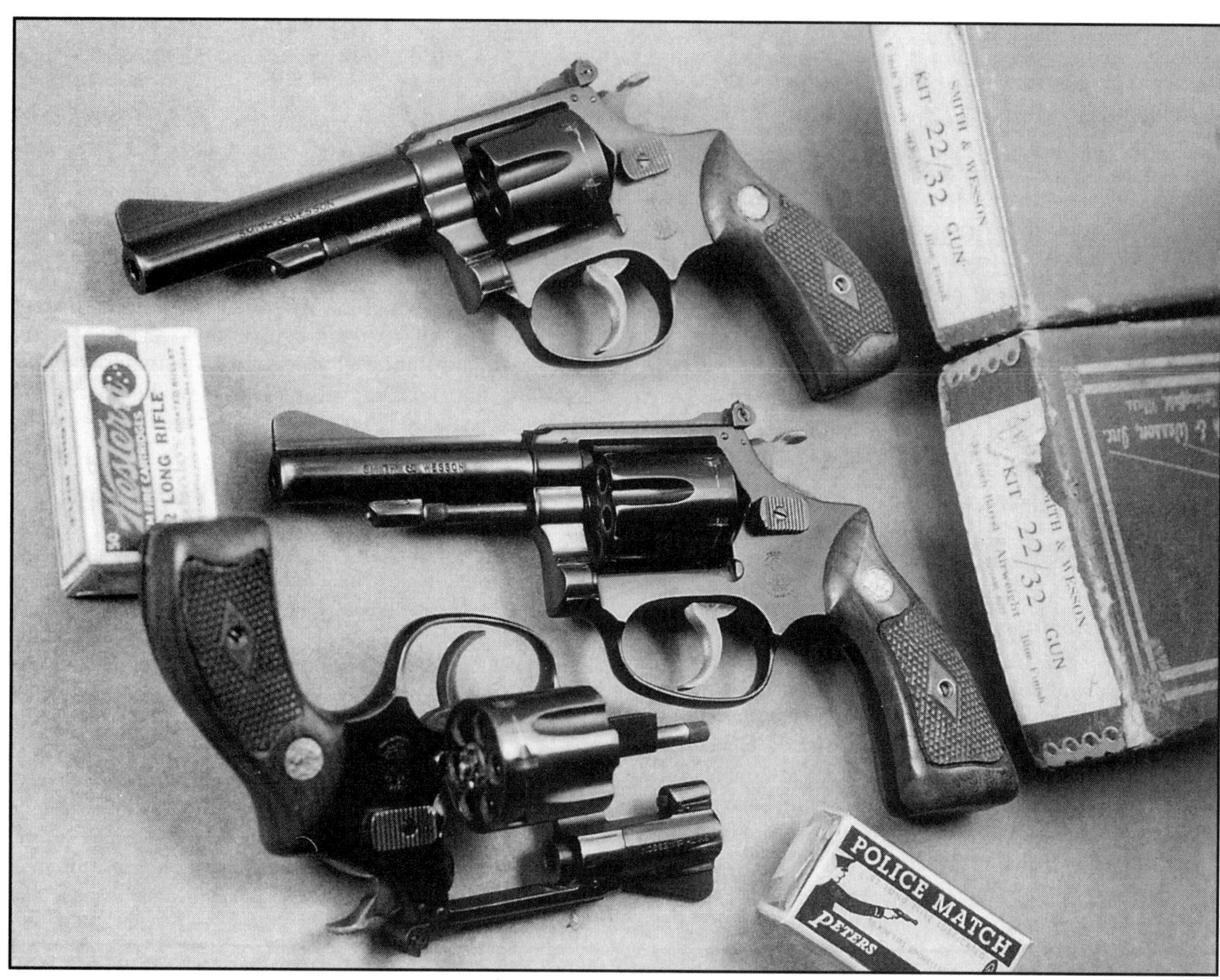

Kit guns, .22/32 Hand Ejectors, top to bottom: early 4-inch with red box, Airweight 3-1/2 inch, and steel frame 2-inch

sight elevation screw threaded into the frame, while others are threaded into the rear leaf, with a T slot cut in the frame much as today's production. Cylinder chambers recessed for case head began in 1935 @ serial number 525600. Approx. Serial number range for true Bekeart Model: 138220-139275. Serial number is viewed on the forestrap without grip removal. Weight 23 oz.

Regular production began at serial 160000 (numbered within the .32 hand ejector Series Model of 1903, 5th change) 1911-1941

ID Key: I frame .22, square butt, s/n on front strap, s/n range

NIB	Exc	VG	Good	Fair	Poor
650	500	300	225	175	125

Variations:

- "True Bekeart": Part of original shipment, add 50-75%

.22/32 TARGET (Postwar):

Cal-.22 Long Rifle, 6" barrel, 6-shot, blue finish, 1/10" or 1/8" Patridge front sight, square notch rear adjustable for windage and elevation, special oversize target stocks of walnut with S&W monograms, non-shrouded extractor rod.

Serial numbered within the .32 Hand Ejector series 1946-1953

ID Key: Similar to above w/hammer block and s/n above 551123

NIB	Exc	VG	Good	Fair	Poor
600	450	275	200	160	120

MODEL OF 1953 .22/32 TARGET:

Cal-.22 Long Rifle, 6" barrel, blue finish, micrometer rear sight, 1/10" Patridge front sight, 6-shot, walnut grips, 5-screw frame, pinned barrel with top rib, flat latch thumbpiece built on the improved I frame and the J frame.

Serial range 101-135465 in the 1953 Kit Gun series 1953-1973

ID Key: Similar to above w/improved I frame, s/n range

NIB	Exc	VG	Good	Fair	Poor
550	375	275	220	150	90

Changes:

1955 Sideplate screw eliminated @ serial 11000
35 1957 *Continued as Model 35*

.22/32 KIT GUN (Prewar):

Cal-.22 Long Rifle, 6-shot fluted cylinder with double action, 4" round barrel, blue or nickel finish, round butt frame with either round or extension type square butt, checkered walnut grips with S&W monograms, pinned barrel, adjustable rear sight, 1/10" Patridge or a USRA pocket revolver front sight, double action on a 5-screw frame, heat treated cylinder with recessed head chambers. Originally built on the 32 HE I frame. Weight 21 oz.

Serial number range 525670-536684 in the 32 Hand Ejector series 1935-1941

ID Key: I frame .22 w/round butt, s/n range

NIB	Exc	VG	Good	Fair	Poor
1250	1000	650	400	275	175

Variations:

- The factory converted many 6" guns to 4" "kit gun" configuration. These guns will have the rework star and date marked on them. Reduces value.

.22/32 KIT GUN (Postwar):

Cal-.22 Long Rifle, 4" barrel, blue or nickel finish, 6-shot round butt frame, 1/10" Patridge or pocket revolver front sight with adjustable rear target sight, stocks are checkered walnut with S&W monograms or small square butt or special target stocks. Initial postwar production identical to prewar, except for s/n range.

Serial number range 536685 within the .32 Hand Ejector series 1946-1952

ID Key: As above, except hammer block and s/n range

NIB	Exc	VG	Good	Fair	Poor
750	600	450	375	250	150

Variations:

- Original 2" barrel scarce, worth premium

MODEL OF 1953 .22/32 KIT GUN:

Cal-.22 Long Rifle, 2" or 4" barrel with square butt or round butt, 6-shot, micrometer rear sights, 2" barrel has a high profile 1/10" serrated ramp front sight, .312" smooth trigger, .375" semi-target hammer, blue or nickel finish, flat latch thumbpiece, 5-screw frame, pinned barrel, walnut grips, built on the improved I frame and the J frame. 2" versions with fixed sights are known to exist as a training gun.

Serial range 101-135465 in the 1953 Kit Gun series 1953-1991

ID Key: Similar to above, except improved I frame or J frame and s/n range

NIB	Exc	VG	Good	Fair	Poor
375	300	200	175	135	85

Variations:

- 5-screw worth 50% premium

Changes:

1955 Delete sideplate screw @ serial 11000
34 1957 *Continued as Model 34*

1955 .22/32 KIT GUN AIRWEIGHT:

Cal-.22 Long Rifle, alloy frame and alloy cylinder, J alloy target frame, 3-1/2" barrel with rare 2" versions known to exist, square butt, 1/10" serrated ramp front sight, micrometer click rear sight, 3-screw frame, 6-shot, blue or nickel finish, narrow top rib with a pinned barrel, walnut grips, counterbored cylinder, flat latch thumbpiece, smooth backstrap, not "Airweight" marked. Also found chambered in .22 MRF in limited production w/ nickel and blue finish.

Original serial number range 5000-135465 in the 1953 Kit Gun series 1954-1974

NIB	Exc	VG	Good	Fair	Poor
375	300	200	175	135	85

Changes:

1957 *Continued as Model 43*

K Frame .22s Background Information

There have been three main concepts driving the manufacture of K frame .22s:

1. They make an ideal "outdoorsman" small game hunting or plinking revolver.
2. For the first half of the twentieth century, K frame revolvers dominated traditional bullseye target shooting. The K frame .22 Target models made ideal companions to the K-.32 and K-.38 revolvers.
3. K frame .22s make ideal training guns for police officers or other individuals whose carry gun is a .38 caliber K frame. The low cost of .22 ammunition, along with its milder report and recoil allow for more training rounds.

MODEL K-22 OUTDOORSMAN (K-22 1st Model):

Cal-.22 Long Rifle, 6-shot fluted cylinder with counterbores, blue finish or nickel on special order, 6" round barrel with no rib, Patridge front sight, adjustable rear sights, KT frame with a floating firing pin, Circassian walnut grips w/large silver medallions on a square butt, non-shrouded extractor rod, has smooth semi-round topstrap with rear leaf sight, 5-screw, double action, pinned barrel, built on the .38 hand ejector frame and numbered within the M&P 1905 4th change series. Weight 38.5 oz.

Serial number range 632132-682419
19,500 mfd. 1931-1940

ID Key: K frame .22, pre-micrometer adj. sights, long action

NIB	Exc	VG	Good	Fair	Poor
550	425	300	250	200	150

Variations:

- Coast Guard Issue: Twenty-five with service sights shipped to the Coast Guard at Curtis Bay, MD in 1935 in a serial range of 650929-650953. May bring as much as 10X standard value or more.
- Earliest production had only one screw holding on rear sight.

K-22 Outdoorsman

MODEL K-22 MASTERPIECE (Prewar, K-22 2nd Model):

Cal-.22 Long Rifle, blue finish or nickel on special order, 6" round barrel with no rib, diamond walnut grips on square butt, short cocking action, 6-shot fluted cylinder with counterbores, the micrometer "click" rear sight was first introduced on this model, KT frame, 5-screw frame, double action, front sight is 1/8" or 1/10" plain Patridge, call gold, or plain bead, anti-backlash trigger.

Serial number range among the M&P series 682420-696952 1067 mfd. 1940-1941

- (See Neal and Jinks for specific serial numbers)

ID Key: K frame .22, micrometer click adjustable sights, short action, no barrel rib

NIB	Exc	VG	Good	Fair	Poor
1600	1200	900	750	450	200

Changes:

1955	Delete sideplate screw
1957	*K-22 Masterpiece continued as Model 17, see next section on numbered hand ejectors*

MODEL K-22 MASTERPIECE (Postwar, 3rd Model):

Cal-.22 Long Rifle, similar to the K-22 Masterpiece with early production having a narrow top rib on the barrel, later changed to a full width rib, and beginning of the "K" serial prefix range @ K101. 1/10" or 1/8" plain Patridge front sight, rear sight is a micrometer click for windage and elevation, blue finish, checkered walnut stocks with S&W monograms, has grooved tangs and trigger, see the Model 17. 1946-1989

ID Key: As above, with ribbed barrel.

	NIB	Exc	VG	Good	Fair	Poor
5-screw	600	425	350	275	225	150
4-screw	450	400	325	275	225	150

THE K-22 COMBAT MASTERPIECE:

Cal-.22 Long Rifle, 4" pinned barrel, blue finish, combat style adjustable rear sight, 1/8" Baughman Quick Draw on plain ramp base front sight, 6-shot, short action, K target frame, square butt, walnut grips, counterbored cylinder, 5-screw, narrow rib, target hammer, target trigger, "K" serial prefix, serrated backstrap, and forestrap. 1949-1985

ID Key: As above, w/4" barrel

NIB	Exc	VG	Good	Fair	Poor
450	400	325	275	225	150

Changes:

1955	Delete sideplate screw
18 1957	*Continued as Model 18*

THE .22 MILITARY & POLICE (Post Office):

Cal-.22 Long Rifle, designated as a training gun for the U.S. Postal Service, the only K frame produced in .22 LR without target sights (other than special orders -- see the 1935 Coast Guard K-22 Outdoorsman order, for example), blue finish, 6-shot, 4" pinned barrel, round blade front sight or serrated ramp w/square notch rear, serial numbered concurrently with the Model 10, 11, and 12 M&P series. Not cataloged. 1948-1978

K-22 Combat Masterpiece and K-22 Target Masterpiece

ID Key: .22 K frame w/fixed sights, s/n range

NIB	Exc	VG	Good	Fair	Poor
800	600	450	300	250	200

Changes:

1948	Introduction @ serial S982000
1948-57	serial range C-1 to C-407400
1957	*Continued as the Model 45*

Models chambered in .22 Long Rifle continued after 1957 and listed in next section, "Numbered Model Revolvers":

Model K-22 Masterpiece - *See Model 17*
Model K-22 Combat Masterpiece - *See Model 18*
Model of 1953 .22/32 Kit Gun - *See Model 34*
Model of 1953 .22/32 Target - *See Model 35*
1955 .22/32 Kit Gun Airweight - *See Model 43*
Military & Police .22 Heavy Barrel ("Post Office Model") - *See Model 45*

.30 Caliber Carbine

.30 CALIBER CARBINE TEST REVOLVER:

Cal-.30 Carbine, S&W did produce on a test basis several revolvers with fixed and target sights, chambered in .30 Carbine, built on the N frame. These were submitted to the army for evaluation in 1944. At least two examples are known to still exist. The revolvers passed an endurance test with no breakages, but shooters objected to the severe muzzle blast and the army did not see a military requirement for purchase. A very few were also reportedly built on the M&P K frame, which proved too light for this cartridge.

> **COLLECTOR'S TIP:** Any of these .30 carbine revolvers are extremely rare among collectors, and would probably bring several thousand dollars.

.32 Caliber Background Information

The I frame (and later the J frame) is considered the traditional size for S&W .32 revolvers. Like the .22, .32s were also made on K frames for those who preferred a larger handgun. In the early twentieth century, the .32 S&W saw considerable service as a police round, but later came to be considered insufficiently powerful for this purpose. Its mild recoil led many to promote it as a good chambering for a "lady's gun." The round enjoyed some popularity in compact self defense revolvers, but the advent of the J frame .38 Special reduced this usage. The .32 S&W cartridge has waned in popularity as the century has progressed.

This has a couple of ramifications for collectors. First, .32 caliber S&Ws can sometimes be picked up at bargain prices, simply because consumer preferences run to .22 rimfires for cheap practice and plinking or .38 Special as a minimum defensive caliber. Secondly, several later variations introduced in .32 caliber were not particularly popular and accordingly saw limited production, resulting in rare and valuable models.

> **COLLECTOR'S TIP:** This is a good field in which to look for "sleepers."

I and J Frame .32s

Model 1896 Background Information

This is the first S&W solid frame revolver with a swing-out cylinder—the hand ejector configuration that continues even today as the backbone of the S&W product line. It also is the first S&W hand ejector purchased by a police department, with 169 units going to the Jersey City, NJ, police, marked "JCP" on the backstrap. Also, guns will be found marked "Newark Police" on the backstrap.

Other interesting features on this key evolutionary model include the method of opening the cylinder by pulling on the end of the ejector rod, and the cylinder stop mounted on the top of the frame (a throwback to the old tip-up designs) rather than in the bottom of the frame as in all subsequent HE models. Also, the patent dates are marked on the cylinder rather than on the top of the barrel. It was also the first S&W made with a circular triggerguard integral to the frame rather than as a separate piece.

Finally, this marked the debut of the S&W .32 long cartridge.

.32 HAND EJECTOR FIRST MODEL DOUBLE ACTION REVOLVER (Model 1 or Model 1896):

Cal-.32 S&W Long, cylinder is unlocked by pulling forward the extractor rod. 3-1/4", 4-1/4", or 6" barrel, blue or nickel finish, round butt or extension type square buttstock of black hard rubber with S&W monogram, no locking lug under the barrel, no thumb latch, 6-shot fluted cylinder, rear service sight was pinned forward in the topstrap above the cylinder, target sight (rare) adjustable for windage and elevation, patent dates stamped on cylinder between flutes. S&W monogram stamped on the sideplate. This model became the basis for the I frame.

Serial number range 1-19712 19,712 mfd. 1896-1903

ID Key: .32 HE w/patents on cylinder and cylinder stop on topstrap

NIB	Exc	VG	Good	Fair	Poor
575	425	325	275	225	125

Variations:

- Short hammer police model worth slight premium
- JCP or Newark marked police guns worth premium
- Target model rare, worth 50-100% premium

.32 HE 1st Model (Model 1896)

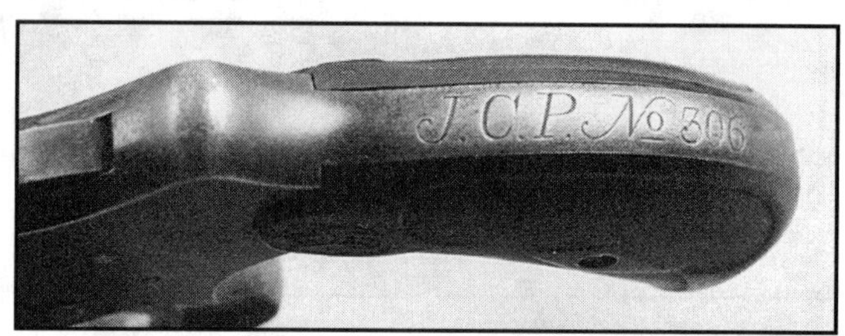

.32 HE 1st Model Jersey City Police marking

.32 HAND EJECTOR MODEL OF 1903 (.32 HE, 2nd Model):

Cal-.32 S&W Long, 3-1/2", 4-1/4", or 6" round barrel, blue or nickel finish, round butt or extension type square buttstock of checkered black hard rubber with S&W monograms, service or target sights, round blade front sight forged into the barrel, cylinder released by a side thumbpiece, now fitted with a locking lug for the extractor rod under the barrel, appears to be the first model with a pinned barrel, 6-shot, I frame with S&W monogram stamped on the sideplate.

Serial number range 1-19425 19,425 mfd. 1903-1904

NIB	Exc	VG	Good	Fair	Poor
450	325	225	175	135	100

Variations:

- Target model worth double above values

.32 HAND EJECTOR MODEL OF 1903 FIRST CHANGE:

Cal-.32 S&W Long, 3-1/4", 4-1/4", or 6" round barrel, blue or nickel finish, black hard rubber stocks, service or target sights, target version had extension stocks of black rubber or walnut with adjustable rear sight, designed like the first model with minor changes, pinned barrel, 6-shot, I frame, S&W monogram stamped on the left frame side.

Serial number range 19426-51126 31,700 mfd. 1904-1906

NIB	Exc	VG	Good	Fair	Poor
400	300	200	150	125	90

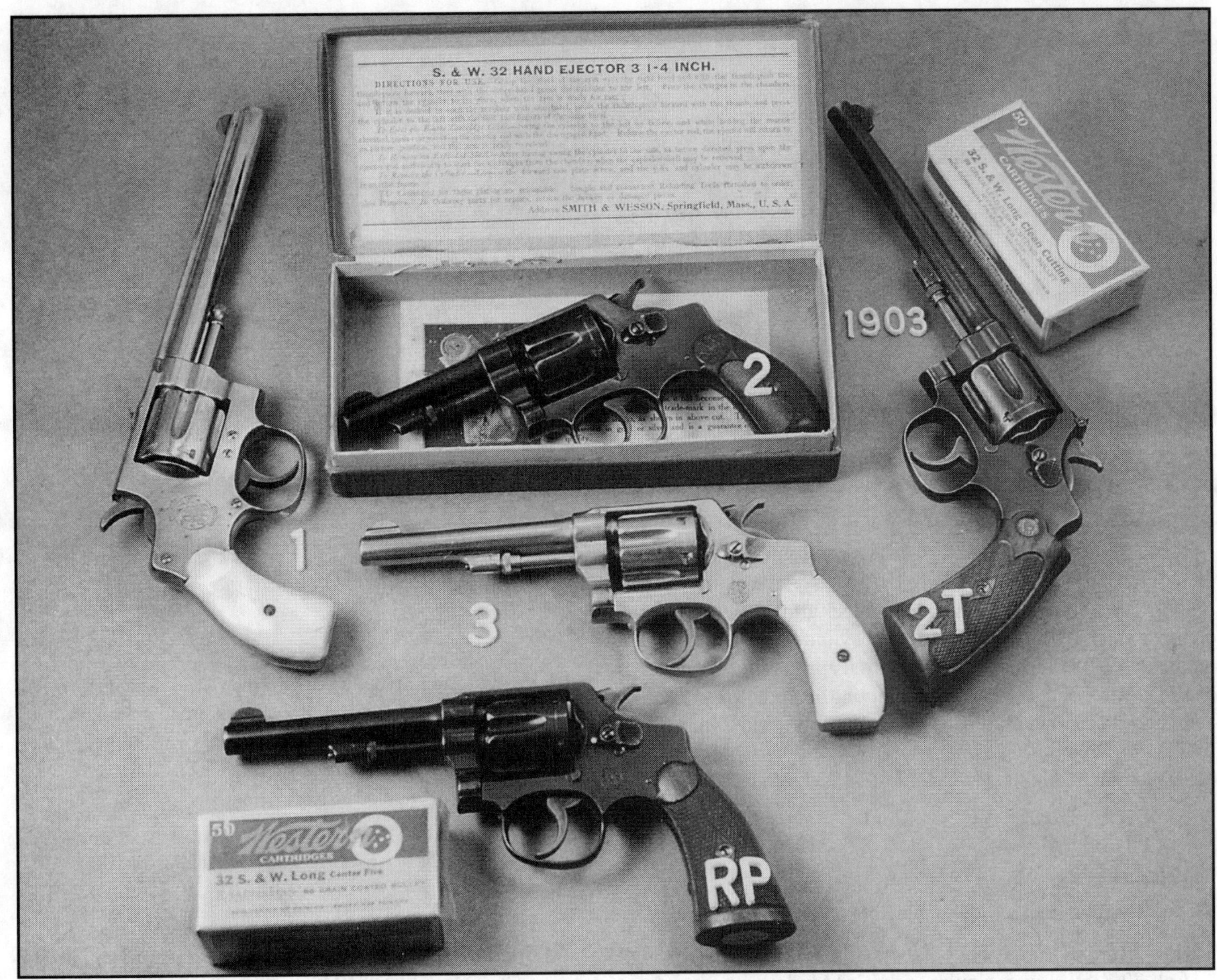

.32 Hand Ejectors: (1) 1st Model; (2) 2nd Model or Model of 1903; (2T) 2nd Model Target; (3) 3rd Model; (RP) Regulation Police

Variations:

- Target model worth double above values

.32 HAND EJECTOR MODEL OF 1903 SECOND CHANGE:

Cal-.32 S&W Long, 3-1/4", 4-1/4", or 6" round barrel, designed like the first change model with minor changes, blue or nickel finish, service or target sights, round butt black rubber stock or walnut extension type, pinned barrel, 6-shot, I frame, target sights were a blade pinned on a raised boss in the front and adj. for windage and elevation on the rear.

Serial number range 51127-95500 44,373 mfd. 1906-1909

NIB	Exc	VG	Good	Fair	Poor
400	300	200	150	125	90

Variations:

- Target model worth double above values

.32 HAND EJECTOR MODEL OF 1903 THIRD CHANGE:

Cal-.32 S&W Long, 3-1/4", 4-1/4", or 6" round barrel, designed like the second change version with minor internal changes blue or nickel finish, pinned barrel, 6-shot, I frame.

Serial number range 95501-96125 624 mfd. 1909-1910

NIB	Exc	VG	Good	Fair	Poor
700	500	375	275	200	150

Variations:

- Target model worth double above values

.32 HAND EJECTOR MODEL OF 1903 FOURTH CHANGE:

Cal-.32 S&W Long, 3-1/4", 4-1/4", or 6" round barrel, designed like the third change version with very minor internal changes, blue or nickel finish, pinned barrel, 6-shot, I frame.

Serial number range 96126-102500 6,374 mfd. 1910

NIB	Exc	VG	Good	Fair	Poor
400	300	200	150	125	90

Variations:

- Target model worth double above values

.32 HAND EJECTOR MODEL OF 1903 FIFTH CHANGE:

Cal-.32 S&W Long, 3-1//4", 4-1/4", or 6" round barrel, designed like the fourth change version with major internal changes, two-piece extractor rod, blue or nickel finish, pinned barrel, I frame, 6-shot.

Serial number range 102501~263000
~160,499 mfd. 1910-1917

NIB	Exc	VG	Good	Fair	Poor
375	275	175	125	100	70

Variations:

- Target model worth double above values

.32 HAND EJECTOR THIRD MODEL:

Cal-.32 S&W Long, 3-1/4", 4-1/4", or 6" round barrel, blue or nickel finish, 6-shot, 5-screw I frame, service sights with round blade front sight, a new hammer block arm was introduced on this model, round butt, heat treated cylinders began in 1920 with serial 320000. Identical in external appearance to Model of 1903 Fifth Change. Serial number found on the butt, cylinder, and barrel. Serial numbered concurrently with the .32 Regulation Police.

Serial range 263001-536684 271,531 mfd. 1911-1942

NIB	Exc	VG	Good	Fair	Poor
400	300	200	150	115	75

Variations:

- Target model worth double above values

THE .32 HAND EJECTOR (Postwar):

Cal-.32 S&W Long, similar to the 3rd Model with postwar improvements—new style rebound hammer block and a change in the extractor rod, 6-shot, blue or nickel finish, 3-1/4", 4-1/4", or 6" barrel, round butt frame, 1/10" round blade front sight, square notch rear sight, checkered walnut stocks with S&W monograms. Serial numbered concurrently with the .32 Regulation Police. Became the Model 30.

Serial range 536685-712953 1946-1960

NIB	Exc	VG	Good	Fair	Poor
375	275	175	125	100	70

Changes:

1948	Postwar production with 3-1/4", 4-1/4", and 6" barrel
1949	Introduce 2" barrel
1955	Eliminate sideplate top screw @ s/n 640980
1957	*.32 HE continued as Model 30*

.32 REGULATION POLICE:

Cal-.32 S&W Long, 3-1/4", 4-1/4", or 6" round barrel, blue or nickel finish, service sights are a round blade front sight, target sights are a square cut blade pinned on a raised boss with rear adj. for windage and elevation. The frame is made with a shouldered backstrap to accept a new style of square walnut buttstocks not interchangeable with previous models, knurled round extractor knob, 6-shot, 5-screw frame, cylinders heat treated in 1920, some production of models with target sights. Serial numbered concurrently with .32 HE Third Model.

Serial number range 331320-536684 1917-1942

NIB	Exc	VG	Good	Fair	Poor
375	275	175	150	120	100

Variations:

- Target model worth double to triple above values.
- Massachusetts State Police: Forty-eight guns shipped to Mass. St. Police in 1929, 4" blue, marked "State Police" on backstrap, s/n's in 508000s and 509000s, worth premium.

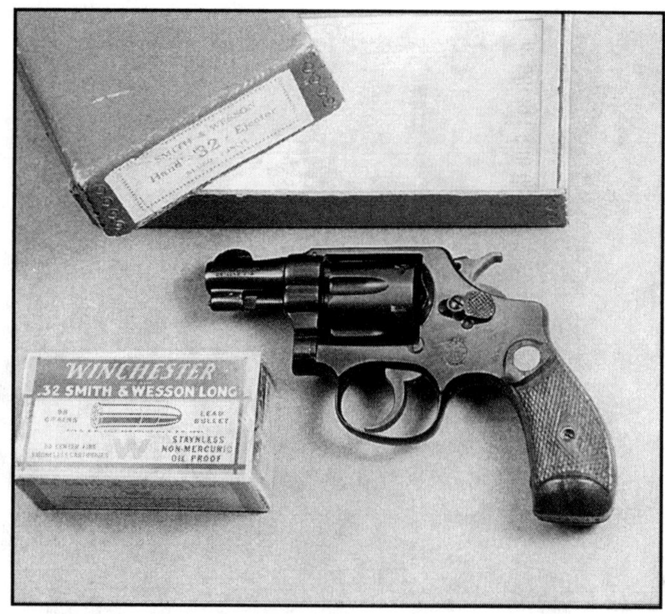

.32 HE, early postwar, 2-inch barrel

.32 REGULATION POLICE (Postwar):

Cal-.32 S&W Long, similar to previous model with postwar design changes: a new design rebound slide hammer block was introduced at serial 536685. 1/10" round blade front sight with a square notch rear, built on the I frame and the improved I frame until 1961 when the J frame was introduced, sideplate top screw eliminated at about serial 640980 in 1956. The serrated front ramp was introduced about 1956. 6-shot, 3-1/4", 4-1/4", or 6" barrel, checkered walnut stocks with S&W monograms, blue or nickel finish, square butt frame. Serial numbered with the .32 Hand Ejector 3rd Model. Became the Model 31.

Serial number range 536685-712953 1946-1960

NIB	Exc	VG	Good	Fair	Poor
350	265	175	150	115	90

Variations:

- .32 Regulation Police Target: 196 made in 1957, double above values

K-32 Masterpiece

Changes:

1948	Postwar production with 3-1/4", 4-1/4", and 6" barrel
1949	Introduce 2" barrel
1955	Eliminate top sideplate screw @ 640,980
1957	196 units built with target sights
1957	*.32 Regulation Police continued as Model 31*

K Frame .32s

.32 MILITARY & POLICE:

Cal-.32 S&W Long, 2", 4", and 5" barrel, a small group of M&P revolvers built to fire the .32 long rather than the .38 and built on the larger .38 M&P frame. K frame.

Serial prefixes of "S" and "C" 4,813 mfd. 1948-1950

- For some reason, very rare and seldom seen. Would be worth substantial premium.

K-32 HAND EJECTOR FIRST MODEL (K-32 Target, K-32 Masterpiece):

Cal-.32 S&W Long, 6" round barrel, 6-shot fluted cylinder, blue finish, KT frame, 1/8" or 1/10" Patridge front sight, with gold bead available, adjustable rear sights, walnut grips on square butt frame, pinned barrel, double action, 5-screw, rare.

Serial number range ~663107~663201 built on the .38 M&P frame of 1905 4th change ~100 mfd. 1936-1941

NIB	Exc	VG	Good	Fair	Poor
5000	2500	1200	800	500	350

K-32 HAND EJECTOR (Postwar):

Cal-.32 S&W Long, short cocking action, anti-backlash trigger, grooved tangs and trigger, 1/8" or 1/10" Patridge front sight, micrometer click rear sight, narrow ribbed barrel, checkered walnut stocks with S&W monograms, now built on the K frame. Quite a scarce gun, with s/n ranges hard to pin down. Known s/n's include all of K-58921 through 58970, and K67601-67670; along with some of the guns in K767574-767599 and K68470-68530 ranges. All of these have the narrow rib. In 1950, the wide rib was introduced, and some K-32s from 1956 will be found in the K271792-271836 s/n range. Additional known s/n ranges listed under Model 16. Weight 38.5 oz. See the Model 16. 1946-1974

NIB	Exc	VG	Good	Fair	Poor
1500	1000	800	650	400	300

.32-20 Hand Ejectors, top to bottom: Model 1902 or 2nd Model, Model 1905 2nd change, Model 1905 4th change

Variations:

- Limited run of 4" barrels in 1949 have been reported—"Combat Masterpiece"

Changes:

1949	Mfd. heavy barrel to Match K-17 and K-38 in weight
1955	Delete sideplate screw
1957	*K-32 Masterpiece continued as Model 16*

.32-20 Winchester Caliber

***Caution:** Do not use modern ammunition designated for rifles in these handguns!*

.32-20 HAND EJECTOR FIRST MODEL:

Cal-.32/20 Win., 4", 5", 6", or 6-1/2" round barrel, 6-shot fluted cylinder, blue or nickel finish, no locking lug under the barrel checkered hard rubber or walnut monogrammed grips, round butt, fixed or target sights were available, round front blade sight, pinned barrel, 4-screw frame, S&W stamped on the sideplate.

Serial number range 1-5311 5,311 mfd. 1899-1902

NIB	Exc	VG	Good	Fair	Poor
800	700	450	350	250	175

Variations:

- Target model worth double above values

.32-20 HAND EJECTOR MODEL 1902 (.32-20 HE 2nd Model):

Cal-.32/20 Win., 4", 5", or 6-1/2" round barrel, blue or nickel finish, similar in design to first model, now made with a locking lug under the barrel and a knurled round extractor rod.

Serial number range 5312-9811 4,499 mfd. 1902-1905

NIB	Exc	VG	Good	Fair	Poor
725	525	435	350	250	175

Variations:

- Target model worth double above values

.32-20 HAND EJECTOR MODEL 1902 1ST CHANGE:

Cal-.32/20 Win., similar to second model with a slightly larger barrel and frame front where the barrel threads in, slight changes in the yoke cut, target version mfd. in 1904, round butt with hard rubber or wood grips, square butt with checkered wood only.

Serial number range 9812-18125 8,313 mfd. 1903-1905

NIB	Exc	VG	Good	Fair	Poor
700	500	425	350	250	150

Variations:

- Target model worth double above values

.32-20 HAND EJECTOR MODEL 1905 (.32-20 HE 3rd Model):

Cal-.32/20 Win., very similar to preceding model with many internal changes, target versions with square butt only, frame drilled for the triggerguard screw, 5-screw frame.

Serial number range 18126-22426 4,300 mfd. 1905-1906

NIB	Exc	VG	Good	Fair	Poor
725	525	425	350	250	150

Variations:

- Target model worth double above values

.32-20 HAND EJECTOR MODEL OF 1905 1ST CHANGE:

Cal-.32/20 Win., 4", 5", 6", or 6-1/2" barrel with various internal changes, new rebound slide introduced, 5-screw frame.

Serial number range 22427~33500 11,073 mfd. 1906-1907

NIB	Exc	VG	Good	Fair	Poor
700	500	425	350	250	150

Variations:

- Target model worth double above values

.32-20 HAND EJECTOR MODEL OF 1905 2ND CHANGE:

Cal-.32/20 Win., similar to preceding model with various internal changes, 5-screw frame, two dowel pins in the star extractor.

Serial number range 33501-45200 11,699 mfd. 1906-1907

NIB	Exc	VG	Good	Fair	Poor
700	500	425	350	250	150

Variations:

- Target model worth double above values

.32-20 HAND EJECTOR MODEL OF 1905 3RD CHANGE:

Cal-.32/20 Win., 4" or 6" barrel, similar to 2nd change model with various internal changes, 5-screw frame.

Serial number range 45201-65700 20,499 mfd. 1909-1915

NIB	Exc	VG	Good	Fair	Poor
650	450	375	275	175	100

Variations:

- Target model worth double above values

.32-20 HAND EJECTOR MODEL OF 1905 4TH CHANGE:

Cal-.32/20 Win., 4", 5", or 6" barrel, blue or nickel finish, flat topstrap, black hard rubber or walnut stocks, 6-shot, target sights on square butt models only, with walnut stocks. Serial number found on butt, cylinder and barrel, heat treated cylinders began at serial number 81287, pinned round barrel, smooth trigger, 5-screw frame.

Serial number range 65701-144684
78,983 mfd. 1915-1940

NIB	Exc	VG	Good	Fair	Poor
600	475	350	250	150	90

Variations:

- Target model worth double above values

.357 Magnum Caliber

"The most important handgun developed in the twentieth century." - Roy Jinks

N Frame .357

.357 Registered Magnum Background Information

The development of the .357 Magnum in 1935 may be viewed as the birth of the modern handgun era. It introduced a power level in handguns unknown before that time. According to the latest statistics on police shootings, the .357 remains unmatched even today as an effective defensive round. The beginning of handgun hunting as something more serious than a stunt can be traced to the power and relatively flat trajectory of the .357.

S&W originally offered the gun on a custom order basis with the gun "registered" with the factory to the purchaser. It was built to specifications and the wide variety of configurations, combined with the .357's significance in handgun history, make the registered magnum a prized collector's item. Possible combinations of features include seven sights, three grips, twenty-three barrel lengths, two finishes, and two hammer styles. Options that were offered for the first time on this model include Magna stocks, Baughman ramp front sight, and humpbacked hammer.

.357 MAGNUM - FACTORY REGISTERED (C&R):

Cal-.357 Magnum, 1st Production of the .357 Magnum. The first production unit was presented to J. Edgar Hoover, Director of the FBI. Barrel lengths available from 3-1/2" to 8-3/4", adjustable micrometer rear sights. Choice of seven front sights, all parts hand fitted and the owner provided with a registration certificate from the factory, the registration number being stamped on the yoke cut preceded by REG- xxxx. Built on the N Target frame with a shrouded extractor rod, ribbed and pinned barrel, with blue or nickel finish, 5-screw frame with serrated backstrap and forestrap, checkered walnut on square butt grips or Magna type with an S&W monogram. Double action, with counterbored cylinders, with a finely checkered topstrap, barrel rib and hammer. .400" hammer and a .312" serrated trigger. "S&W .357 Magnum" on the barrel's right side. Numbered in the .44 Hand Ejector 3rd model series.

Serial number range 45768-62489 ~5,500 mfd. 1935-1938

NIB	Exc	VG	Good	Fair	Poor
2500	1750	1250	900	700	500

Registered Magnum

Variations:

- Add 20% for original registration certificate accompanying gun.
- Barrel lengths: Available in 1/4" increments, most popular lengths, in order, were 6-1/2", 5", 6", 8-3/4", 3-1/2", and 4". Premiums are paid for scarcity of barrel length.
- Nickel finish worth premium, only 174 made.
- Humpbacked hammer: 25% had this option.
- In 1937, the logo was changed from a small logo on the left of the frame to a large logo on the right side.
- Special features worth premiums: Pearl, ivory, or stag grips. Factory inscribed (47 made). Full factory engraving (11 made). One gun was custom made in .22 long rifle caliber.

.357 MAGNUM PREWAR (C&R):

Same as above but without registered number. Actually scarcer than the registered version, but tends to bring less on the collector market.

Numbered in the same serial range as above

1,142 mfd. 1938-1941

NIB	Exc	VG	Good	Fair	Poor
1200	750	600	400	300	225

.357 MAGNUM POSTWAR:

Cal-.357 Magnum, reintroduced with a "S" serial prefix at S-71801 in December 1948 with a new rebound slide operated hammer block and a short throw hammer. Choice of any standard target sights, checkered walnut stocks with S&W monograms, blue or nickel finish, finely checkered topstrap with matching barrel rib and checkered front and rear straps. S&W grooving on the trigger, shrouded extractor rod, 5-screw N Target frame. The "S" prefix continued until 1969 when it was changed to an "N" prefix. Barrels were then standard at 3-1/2", 5", 6", 6-1/2", and 8-3/8". Some production of humpback hammers, a very popular arm with police depts. and the F.B.I. in 3-1/2" and 5" versions. Sideplate screw eliminated after Serial S-171584 in 1956. Became the Model 27 in 1957. 1946-DATE

NIB	Exc	VG	Good	Fair	Poor
700	500	375	275	225	150

Variations:

- "Transitional" models with s/n below S-75000 worth about double standard values

Changes:

1949	Begin "S" serial prefix @ S-72000
1955	Delete upper sideplate screw @ S-171584
1957	*The .357 Magnum continued as Model 27*

THE HIGHWAY PATROLMAN:

See the Model 28 in the next section for full description

Changes:

1954 Begin "S" serial prefix @ S103500
1955 Delete sideplate screw @ S171584
1957 *Highway Patrolman continued as Model 28*

K Frame .357 Background Information

Well-known border patrolman and exhibition shooter Bill Jordan, among others, urged S&W to offer the power of the .357 cartridge in a more compact package than the big N frame. The result was the K frame .357 Combat Magnum, which was continued as the Model 19.

THE .357 COMBAT MAGNUM:

Cal-.357 Magnum, K Target frame, blue or nickel finish, originally available in 4" only with a 1/8" Baughman Quick Draw on plain ramp base front sight with adjustable rear sight, built on a frame that is slightly larger than a standard K frame in the yoke area. 1955-DATE

NIB	Exc	VG	Good	Fair	Poor
500	350	250	185	150	100

Variations:

- Initial production was shipped in dark blue presentation cases, marked "COMBAT MAGNUM" on top.

Changes:

1955 Introduction @ K-260001
1957 *The .357 Combat Magnum continued as the Model 19*

.38 Caliber and .38 Special Caliber

(Listed chronologically within frame size)

K frame .38 Background Information

The introduction of the .38 HE Military & Police marks the beginning of what would become the quintessential police handgun of the twentieth century and the workhorse of S&W production for many decades—the K frame revolver chambered for a .358" diameter bullet. Also especially significant is the introduction of what has probably become the most used centerfire cartridge in America, the .38 Special. The basic design of this gun has been continuously improved over nearly a century, and in its current variations such as the Models 10, 19, and 66, is still considered by many expert authorities to be the finest personal defense or police handgun available.

.38 HE M&P 1st Model, U.S. Army issue

.38 MILITARY & POLICE 1ST MODEL (Model 1899 Army-Navy Revolver):

Cal-.38 S&W Special or .38 Long Colt (U.S. Service Cartridge), 6-shot fluted cylinder, 4", 5", 6", or 6-1/2" round pinned barrel, earliest of the S&W models with a swing-out cylinder in this caliber, no locking lug present on the barrel bottom, service or target sights, blue or nickel finish, checkered hard rubber stocks w/S&W monograms or plain walnut, round butt, square cut round blade front sight on a raised boss. Believe it or not, this gun can be considered a "Pre-5-screw 4-screw model" since the 5th frame screw was added to the basic hand ejector design about 1905.

Serial number range 1-20975 20,975 mfd. 1899-1902

NIB	Exc	VG	Good	Fair	Poor
1000	700	600	500	350	250

Variations:

- Target model worth double above values.
- **U.S. Navy Model:** Cal-.38 Long Colt, 1,000 marked "U.S.N." with an anchor and Navy serial number on the butt, 6" barrel. Navy serial number range 1-1000, S&W serial number range 5001-6000, 1900.

NIB	Exc	VG	Good	Fair	Poor
n/a	1400	1000	700	500	300

- **U.S. Army Model:** Cal-.38 Long Colt, 1,000 marked "U.S. ARMY MODEL 1899" on the butt, 6" barrel. Army Issue has the inspectors initials in the grip circles, with lanyard ring. S&W serial number range 13001-14000, 1901.

NIB	Exc	VG	Good	Fair	Poor
n/a	1250	800	600	450	300

- Coast Guard shipment: s/n 20752-20801 shipped to the U.S. Coast Guard, Revenue Cutter Service in 1902. Total fifty guns, worth substantial premium.

.38 MILITARY & POLICE 2ND MODEL (Model of 1902):

Cal-.38 S&W Special, 6-shot fluted cylinder, 4", 5", 6", or 6-1/2" pinned barrel, blue or nickel finish, checkered hard rubber grips or walnut, round butt, built similar to the first model

Early .38 HE M&P commercial models, top to bottom: 1st Model, Model of 1902, Model of 1905 2nd change, Model of 1905 4th change

and now fitted with a locking lug on the barrel bottom, with minor internal changes, service or target sights.

Serial number range 20976-33803 12,827 mfd. 1902-1903

NIB	Exc	VG	Good	Fair	Poor
550	475	375	275	200	125

Variations:

- Target model worth 50% premium.
- **U.S. Navy Model:** Cal-.38 Long Colt, Navy serial number range 1001-2000 continued from 1st order in 1900. Marked "U.S.N." with an anchor on the butt. S&W Serial number range is 25001-26000 found on the front tang, 1902.

NIB	Exc	VG	Good	Fair	Poor
—	1100	700	500	400	300

.38 MILITARY & POLICE MODEL OF 1902 1ST CHANGE:

Cal-.38 S&W Special, 6-shot fluted cylinder, 4", 5", 6-1/2" barrel, checkered hard rubber grips with S&W monograms, or checkered walnut, blue or nickel finish. Changes are an enlarged barrel thread diameter and the corresponding change to the frame, also changes to the yoke and yoke cut, pinned barrel, 4-screw frame (pre-5-screw 4-screw). The first square butt K frames show up in the middle of this model s/n range.

Serial number range 33804-62449 28,645 mfd. 1903-1904

NIB	Exc	VG	Good	Fair	Poor
525	450	350	260	185	115

Variations:

- Target model worth 50% premium

.38 MILITARY & POLICE MODEL OF 1905 (.38 HE M&P, 3rd Model):

Cal-.38 S&W Special, similar to 1902 1st change with round or square butt, changes in the cylinder stop cut and the frame stop cut. Triggerguard screw added, making this the first "5-screw" model.

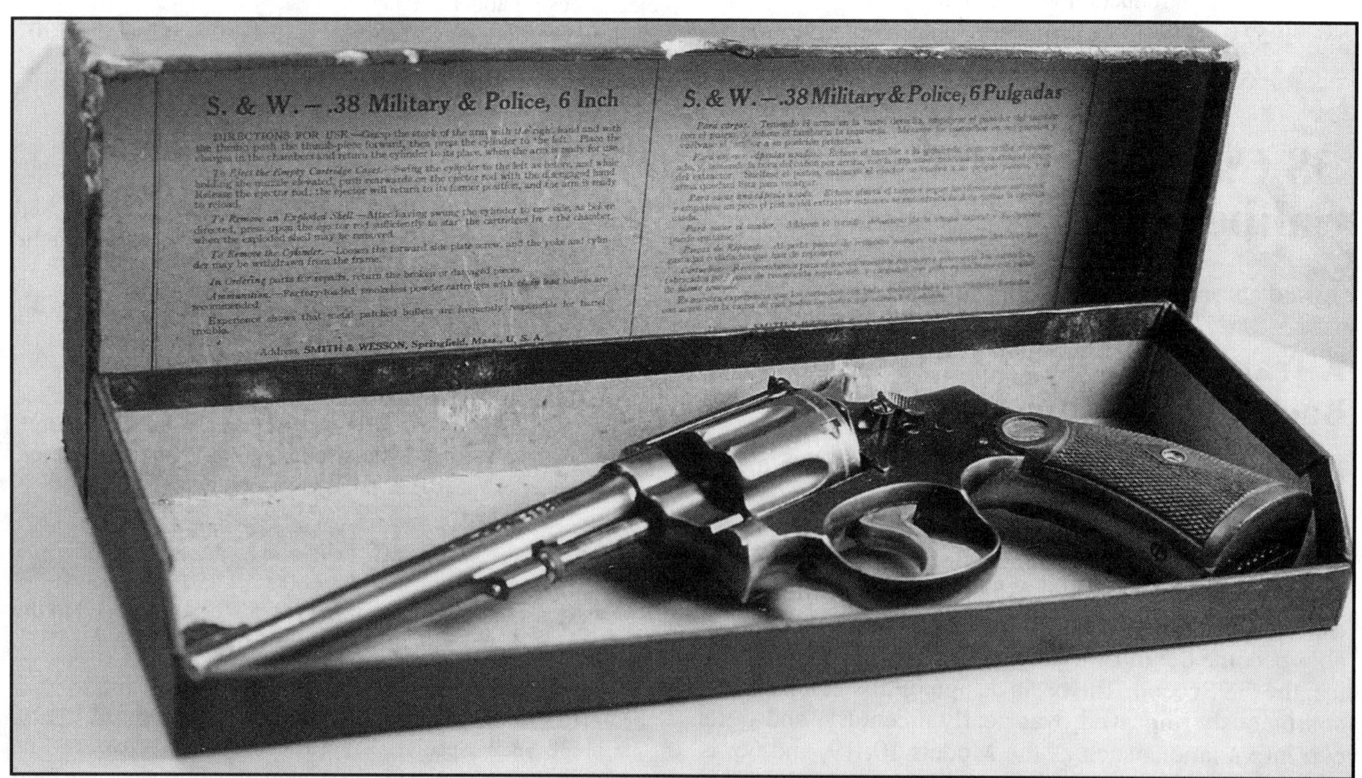

Early .38 M&P Target Model

Serial number range 62450-73250 10,800 mfd. 1905-1906

NIB	Exc	VG	Good	Fair	Poor
600	500	385	300	225	135

Variations:

- Target model worth 50% premium

.38 MILITARY & POLICE MODEL 1905 1ST CHANGE:

Cal-.38 S&W Special, 6-shot fluted cylinder, with 4", 5", 6", or 6-1/2" barrel, designed like the previous model with various internal changes, round or square butt, blue or nickel finish. Serial number range overlaps with the 2nd change model.

Serial number range 73251-146899 73,648 mfd. between 1st and 2nd change 1906-1909

NIB	Exc	VG	Good	Fair	Poor
350	285	200	150	125	80

Variations:

- Target model worth 50% premium

.38 MILITARY & POLICE MODEL 1905 2ND CHANGE:

Cal-.38 S&W Special, identical to 1st change with minor changes with 4", 5", 6", or 6-1/2" barrel, two dowel pins in star extractor.

Serial number range 73251-146899 overlapping with the 1st change model 1906-1909

NIB	Exc	VG	Good	Fair	Poor
350	285	200	150	125	80

Variations:

- Target model worth 50% premium

.38 MILITARY & POLICE MODEL 1905 3RD CHANGE:

Cal-.38 S&W Special, 6-shot fluted cylinder, 4" or 6" barrel, round or square butt, blue or nickel finish, minor internal changes, knurled extractor knob now a solid piece.

Serial number range 146900-241703
94,803 mfd. 1909-1915

NIB	Exc	VG	Good	Fair	Poor
350	285	200	150	125	80

Variations:

- Target model worth 25% premium

.38 MILITARY & POLICE MODEL 1905 4TH CHANGE:

Cal-.38 S&W Special, 6-shot fluted cylinder, 2", 4", 5", or 6" barrel, round or square butt, hard rubber or walnut stocks, changes are primarily internal, heat treated cylinders began @ s/n 316648. Tangs on target models are serrated, early style hammer block.

Serial number range 241704-1000000
758,296 mfd. 1915-1942

NIB	Exc	VG	Good	Fair	Poor
300	250	175	140	115	70

Variations:

- Target model worth 25% premium.
- Texas State Prison: Nickel, 5", well-used, a small number of guns purchased 1927-1930 scattered between s/n's 500000 and 630000, marked Texas State Prison, worth premium.
- USNCPC marked: 3000 guns total in the 748000 - 760000 s/n range, "U.S. Navy Civilian Police Corps" abbreviation on backstrap, worth double to triple standard values.
- USMC: In 1932, 1000 guns shipped to marines, 6" blue SB, broad s/n range, markings not reported. Worth premium.
- Other U.S.: 4", 5", and 6" guns were bought by the army in 1941-1942. Often marked "U.S." on left frame. Worth 50-100% premium.

.38/200 BRITISH SERVICE REVOLVER (Model K-200, S&W Pistol # 2):

Cal-.38 S&W w/200 grain bullet, 4", 5", or 6" barrel, 6-shot fluted cylinder, bright blue, brush blue, sandblast blue, and sandblast parkerized finishes are found, round blade front sight and notch cut rear service sights, square butt with checkered walnut grips with S&W monograms for the commercial version, smooth walnut without monograms with lanyard ring for the service version, 5-screw frame, pinned barrel. The serial range continues from the M&P series 1905 4th change, in a range of 700000 to 1000000. Then the gun was numbered with a "V" prefix (for "Victory") in the same s/n range as the .38 Special Victory Models from V-1 to V-769000. Early Lend Lease guns were marked "UNITED STATES PROPERTY." Later guns were marked same as the Victory Model. When a new style hammer block was introduced, the serial prefix was again changed, this time to an "SV." The serial number range runs from SV-769001 to SV-811119 and is concurrent with the Victory Model chambered in .38 S&W Special. It is reported that a "VS" serial prefix exists but the authors have never confirmed this. 568,204 mfd. 1940-1945

NIB	Exc	VG	Good	Fair	Poor
300	225	160	120	100	60

Variations:

- Non-factory converted to .38 Special: Will detract from the value, and should be checked out by a competent gunsmith, as some of these conversions are poorly and unsafely done.

Changes:

1947	Begin S serial prefix
1948	Begin C serial prefix
1955	Delete upper sideplate screw
1957	*Continued as Model 11*

Typical .38-200 British markings

.38-200 British service revolvers w/plastic case as used by British paratroopers

.38 MILITARY & POLICE VICTORY MODEL:

Cal-.38 S&W Special, 2" or 4" round pinned barrel, 6-shot, lanyard ring, sandblast blue or parkerized finish, 5-screw frame, non-shrouded extractor, round blade front sight w/square notch rear sight, smooth wood grips on a square butt frame, introduced with a "V" serial prefix (for "Victory") from V-40001 to V-769000 at which time a new design hammer block was introduced and the serial prefix became an "SV" added to indicate this change. It is reported that a "VS" serial prefix exists but the authors have never confirmed this. "U.S. Property" stamped on the topstrap with a "GHD" inspector's stamp elsewhere on the frame.

.38 M&P Victory Model; note navy markings on top gun

Serial numbers V-1 to V-769000 and SV-769001 to SV-811119 numbered concurrently with the 38/200 British Service Model. ~242,291 mfd. 1942-1945

NIB	Exc	VG	Good	Fair	Poor
400	350	225	185	160	90

Variations:

- 2" barrel scarce, worth 6X premium. It is known that 300 with 2" barrels went to the Dept. Of Justice.
- A very few reported with Israeli markings, worth premium.
- "U.S. NAVY" marked worth 10-25% premium.

- Many interesting variations and markings found: USMC, Bavarian Rural Police, Australia, New Zealand, South Africa, etc.
- Unmarked: Many were sold to civilian users (defense plants, post office, etc.) and do not have U.S. or inspector markings.

.38 MILITARY & POLICE (Postwar):

Cal-.38 S&W Special, a continuation of the previous model without the "V" serial prefix or the lanyard ring, beginning about Sept. 1945 with an "S" serial prefix at S 811120 to about S 990184 when a new short throw hammer was introduced, becoming the now familiar Model 10. After the production of the second million M&P revolvers, the serial prefix was changed again to a "C" prefix in 1948 and was numbered concurrently with the M&P Airweights and the Model 45. The "C" continued until 1967 when a "D" serial prefix was introduced after C 999999. Available in 2", 4", 5", or 6" barrel, 1/10" fixed round blade front sight with a square notch rear, blue or nickel finish, 5-screw frame on a square butt, pinned barrel, .240" serrated trigger, checkered walnut grips with S&W monograms, round butt available in late 1947. Became the Model 10 in 1957. 1946-DATE

NIB	Exc	VG	Good	Fair	Poor
500	425	350	220	170	125

Variations:

- **"1946 (Mexican) Target":** 2901 units shipped in 1945 and 1946 in s/n range 812000-817000

Changes:

1945	Begin "S" serial prefix @ S 811120 to S 999999
1948	Begin "C" serial prefix @ C 1 to C 999999
1952	Change front sight from round blade to ramp
1955	Delete upper sideplate screw
1957	*Continued as Model 10*

.38 M&Ps: scarce 5-inch bbl. and 2-inch marked "U.S. Army"

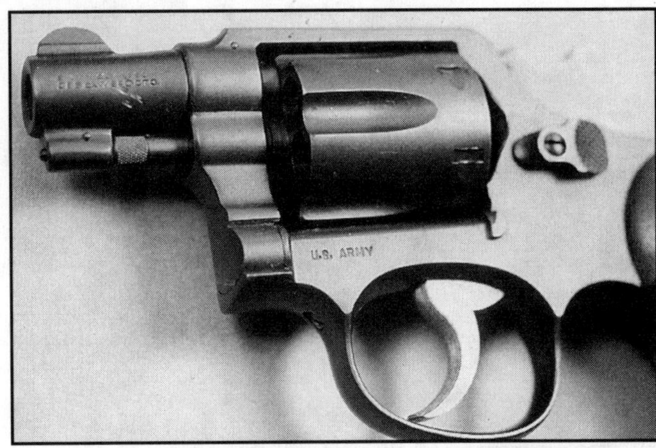

Close-up "U.S. Army" marking on .38 M&P below left

.38 M&P Airweight.

.38 M&P AIRWEIGHT:

See above and see Model 12 in next section, "Numbered Model Revolvers"

Changes:

1952	Introduction @ C 223999
1954	Alloy cylinder changed to steel due to cracking
1955	Delete sideplate screw
1957	*Continued as Model 12*

USAF-M13 (The "Aircrewman"):

Cal-.38 Special, alloy frame and alloy cylinder, 6-shot, blue finish, 2" pinned barrel, .240" hammer with .240" serrated trigger, round butt with walnut grips, serrated ramp front sight w/square notch rear, a flat latch with three variations, 4-screw frame, similar to the Model 12, has "Revolver, Lightweight, M-13" stamped on the topstrap, "Property of U.S. Air Force" stamped on the backstrap. Most were destroyed by the government. Has a "C" serial prefix in a range of C-247000 to C-405363. Numbered concurrently with Model 10, 11, 12, and 45. 605 early versions were serial numbered with an "A.F.NO" prefix . (A.F.NO. 1190 - A.F.NO. 1794) These are a 5-screw variation with "Aircrewman" on the barrel, but with no topstrap markings and

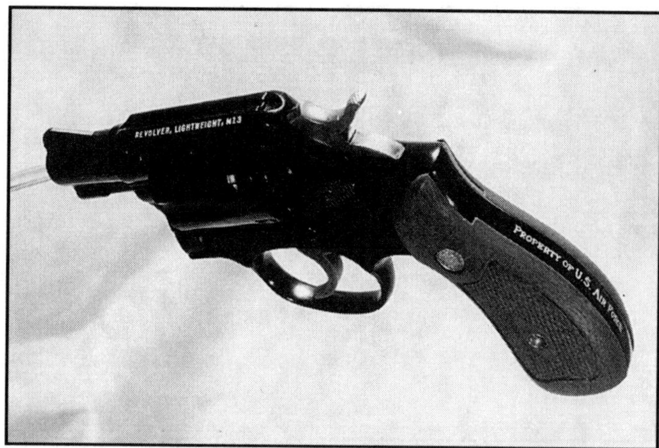

USAF M-13 Aircrewman

have air force medallions in the grip circles with a smooth backstrap. "P" inspector's stamp on left side of the frame above the triggerguard. Genuine Aircrewmans have all matching serial numbers on the frame, cylinder face, grips, and barrel. Many were repaired by military armorers who interchanged parts, especially cylinders with non-matching numbers. Nine variations of the Aircrewman are known to exist. Weight 14.5 oz.

~40,000 mfd. (but most destroyed) 1951-1957

COLLECTOR'S TIP:
1) Counterfeit and reworked Aircrewmans are commonplace.
2) Unlike the Model 12, few original examples w/steel cylinders are known to exist.

NIB	Exc	VG	Good	Fair	Poor
1000	850	600	450	325	200

Variations:

- Guns with an "AF" prefix may bring 4X to 5X standard value

K-38 TARGET MASTERPIECE:

Cal-.38 S&W Special, 6" barrel, 1/8" or 1/10" Patridge front sight with a new micrometer click rear sight, blue finish, narrow ribbed barrel, anti-backlash trigger, short cocking action, short throw hammer, checkered Magna style walnut grips with S&W monograms, "K" serial prefix, became the Model 14. Weight 38.5 oz.

Introduced @ serial K-1661 1946-1982

NIB	Exc	VG	Good	Fair	Poor
425	300	250	180	135	90

Changes:

1947	Begin production @ serial K-1661
1949	mfd. heavy barrel to match K-17 and K-32 in weight
1955	Delete sideplate screw
1957	*Continued as Model 14*

K-38 COMBAT MASTERPIECE:

Cal-.38 Special, adjustable rear sights, 6-shot, K Target frame, originally made with a 4" barrel then 2", 6", or 8-3/8" (5" rare), pinned and narrow ribbed barrel, blue or nickel finish, .375" or .500" target hammer, 1/8" Baughman Quick Draw on plain ramp base front sight, 5-screw frame, square butt with walnut grips, .312" smooth combat trigger on 2" and 4", .265" serrated service trigger on 6" and 8 3/8", .400" target trigger on 4" barrel. Serrated backstrap and forestrap. Original "K serial prefix. 1949-DATE

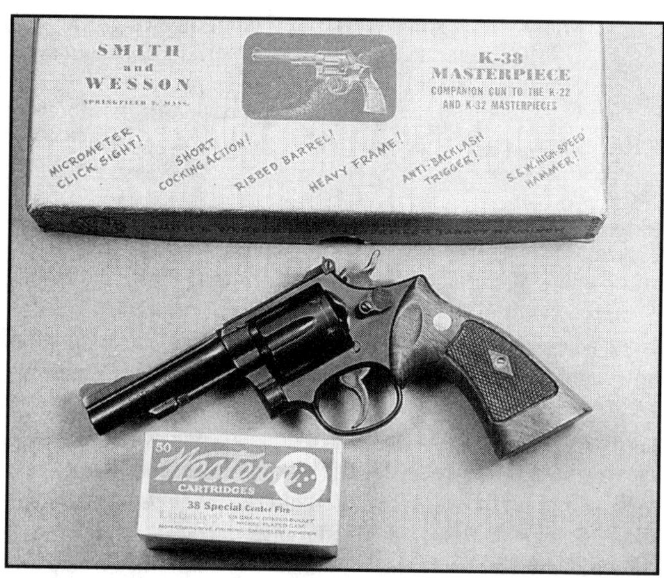

K-38 Combat Masterpiece

NIB	Exc	VG	Good	Fair	Poor
425	300	250	175	135	85

Changes:

1955	Delete upper sideplate screw
1957	*K-38 Combat Masterpiece continued as Model 15*

I frame .38 Background Information

The .38 Regulation Police and the .38/32 Terrier are 5-shot revolvers chambered for the shorter, older, and less powerful .38 S&W round. (.38/32 designation refers to a .38 caliber chambering on a frame designed for .32 caliber.) The I frame was too small for the .38 Special round and was eventually discontinued and replaced by the J frame, which would accommodate both 5-shot .38 Special and 6-shot .32 configurations.

.38 REGULATION POLICE (Prewar):

Cal-.38 S&W, 5-shot fluted cylinder, built on the .32 hand ejector frame w/larger cylinder cut for the increased diameter, 1-1/4" long cylinder, 4" round pinned barrel, checkered walnut grips with S&W monograms on a square butt frame, this frame is cut to accept the stocks in a shoulder recess, blue finish, round blade front sight with a notch cut rear sight. The serial number is found on the front tang or forestrap. "Regulation Police" with ".38 S&W ctg" marked on the barrel's right side, 5-screw frame.

Serial number range 1-54474 54,474 mfd. 1917-1940

ID Key: 5-shot .38 S&W square butt

NIB	Exc	VG	Good	Fair	Poor
375	300	225	160	125	80

Variations:

- Target model worth 50% premium.
- **.38 Regulation Police Post Office Version:** Cal-.38 S&W, 500 made with a 2" barrel and a small steel plate fastened to the grip butt to add weight, blue finish, marked: "R.M.S. P.O. DEPT" on the backstrap. Serial range 47440-48127 in the .38 Regulation Police series, 500 mfd., 1938. Double or triple above value.

.38 REGULATION POLICE (Postwar):

Cal-.38 S&W, similar to prewar production with postwar design hammer block, and a flat latch, 4" barrel, 1/10" round blade front sight with a square notch rear, blue or nickel finish, checkered walnut stocks with S&W monograms on a square butt frame, postwar versions are found with the I frame and improved I frame with a coil mainspring rather than the leaf spring. Later built on the slightly longer J frame. "Regulation Police" markings are now deleted as existing stock was used. Became the Model 33.

Serial number range 54475-122678 1949-1969

NIB	Exc	VG	Good	Fair	Poor
350	285	200	150	125	80

Changes:

1949	Begin postwar production
1955	Sideplate screw eliminated
1957	*.38 Regulation Police continued as Model 33*

.38/32 TERRIER:

Cal-.38 S&W, 5-shot fluted cylinder, 2" pinned barrel, blue or nickel finish, round butt frame with stocks of walnut with S&W monograms, 1/10" round blade front sight, square notch cut rear, the .38/32 indicates this is built on the .32 hand ejector frame in .38 caliber, 2" version of the .38 Regulation Police on a round butt frame. Became the Model 32.

Prewar serial number range 38976-54474 in the .38 Regulation Police series 1936-1940

ID Key: 5-shot .38 S&W round butt 2"

NIB	Exc	VG	Good	Fair	Poor
350	275	200	150	125	80

Changes:

1955	Sideplate screw eliminated
1957	*.38/32 Terrier continued as Model 32*

N Frame .38 Background Information

When S&W began development of a more powerful round than the standard .38 Special (a process that eventually culminated in the development of the .357 Magnum), they wanted a stouter platform than the standard K frame. The obvious choice was the big N frame, originally developed for .44 caliber rounds. The .38/44 (.38 caliber on a .44 frame) Heavy Duty and Outdoorsman series was the result. The .38/44 round was basically a hot-loaded .38

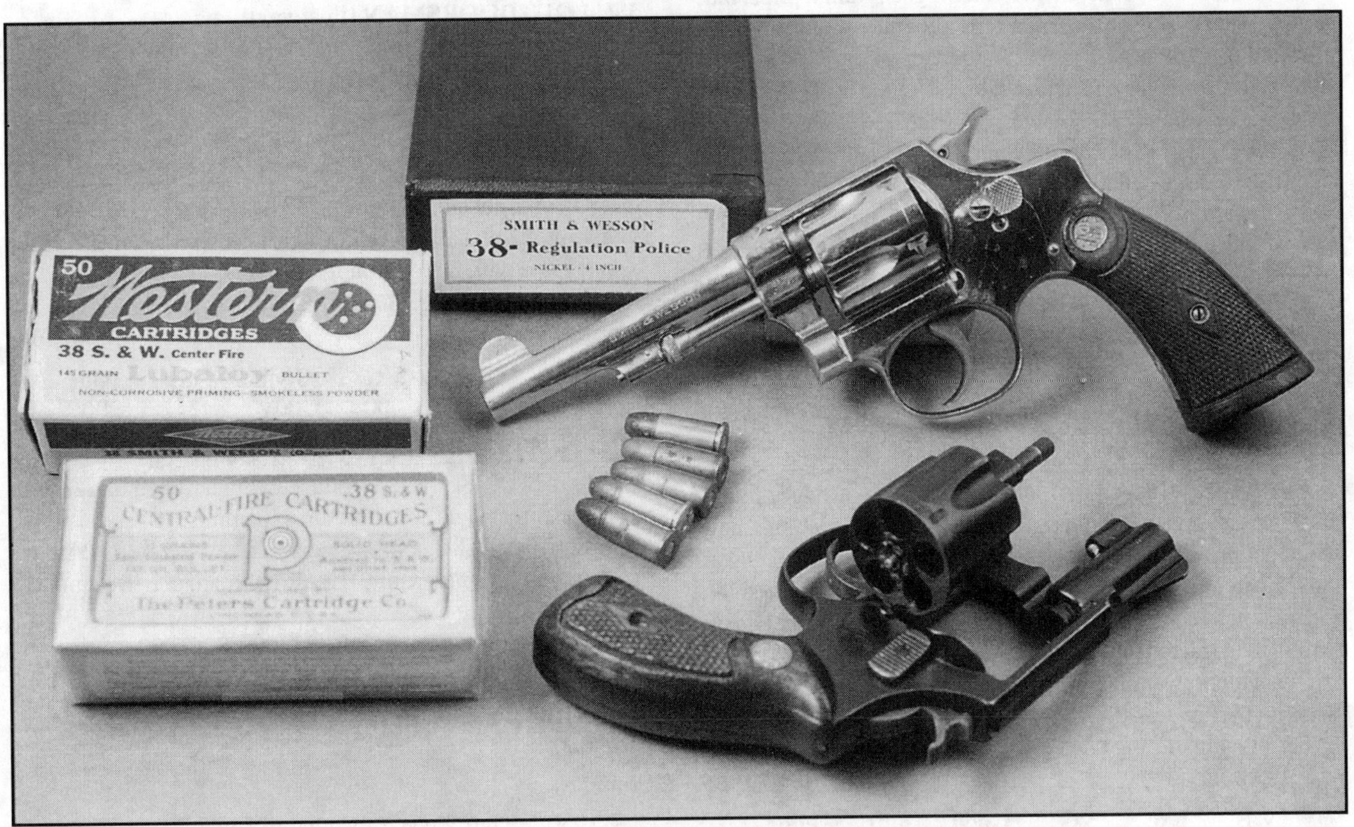

I frame .38/32s in .38 S&W: Regulation Police (top) and Terrier (bottom)

N-frame .38-44 Heavy Duty (top and middle) and .38-44 Outdoorsman (bottom)

Special, and was also called the .38 Super Police. This round should not be confused with the older .38/44 target round developed for the New Model #3 Target Model (see comments under that model listing in the top-break section). "Heavy Duty" is fixed sight, "Outdoorsman" is adjustable sight version.

.38/44 HEAVY DUTY (Prewar) (.38 Super Police):

Cal-.38 S&W Special, 6-shot, fixed sights, walnut grips, blue or nickel finish, built on the larger N frame with 4-screw sideplate, 5" round pinned barrel, with some production of 3-1/2", 4", 6", and 8-3/4" barrels, shrouded extractor rod, round blade front sight with square notch rear, smooth backstrap, ".38 S&W Special CTG" on right side of barrel, "Smith & Wesson" on left barrel side, 1-9/16" long cylinder. This model has a small spring loaded ball bearing on the crane, visible by disassembly only, twelve chambered in .45 Colt. Built for a special high-powered .38 special round, predecessor of the .357 Magnum. Weight 41 oz.

Serial number range 35037-62023 in the .44 Hand Ejector series 11,111 mfd. 1930-1941

NIB	Exc	VG	Good	Fair	Poor
800	650	425	300	250	200

.38/44 HEAVY DUTY (Postwar):

Cal-.38 S&W Special, 4" and 5" barrels, reintroduced with an "S" serial prefix beginning @ S62940, incorporating a new slide action hammer block. A short throw hammer was introduced in 1948 @ S72300. 1/10" round blade front sight, square notch rear, blue or nickel finish, checkered walnut grips, shrouded extractor rod, N frame. Some early postwar guns are known with prewar magnum ribbed barrels and checkered ribs. Became the Model 20.

Serial number range S62940-S256133
9,493 mfd. 1946-1966

NIB	Exc	VG	Good	Fair	Poor
675	500	325	275	200	135

Changes:

1955	Delete upper sideplate screw
1957	*.38/44 Heavy Duty continued as Model 20*

Variations:

- "Austin Police Dept" marked: 130 4" nickel guns shipped 1952 and 1959, with s/n's in the S-88XXX, 89XXX, and 14XXXX ranges

.38/44 HEAVY DUTY - ALLOY FRAME:

Cal-.38/44 S&W Special, a small group (about 10) of aluminum alloy N frame Heavy Duties were made on a special basis about 1955, with a steel cylinder, 4" and 5" barrels, target sights with barrel shroud and barrel rib. "S" serial prefix. It is reported that both target and fixed sight models were made in blue and nickel finish. Also known as "The Light Heavy Duty" this was made for the police market on a test basis. Four are known in private collections. Value would be several thousand dollars.

.38/44 OUTDOORSMAN (Prewar):

Cal-.38 S&W Special or .38/44 S&W Special, target version of the Heavy Duty, 6-1/2" round or 8-3/4" ribbed and pinned barrel, 6-shot, blue or nickel finish, square butt with checkered Magna style walnut stocks, Patridge front sight, N Target frame, adjustable rear sight, shrouded extractor rod.

Serial number range 35037-62483 in the .44 Hand Ejector series 4,761 mfd. 1931-1941

NIB	Exc	VG	Good	Fair	Poor
900	700	500	375	250	200

.38/44 OUTDOORSMAN (Postwar):

Cal-.38 S&W special, reintroduced with a new slide hammer block and an "S" serial prefix beginning @ S 62940. 6-1/2" barrel, 1/8" or 1/10" Patridge front sight, square notch rear sight adjustable for windage and elevation, barrel is ribbed and pinned, marked with "Smith & Wesson" on left side, "38 S&W Special" on right side. Cylinder is 1-9/16" long, .312" grooved trigger, blue finish (nickel rare), shrouded extractor, checkered walnut grips with S&W monograms.

Serial number range S62940-S75000 Approx. postwar production 2,326 mfd. 1946-1949

NIB	Exc	VG	Good	Fair	Poor
700	550	400	300	225	200

.38/44 OUTDOORSMAN MODEL OF 1950:

Cal .38 S&W Special, introduced with a ribbed barrel and a micrometer rear sight and short throw hammer. "S" serial prefix, Patridge front sight, shrouded extractor, 5-screw NT frame, .500" target hammer with .312" smooth trigger. Became the Model 23.

Approx. serial number range S75000-S261999
6,039 mfd. 1950-1966

NIB	Exc	VG	Good	Fair	Poor
600	525	350	250	185	135

Changes:

1950	Introduce ribbed barrel and micrometer rear sight

1955	Delete upper sideplate screw
1957	*.38/44 Outdoorsman continued as Model 23*

J frame .38 Background Information

The J frame was developed as an attempt to package the power of the .38 Special cartridge in a small, "pocket-sized" revolver. The I frame was too small, although it would accommodate 6-shot .32 or 5-shot .38 S&W configurations. Introduced initially with the Chiefs Special, the J frame was eventually standardized as the smallest frame modern production S&W.

J frame S&Ws are often cited as the smallest concealable handgun that chambers an effective defensive round. They have been immensely popular over the decades as police back-up and off-duty guns, as well as civilian concealed carry defensive handguns, and are generally the standard by which all such guns are measured.

The variations that have evolved from the original Chiefs Special have most often been attempts to further enhance the concealability or ease of carry of this gun. The alloy frame "Airweight" variations reduce the weight by several ounces—a very significant improvement in a gun that is carried daily but fired seldom. The shrouded hammer of the Bodyguard configuration keeps the hammer spur from snagging on clothing, yet allows the gun to be carefully cocked for single-action deliberate aimed fire if necessary. The stainless steel variations, beginning with the Model 60, provide rust resistance in a gun that is often carried close to the body and subject to the corrosive effect of perspiration.

The Centennial series deserves some particular commentary. The name comes from its introduction in S&Ws 100th year. Its initial configuration was basically that of a hand ejector version of the old "lemon squeezer" top-break, a "hammerless" (actually a concealed hammer) "double action only" revolver with a grip safety. When the Centennial models were discontinued in the mid 1970s, their passage was loudly lamented by many, and the little guns were eagerly sought after both by collectors and individuals wanting the best in a "pocket" revolver. Demand must generate supply, because the Centennials were reintroduced in the 1990s, without the grip safety device, to critical acclaim. Most recently, the Model 640-1 has been introduced, chambered for the powerful .357 Magnum cartridge, and arguably offering the most power per ounce of gun of any defensive handgun made.

SAFETY NOTE: The term "pocket pistol" does not mean it is safe or advisable to carry a loaded revolver loose in the pocket! A gun carried in such a manner will seldom stay in a convenient accessible position, and more importantly, may be accidentally fired with fatal consequences. There are pocket holsters available that cover the triggerguard and position the revolver properly in the pocket and enhance safety considerably.

See photos in next section on Numbered Models - modern hand ejectors.

CHIEFS SPECIAL:

Cal-.38 S&W Special, 5-shot, 2" barrel with round butt or 3" barrel with square butt, blue or nickel finish, J frame (very early production versions are found with a round blade front sight, 5-screw frame, with a standard thumbpiece on a round butt, smooth backstrap, round triggerguard; transitional variations are found with 3-, 4- and 5-screw frames with ramp front sight), w/flat latch thumbpiece, walnut grips, pinned barrel, 1/10" serrated ramp front sight w/square notch rear sight, .240" service hammer, w/.240" serrated trigger, later changed to .312" smooth combat trigger. Approx. 1,740 mfd. with target sights (see the Model 50). Earliest production had shorter grips and grip frame, no barrel rib, half round front sight blade, more rounded triggerguard, 5-screw. Most of that had changed by 1952 or 1953.

Serial number range 1-786544 numbered in an original series 1951-DATE

NIB	Exc	VG	Good	Fair	Poor
400	300	225	175	150	100

Changes:

1952	Intro square butt @ serial 21,342
1953	Elimination of screw in triggerguard (4-screw)
1955	Delete sideplate screw @ serial 75,000 (3-screw)
1957	*Chiefs Special continued as Model 36*

CHIEFS SPECIAL TARGET:

See Model 50 in next section for details.

CHIEFS SPECIAL AIRWEIGHT:

Cal-.38 S&W Special, 5-shot, originally built with alloy frame and alloy cylinder weighing 10-3/4 ounces, later built w/steel cylinder, JA frame, 2" barrel with round butt and square butt or 3" barrel with square butt only, blue or nickel finish, early versions have a .240" service hammer w/.240" serrated trigger, later versions have a .312" smooth combat trigger, 4-screw alloy frame, pinned barrel, serrated ramp front sight w/square notch rear, original flat latch, checkered walnut grips. 3,777 mfd. with an alloy cylinder below serial 35000. Earliest production may have a small lock screw on the upper sideplate screw. "Airweight" marked.

Original serial number range 1-786544 numbered in the Chiefs Special series 1952-DATE

NIB	Exc	VG	Good	Fair	Poor
400	325	225	185	125	75

Changes:

1954	Alloy cylinder replacement with steel
1954-55	312 mfd. with target sights and 3-1/2" barrel
1955	Eliminate upper sideplate screw
1957	*Continued as the Model 37*

CHIEFS SPECIAL AIRWEIGHT: THE "AIRCREWMAN" (Baby Aircrewman):

Cal-.38 S&W Special, 5-shot w/alloy frame and cylinder, fixed sight, 605 "Aircrewman" versions, serials "A.F.NO. 1795 -A.F.NO.2399," were shipped to the U.S. Air Force in 1953. Marked with "AIRCREWMAN" on the barrel and "PROPERTY OF U.S. AIR FORCE" on the smooth backstrap, "P" proof mark over the triggerguard with air force medallions in the grip circles. Most were destroyed! Few authentic examples exist! Weight 10.5 oz. 1953

THE BODYGUARD AIRWEIGHT:

Cal-.38 S&W Special, 5-shot, alloy frame, steel barrel and cylinder, shrouded hammer, 2" barrel with some production of 3" barrels, JAC frame, blue or nickeled aluminum finish, walnut grips, pinned barrel, 4-screw frame, flat latch thumbpiece, round butt, "Airweight" stamped on barrel, also found in combinations of nickel cylinder with blue frame and barrel, serrated ramp front sight, .240" shrouded service hammer, .312" smooth trigger.

Serial range 66000-786544 in the Chiefs Special series 1955-DATE

NIB	Exc	VG	Good	Fair	Poor
400	300	250	175	125	75

Changes:

1956 Eliminate upper sideplate screw

38 1957 *Continued as the Model 38*

THE CENTENNIAL:

Cal-.38 S&W Special, 5-shot, blue or nickel finish, 2" barrel, grip safety on the backstrap, fully concealed hammer, JS frame, double action only, walnut or smooth wood high horned grips, smooth backstrap, .240" serrated trigger (some early versions w/smooth trigger), pinned barrel, flat latch thumbpiece, 1/10" serrated ramp front sight w/square notch rear, 4-screw frame. This model has a pin stored under the grip to lock the backstrap safety down. Numbered concurrently with the Model 42. Weight 19 oz.

Serial number range 1-30160 1952-1974

NIB	Exc	VG	Good	Fair	Poor
550	475	300	225	185	125

Changes:

1955 Eliminate upper sideplate screw

40 1957 *Continued as Model 40*

THE CENTENNIAL AIRWEIGHT:

Cal-.38 S&W Special, 5-shot, alloy frame, steel cylinder (37 mfd. with alloy cylinder), blue or nickel finish, 2" barrel, grip safety on the backstrap, JSA frame with 4 screws, double action only, pinned barrel, walnut or smooth wood high horned grips, fully concealed hammer, .240" serrated trigger, flat latch thumbpiece. This model has a pin stored under the grip to lock the backstrap safety down, "Airweight" on barrel. Numbered concurrently with Model 40. Very early production may have a small lock screw on the upper sideplate screw.

Centennials, top to bottom: early steel frame, Airweight, and Model 42 Airweight (listed in next section)

Serial range of 1-30160 in an original series 1952-1974

NIB	Exc	VG	Good	Fair	Poor
500	450	300	200	150	100

Variations:

- Nickel: 2X blue value

Changes:

1955 Eliminate upper sideplate screw
42 1957 *Continued as Model 42*

.38 Special and .38 S&W revolvers introduced as named model hand ejectors prior to 1957 and continued as numbered models in the S&W product line after 1957:

.38 M&P - *See Model 10*
.38/200 British Service -1947 - *See Model 11*
M&P Airweight -1952 - *See Model 12*
K-38 Target Masterpiece -1946 - *See Model 14*
K-38 Combat Masterpiece -1949 - *See Model 15*
.38/44 Heavy Duty -1946 - *See Model 20*
.38/44 Outdoorsman -1946 - *See Model 23*
.38/32 Terrier -1946 - *See Model 32*
.38 Regulation Police -1946 - *See Model 33*
.38 Chiefs Special -1950 - *See Model 36*
.38 Chiefs Special Airweight -1952 - *See Model 37*
Bodyguard Airweight -1955 - *See Model 38*
Centennial -1953 - *See Model 40*
Centennial Airweight -1952 - *See Model 42*
Chiefs Special Target -1955 - *See Model 50*

.44 Special Caliber Background Information

Forty-four caliber has always been S&Ws first choice in full-size service revolvers. All of the big .44s seem to have a special appeal for collectors. The .44 Triple Lock in particular has something of a cult following. A number of knowledgeable individuals have called it the finest revolver ever made. It also marked the introduction of the acclaimed .44 Special cartridge, predecessor of the .44 Magnum.

.44 HAND EJECTOR FIRST MODEL (New Century, Triple Lock, .44 Military - Model Of 1908):

Cal- various calibers including: .44 S&W special, .44 S&W Russian, .44-40 Win., .455 Mark II, .38-40 Win., .45 S&W Special. Twenty-one reported mfd. in .45 Colt; 1226 reported mfd. in .450 Eley; 13,753 reported mfd. in .44 S&W Special. Also reported that a small quantity were made in .22 long rifle. A 6-shot fluted cylinder with 4", 5", 6-1/2", or 7-1/2" barrel lengths. The first sideswing cylinder in the .44 Hand Ejector series. This model has a third lock at the crane giving this its unique name, blue or nickel finish on a square butt frame, walnut grips, service or target sights. Five-screw frame with a shrouded extractor rod, round blade front sight on a round barrel, on fixed sight versions, .260" hammer and smooth backstrap.

Serial number range 1-15375 in the .44 Hand Ejector series 15,375 mfd. 1907-1915

NIB	Exc	VG	Good	Fair	Poor
1400	900	700	500	350	250

Variations:

- Calibers other than .44 Special worth 75-100% more. In the 12000 to 13000 s/n range some .45 caliber guns will be found—most originally .455, some converted to .45 Colt, possibly by the factory.
- See also .455 HE 1st Model.
- Target model: Target versions have a Patridge pinned front sight, serrated backstrap and serrated front tang, with a smooth trigger and smooth rear sight blade. Target models worth 75-150% premium.

.44 HAND EJECTOR SECOND MODEL:

Standard cal-.44 S&W Special, some also made in .44-40 Win., .45 Colt, or .38-40 Win. Similar to the .44 First Model New Century except the triple lock feature was eliminated along with the shrouded extractor. Blue or nickel finish, 4" (rare), 6-1/2" (standard), and 5"(scarce) round barrel, square butt walnut stocks, service sights. Target versions are a Patridge blade on a raised pinned boss. 5-screw frame, .260" hammer, 727 mfd. in .45 Long Colt with a 6-1/2" barrel.

Serial number range 1376-about 50000 in the .44 Hand Ejector series 34,624 mfd. 1915-1937

NIB	Exc	VG	Good	Fair	Poor
800	550	400	335	250	200

Variations:

- Calibers other than .44 Special worth 75-100% more. Only 565 made in .44-40, including thirty-two 5" blued in s/n range 30052-30204 and twenty-three 6-1/2" nickel in s/n range 33763-33834.
- Target Models: Patridge front sight on a raised and pinned boss, serrated backstrap and serrated front grip tang, smooth trigger, and smooth rounded rear leaf sight, add 50-75%.

.44 HAND EJECTOR THIRD MODEL (Model 1926 Hand Ejector, Prewar):

Cal-.44 S&W Special, .44-40,.45 Colt, 6-shot fluted cylinder, 4", 5", or 6-1/2" round barrel, blue or nickel finish, checkered walnut square buttstocks, service or target sights, shrouded extractor rod, some found with lanyard ring, 5-screw, not cataloged until 1940.

Serial number range 28358- 61412 in the .44 Hand Ejector series 4,976 mfd. 1926-1940

NIB	Exc	VG	Good	Fair	Poor
1750	1000	650	450	350	200

Variations:

- Calibers other than .44 Special worth 75-100% more.
- Prewar Target model: Micrometer rear sight, estimated less than fifty made prewar. Add 150%.

.44 Hand Ejectors: (1) 1st Model Triple Lock; (2) 2nd Model, standard and target; (3) 3rd Model; (4) 4th Model, Model of 1950

.44 HAND EJECTOR THIRD MODEL POSTWAR (The 1926 Model .44 Military):

Cal-.44 S&W Special, reintroduced with a new slide activated hammer block and an "S" serial prefix. 4", 5", or 6-1/2" round barrel, blue or nickel finish, 1/10" round blade front sight with a square notch cut rear sight, checkered walnut grips with S&W monograms.

Serial range S62489-S75000 1,473 mfd. 1946-1950

NIB	Exc	VG	Good	Fair	Poor
1500	700	375	325	250	200

Variations:

- **1926 Model .44 Target (Postwar):** Cal-.44 S&W Special, 6-1/2" barrel (4" and 5" very rare), blue finish, 1/8" or 1/10" Patridge front sight with square notch rear adjustable for windage and elevation, 6-shot, NT frame, "S" serial prefix, checkered walnut grips with S&W monograms, grooved tangs and trigger, estimated less than 100 produced. Worth double to triple standard value. Serial range S 62489-S75000 in the postwar .44 Hand Ejector series, 1946-1950.

.44 HAND EJECTOR FOURTH MODEL OF 1950 (The Model 1950 .44 Target):

Cal-.44 S&W Special, 6-1/2" barrel standard with top rib (4" scarce, 5" rare), micrometer click rear sight, Patridge front sight, short throw hammer, introduced @ serial S75000. Became the Model 24.

Serial number range S75000-S263000
5,050 mfd. 1950-1966

NIB	Exc	VG	Good	Fair	Poor
800	550	400	335	250	200

Changes:

1955	Delete sideplate screw @ serial S-175000
1957	*Model of 1950 .44 Target continued as Model 24*

.44 HAND EJECTOR FOURTH MODEL OF 1950, MILITARY (The Model 1950 .44 Military):

Cal-.44 S&W Special, 6-shot, fixed rear sight with round blade front sight, 4", 5", 6-1/2" round barrel, blue or nickel finish, shrouded extractor rod, walnut grips, became the Model 21.

Serial number range S75000-S263000
1,200 mfd. 1950-1966

NIB	Exc	VG	Good	Fair	Poor
1200	750	600	450	350	250

Changes:

1955	Delete sideplate screw
1957	*Model 1950 .44 Military continued as Model 21*

.44 Magnum Caliber Background Information

In many ways the .44 Magnum, currently manufactured as the Model 29 and Model 629, is the flagship of the S&W product line.

The concept evolved from experimentation with heavy .44 Special loads in N frame hand ejectors by individuals such as Elmer Keith. As developed by Remington and S&W, the .44 Magnum round was a lengthened .44 Special case loaded to a power level previously unknown in revolvers. A strengthened N frame revolver was designed to handle the new pressure levels.

The combination was an instant hit, and with the help of the Clint Eastwood "Dirty Harry" movies the gun and cartridge acquired a mystique unequaled by any other modern revolver. Although its power level has been surpassed in recent years by single-shot "hand rifles" and huge single action revolvers, it remains ensconced in the collective consciousness as "the most powerful handgun ever made." In practice, many found that extended shooting of full power loads could be punishing to both gun and shooter. In the early days, .44 Magnums were hard to find new, but were often found used in nearly new condition, offered with a box of ammo consisting of forty-four loaded cartridges and six empty cases. The .44 Magnum increased the popularity of handgun hunting, with most authorities finding it adequate for deer-sized game, and some using it for larger game. Many .44 Magnum shooters take advantage of the fact that any .44 Magnum will also chamber the less powerful .44 Special for more pleasant plinking and practice, or for defensive applications where the over-penetration of a magnum load could present dangers to innocent bystanders.

S&W has continually improved the design, and current production guns include recent engineering changes that have significantly enhanced the durability of the gun. Variations range from heavy lugged barrels and unfluted cylinders that add recoil damping weight, to the Mountain Revolver, a lightweight stainless 629 for those who need a powerful handgun in the lightest possible configuration. These recent variations are detailed in the next section, "Numbered Model Revolvers."

THE .44 MAGNUM:

Cal-.44 Magnum, 4", 6-1/2", or 8-3/8" (5" rare) barrel, pinned barrel, blue or nickel finish, Red Ramp front sight, white outline rear blade, black presentation case, shrouded extractor rod, N Target frame, 6-shot, walnut stocks, counterbored cylinder, .500" target hammer, .400" or .500" target trigger. 6,500 mfd. with 4-screw sideplate in a serial range of S130000 to S167500, and are C&R. 1955-DATE

	NIB	Exc	VG	Good	Fair	Poor
5-screw	1600	1100	850	600	350	200
4-screw	750	550	400	350	300	200

U.S. Model of 1917 .45ACP Hand Ejector

Variations:

- Original 5" barrel worth double above values in blue, triple in nickel

Changes:

1955	Begin production @ "S" serial S130000
1956	Delete upper sideplate screw @ serial S-167500
1957	*The .44 Magnum continued as Model 29*

.45 Caliber

.45 HAND EJECTOR U.S. SERVICE, MODEL OF 1917:

Cal-.45 ACP or .45 Auto Rim, 5-1/2" round barrel, heat treated cylinders, blue finish, round blade front sight, rear sight was a notch cut into the topstrap, supplied with half moon clips and a lanyard ring. The cylinder was 6-shot with a square cut shoulder to allow the use of the rimless cartridge without half moon clips if necessary. Approx. 163,000 were made for the U.S. Army between 1917-1919, the frame was stamped "U.S. ARMY MODEL 1917" on the butt. "UNITED STATES PROPERTY" is stamped under the barrel. "S&W D.A. 45" stamped on the barrel's right side. U.S. ARMY serial range is approx. 1-169000. Bluing on military guns is a lighter shade than standard commercial bluing. Usually a U.S. ordnance "flaming bomb" mark is found on the side of the frame in front of the hammer. Plain walnut stocks on U.S. issue models, checkered walnut with S&W monogram on commercial models. Magna type stocks were supplied after 1938. At serial 185000 a new hammer block was added to this model. Serial number on the butt, cylinder face, barrel, yoke, and back of the extractor star. The S&W trademark was not stamped on military frames.

Serial number range 1-209791 1917-1946

NIB	Exc	VG	Good	Fair	Poor
700	475	325	300	250	175

Variations:

- Target model variation: 5,050 produced. Worth premium.
- Commercial variation: 1,200 produced. Worth double standard values in higher condition grades. A few shipped with nickel finish worth additional premium.
- Brazilian Contract: 25,000 were made for the Brazilian government and stamped with the Brazilian crest on the sideplate. A 1938 shipment included most guns in s/n range 181983-207043, and a 1946 shipment included most guns in s/n range 207196-207989. A large quantity was imported in 1990 and will bear an importer's mark.

NIB	Exc	VG	Good	Fair	Poor
----	300	285	250	185	135

THE 1917 ARMY (Postwar):

Cal-.45 ACP or .45 Auto Rim, 5-1/2" barrel, 1/10" round blade front sight with a square notch rear, N frame, non-shrouded extractor, with half moon clips, checkered walnut grips with S&W monograms, blue finish, a commercial version of the 1917 Army. 10,000 frames stamped in the 1930s were located, assembled, and sold as late as 1949-50 as the Model 1917 Army. 991 commercial versions were made in a serial number range of S209792-S210782 with an "S" serial prefix to indicate a new postwar hammer block, and continuing the 1917 serial number range. The commercial versions had the S&W trademark on the sideplate. 1946-1950

NIB	Exc	VG	Good	Fair	Poor
1200	650	400	325	250	175

Variations:

- Target model worth double to triple standard value

.45 HAND EJECTOR MODEL OF 1950, MILITARY (1950 Army):

Cal-.45 ACP, similar to the 1917 Model with a new short throw hammer and a new slide action hammer block, 5-1/2" round barrel lanyard ring was now discontinued, Magna style walnut grips, round blade front sight with square notch rear, N frame, 203 were chambered in .45 Colt at serial S103000. This model can be marked "45 CAL MODEL 1950" or "S&W D.A. 45." Became the Model 22.

Serial number range S8500-S236000 in the N frame series 3,976 mfd. 1951-1966

NIB	Exc	VG	Good	Fair	Poor
1500	900	650	500	350	200

Changes:

1952	203 Chambered in .45 Colt
1955	Delete
1957	*Model 1950 .45 Army continued as Model 22*

THE 1950 .45 TARGET MODEL:

Cal-.45 ACP, .44 Special, or .45 Colt, 6-shot, blue finish, Patridge front sight, micrometer rear sight, Magna type walnut grips, .500" target hammer, .500" target trigger, shrouded extractor rod, 6-1/2" barrel with top rib and pinned, 5-screw frame. Barrel marked ".45 CAL MODEL 1950." NT frame, 200 chambered in .45 Colt in 1953. Diamond walnut stocks, or smooth rosewood target stocks, "S" serial prefix. .45 ACP caliber became the Model 26, while the .44 Special caliber became the Model 24. Earliest production may lack caliber marking on side of barrel.

Serial number range S76212-S211000
2,768 mfd. 1950-1961

NIB	Exc	VG	Good	Fair	Poor
750	675	550	450	300	200

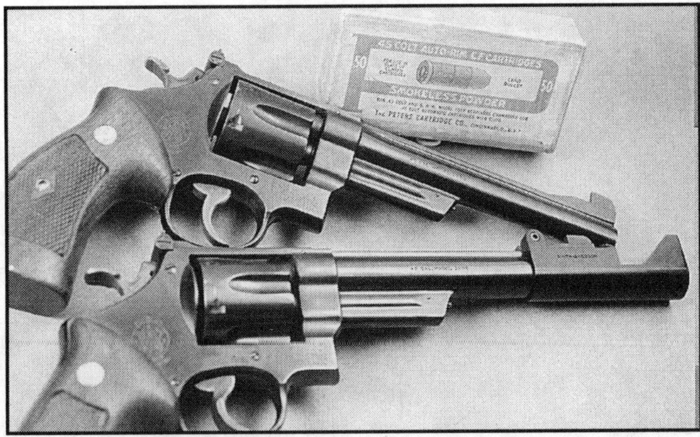

.45 Target Models, top to bottom: Model 1950, Model 1955 w/S&W detachable muzzle brake

Variations:

- .45 Long Colt worth 2X to 4X standard .45 ACP values

Changes:

1953	200 chambered for .45 Long Colt
1955	Delete sideplate screw
1957	*1950 Model .45 Target Light Barrel continued as Model 26*

THE 1955 .45 TARGET MODEL:

Cal-.45 ACP, 6-1/2" heavy barrel version of the 1950 Target Model, with .500" target hammer and .500" target trigger, target stocks, shrouded barrel marked "45 CAL. MODEL 1955," supplied with half moon clips, on a 5-screw N Target frame with a Patridge front sight, "S" serial prefix, designated the Model 25 in 1957. About twenty were mfd. in .45 Colt caliber in early production.

Approx. serial number range S150000-S333454, continued with the "N" serial prefix in 1969 1955-1992

NIB	Exc	VG	Good	Fair	Poor
500	350	300	260	200	175

Changes:

1955	Introduction @ S150000
1956	Delete sideplate screw
1957	*1955 Model Target Heavy Barrel continued as Model 25*

.455 Mark II Caliber

.455 MARK II HAND EJECTOR FIRST MODEL:

Cal-.455 Mark II cartridge, 6-1/2" round barrel, blue finish, square butt checkered walnut stocks, round blade front sight, rear sight is a notched cut in the rear of the topstrap, shrouded extractor rod, 5-screw N frame, 6-shot fluted cylinder, with a lanyard ring, was designed identical to the .44 Hand Ejector First Model (Triple Lock) with a .45 cal barrel, no caliber stamping on the barrel, only the company name and patent dates. Many were converted to the .45 Colt cartridge as war surplus, these conversions usually are identified by frames having British proof markings and caliber overstampings. The first 100 units went to Wilkinson Sword as commercial guns. Remainder of production was military.

Serial number range 1-5000 5,000 mfd. 1914-1915

NIB	Exc	VG	Good	Fair	Poor
900	700	575	400	300	200

Variations:

- Commercial model worth premium

.455 MARK II HAND EJECTOR SECOND MODEL:

Cal-.455 Mark II, 6-1/2" round barrel, 6-shot fluted cylinder, similar to the first model without the extractor shroud, inside frame dimensions were slightly increased, caliber marking of "Smith & Wesson .455," extractor rod changed, round blade front sight w/notch cut rear sight, butt swivel. As with the first model many were converted to .45 Colt. Approx. 691 first model

.455 MK II Hand Ejectors, top to bottom: 1st Model Triple Lock, 2nd Model

frames were assembled and stamped in the second model serial range. From both Models 59,150 were mfd. for English service and 14,500 for the Canadian service. A few commercial guns were made, with 13 known in the late 13000-early 16000 s/n range.

Serial number range 5001-74755 69,754 mfd. 1915-1917

NIB	Exc	VG	Good	Fair	Poor
600	450	300	260	225	175

NUMBERED MODEL REVOLVERS (Modern Hand Ejectors, 1957-Present)

Contents

Stainless Steel and Alloy J Frame .32 Magnums:

Model 631: .32 Magnum Target Stainless
Model 632: .32 Magnum Centennial Airweight Stainless

Stainless Steel and Alloy J Frames, Continued:

Model 637: .38 Chiefs Special Airweight Stainless
Model 638: .38 Bodyguard Airweight Stainless
Model 640: .38 Centennial Stainless; Specials
Model 640-1: .357 Magnum Centennial Stainless
Model 642: .38 Centennial Airweight Stainless

Stainless Steel K Frames:

Model 648: .22 Magnum Rimfire Stainless

Stainless Steel J Frames, Continued:

Model 649: .38 Bodyguard Stainless
Model 650: .22 M.R.F. Service Kit Gun
Model 651: .22 M.R.F. Target Kit Gun

Stainless Steel N Frames, Continued:

Model 657: The .41 Magnum Stainless

Stainless Steel L Frames:

Model 681: The .357 Distinguished Service Magnum Stainless
Model 686: The .357 Distinguished Combat Magnum Stainless; Specials

J Frames Stainless:

Model 940: 9mm Centennial Stainless; Special

Revolver frame sizes and designations used in this guide:

M frame	early LadySmiths
I frame	predecessor of the J frame with a leaf mainspring and strain screw
J frame	steel frame with fixed sights
JAC frame	shrouded hammer w/alloy frame
JC frame	shrouded hammer w/steel frame
JA frame	alloy frame with fixed sights
JAT frame	alloy frame with target sights
JS frame	fully concealed hammer
JT frame	steel frame with target sights
K frame	steel frame with fixed sights
KA frame	alloy frame with fixed sights
KAT frame	alloy frame with target sights
KT frame	steel frame with target sights
KTC	target centerfire .22 Magnum
KTM	target rimfire magnum
L frame	larger and heavier than a K frame, with a full underlug barrel on a steel frame with fixed sights
LT frame	steel frame full lug with target sights
N frame	largest of the current frames, steel frame with fixed sights
NT frame	steel frame with target sights

Modern revolver feature codes used in this guide:

(For auto features see the section on autoloaders)

AA	aluminum alloy
AF	adjustable front sight
AM	ambidextrous safety
AS	adjustable sights
B	blue finish
CG	combat grips
CH	concealed hammer
CS	combat stocks
CT	combat trigger
DA	double action only
DT	drilled and tapped
FL	full underlug barrel
FS	fixed sights
GS	glass beaded
HB	heavy barrel
HP	high profile front sight
IFS	interchangeable front sights
LP	low profile front sight
LS	LadySmith
N	nickel finish
PBP	pinned black Patridge
PP	power port
RB	round butt
RR	red ramp front sight insert
S	stainless finish
SA	single action
SB	square butt
SG	synthetic grips
SH	shrouded hammer
SKU	stock keeping unit, i.e. product code
SM	scope mount
SS	stainless steel
ST	semi-target trigger
TG	target grips
TH	target hammer
TS	target stocks
TT	target trigger
WG	wood grips
WO	white outline on the rear sight blade
WTS	walnut target stocks
w/	with
~	approximately

Numbered Model Revolver Background Information

Beginning in 1957, Smith and Wesson stamped a model number inside the yoke cut of all revolvers. Many retained their descriptive names as well as a model number assignment. The serial number may be found on the butt end of the revolver and the yoke cut for K frames, N frames, and L frames. J frames have the serial number only on the butt. Engineering changes are designated by a model number with a - (dash) and a number stamped in the yoke cut (for example: Mod 53-2). In most cases, there were no design changes associated with the new model numbers in 1957. For example, the last "pre-model 29" .44 Magnum would be no different from the first .44 Magnum marked Model 29.

Please refer to the previous section for background information on numbered model hand ejectors that were introduced as named models prior to 1957.

Some of the more significant developments in the hand ejector line since 1957 include the following:

1964: .41 Magnum introduced, background information at Model 57 listing

1965: Stainless steel guns, background information at Model 60 listing

1981: L frame developed, background information at Model 581 listing

1982: Pinned barrel and recessed cylinder discontinued

1990: Centennial reintroduced, background information at Centennial listing in previous section

Around 1988, S&W introduced some engineering changes called the endurance package that were especially significant for the .44 Magnum models.

Beginning in late 1993 and currently now in production, S&W made a few obvious changes to the frames of the target handguns (K, L, and N frames). The most easily spotted change is the rounding of the rear sight leaf toward the muzzle. Under this new leaf are now a pair of drilled and tapped holes for scope mounting. S&W has introduced CNC machining to their manufacturing process and now the sideplate lines are as tight fitting as ever.

The second most noticeable change is the shape of the star extractor. The extractor rod is now made without the groove and instead has a flat side to guide it. Other changes are not so readily noticeable and are mostly internal. Also, S&W is now in the process of eliminating the square butt configuration from revolver productions.

For the past several years, there have been excellent buys available in .38 and .357 caliber hand ejectors as some police agencies switched to semiautos and traded in their service revolvers. Many of these may show extensive holster wear, but remain in excellent to very good mechanical condition. In addition to their value as shooters, a fascinating collection could be assembled of various department marked or issued guns. A few of these variations have been mentioned throughout this book as they came to the authors' attention, but these represent only the tip of the iceberg.

Note that due to durability of finish, most stainless steel guns will be found in excellent to very good condition. In fact, most guns produced in the last twenty years or so will usually be found in good or better condition.

Model 10, top to bottom: three-inch for Michigan Police, later adopted by F.B.I.; Royal Hong Kong Police

COLLECTOR'S TIPS: Readers should note that in NIB or excellent condition, 5-screw guns will nearly always bring a premium, 4-screw guns will bring a lesser premium, and pinned and recessed guns will bring a small premium over current production counterparts. Collectors of more recent guns tend to only pay premiums for rare variations on higher condition guns.

NOTE: Many of these numbered model revolvers were introduced prior to 1957 as named models. When researching an early numbered model revolver, be sure to check the information under its model name in the previous section on early hand ejectors.
S&W product codes are listed for models in production beginning in 1984.

Serial Numbers: Early handgun serial numbers may be found in the following locations: on the butt, on the face of the cylinder, behind the star extractor, on the crane face, on the barrel flat, inside the extractor shroud (on shrouded barrels), and usually on the inside of the right grip, either stamped or usually written in chalk or pencil. More modern handguns have the serial number only stamped on the butt and the yoke cut or laser etched under the topstrap.

MODEL 10: THE .38 MILITARY & POLICE (Postwar):

Cal-.38 Special, a continuation of the .38 Military & Police Victory Model, this popular model is now fitted with a new hammer block and continued with an "S" serial prefix. K frame, fixed sight, 2", 4", 5", or 6" pinned barrel on a round or square butt, blue or nickel finish, 6-shot w/fluted cylinder, checkered walnut grips, 5-screw frame, 1/10" serrated ramp front sight, square notch rear sight, smooth backstrap. Early postwar versions are found with a round blade front sight, .312" smooth combat trigger, .265" service hammer, continued from the

Royal Hong Kong Police marking on Model 10

postwar .38 M&P series and now numbered concurrently with the Model 11, 12, 45, and Aircrewman. Retail $383-$390.

1945-DATE

NIB	Exc	VG	Good	Fair	Poor
325	250	185	160	125	75

Specials and variations:

Numerous examples and variations of this popular sidearm are found. The following is a partial list.

- Premium for 5-screw (40%), 4-screw (20%).
- Slight premium for nickel.
- **Post Office Dept.:** 150 in 1958, 4" SB, blue, TS, stamped "PO DEPT," in s/n range C428783-478929. See also Model 45.
- **Robbins Air Force Base:** 922 in 1960, 2" RB, s/n range early C510000s-530000s.
- **Rhode Island State Police:** 29 guns in 1964, 6" blue SB, s/n range C707629-712998.
- 1967: Special run of 3" w/pencil barrel, square butt, sold by H.H. Harris, Chicago.
- **FBI Issue:** 2-1/2" heavy barrel versions were sold to the FBI in 10-6 and 10-8 heavy barrel models.
- **Hong Kong Police:** This version stamped "RHKP" with number on the backstrap w/lanyard ring, 4", blue with std. barrel. Around 1983.
- **.357 NYSP:** Several thousand chambered in .357 MAG for NYSP w/4" heavy barrel. Predecessor to the Model 13 with a counterbored cylinder and pinned barrel. Marked 10-6. 1972.
- **Peru Police:** 10-7, Peru Police Crest stamped on the sideplate, 2" barrel, round butt, blue finish, smooth trigger. Marked "Policia de investigaciones del Peru." Product Code: 100101, AEV 9xxx. 1984.
- **Ohio Highway Patrol Commemorative:** 4" barrel with wood presentation case, blue, 2025 mfd., 1973.
- **Military Purchase:** Over a period of 12 years, over 133,000 Model 10s have been purchased by the U.S. Military. Most commonly found with "U.S." on the backstrap.
- **"Saudi-Crest Marked":** 4" pencil barrel, Mod. 10-5 square butt blue finish, "D" serial prefix.
- **Brazilian Contract:** Model 10-10 with full lug 3" barrel and full-length extractor rod, round butt, special production 1995. Product Code: 100135.

Chronology of Changes - Model 10:

Mod.	Year	Change
	1945	Begin "S" serial prefix @ S811120 to S999999
	1948	Begin "C" serial prefix @ C1 to C999999
	1952	Change front sight from round blade to ramp
	1955	Delete upper sideplate screw
	1957	*Continued as Model # 10*
10	1957	Stamping of model number
10-1	1959	Introduction of 4" heavy barrel
10-2	1961	Extractor rod change: right to left hand thread
10-3	1961	Extractor rod change on heavy barrel and front sight changed from 1/10" to 1/8" on heavy barrel
10-4	1962	Triggerguard screw eliminated on std. barrel
10-5	1962	Sight changed from 1/10" to 1/8" on std. barrel
10-6	1962	Triggerguard screw eliminated on heavy barrel
	1967	Begin "D" serial prefix @ D1
10-7	1977	Gas ring change from yoke to cylinder on std. barrel
10-8	1977	Gas ring change on heavy barrel model
	1981	Logo moved from sideplate to right side of frame
	1982	Eliminate pinned barrel, start three-letter serial prefix
10-9	1988	New yoke retention system/radius stud pkg - std. barrel
10-10	1988	New yoke retention system/radius stud - heavy barrel
	1992	Blue finish only
	1993-94	Synthetic grips / change extractor

Product Codes:

code	config	year	comment
100101 2"	B RB	84	Special for Peru police
100102 2"	B RB	84-96	28 oz.
100104 2"	B SB	84-86	
100108 4"	B SB	84-94	30.5 oz.
100114 2"	N RB	84-86	
100115 2"	N SB	84-87	
100117 4"	N SB	84-86	
100121 3"	HB B RB	84-87	30.5 oz.
100123 4"	HB B RB	84-91	33.5 oz.
100125 4"	HB B SB	84-96	
100127 3"	HB N RB	84-87	
100129 4"	HB N SB	84-91	
100135 3"	FL B	94	Special Brazilian contract

MODEL 11: .38/200 MILITARY & POLICE:

Cal-.38 S&W, 200 grain round nose bullet, manufactured mainly for the British Commonwealth countries. K frame, 4", 5", or 6" barrel lengths, 6-shot, fixed sights, 5-screw frame, round blade front sight, early versions were bright blue, later versions a sandblast parkerized finish, smooth wood grips, lanyard ring, pinned barrel. 568,204 mfd. from 1938-1945, and again from 1947 to 1965 in various quantities, with and without British markings. 1938-1945 serial range 700000-1000000 and V1-V800000, then SV800001-SV850000. This model was mfd. and numbered concurrently with the U.S. Victory Model. Postwar serial numbered with the Model 10, 12, 45, and Aircrewman. Not cataloged.

1938-1965

Model 12, two-inch square butt, nickel

NIB	Exc	VG	Good	Fair	Poor
300	225	175	140	100	65

Changes:

	1947	Begin "S" serial prefix
	1948	Begin "C" serial prefix
	1955	Delete upper sideplate screw
11	1957	Stamping of model number
11-1	1961	Change extractor rod thread
11-2	1962	Change front sight blade
11-3	1962	Eliminate triggerguard screw
11-4		Change gas ring (Note: this model not verified)

MODEL 12: THE .38 MILITARY & POLICE AIRWEIGHT:

Cal-.38 Special, similar to Model 10 but has an alloy frame and originally an alloy cylinder, later changed to steel. KA frame, 6-shot, blue or nickel finish, serrated ramp front sight w/square notch rear, 2", 4", 5", or 6" pinned barrel, round or square butt, checkered walnut grips, 5-screw frame, flat latch thumbpiece, .240" hammer and trigger, numbered with the Model 10, 11, 45, and Aircrewman. This alloy frame is slightly thinner than a standard K frame by .080", smooth backstrap. A .265" serrated hammer and .312" smooth combat trigger were added in 1984 with the frame thickness change. An all alloy frame and cylinder in 2" weighs 14.5 oz. Not to be confused with the Aircrewman. 1952-1986

NIB	Exc	VG	Good	Fair	Poor
350	275	220	175	125	75

Variations:

- Slight premium for nickel.
- 1966: Special production w/safety latch: Mounted into the sideplate for the French police. Estimated 12-18 in the U.S. 3" barrel w/round butt, blue finish. The safety device locks the hammer and trigger when pushed forward.

Changes:

	1952	Introduction @ C223999
	1954	Alloy cylinder changed to steel due to cracking
	1955	Delete sideplate screw
	1957	*Continued as Model 12*
12	1957	Stamping of model number
	1959	Introduce 4", 5", and 6" barrel
	1960	Delete 5" and 6" barrel lengths
12-1	1962	Eliminate triggerguard screw; extractor rod changed from right to left hand thread
12-2	1962	Front site changed from 1/10" to 1/8" blade
	1966	Thumbpiece changed
	1967	Begin "D" serial prefix
12-3	1977	Change gas ring from yoke to cylinder
12-4	1984	Change to standard K frame thickness

Product Codes:

100202	2"	B RB	84-85	18.5 oz.
100204	2"	B SB	84-85	
100206	4"	B RB	84-85	19.5 oz.
100208	4"	N RB	84-85	
100210	2"	N RB	84-85	
100211	2"	N SB	84-85	
100212	2"	B RB	86 only	
100215	4"	B SB	86 only	

Look closely at this Model 12. Is the cylinder latch on the wrong side? Not really! This is a manual safety installed for special French order.

MODEL 13: THE .357 MAGNUM MILITARY & POLICE HEAVY BARREL:

Cal-.357 Magnum, heavy barrel with non-shrouded extractor rod, fixed sight, 3" pinned barrel with round butt or 4" pinned

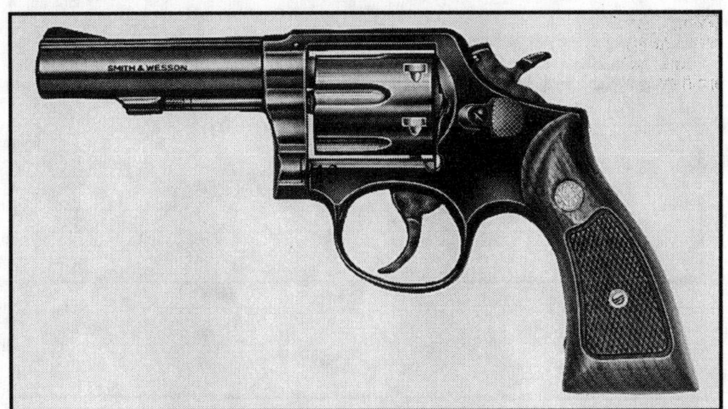

Model 13

heavy barrel with square butt, blue finish, service walnut grips, K frame, 6-shot, serrated ramp front sight w/square notch rear sight, counterbored and fluted cylinder, .312" smooth combat trigger, .265" service hammer, original "D" serial prefix. Popular F.B.I. issue sidearm in 1974 and 1986-87. Successor to Model 10-6 in .357. Retail $394. 1974-DATE

Note: Not to be confused with the M-13 Aircrewman, listed in previous section.

NIB	Exc	VG	Good	Fair	Poor
350	260	220	185	150	100

Variations:

- Premium for nickel or for N.Y.S.P. marked gun (1200 made).
- Model PC-13 .357: Cal-.357 Magnum, production of 400 units from the Performance Center for Lew Horton. "A very serious carry revolver." Four Magna ports on a 3" barrel, fixed sight rear sight w/ramp front sight, Secret Service boot grips on a K frame, 6-shot, bobbed hammer, double action only, matte blue finish with beveled cylinder latch, trigger, and charge holes. Shrouded extractor rod, trigger has overtravel stop. 1995.

Changes:

13-1	1974	Introduced this year for N.Y.S.P.
13-2	1977	Change gas ring from yoke to cylinder
13-3	1982	Eliminate cylinder counterbore and pinned barrel
13-4	1988	New yoke retention system/radius stud package
	1994	Synthetic grips; change extractor

Product Codes:

100304 3"	HB B RB	84-96	31 oz.
100306 4"	HB B SB	84-96	34 oz.
100308 3"	HB N RB	84-86	
100310 4"	HB N SB	84-86	

MODEL 14: THE K-38 TARGET MASTERPIECE (Postwar):

Cal-.38 Special, target model, 6-shot, 6" or 8-3/8" pinned and ribbed barrel, blue finish (nickel rare), adjustable rear sight, K Target frame, double action, 5-screw frame, 1/8" Patridge front sight, checkered walnut grips, with .500" serrated trigger, .500" target hammer, serrated backstrap and forestrap. Matched in weight with K-22 Masterpiece and K-32 Masterpiece and offered as a matching companion gun. 1947-1982

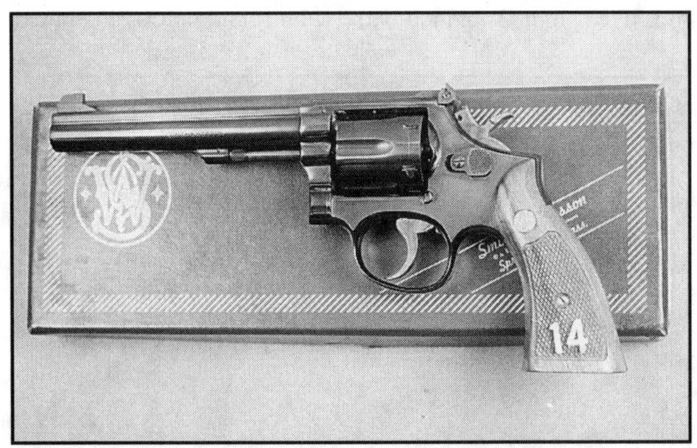

Model 14

NIB	Exc	VG	Good	Fair	Poor
385	285	225	185	150	85

Variations:

- 20% premium for 5-screw model

Changes:

	1947	Begin production @ serial K-1661
	1949	mfd. heavy barrel to match K-17 and K-32 in weight
	1955	Delete sideplate screw
14	1957	*Continued as Model 14*
	1957	Stamping of model number
14-1	1959	Right hand to left hand thread extractor rod
	1959	Introduce 8-3/8" barrel
14-2	1961	Cylinder stop changed, delete triggerguard screw
	1965	Production of 184 with a 4" barrel, serial number range of K623343-K624495
14-3	1967	Relocation of rear sight leaf screw
	1968	Begin "D" serial prefix
14-4	1977	Change gas ring from yoke to cylinder

MODEL 14: THE K-38 MASTERPIECE SINGLE ACTION:

Cal-.38 Special, as above with single action only. Internal deletion of parts allow single action only, pulling the trigger only rotates the cylinder, but does not lift the hammer. 1961-1982

NIB	Exc	VG	Good	Fair	Poor
425	325	250	185	135	85

MODEL 14: THE K-38 HEAVY BARREL FULL LUG:

Cal-.38 Special, 6" full lug barrel, K Target frame, 6-shot, square butt, .500" target hammer, wood combat grips, blue finish, ribbed barrel, adjustable rear sight, .312" smooth combat target trigger, pinned Patridge front sight on ramp base. Serrated backstrap and forestrap. Retail $465. 1991-DATE

NIB	Exc	VG	Good	Fair	Poor
375	275	210	175	135	85

Variations:

- Special 1995: Production of 4" barrel for Perry & Assoc. for pistol teams. Accurized from the Performance Center. Limited production.
- "Last Stand": See Twelve Revolvers under "Commemoratives and Specials."

Changes:

14-5	1991	Full lug barrel initial run of 2,000 @ introduction
	1992	Became std. production
14-6	1994	Synthetic grips, drill and tap, change extractor, change rear sight

Product Code:

100338 6"	B FL SB AS 91-96	47 oz.

Model 15

MODEL 15: THE K-38 COMBAT MASTERPIECE:

Cal-.38 Special, adjustable rear sights, 6-shot, K Target frame, originally made with a 4" barrel then 2", 6", or 8-3/8", (5" rare) pinned and narrow ribbed barrel, blue or nickel finish, .375" or .500" target hammer, 1/8" Baughman Quick Draw on plain ramp base front sight, 5-screw frame, square butt with walnut grips, .312" smooth combat trigger on 2" and 4", .265" serrated service trigger on 6" and 8 3/8", .400" target trigger on 4" barrel. Serrated backstrap and forestrap. Original "K" serial prefix. 1949-DATE

NIB	Exc	VG	Good	Fair	Poor
375	275	200	165	135	85

Variations:

- **U.S.A.F.** Issue: In 1966, approx. 2000 Model 15s with 4" barrel were shipped to Warner Robbins A.F.B. w/"U.S.A.F." on left of frame, other markings unknown. Model 15-2. Worth 4X standard model in higher condition grades, double in lower grades.
- 1989 4" heavy barrel: With red ramp, mfd. for D.C. police.

Changes:

	1955	Delete upper sideplate screw
	1957	*K-38 Combat Masterpiece continued as Model 15*
15	1957	Stamping of model number
15-1	1959	Right hand to left hand thread extractor rod
15-2	1961	Delete triggerguard screw, change cylinder stop
	1964	Introduce 2" heavy barrel
15-3	1967	Relocation of rear sight leaf screw
15-4	1977	Change gas ring from yoke to cylinder
	1982	Pinned barrel eliminated
15-5		Various internal changes
	1986	Introduction of 6" and 8-3/8" barrel
15-6	1988	New yoke retention system/radius stud package
	1988	Discontinue 8-3/8" and 2" barrel
	1992	Discontinue 6" barrel, blue finish only
15-7	1994	Synthetic grips, drill and tap, change rear sight, change extractor

Product Codes:

100402 2"	B SB	84-87	30 oz.
100404 4"	B SB	84-86	32 oz.
100405 4"	B SB TT TH	84-86	
100407 2"	N SB	84-86	
100409 4"	N SB	84-87	
100411 6"	B SB	86-92	35 oz.
100413 8-3/8"	B SB	86-87	39 oz.
100419 4"	B SB CT TH	87-96	

MODEL 16: The K-32 MASTERPIECE (Postwar) (C&R):

Cal-.32 S&W Long, K Target frame, this postwar model now incorporates a new hammer block and a barrel rib, adjustable rear sight, 6-shot w/fluted cylinder, 6" pinned barrel with rib, checkered walnut grips, blue finish, 4" barrel rare, being designated as the .32 Combat Masterpiece, square butt, 5-screw frame, non-shrouded extractor rod, 1/8" or 1/10" plain Patridge front sight, matched in weight with the K-22 and K-38 Masterpiece, serrated backstrap and forestrap. "K" serial prefix. Scarce gun with s/n's hard to track. See listings under K-32 in previous section. Also, some Model 16-2s known in s/n range K827718-827829 and some 16-3s known in s/n range 3K29411-30791. 3630 mfd. 1947-1974

Previously produced as K-32 Masterpiece

NIB	Exc	VG	Good	Fair	Poor
1250	1000	700	450	300	250

Changes:

	1949	Mfd. heavy barrel to Match K-17 and K-38 in weight
	1955	Delete sideplate screw
16	1957	Stamping of model number
16-1	1959	Right hand to left hand thread extractor rod
16-2	1961	Delete triggerguard screw, change cylinder stop
16-3	1967	Relocation of rear sight leaf screw

MODEL 16: THE K-32 REINTRODUCTION - FULL LUG:

Cal-.32 H&R MAG, 4", 6", or 8-3/8" full lug barrel, 6-shot, blue finish, target hammer, target trigger, Goncalo Alves combat wood combat grips, adjustable rear sight, K Target frame, ribbed barrel, Patridge front sight, 4" w/.375" semi-target hammer and .312" smooth combat trigger, 6" and 8-3/8" with .500" target hammer and .400" serrated target trigger, serrated backstrap and forestrap. Three-letter serial prefix. 1989-1992

NIB	Exc	VG	Good	Fair	Poor
425	300	250	175	135	85

Changes:

16-4	1989	Intro full lug barrel
	1992	Discontinue 4" and 8-3/8" barrel

Product Codes:

100558 4"	B CS SB ST CT FL	90	42 oz.
100560 6"	B CS SB TH TT FL	90-92	47 oz.
100562 8-3/8"	B CS SB TH TT FL	90	54 oz.

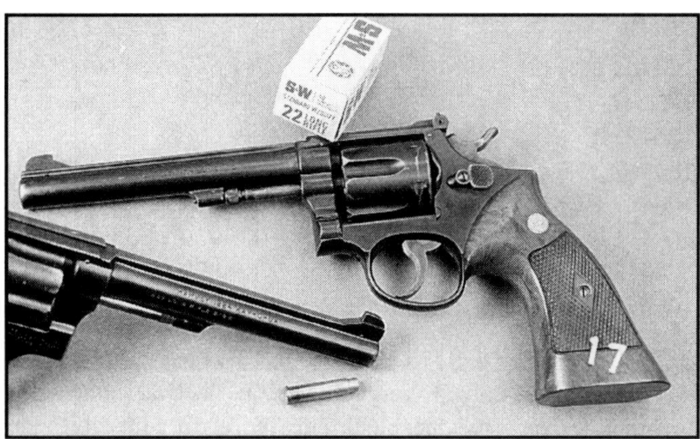

Model 17, .22 LR. Note barrel of bottom gun marked "Harvey .224 Kay-Chuk." These custom .22 high power centerfire conversions of Model 17s paved the way for the Model 53 Jet.

MODEL 17: THE K-22 MASTERPIECE (Postwar):

Cal-.22 Long Rifle, this postwar model now incorporates a new hammer block, 6-shot, blue finish, original mfd. with a 6" barrel (5" rare), walnut grips, adjustable micrometer rear sight, Patridge front sight, K Target frame, square butt, ribbed and pinned barrel, counterbored cylinder, 5-screw, .375" semi-target or .500" target hammer, .312" smooth combat trigger or .400" and .500" serrated trigger. Serrated backstrap and forestrap. Original "K" serial prefix. 1946-1989

NIB	Exc	VG	Good	Fair	Poor
400	300	250	175	135	85

Variations:

- Rare configuration: In 1975, fifteen made in 6" nickel, SB, TH, TT, in s/n range 1K3034-3655
- This model was the basis for conversions to the centerfire wildcat .224 Harvey K Chuck round, the predecessor of the Model 53 Jet

Changes:

	1955	Delete sideplate screw
17	1957	Stamping of model number
	1958	Introduce 8-5/8" barrel (4-screw)
17-1	1959	Right hand to left hand thread extractor rod
	1960	Introduce 8-3/8" barrel
17-2	1961	Delete triggerguard screw, change cylinder stop
17-3	1967	Relocation of rear sight leaf screw
17-4	1977	Change gas ring from yoke to cylinder
	1982	Eliminate pinned barrel
	1986	Introduce 4" barrel w/serrated ramp on ramp base, heavy barrel
17-5	1988	New yoke retention system/radius stud package

Product Codes:

100502 6"	B SB	84-86	39 oz.
100503 6"	B TS TT TH	84-86	
100505 8-3/8"	B SB	84-86	43 oz.
100506 8-3/8"	B TS TT TH	84-86	
100508 4"	B SB HB	86-89	36 oz.
100510 6"	B SB	87-89	
100512 6"	B TS TT TH	87-89	
100516 8-3/8"	B TS TT TH	87-89	

MODEL 17: THE K-22 MASTERPIECE - FULL LUG BARREL:

Cal-.22 Long Rifle, 6-shot, 4", 6", or 8-3/8" full lug ribbed barrel, blue finish, wood combat style grips, .375" semi or .500" full target hammer, .400" target or .312" combat trigger, adjustable rear sight, K Target frame, square butt, counterbored cylinder, pinned Patridge front sight on ramp base, early 17-6 variations are found without the full lug. Serrated backstrap and forestrap. 1990-1994

NIB	Exc	VG	Good	Fair	Poor
375	300	235	185	150	100

Variations:

- "The Revolver": See Twelve Revolvers in "Specials and Commemoratives" section
- Fifty reported made in two-tone w/stainless cylinder

Changes:

17-6 1990	Full lug barrel
1993	Discontinue 8-3/8" barrel
17-7 1994	Drill and tap, change rear sight, change extractor

Product Codes:

100538 4"	B CT ST SB CS FL	90-94	42 oz.
100540 6"	B CT ST SB CS FL	90	
100542 6"	B TT TH SB CS FL	90-94	48 oz.
100544 8-3/8"	B TT TH SB CS FL	90-92	54 oz.
100509 6"	B TT TH SB CS FL	94 w/stainless cyl. special	

MODEL 18: THE K-22 COMBAT MASTERPIECE:

Cal-.22 Long Rifle, 4" pinned barrel, blue finish, combat style adjustable rear sight, 1/8" Baughman Quick Draw on plain ramp base front sight, 6-shot, short action, K Target frame, square butt, walnut grips, counterbored cylinder, 5-screw, narrow rib, target hammer, target trigger, "K" serial prefix, serrated backstrap and forestrap. 1949-1985

NIB	Exc	VG	Good	Fair	Poor
400	335	240	175	135	85

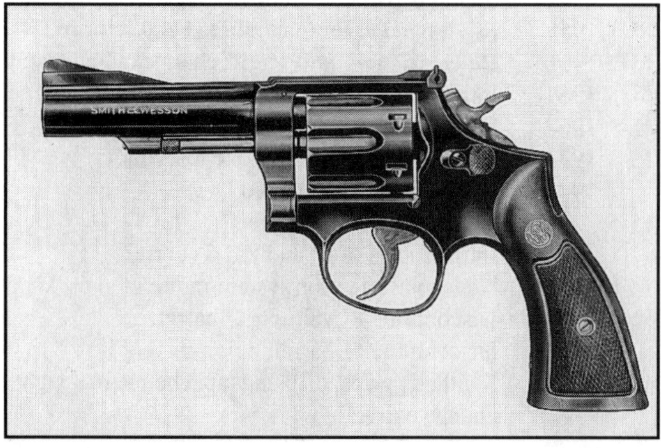

Model 18

Variations:

- 5-screw, add 10-20%
- Nickel finish not cataloged, but produced, add 50-75%

Changes:

	1955	Delete sideplate screw
18	1957	Stamping of model number
18-1	1959	Right hand to left hand thread extractor rod
18-2	1961	Cylinder stop changed, delete triggerguard screw
18-3	1967	Relocation of rear sight leaf screw
18-4	1977	Change gas ring from yoke to cylinder
	1982	Eliminate pinned barrel

Product Codes:

100602 4" B SB	84-85	36 oz.
100603 4" B SB TT TH	84-85	

MODEL 19: THE .357 COMBAT MAGNUM:

Cal-.357 Magnum, K Target frame, blue or nickel finish, originally available in 4" only with a 1/8" Baughman Quick Draw on plain ramp base front sight with adjustable rear sight, later versions with 2-1/2" (3" very rare, 5" rare) or 6" pinned barrel and Patridge sight, found with .400" target trigger, .265" service trigger or .312" smooth combat trigger, .375" semi or .500" full target hammer, target stocks, later versions with red ramp and white outline, round butt on 2-1/2" version only, shrouded extractor rod, original 4-screw frame, ribbed barrel and counterbored cylinder, serrated backstrap and forestrap. The Model 19 is built on a frame that is slightly larger than a standard K frame in the yoke area. Retail $430-$416.

1955-DATE

NIB	Exc	VG	Good	Fair	Poor
340	260	220	185	150	100

Commemoratives and variations:

- **The Texas Ranger Commemorative 1823-1973 (C&R):** Cal-.357 Magnum, 4" barrel, red ramp, white outline, target hammer, smooth trigger, counterbored cylinder and pinned, "Texas Rangers" marked on barrel, rosewood or walnut grips, knife serial matches revolver, presentation case with the Texas Ranger seal on top, triggerguard narrowed on right side. Production overruns with a narrow triggerguard were sold as a Model 19-3. Eight thousand sets sold with the Bowie Knife; 1,950 sold with a presentation case only, fifty were class A engraved, with a knife and case. Model 19-3 serial number range TR1-TR10000, 1973. New in the case w/knife value $650. Add 10% premium for serial numbers under 1000, and those sold through the Texas Ranger Commission.

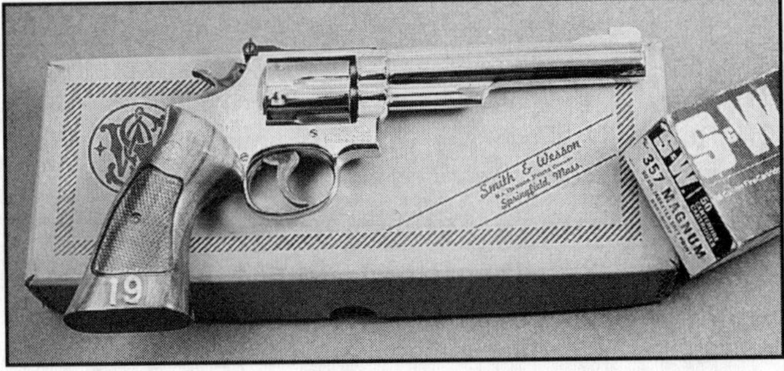

Model 19, nickel square butt, gray box

Model 19, 2-1/2-inch round butt

- **California Highway Patrol Commemorative (C&R):** 5000 made 1978-1979, 6" blue. NIB $650.
- **City of Los Angles 200th Anniversary (C&R).**
- **Fairfax Co. VA Police.**
- **Fraternal Order of Police:** Engraved with "Law Enforcement Hero's Memorial," "1986 Limited Edition." "S&W 357 Magnum." 4" with presentation case, 381 mfd., 1986.
- **Kentucky State Police Commemorative:** 4" blue, 917 mfd., 1978-1979.
- **Maryland State Police Commemorative:** 50th Anniversary, 6" barrel, gold inlays, presentation cased.
- **New Mexico State Police:** 19-4, 4" blue, 400 mfd. in 1975 w/wood presentation case.
- **Office of Naval Intelligence (ONI) Issue**: Cal-.357 Magnum, 1965, ONI marked, blue finish, 4" round butt, red ramp w/white outline. 1000 mfd. and issued to the ONI and FBI w/service trigger, standard hammer, grip adapter, found in s/n range K544000-624000.
- **1966:** Two hundred issued w/yellow ramp and white outline. Marked "NIS" w/smooth combat trigger (aka "Ranger Trigger").
- **Oregon State Police Commemorative:** Presentation case with belt buckle, 6" blue, 1100 made in 1981, NIB $900.
- **Pennsylvania State Police Commemorative:** 19-4, 75th Anniversary, 1905-1980. Gold inlays, w/wood presentation case, 4", 3000 mfd., 1980.
- **Prince William Co. VA Police**
- **Tenn Highway Patrol:** 19-4, 4", 600 mfd. in 1979 w/wood presentation case.
- **U.S. Customs Commemorative** 19-4, 4" blue, 813 mfd. in 1978 w/wood presentation case.
- **Washington State Penitentiary Commemorative:** 100 Years, 1886-1986, 6" with case.

- **West Virginia State Police Commemorative:** 4" blue, 627 mfd., 1979.
- **Model 19 9mm:** Model 19 variations exist chambered in 9mm—a forerunner of the Model 547 for European export.
- **Model 19-P:** Variations were built in a fixed sight configuration for export to South America (Peru) in limited quantities with 2-1/2" barrel w/round butt and 4" barrel on a square butt.
- **1995 Special for Lew Horton:** 3" Magna ported full lug barrel. Approx. 75 mfd., Product Code: 100701.
- **Model 19-3 w/optical sight:** 4" barrel, several made on a test basis.
- **"Hands Off":** See Twelve Revolvers under "Commemoratives and Specials" section.

Changes:

	1955	Introduction @ K-260001
19	1957	Stamping of model number
19-1	1959	Right hand to left hand thread extractor rod
19-2	1961	Cylinder stop changed, delete triggerguard screw
	1963	Introduce 6" barrel
	1963	Fifty mfd. with 2-1/2" barrel in a serial range of K544672-K544721
	1966	Introduce 2-1/2" barrel
19-3	1967	Relocation of rear sight leaf screw
19-4	1977	Change gas ring from yoke to cylinder
19-5	1982	Eliminate cylinder counterbore and pinned barrel
19-6	1988	New yoke retention system/radius stud package
	1992	Blue finish only
19-7	1994	Synthetic grips, grill and tap, change extractor, change rear sight

Product Codes:

100701	3"	FL B RB	Special 95	
100702	2-1/2"	B RB ST	84-96	30.5 oz.
100703	2-1/2"	B RB RR WO	84-91	
100705	4"	B TS SB	84-96	36 oz.
100706	4"	B TS TT TH	84-86	
100707	4"	B TS SB RR WO	84-94	
100708	4"	B TS TT TH RR WO	84-86	
100710	6"	B TS SB	84-96	39 oz.
100711	6"	B TS TT TH	84-86	
100712	6"	B TS TT TH RR WO	84-91	
100714	2-1/2"	N RB	84-86	
100715	2-1/2"	N RB RR WO	84-86	
100717	4"	N TS	84-91	
100718	4"	N TS RR WO	84-86	
100719	4"	N TS TT TH RR WO	84-86	
100721	6"	N TS	84-91	
100722	6"	N TS TT TH	84-86	
100723	6"	N TS TT TH RR WO	84-86	

MODEL 19: .357 MAGNUM K COMP:

Cal-.357 Magnum, K Target frame w/round butt, 6-shot, 3" full lug ported barrel, counterbored cylinder, smooth combat trigger, front sight is set back w/dot tritium night sight on post, black blade adj. rear sight, contoured thumbpiece, rubber combat grips, blue matte finish, from the S&W Performance Center, limited production, weight 36 oz. New value: $800.

1994

Product Code:

170025

MODEL 20: THE .38/44 HEAVY DUTY (Postwar):

Cal-.38 Special, this postwar model now incorporates a new hammer block, fixed sights, blue or nickel finish, 6-shot, walnut grips, 4", 5", or 6-1/2" round pinned barrel, N frame 5-screw, new rebound hammer, shrouded extractor rod, 1/10" round blade front sight, square notch rear sight, checkered walnut Magna stocks with S&W monograms.

Postwar serial number range S62940-S263000

9,493 mfd. 1946-1966

NIB	Exc	VG	Good	Fair	Poor
400	300	225	185	150	100

Changes:

	1949	Introduce 6-1/2" barrel
	1955	Delete upper sideplate screw
	1957	*.38/44 Heavy Duty continued as Model 20*
20	1957	Stamping of model number
20-1	1960	Right hand to left hand thread extractor rod
20-2	1961	Cylinder stop changed, eliminate triggerguard screw

MODEL 21: THE MODEL 1950 .44 MILITARY (C&R):

Cal-.44 S&W Special, successor to the 1926 .44 Military with new hammer block, 6-shot, blue or nickel finish, N frame, 4", 5", or 6-1/2" barrel, 5-screw frame, round pinned barrel, shrouded extractor rod, 1/10" round blade front sight w/square notch rear sight, checkered walnut Magna stocks with S&W monograms.

Serial number range S75000-S263000

1,200 mfd. 1950-1966

NIB	Exc	VG	Good	Fair	Poor
1600	1000	750	600	350	250

Changes:

	1955	Delete sideplate screw
	1957	*Model 1950 .44 Military continued as Model 21*
21	1957	Stamping of model number
21-1	1960	Right hand to left hand thread extractor rod
21-2	1961	Cylinder stop changed, eliminate triggerguard screw

MODEL 22: THE MODEL 1950 .45 ARMY:

Cal-.45 ACP, similar to Model of 1917, 5-1/2" barrel, short throw hammer, Magna style walnut grips with S&W monograms, new hammer block, lanyard ring discontinued, N frame, 5-screw frame, blue finish, 6-shot, pinned barrel, 1/10" round blade front sight, square notch rear sight, ".45 CAL

MODEL 1950" stamped on the upper sideplate screw barrel, non-shrouded extractor rod.

Serial number range S76000-S263000

3,976 mfd. 1950-1966

NIB	Exc	VG	Good	Fair	Poor
1400	1000	700	450	325	200

Changes:

	1952	203 chambered in .45 Colt
	1955	Delete upper sideplate screw
	1957	*Model 1950 .45 Army continued as Model 22*
22	1957	Stamping of model number
22-1	1960	Right hand to left hand thread extractor rod
22-2	1961	Cylinder stop changed, eliminate triggerguard screw

MODEL 23: THE .38/44 OUTDOORSMAN (Postwar):

Cal-.38 S&W Special, target sights, 1/8" Patridge front sight, adjustable rear sights, blue finish, 6-shot, N Target frame, 6-1/2" barrel (4" and 5" rare), walnut Magna stocks, pinned barrel, shrouded extractor rod, 5-screw frame, new hammer block.

Serial number range S62484-S263000

Postwar	2,326 mfd.	1946-1950
1950 style design	6,039 mfd.	1950-1966

NIB	Exc	VG	Good	Fair	Poor
600	450	350	250	175	100

Changes:

	1950	Introduce ribbed barrel and micrometer rear sight
	1955	Delete upper sideplate screw
	1957	*.38/44 Outdoorsman continued as Model 23*
23	1957	Stamping of model number
23-1	1960	Right hand to left hand thread extractor rod
23-2	1961	Cylinder stop changed, eliminate triggerguard screw

MODEL 24: THE MODEL OF 1950 .44 SPECIAL TARGET:

Cal-.44 S&W Special, successor to the 1926 Model .44 Target with a new short throw hammer, 6-1/2" (4" and 5" rare) pinned and ribbed barrel, micrometer rear sight, blue finish, 6-shot, N Target frame, 1/8" Patridge front sight, shrouded extractor rod, 5-screw frame, checkered walnut Magna stocks.

Serial number range S75000-S263000

5,050 mfd. 1950-1967

NIB	Exc	VG	Good	Fair	Poor
750	600	450	300	200	150

Variations:

- 4" or 5", add 75-100%
- 5-screw rare, worth premium

Changes:

	1955	Delete sideplate screw @ serial S175000
	1957	*Model of 1950 .44 Target continued as Model 24*
24	1957	Stamping of model number
24-1	1960	Right hand to left hand thread extractor rod
24-2	1961	Cylinder stop changed, eliminate triggerguard screw

MODEL 24: 1950 .44 TARGET REINTRODUCTION:

Cal-.44 Special, 4" or 6-1/2" barrel (5" rare), blue finish, 6-shot, target stocks, .265" serrated target trigger w/.400" target hammer on 4" barrel with Baughman front sight, .500" target hammer w/.400" target trigger on 6-1/2" barrel with Patridge front sight, N Target frame, square butt, three-letter serial prefix, shrouded extractor rod, first 100 were factory engraved w/smooth walnut stocks and silver S&W medallions in the grips.

7,500 mfd. 1983-1984

NIB	Exc	VG	Good	Fair	Poor
425	360	300	225	190	150

Variations:

- Model 24-3 1983 introduction w/no barrel pin Lew Horton Special: 3" barrel, round butt, adjustable rear sight, blue finish, limited edition. 5,000 mfd., 1983-1984. $475.
- "Through the Line": See Twelve Revolvers in "Commemoratives and Specials" section.

Product Codes:

100782 4"	B TS	84	41.5 oz.
100785 6-1/2"	B TS TT TH	84	43 oz.

MODEL 25: THE 1955 MODEL .45 TARGET HEAVY BARREL:

Cal-.45 ACP or .45 Long Colt, N Target frame, blue or nickel finish, 6-shot, 5-screw, 6-1/2" ribbed and pinned barrel, target sights, .500" target hammer, .400" or .500" target trigger, checkered target Magna style grips, shrouded extractor rod, 1/8" Patridge front sight, later versions with 4", 6", or 8-3/8" barrel with a red ramp insert on ramp base, half moon clips with .45 ACP version marked "45 CAL. MODEL 1955," "S" serial prefix, muzzle brake options are found. 5" barrel rare. Model 25 commemoratives are curio and relic as defined by the Bureau of Alcohol, Tobacco, and Firearms. 1955-1991

	NIB	Exc	VG	Good	Fair	Poor
4-screw	550	450	335	225	195	150
3-screw	400	350	300	225	195	125

Variations:

- Montana Centennial Commemorative: 200 guns in 1988, logo on sideplate, wood case.

Model 25

- **Model 25: The 125th Anniversary Commemorative:** Cal-.45 Colt, to commemorate the 125th year of Smith & Wesson. This model was made in three editions:
  *** Standard Edition:** 9948 units, 6-1/2" barrel, bright blue finish, barrel marking: "Smith & Wesson 125th Anniversary," gold filled. Sideplate mark: 125th commemorative seal. Gold filled smooth Goncalo Alves target grips with nickel plated S&W medallions, red ramp front sight w/white outline rear. Mahogany presentation case w/rosewood finish, nickel silver 125th anniversary medallion. Book by Roy G. Jinks: *125 Years with Smith & Wesson.* Serial number range S&W 00001 to S&W 10000, except as allocated below. NIB $500.
  *** Deluxe Edition:** Fifty units, class A engraved, ivory stocks w/nickel plated S&W medallion, 125th seal hand engraved on the sideplate. Anniversary medallion is sterling silver, book is leather-bound. Serial number range S&W 00010, S&W 00020 etc. to S&W 00500. Retail $1,500.
  *** Custom Deluxe Edition:** Two units, class A engraved with gold inlays, genuine ivory stocks w/nickel plated S&W medallions, 125th sideplate seal is gold inlaid. Serial numbers S&W 00001 and S&W 00125. Retail $25,000 (not for sale).

Changes:

	1955	Introduction @ S150000
	1956	Delete sideplate screw
	1957	*1955 Model Target Heavy Barrel continued as Model 25*
25	1957	Stamping of model number
25-1	1960	Change extractor rod, right to left hand thread
25-2	1961	Eliminate triggerguard screw
	1969	Begin "N" serial prefix
25-3	1977	.45 ACP 3" version mfd. for Lew Horton
25-3	1977	.45 Colt Anniversary Edition - short cylinder
25-4	1977	.45 Colt Deluxe Anniversary Edition - short cylinder 25-3 and 25-4 had short cylinders not used on 25-5
25-5	1978	.45 Colt caliber std. production, long cylinder now available with 4", 6", or 8-3/8" barrel
	1982	Delete pinned barrel
25-6	1988	New yoke retention system - unfluted cylinder .45 ACP
25-7	1988	New yoke retention system - unfluted cylinder .45 Colt
25-8	1990	Longer stop notch in cylinder -.45 ACP
25-9	1990	Longer stop notch in cylinder -.45 Colt

Product Codes:

100902 4"	B TS TT TH RR WO .45LC	84-91	44 oz.
100904 6"	B TS TT TH RR WO .45LC	84-91	46 oz.
100906 8-3/8"	B TS TT TH RR WO .45LC	84-91	50 oz.
100907 4"	N TS TT TH RR WO .45LC	84-86	
100908 6"	N TS TT TH RR WO .45LC	84-86	
100909 8-3/8"	N TS TT TH RR WO .45LC	84-86	
100924 5"	Glass bead finish, unfluted cylinder, 2000 mfd. in .45LC, all laser engraved, 1989		
100902 4"	barrel reported in fixed sight variation for RSR		

MODEL 26: THE 1950 MODEL .45 TARGET LIGHT BARREL:

Cal-.45 ACP, micrometer rear sight, 6-1/2" ribbed barrel, (4" and 5" rare), short throw hammer, shrouded extractor rod, N Target frame, blue finish, 5-screw, marked ".45 CAL MODEL 1950," 6-shot, 1/8" Patridge front sight, checkered walnut stocks.

Serial number range S76000-S263000
2,768 mfd. 1950-1966

NIB	Exc	VG	Good	Fair	Poor
850	700	575	400	300	200

Variations:

- 26-1 1989: Special production for Georgia State Patrol, w/lanyard, 5" tapered barrel w/rib, chambered in .45 Long Colt, w/Baughman front sight, adjustable rear sight, three-letter serial prefix, approx. forty available outside the contract. Blue finish.

Product Code:

100920 5" .45LC AS.

Changes:

	1953	200 chambered for .45 Long Colt
	1955	Delete sideplate screw
	1957	*1950 Model .45 Target Light Barrel continued as Model 26*
26	1957	Stamping of model number
26-1	1960	Change extractor rod, right hand to left hand thread
26-2	1961	Cylinder stop changed, eliminate triggerguard screw

MODEL 27: The .357 MAGNUM (Postwar):

Cal-.357 Magnum, this model now incorporates a new hammer block and postwar improvements, 6-shot, blue or nickel finish, original barrel lengths of 3-1/2" and 5", 4", 6", 6-1/2",

Model 27; bottom is "Outnumbered" from "Twelve Revolvers" series

or 8-3/8" barrel lengths in later production, micrometer rear sight, diamond walnut Magna stocks, shrouded extractor rod, N Target frame, square butt, ribbed and pinned barrel, finely checkered topstrap on early versions, choice of any front sight, 5-screw, counterbored cylinder, grooved backstrap and forestrap, .400" serrated trigger, .500" target hammer, red ramp on ramp base on 4" w/white outline rear sight, Patridge on 6" and 8-3/8" w/plain rear blade. Also see the Registered Magnum and related models in previous section, " Early Hand Ejectors - Named Model Revolvers." 1949-1994

	NIB	Exc	VG	Good	Fair	Poor
4-screw	450	325	250	200	150	100
3-screw	350	275	225	200	150	100

Commemoratives and variations:

- **Texas Department of Public Safety Commemorative:** 400 made in 1979, 5" blue.
- **Model 27: The .357 Magnum 50th Year Commemorative (C&R):** Cal-.357 Magnum, 5" barrel, target hammer, target trigger, 6-shot, blue finish with gold inlay, smooth wood grips, ramp on ramp base front sight, adjustable rear sight, finely checkered topstrap, wood presentation case with a registration certificate "50th Anniversary 1935-1985" stamped on barrel, sideplate stamped "The First Magnum - April 8 1935." 27-3, $475. Serial number range REG 0001-REG 2500, 2500 mfd., 1985.
- **Model 27: .357 Magnum Reintroduction:** Cal-.357 Magnum, a special production run of 3-1/2" and 5" barrels, blue finish only, 6-shot, "like the original." .400" semi-target hammer, N Target frame, .312" smooth combat trigger, pinned black front ramp sight, morado wood target stocks, production run of 1,500. Model 27-5. Special for 1991. $450 NIB.

  Product Codes:

100998 3-1/2"	B	43.5 oz.
100996 5"	B	44.5 oz.

- **Model 27: The General Patton Commemorative:** Cal-.357 Magnum, in 1993 a collector edition of the General Patton Model 27 was mfd. for the American Historical Foundation in Richmond, VA with 4" barrel. One hundred Deluxe Editions mfd. with sterling silver plating and full engraving, serial range P001D to P100D. 950 collector editions mfd. with blue frame and silver plated cylinder with military insignia and General officer's rank. Serial range P001C-P950C. General Patton's original sidearms are in the Patton Museum at Fort Knox Ky. 1994.
- **Model 27 The F.B.I. Commemorative:** Cal- .357 Magnum, Model 27-3 w/special serial range prefix of FBI xxxx, commemorating fifty years, marked: "1934 Federal Bureau of Investigation" on the right side of a 5" barrel, FBI seal on sideplate, target hammer, target trigger, "FBI" on left side of frame, Baughman front sight, basswood case w/FBI seal. 1983.
- **"Outnumbered":** See Twelve Revolvers in "Commemoratives and Specials" section.

Changes:

	1949	Begin "S" serial prefix @ S72000
	1955	Delete upper sideplate screw @ S171584
27	1957	Stamping of model number
27-1	1960	Change from right to left hand extractor rod
27-2	1961	Cylinder stop changed, eliminate triggerguard screw
	1969	Change to "N" serial prefix
	1975	Target trigger, target hammer, red ramp/white outline introduced with Goncalo Alves target stocks and case 3-1/2" and 5" barrel discontinued
27-3	1982	Eliminate cylinder counterbore and pinned barrel
	1987	Discontinue nickel finish
27-4	1988	New yoke retention system/radius stud package
27-5	1990	Longer stop notch in cylinder
	1992	Discontinue 4" and 8-3/8" barrel
27-6	1994	Hogue grips, drill and tap, change rear sight, change extractor

Product Codes:

101002 4"	B TS TT TH RR WO	84-91	41oz.
101004 6"	B TS TT TH	84-94	
101006 8-3/8"	B TS TT TH	84-91	47oz.
101008 4"	N TS TT TH RR WO	84-86	
101010 6"	N TS TT TH	84-86	44oz.
101012 8-3/8"	N TS TT TH	84-86	

MODEL 28: THE HIGHWAY PATROLMAN

Cal-.357 Magnum, "Highway Patrol," a utility model, dull blue finish, adjustable rear sight leaf that is non-serrated, 6-shot, 4" or 6" pinned and ribbed barrel, Magna or target walnut grips, NT frame, counterbored cylinders, has "Highway Patrol" stamped in the barrel, 5-screw, 1/8" Baughman Quick Draw front sight, shrouded extractor rod, .400" semi-target hammer, .265" serrated trigger, original test production marked "PATROLMAN." The name change was suggested by Mrs. Florance Van Orden of "The Evaluators Ltd." to then president

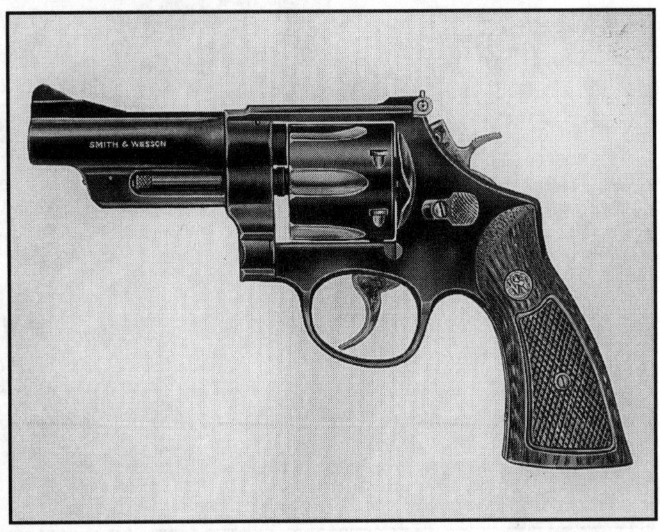

Model 28

Carl Helstrum. *Previously produced as "The Highway Patrolman."* 1954-1986

NIB	Exc	VG	Good	Fair	Poor
350	250	200	175	135	85

Variations:

- **Massachusetts State Police:** Twenty-five guns in 5" nickel marked FHP 32 through 56 in 1959
- **Washington State Police Commemorative:** 762 guns in 1981, 6" blue
- A few made with dull nickel finish, reportedly as salesman's samples

Changes:

	1954	Begin "S" serial prefix @ S103500
	1955	Delete sideplate screw @ S171584
	1957	*Highway Patrolman continued as Model 28*
28	1957	Stamping of model number
28-1	1960	Change from right to left hand extractor rod
28-2	1961	Cylinder stop changed, eliminate triggerguard screw
	1969	Change to "N" serial prefix
28-3	1982	Eliminate cylinder counterbore and pinned barrel

Product Codes:

101102 4"	B SB	84-86	42 oz.
101103 4"	B TS	84-86	
101105 6"	B SB	84-86	44 oz.
101106 6"	B TS	84-86	

MODEL 29: The .44 MAGNUM:

Cal-.44 Magnum, 4", 6-1/2", or 8-3/8" (5" rare) barrel, pinned barrel, blue or nickel finish, red ramp front sight, white outline rear blade, black presentation case, shrouded extractor rod, N Target frame, 6-shot, walnut stocks, counterbored cylinder, .500" target hammer, .400" or .500" target trigger. 6,500 mfd. with 4-screw sideplate in a serial number range of S130000 to S167500 and are C&R. Retail $554-$566. 1955-DATE

	NIB	Exc	VG	Good	Fair	Poor
4-screw	700	550	400	350	300	200
3-screw	500	400	350	325	285	200

Model 29; lower two guns are "Hostiles" and "The Attack" from "Twelve Revolvers" series

Variations:

- Original 5" barrel: About 200 made as 4-screw Model 29, remainder as 3-screw Mod. 29-1 or 29-2. Worth double above values.
- 5-screw nickel worth 2X to 4X standard value; 4-screw nickel worth 50-75% premium.

Changes:

	1955	Begin production @ "S" serial S130000
	1956	Delete upper sideplate screw @ serial S167500
	1957	*The .44 Magnum continued as Model 29*
29	1957	Stamping of model number @ serial S179000
	1958	8-3/8" barrel introduced, 500 5" barrels mfd.
29-1	1960	Change extractor rod, thread changed to left hand to prevent unscrewing under recoil @ serial S270000
29-2	1961	Cylinder stop changed, eliminate triggerguard screw
	1969	Change to "N" serial prefix @ serial S333454
	1979	6-1/2" barrel length dropped in favor of 6" as standard barrel length
29-3	1982	Eliminate cylinder counterbore and pinned barrel
29-4	1988	New yoke retention system/radius stud package; integral scope mounts on 8-3/8"
29-5	1990	Longer stop notch in cylinder, new bolt block
29-6	1994	Hogue grips, drill and tap, change rear sight, change extractor

Product Codes:

101204 4"	B TS TT TH RR WO	84-92	44 oz.
101206 6"	B TS TT TH RR WO	84-96	
101208 8-3/8"	B TS TT TH RR WO	84-96	51.5 oz.
101210 4"	N TS TT TH RR WO	84-91	
101212 6"	N TS TT TH RR WO	84-91	7 oz.
101214 8-3/8"	N TS TT TH RR WO	84-91	

MODEL 29: The "SILHOUETTE":

Cal-.44 Magnum, 10-5/8" ribbed barrel, blue finish, adjustable four-position front sight, adjustable rear sight has narrow white outline blade, 6-shot, Goncalo Alves grips, NT frame, .400" target trigger, .500" target hammer, shrouded extractor, not known if any were mfd. w/counterbored cylinder and barrel pin. Special presentation case available. First guns had "N" prefix s/n's. 1983-1991

NIB	Exc	VG	Good	Fair	Poor
600	525	385	325	275	200

Changes:

29-3 1983	Cylinder counterbore eliminated
29-4 1988	New yoke retention system/radius stud package -- early models marked 29-3E for endurance package
29-5 1990	Longer stop notch in cylinder, new bolt block

Product Code:

101202 10-5/8"	B TS TT TH	84-91	57.5 oz.

MODEL 29: "The .44 CLASSIC":

Similar to standard Model 29 but with full lug barrel. Cal-.44 Magnum, 5", 6-1/2", 8-3/8" barrel, blue finish, 6-shot, interchangeable front sights, white outline rear sight, .500" target hammer, .400" serrated target trigger, Hogue grips on a round butt frame, chamfered cylinder, NT frame, lasersmith engraved, drilled and tapped for scope mount under the rear sight strap. Serial number laser etched under the topstrap, 29-5 1991. 1991-1994

NIB	Exc	VG	Good	Fair	Poor
500	400	350	300	250	200

Changes:

29-6 1994	Change rear sight, change extractor, drill and tap

Product Codes:

101274 5"	B FL SB IFS SG WO	91-94	51 oz.
101276 6-1/2"	B FL SB IFS SG WO	91-94	52 oz.
101270 8 3/8"	B FL SB IFS SG WO	91-94	54 oz.

MODEL 29: "The .44 CLASSIC DX":

Deluxe version of .44 Classic. Cal-.44 Magnum, with features like the Classic, 6-1/2" or 8-3/8" barrel, with combat hardwood grips or Hogue square butt conversion grips on a round butt frame, five front sights included, frame drilled and tapped, Lasersmith engraved. 1991-1992

NIB	Exc	VG	Good	Fair	Poor
550	500	450	375	250	200

Changes:

29-5 1992	Introduce 5" barrel

Product Codes:

101266 5"	B FL IFS SG WO CS	92	51 oz.
101278 6-1/2"	B FL IFS SG WO CS	91-92	52 oz.
101272 8-3/8"	B FL IFS SG WO CS	91-92	54 oz.

MODEL 29: "The .44 MAGNA CLASSIC":

Cal-.44 Magnum, with all of the above features, 7-1/2" full lug barrel, .500" target hammer, .400" serrated trigger w/trigger works, non-chamfered cylinder, cherrywood presentation case, black leather sight box, "1 of 3000" lasersmith engraved on barrel, accurized with a test target and registration certificate. 29-5 1990. Serial number range MAG0001-MAG3000 concurrent with the 629 Magna Classic. Run of 1,800 in blue. 1990

Product Code:

101264

NIB	Exc	VG	Good	Fair	Poor
900	600	475	375	300	200

Specials and variations all inclusive for the Model 29:

- All listed product codes for the Model 29

101202 10-5/8"	Silhouette	83-91	57.5 oz.
101204 4"	Blue	84-92	
101205 6"	Special	94	
101206 6"	Blue	84-94	
101208 8-3/8"	Blue	84-94	

101210 4"	Nickel	84-91
101212 6"	Nickel	84-91
101214 8-3/8"	Nickel	84-91
101230 6"	Classic Hunter	87
101233 8-3/8"	Scope Mount	89
101249 5"	Hill Country	89
101251 3"	Special	89
101254 8-3/8"	Classic Hunter	89
101256 7-1/2"	Accusport	89
101264 7-1/2"	Magna Classic	90
101266 5"	Classic DX	91-92
101270 8-3/8"	.44 Classic	91-94
101272 8-3/8"	Classic DX	91-92
101274 5"	.44 Classic	91-94
101276 6-1/2"	.44 Classic	91-94
101278 6-1/2"	Classic DX	91-92
101282 6"	Classic Hunter	91

- **The Tunnel Gun:** (A non-S&W product) A highly modified N (29-2) frame with a 1.3" smooth barrel, blue finish, chambered for a "very" special .500" noiseless shot shell. Mfd. for armed forces use in Southeast Asia by the A.A.I. Corp. Also called the Tunnel Weapon or "QSPR" (Quiet Special Purpose Revolver). On display at The Military Ordnance Museum, Aberdeen, MD. Approx. 17 mfd., 1969.
- **North Carolina Highway Patrol Commemorative:** Model 29-2, 6" barrel w/wood presentation case, "1929-1979" w/seal on sideplate, red ramp w/white outline, nickel finish, 1200 mfd., 1979. NIB $1500.
- **Model 29 Lew Horton Special:** Cal-.44 Magnum, Combat Magnum 3" barrel, contoured wood grips, adj. rear sight, red ramp front sight, white outline, smooth combat trigger, semi-target hammer. Product code: 101224. 1984.
- **Model 29-3: Elmer Keith Commemorative Edition (C&R):** Cal-.44 Magnum, blue finish, 6-shot, target hammer, target trigger, red ramp on ramp base front sight, adjustable rear sight, 4" barrel, engraved picture on sideplate, "1899-1984," "Outstanding Handgunner," and "Salmon Idaho" on the cylinder. Serial number range EMK001-EMK2500, 2,500 mfd., 1985. NIB $800.
- **Elmer Keith Deluxe Edition:** S/n EMK001-EMK100 worth 2X to 3X above value.
- **29-3 The Classic Hunter:** Lew Horton special, Cal-.44 Magnum, 6-shot nonfluted cylinder, 6" full lug barrel, adjustable four-position front sight, white outline rear blade, blue finish, Hogue rubber combat grips, N Target frame, square butt. Product code: 101230. Run of 5,000, 1987. NIB $550 Exc $500.
- **29-4 5" Full Lug Barrel**: Unfluted cylinder, square butt, Hogue grips, mfd. for Hill Country Dist. Product code: 101249. 500 mfd., 1989. NIB $525 Exc $500.
- **29-4 3" Full Lug Barrel**: Unfluted cylinder, Pachmayr SKGR grips. .500" target hammer, .400" serrated target trigger, red ramp front sight w/white outline rear sight, 43.5 oz. Product code: 101251. 3200 mfd., 1989. NIB $450.
- **29-4 Classic Hunter:** 8-3/8" barrel, full lug, unfluted cylinder w/red ramp/white outline, .400" target trigger, .500" target hammer, square butt w/Hogue grips. Product code: 101254. 2500 mfd., 1989. NIB $475.
- **29-5 7-1/2" Full Lug Barrel:** Unfluted cylinder, mfd. for Accusport, interchangeable front sight, round butt. Product code: 101256. 500 mfd., 1989. NIB $535.
- **29-5 Classic Hunter Reintroduction:** 6" barrel, .400" target trigger, .500" target hammer, full lug barrel, non-fluted cylinder, red ramp, white outline, Hogue soft rubber combat grips. Product code: 101282. 51.75 oz. Limited production, 1991. NIB $450.
- **Model 29 w/Scope Mount:** 8-3/8" barrel with factory broaching to accommodate S&W scope mounting system, .500" target hammer, .400" serrated target trigger, red ramp front sight w/white outline rear sight, rings and bases included. Product code: 101233. 54.5 oz. 1989. NIB—mixed reports on NIB price, ranging from $1500 to $400—more info needed.
- **29-5 6" w/Tapered Barrel:** Ramp on ramp base front sight, target hammer, target trigger, Hogue grips, blue finish, unfluted cylinder, with counterbored cylinder. Product code: 101205. Approx. 9 mfd., 1994. NIB $1500.
- **Alaskan 25th Anniversary Commemorative:** 6", NIB $650.
- **S&W Collectors Association 25th Anniversary:** "Mountain Gun" configuration in blue, 4" light tapered barrel, chambered cylinder, round butt. NIB $670.
- **"Hostiles":** See Twelve Revolvers in "Commemoratives and Specials" section.
- **"The Attack":** See Twelve Revolvers in "Commemoratives and Specials" section.

MODEL 30: THE .32 HAND EJECTOR (Postwar):

Cal-.32 S&W Long, 6-shot, 2", 3", 3-1/4", 4", 4-1/4", or 6" pinned barrel, blue or nickel finish, walnut or hard rubber grips, built on the I frame, improved I frame and the J frame, original 5-screw frame, flat latch thumbpiece, round blade front sight later changed to a 1/10" serrated ramp front sight w/square notch rear sight, round butt. Postwar serial number range 536685-826977 in the .32 Hand Ejector series with postwar improvements. 1948-1976

Previously produced as "The .32 Hand Ejector"

NIB	Exc	VG	Good	Fair	Poor
325	250	200	175	135	85

Changes:

	1948	Postwar production with 3-1/4", 4-1/4", and 6" barrel
	1949	Introduce 2" barrel
	1955	Eliminate sideplate top screw @ 640980
30	1957	Stamping of model number
	1957	2", 3", 4" barrel lengths now standard
30-1	1961	J frame production @ serial 712954
	1966	Change thumbpiece
	1969	Begin "H" serial prefix

MODEL 31: THE .32 REGULATION POLICE (Postwar):

Cal-.32 S&W Long, fixed sights, 6-shot, 2", 3", 3-1/4", 4", or 4-1/4" pinned barrel, blue or nickel finish, round blade front sight later changed to a 1/10" serrated ramp front sight,

Model 31

checkered walnut grips, .240" service hammer, .312" smooth trigger, original 5-screw frame with a flat latch thumbpiece, square butt, some variations are found with target sights, built on the I frame, improved I frame and the J frame. Serial number range 331320-826977 beginning in the original .32 Hand Ejector series.

Postwar serial number range: 536685-826977 1948-1991

Previously produced as the .32 Regulation Police

NIB	Exc	VG	Good	Fair	Poor
325	250	200	175	135	65

Changes:

	1948	Postwar production with 3-1/4", 4-1/4", and 6" barrel
	1949	Introduce 2" barrel
	1955	Eliminate top sideplate screw @ 640980
	1957	196 units built with target sights
31	1957	Stamping of model number
	1957	2", 3", 4" barrel now standard
31-1	1961	J frame production @ serial 712954
	1966	Change thumbpiece
	1969	Begin "H" serial prefix
	1978	Delete 4" barrel
	1982	Delete pinned barrel
31-2	1988	New yoke retention system/radius stud package
31-3	1990	New sight width on frame and barrel

Product Codes:

101302 2"	B SB	84-91	19 oz.
101304 3"	B SB	84-91	20 oz.

MODEL 32: THE .38/32 TERRIER (Postwar):

Cal-.38 S&W, 5-shot, 2" pinned barrel, walnut or rubber grips, blue or nickel finish, fixed sights, round butt, 5-screw frame, 1/10" serrated ramp front sight w/square notch rear, flat latch thumbpiece, built on the I frame, improved I frame and the J frame, w/3-, 4-, and 5-screw variations. Weight 17 oz.

Serial range 38976-122678 in the .38 Regulation Police series; postwar serial range 54474-122678 1948-1974

Previously produced as .38/22 Terrier

NIB	Exc	VG	Good	Fair	Poor
365	275	200	175	135	65

Changes:

	1955	Sideplate screw eliminated
	1957	*.38/32 Terrier continued as Model 32*
32	1957	Stamping of model number
32-1	1961	J frame production
	1966	Change thumbpiece
	1969	Begin "R" serial prefix

MODEL 032: .32 MAGNUM CENTENNIAL AIRWEIGHT:

Cal-.32 H&R Magnum, 6-shot, 2" barrel, alloy frame, steel cylinder and barrel, "Airweight" marked, round butt with Uncle Mike's grips, flat blue finish, .312" smooth trigger, concealed hammer, serrated ramp front sight, square notch rear sight, JA frame, serial number laser etched under the topstrap. Marked "MOD.032," contoured thumbpiece, limited production, not cataloged. 1992

NIB	Exc	VG	Good	Fair	Poor
425	350	250	200	150	75

Product Code:

103678 2" B RB FS

MODEL 33: THE .38 REGULATION POLICE (Postwar):

Cal-.38 S&W, 5-shot, blue or nickel finish, 4" pinned barrel, round blade front sight later changed to a 1/10" serrated front ramp w/square notch rear, 5-screw frame, flat latch thumbpiece, walnut stocks, built on the I frame, the improved I frame, and the J frame. 1949-1974

Serial number range 1-122678 in the original .38 Regulation Police series

Postwar serial number range 54474-122678

Previously produced as the .38 Regulation Police

NIB	Exc	VG	Good	Fair	Poor
350	285	225	175	135	65

Changes:

	1949	Begin postwar production
	1955	Sideplate screw eliminated
	1957	*.38 Regulation Police continued as Model 33*
33	1957	Stamping of model number
33-1	1961	J frame production
	1966	Change thumbpiece
	1969	Begin "R" serial prefix

MODEL 34: The MODEL of 1953 .22/32 KIT GUN:

Cal-.22 Long Rifle, 2" or 4" barrel with square butt or round butt, 6-shot, micrometer rear sights, 2" barrel has a high profile 1/10" serrated ramp front sight, .312" smooth trigger, .375" semi-target hammer, blue or nickel finish, flat latch thumbpiece, 5-screw frame, pinned barrel, walnut grips, built on the improved I frame and the J frame. 2" versions with fixed sights are known to exist as a training gun.

Serial number range 101-135465 in the 1953 Kit Gun series 1953-1991

Previously produced as the Model of 1953 .22/32 Kit Gun

Model 34

NIB	Exc	VG	Good	Fair	Poor
375	300	225	175	135	85

Changes:

	1955	Delete sideplate screw @ serial 11000
34	1957	Stamping of model number
	1957	Introduce 2" barrel
34-1	1960	J frame production @ serial 70000
	1966	Change thumbpiece
	1969	Begin "M" serial prefix @ M1
	1982	Eliminate pinned barrel
34-2	1988	New yoke retention system

Product Codes:

101402 2"	B RB	84-91	
101404 2"	B SB	84-86	22 oz.
101406 4"	B RB	84-86	
101408 4"	B SB	84-91	24 oz.
101410 2"	N RB	84-86	
101412 2"	N SB	84-86	
101414 4"	N RB	84-86	
101416 4"	N SB	84-86	

MODEL 35: The MODEL of 1953 .22/32 TARGET:

Cal-.22 Long Rifle, 6" barrel, blue finish, micrometer rear sight, 1/10" Patridge front sight, 6-shot, walnut grips, 5-screw frame, pinned barrel with top rib, flat latch thumbpiece built on the improved I frame and the J frame.

Serial range 101-135465 in the 1953 Kit Gun series 1953-1973

NIB	Exc	VG	Good	Fair	Poor
450	320	250	200	150	90

Changes:

	1955	Sideplate screw eliminated @ serial 11000
35	1957	Stamping of model number
35-1	1960	J frame production @ serial 70000
	1966	Change thumbpiece
	1969	Begin "M" serial prefix @ M1

MODEL 36: The .38 CHIEFS SPECIAL:

Cal-.38 S&W Special, 5-shot, 2" barrel with round butt or 3" barrel with square butt, blue or nickel finish, J frame (very early production versions are found with a round blade front sight, 5-screw frame, with a standard thumbpiece on a round butt, smooth backstrap, round triggerguard; transitional variations are found with 3-, 4-, and 5-screw frames with ramp front sight), w/flat latch thumbpiece, walnut grips, pinned barrel, 1/10" serrated ramp front sight w/square notch rear sight, .240" service hammer, w/.240" serrated trigger, later changed to .312" smooth combat trigger. Approx. 1,740 mfd. with target sights (see the Model 50). Earliest production had shorter grips and grip frame, no barrel rib, half round front sight blade, more rounded triggerguard, 5-screw. Most of that had changed by 1952 or 1953. Retail $377.

Serial number range 1-786544 numbered in an original series 1950-DATE

Previously produced as the Chiefs Special

NIB	Exc	VG	Good	Fair	Poor
325	250	200	175	150	100

Variations:

- Premium for flat latch models.
- **U.S. Marked:** A small group (about 2,000) of Model 36s were marked with "U.S." on the backstrap and fitted with a lanyard ring, about 1977, and sold to the army. Production overruns (about 112) are found w/"Made in U.S. A." on the backstrap.
- **USAF Office of Special Investigations:** 3" heavy barrel, stamped "OSI" on sideplate and frame.
- **Chiefs Special Target:** Model 36-1 Chiefs Target worth double standard value (total 202 shipped). Also see Model 50.

Changes:

	1952	Introduce square butt @ serial 21342
	1953	Elimination of screw in triggerguard (4-screw)
	1955	Delete sideplate screw @ serial 75000 (3-screw)
	1957	*Chiefs Special continued as Model 36*
36	1957	Stamping of model number @ serial 125000
	1962	Internal hammer alteration @ serial 295000
	1966	Thumbpiece change
36-1	1967	Indicates 3" heavy barrel
	1969	Begin J serial prefix @ J1
	1975	Heavy barrel std.
	1982	Eliminate pinned barrel
36-2	1988	New yoke retention system – tapered barrel
36-3	1988	New yoke retention system – heavy barrel
36-4	1989	LadySmith version
36-5	1989	LadySmith version
36-6	1989	Target version – special production
36-7	1990	New sight width on frame and barrel
36-8	1990	New sight for heavy barrel
	1991	Limited edition with full lug and target sights
	1992	2" and 3" HB in round butt only
	1994	Synthetic grips, change extractor

Product Codes:

101502 2"	B RB	84-96	19.5 oz.
101504 2"	B SB	84-91	
101506 2"	N RB	84-92	

Model 36 and 37 Chiefs Specials, top to bottom: Model 36 two-inch, Model 36 three-inch square butt, and Model 37 Airweight two-inch

101508 2"	N SB	84-87	
101510 3"	HB B RB	84-94	21.5 oz.
101512 3"	HB B SB	84-91	
101514 3"	HB N RB	84-86	
101516 3"	HB N SB	84-86	
101517 3"	LadySmith version		
101518 2"	LadySmith version		
101520 2"	DA RB CS Bobbed Hammer	2000 mfd. 1989 Special Edition	
101522 3"	DA RB SG Bobbed Hammer	2000 mfd. 1989 Special Edition	
101524 2"	RB AS SG Bobbed Hammer	2000 mfd. 1989 Special Edition	
101549 3"	HB FL AS SG Glass Bead	3200 mfd. 1989 Special Edition	
101554 3"	LadySmith version		
101556 2"	LadySmith version		

MODEL 36LS: The .38 LADYSMITH:

Cal-.38 S&W special, 5-shot, 2" regular or 3" heavy barrel, blue finish, grips are anatomically designed for women, round butt on 2", wood combat grips on 3", J frame, .312" smooth combat trigger w/beveled edges, .240" service hammer, serrated

Model 36-1 Chiefs Special Target

ramp front sight w/square notch rear, redesigned double action, has "LADYSMITH" engraved on the frame. Early production with a hard plastic case, later production with a softside LadySmith case. Retail $412-$428. 1989-DATE

NIB	Exc	VG	Good	Fair	Poor
350	270	200	175	135	85

Changes:

36-4 1989	2" regular barrel
36-5 1989	3" heavy barrel
1992	Discontinue 3" barrel; softside LadySmith case
1994	Laminate rosewood grips, change extractor

Product Codes:

101490 2"	B RB LS w/soft case	92-96	20 oz.
101518 2"	B RB LS w/case	89-91	
101517 3"	HB B RB LS w/case	89-91	23 oz.
101556 2"	B LS wo/case	91	
101554 3"	HB B LS wo/case	91	

MODEL 37: The .38 CHIEFS SPECIAL AIRWEIGHT:

Cal-.38 S&W Special, 5-shot, originally built with an alloy frame and alloy cylinder weighing 10-3/4 ounces, later built w/steel cylinder, JA frame, 2" barrel with round butt and square butt or 3" barrel with square butt only, blue or nickel finish, early versions have a .240" service hammer w/.240" serrated trigger, later versions have a .312" smooth combat trigger, 4-screw alloy frame, pinned barrel, serrated ramp front sight w/square notch rear, original flat latch, checkered walnut grips. 3,777 mfd. with an alloy cylinder below serial 35000. Earliest production may have a small lock screw on the upper sideplate screw. "Airweight" marked. Retail $412-$428.

Original serial number range 1-786544 numbered in the Chiefs Special series 1952-DATE

Chiefs Special Airweight: The "Aircrewman" (Baby Aircrewman): See listing in previous section, " Early Hand Ejectors – Named Model Revolvers."

NIB	Exc	VG	Good	Fair	Poor
350	285	225	185	125	75

Changes:

1954	Alloy cylinder replacement with steel

Model 37, 1994 production

	1954-55	312 mfd. with target sights and 3-1/2" barrel
	1955	Eliminate upper sideplate screw
37	1957	Stamping of model number
	1962	Internal hammer alteration
	1966	Thumbpiece change
	1969	Begin "J" serial prefix
	1982	Eliminate pinned barrel
	1988	Delete 3" barrel
37-1	1988	New yoke retention system/radius stud package
37-2	1990	New sight width on frame and barrel to 1/8"
	1992	Introduce flat matte blue and satin nickel finish
	1993	Delete "Airweight" markings on barrel
	1994	Laser inscribe "Airweight" on sideplate, synthetic grip, change extractor

Product Codes:

101601 2"	B RB	84 Special for Peru police, 250 mfd.		
101602 2"	B RB	84-96	13.5 oz.	
101604 2"	B SB	84-87		
101605 3"	B RB	84-86	14.5 oz.	
101607 3"	B SB	84-86		
101609 2"	N RB	84-95		
101611 2"	N SB	84-87		

MODEL 38: The BODYGUARD AIRWEIGHT:

Cal-.38 S&W Special, 5-shot, alloy frame, steel barrel and cylinder, shrouded hammer, 2" barrel with some production of 3" barrels, JAC frame, blue or nickeled aluminum finish, walnut grips, pinned barrel, 4-screw frame, flat latch thumbpiece, round butt, "Airweight" stamped on barrel, also found in combinations of nickel cylinder with blue frame and barrel, serrated ramp front sight, .240" shrouded service hammer, .312" smooth trigger. Retail $444-$460.

Serial number range 66000-786544 in the Chiefs Special series 1955-DATE

NIB	Exc	VG	Good	Fair	Poor
350	275	210	175	125	75

Changes:

	1956	Eliminate upper sideplate screw
38	1957	Stamping of model number
	1962	Internal hammer alteration
	1966	Thumbpiece change
	1968	Begin "J" serial prefix
		Sales to Mich. Police Supply w/stainless cylinder
	1982	Eliminate pinned barrel
38-1	1988	New yoke retention system/radius stud package
38-2	1990	New sight width on frame and barrel
	1993	Change to matte blue and satin nickel finish, delete "Airweight" marking on barrel
	1994	Laser inscribe "Airweight" on sideplate, change extractor

Product Codes:

101702 2"	B RB	84-96	14 oz.
101704 2"	N RB	84-95	

MODEL 39:

See Autoloaders

Model 37, scarce three-inch nickel square butt

Model 38 Airweight Bodyguard

MODEL 40: The CENTENNIAL:

Cal-.38 S&W Special, 5-shot, blue or nickel finish, 2" barrel, grip safety on the backstrap, fully concealed hammer, JS frame, double action only, walnut or smooth wood high horned grips, smooth backstrap, .240" serrated trigger (some early versions w/smooth trigger), pinned barrel, flat latch thumbpiece, 1/10" serrated ramp front sight w/square notch rear, 4-screw frame. This model has a pin stored under the grip to lock the backstrap safety down. Weight 19 oz.

Numbered concurrently with the Model 42 in a serial number range of 1-30160 1952-1974

NIB	Exc	VG	Good	Fair	Poor
450	400	325	225	185	125

Changes:

	1955	Eliminate upper sideplate screw
40	1957	Stamping of model number
	1966	Change thumbpiece
	1971	Begin "L" serial prefix @ L1

MODEL 41:

See Autoloaders

MODEL 42: The CENTENNIAL AIRWEIGHT:

Cal-.38 S&W Special, 5-shot, alloy frame, steel cylinder (37 mfd. with alloy cylinder), blue or nickel finish, 2" barrel grip safety on the backstrap, JSA frame with 4 screws, double action only, pinned barrel, walnut or smooth wood high horned grips, fully concealed hammer, .240" serrated trigger, flat latch thumbpiece, "Airweight" on barrel. This model has a pin stored under the grip to lock the backstrap safety down. Very early production may have a small lock screw on the upper sideplate screw.

Numbered concurrently with Model 40 in a serial number range of 1-30160 in an original series 1952-1974

NIB	Exc	VG	Good	Fair	Poor
450	400	325	225	185	100

Variations:

- Nickel: 2X blue value

Changes:

	1955	Eliminate upper sideplate screw
42	1957	Stamping of model number
	1966	Change thumbpiece
	1971	Begin "L" serial prefix @ L1

MODEL 042: CENTENNIAL AIRWEIGHT:

Cal-.38 S&W Special, matte or polished blue finish, JA frame, 5-shot, alloy frame with 2" steel barrel and cylinder, concealed hammer, double action only, Uncle Mike's grips, not "Airweight" marked, serrated ramp front sight w/square notch rear, serial number also laser etched under the topstrap, without the grip safety, marked "MOD.042," .312" smooth trigger, not cataloged. 1992

NIB	Exc	VG	Good	Fair	Poor
450	350	275	225	175	100

Product Code:

103792 2" B RB 92 15.8 oz.

MODEL 43: The 1955 .22/.32 KIT GUN AIRWEIGHT:

Cal-.22 Long Rifle, alloy frame and alloy cylinder, J alloy target frame, 3-1/2" barrel with rare 2" versions known to exist, square butt, 1/10" serrated ramp front sight, micrometer click rear sight, 3-screw frame, 6-shot, blue or nickel finish, narrow top rib with a pinned barrel, walnut grips, counterbored cylinder, flat latch thumbpiece, smooth backstrap, not "Airweight" marked. Also found chambered in .22 MRF in limited production w/nickel or blue finish with 2" barrel.

Original serial number range 5000-135465 in the 1953 Kit Gun series 1954-1974

NIB	Exc	VG	Good	Fair	Poor
375	300	250	175	135	85

Changes:

43	1957	Stamping of model number
	1966	Change thumbpiece
	1969	Begin "M" serial prefix @ M1

MODEL 44:

See Autoloaders

Model 42

Model 43

Model 45s

MODEL 45: THE .22 MILITARY & POLICE (Post Office):

Cal-.22 Long Rifle, designated as a training gun for the U.S. Postal Service, the only K frame produced in .22 LR without target sights (other than special orders -- see the 1935 Coast Guard K-22 Outdoorsman order for example), blue finish, 6-shot, 4" pinned barrel, round blade front sight or serrated ramp w/square notch rear, serial numbered concurrently with the Model 10, 11, and 12 M&P series. Not cataloged. 1948-1978

Previously produced as the .22 M&P (Post Office)

NIB	Exc	VG	Good	Fair	Poor
700	575	450	300	250	175

Changes:

	1948	Introduction @ serial S982000
	1948-57	Serial number range C1 to C407400
	1957	Stamping of model number
45-1	1960	Change extractor rod thread
45-2	1963	Eliminate triggerguard screw, 500 mfd. approx. start of serial range @ C622641
45-2	1966	Unknown quantity mfd. C-800xxx range
45-3	1977-78	Quantity unknown, possible "2D" prefix

MODEL 46:

See Autoloaders

MODEL 47:

Experimental, also see 147A in the auto section

MODEL 48: The K-22 MASTERPIECE MAGNUM RIMFIRE:

Cal-.22 Win. Magnum Rimfire, 6-shot, K Target Magnum frame, 4", 6", or 8-3/8" barrel, blue finish, micrometer rear sight, auxiliary .22 LR cylinder and yoke also available, pinned barrel with top rib, walnut grips, .312" smooth trigger, .375" semi-target hammer, 4-screw frame, counterbored cylinder, 1/8" Patridge front sight. 1959-1986

Model 48s

NIB	Exc	VG	Good	Fair	Poor
375	275	200	160	125	80

Variations:

- 4-screw, add 25%
- Nickel models exist, not cataloged, worth premium
- 135 made in 1978 with no model markings, in C883000 s/n range

Changes:

48	1959	Begin production @ K35000
48-1	1960	Change extractor rod thread
48-2	1962	Eliminate screw in triggerguard
48-3	1968	Relocation of rear sight leaf screw
48-4	1977	Change gas ring from yoke to cylinder
	1982	Delete pinned barrel

Product Codes:

101902 4"	B SB	84-86	36 oz.
101904 6"	B SB	84-86	39 oz.
101906 8-3/8"	B SB	84-86	3 oz.

MODEL 49: The BODYGUARD:

Cal-.38 S&W Special, identical to the Model 38, except with heavier steel frame, JC frame, blue or nickel finish, round butt, flat latch, 3" barrel rare, .240" shrouded service hammer, .312" smooth trigger, serrated ramp front sight w/square notch rear. Retail $409.

Serial number range 163051-786544 in the Chiefs Special series 1959-DATE

NIB	Exc	VG	Good	Fair	Poor
350	275	210	175	135	100

Variations:

- A blue finish w/stainless cylinder version was mfd. for the Michigan Police Supply Co.

Changes:

49	1959	Introduction
	1966	Change thumbpiece
	1969	Begin "J" serial prefix @ J1
	1982	Delete pinned barrel
49-1	1988	New yoke retention system/radius stud package
49-2	1990	New sight width on frame and barrel 1/8"
	1993	Change to matte finish
	1994	Synthetic grips, change extractor

Product Codes:

102002 2"	B SG RB	84-96	20 oz.
102004 2"	N RB	84-86	

MODEL 50: The .38 CHIEFS SPECIAL TARGET:

Cal-.38 S&W Special, 2" barrel with round butt or 3" barrel with square butt, .240" service hammer, .240" serrated trigger, J Target frame, blue or nickel finish, 5-shot, pinned barrel, 2" barrel has a 1/10" high profile serrated ramp front sight, 3" barrel has a normal profile 1/10" front sight, smooth backstrap, also found with red ramp/white outline/target trigger, adjustable rear sight, random limited production. 1955-1975

Model 49 Bodyguard

NIB	Exc	VG	Good	Fair	Poor
600	500	325	250	200	125

Variations:

- In 1978, 37 were made w/ 2" barrel and square butt, s/n prefixes in 933J-936J range

Changes:

1955	100 mfd. serial number range 55050-57919
1956	14 mfd.

Model 50

36	1957	Stamping of model number 36
36	1959	198 mfd. serial range number 149811-149941
50	1965-75	Stamping of model number 50
50	1966	Change thumbpiece
50	1966	1006 mfd. serial number range 391773-392778
50	1969	Begin "J" serial prefix
50	1973	568 mfd. serial number range 930J45-936J19
36-1	1975	213 mfd. with 3" square butt with Model 36-1 stamping in a serial number range 2J3134-2J3347

MODEL 51: 1960 .22/32 KIT GUN MAGNUM RIMFIRE:

Cal-.22 Win. Magnum Rimfire, J Target Magnum frame, 3-1/2" pinned barrel, 6-shot, micrometer rear sight, blue or nickel finish, walnut grips, square butt with approx. 600 round butt mfd., counterbored cylinder, flat latch thumbpiece, 1/10" serrated ramp front sight, also found with .22 Long Rifle Aux. cylinder, bi-color w/nickel cylinders are rare.

Serial number range 52637-135465 in the 1953 Kit Gun series 1960-1974

NIB	Exc	VG	Good	Fair	Poor
450	325	250	175	125	75

Variations:

- Aux. .22 LR cylinder, add $50
- Nickel finish, add 50%
- Square butt worth 2X to 3X standard value

Changes:

51	1960	Introduction
	1966	Change thumbpiece
	1969	Begin "M" serial prefix @ M1

MODEL 52:

See Autoloaders

MODEL 53: THE .22 CENTERFIRE MAGNUM JET (C&R):

Cal-.22 Remington Jet, .22 Long Rifle, blue finish, 4", 6", or 8-3/8" barrel (5" rare), 6-shot, walnut or smooth rosewood stocks, micrometer rear sight, auxiliary .22 LR cylinder was available, shrouded extractor rod, all supplied with nickel wash-coated steel inserts to fire the .22 Long Rifle, K Target Centerfire frame, mfd. with a "switch" on the hammer to select the dual firing pins, ".22 Magnum" stamped on the barrel, counterbored cylinder, ribbed and pinned barrel, serrated backstrap, boxed with punchouts for aux. cylinder and inserts, tools optional, also found with red ramp and white outline rear sight, target hammer, target trigger also found, 1/8" Baughman Quick Draw front sight, two styles of front ramp have been noted with the 4" barrel having a ramp on ramp base, factory nickel finish is rare. Model 53-1 is not found due to extractor rod change prior to manufacture in 1960.

14,956 mfd. 1961-1974

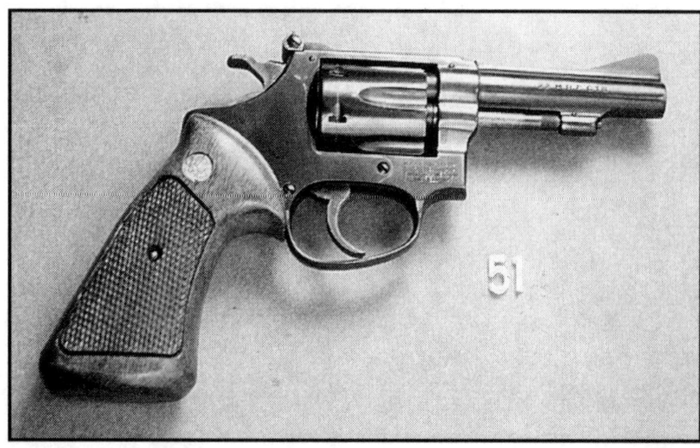

Model 51

Background: This high speed .22 centerfire cartridge and revolver were developed after conversions of the Model 17 to Wildcat .224 Harvey Kay Chuk had proven popular. However, popularity suffered when it was discovered that the chambers had to be kept scrupulously clean and dry to prevent the bottlenecked cartridges from backing out of chambers against the recoil shield when fired, tying up the revolver.

	NIB	Exc	VG	Good	Fair	Poor
4-screw	1000	750	450	350	250	200
3-screw	800	650	450	350	250	175

Variations:

- Add $150 for auxiliary .22 LR cylinder. Deduct $75 from NIB or excellent guns that do not include individual chamber inserts.

Changes:

53	1961	Introduction @ serial K429000
53-2	1962	Eliminate screw in triggerguard
	1989-90	Jet" ammunition discontinued by Remington

MODEL 54:

Experimental

MODEL 55:

Experimental

MODEL 56: KXT-38 USAF (C&R):

Cal-.38 S&W Special, K Target frame, 2" heavy barrel, target sights, non-serrated rear sight bar extends to the base of the front sight, which is a serrated ramp on a ramp base, 6-shot, blue finish, pinned barrel, walnut grips, square butt, became the basis for the Model 15-2. "U.S." marked on the smooth backstrap, this is an exception where the backstrap is smooth on a target revolver rather than serrated. Believed that most were destroyed by the government in Brunswick, GA. Four are archived in the Springfield Armory Museum N.H.S.

Serial number range K500001-K515205
15,205 mfd., most destroyed 1962-1963

NIB	Exc	VG	Good	Fair	Poor
2500	1750	1250	1000	650	300

.41 Magnum Background Information

The .41 Magnum was originally conceived as an ideal police round, offering a larger diameter bullet than a .357 Magnum without the overpenetration and heavy recoil of the .44 Magnum. After its introduction, however, the mid-velocity police loading was overshadowed by the full power magnum loading, and it never really caught on as

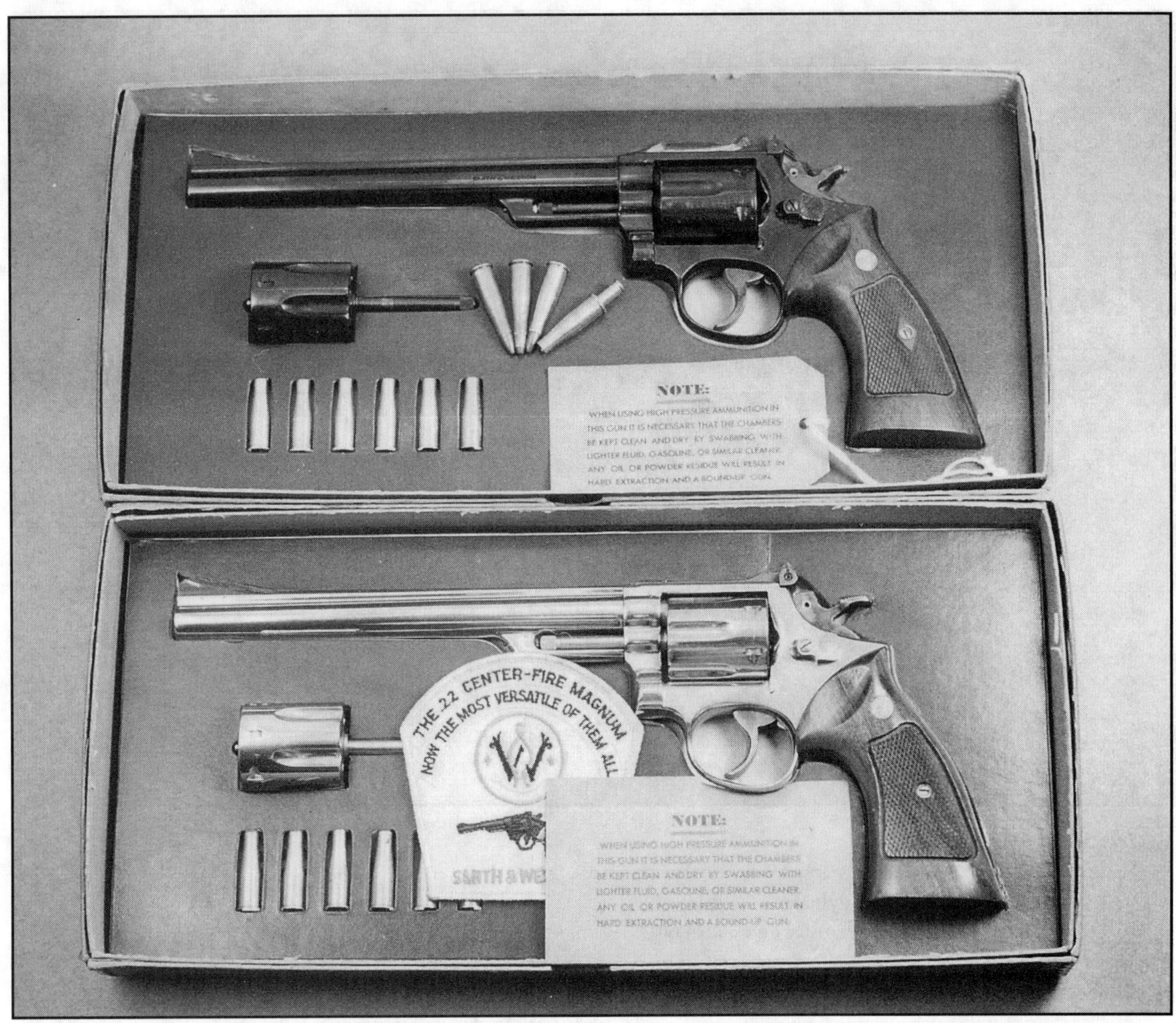

Model 53 Jet, blue and nickel, 8-3/8" barrel, in their proper box

a police round. Some handgun hunters like the round, believing it to be adequate for most medium game and easier on the shooter than the .44 Magnum.

Perhaps the .41 Magnum was just ahead of its time. The .40 S&W round comes close to the original concept (although applied to autoloaders instead of revolvers) and is making tremendous inroads in the law enforcement market.

S&W .41 Magnum revolvers include the adjustable sight Model 57 and fixed sight Model 58, along with their stainless steel counterparts, the 657 and 658.

MODEL 57: The .41 MAGNUM TARGET:

Cal-.41 Magnum, N Target frame, blue or nickel finish, 6-shot, 4", 6", or 8-3/8" barrel, micrometer rear sights, 1/8" red ramp on ramp base w/white outline rear sight, special oversize Goncalo Alves stocks, pinned barrel, shrouded extractor rod, counterbored cylinder, .500" target hammer, .400" or .500" target trigger, original "S" serial prefix.

First gun was s/n S236941 1963-1993

NIB	Exc	VG	Good	Fair	Poor
450	375	300	250	185	125

Variations:

- "S" prefix s/n, add 25-75%
- "Last Cartridge": See Twelve Revolvers in "Commemoratives and Specials" section

Changes:

57	1964	Introduction @ S227750
	1969	Change to "N" serial prefix @ S333454
57-1	1982	Eliminate cylinder counterbore and pinned barrel
57-2	1988	New yoke retention system/radius stud/floating hand

Models 57 and Model 58

57-3	1990	Longer stop notch in cylinder
	1992	Delete 4" and 8-3/8" barrels, blue finish only

Product Codes:

102202 4"	B TS TT TH RR WO	84-91	44.2 oz.
102204 6"	B TS TT TH RR WO	84-93	
102206 8-3/8"	B TS TT TH RR WO	84-91	52.5 oz.
102208 4"	N TS TT TH RR WO	84-86	
102210 6"	N TS TT TH RR WO	84-86	48 oz.
101212 8-3/8"	N TS TT TH RR WO	84-86	

MODEL 58: The .41 MAGNUM MILITARY & POLICE:

Cal-.41 Magnum, 6-shot, blue or nickel finish, 4" pinned barrel, walnut Magna grips, N frame, counterbored cylinder, .260" service hammer, .312" smooth trigger, smooth backstrap, 1/8" serrated ramp front sight w/square notch rear fixed sight, non-shrouded extractor rod.

Original introduction serial number range of S256500-S260632 1964-1978

NIB	Exc	VG	Good	Fair	Poor
400	325	250	185	150	100

Changes:

58	1964	Introduction @ S256500
	1969	Change to "N" serial prefix

Stainless Steel Revolver Background Information

Before the introduction of the Model 60, revolvers were made of carbon steel (some "airweight" models with an aluminum alloy frame to reduce weight). They were either blued or, if additional corrosion resistance was desired, nickel plated. In 1965, S&W began a revolution in handgun marketing with the introduction of a stainless steel Chiefs Special. Although there was some initial resistance from traditionalists, the reduced maintenance and increased finish durability of stainless steel has since resulted in it becoming the material of choice for most handgun buyers.

The only exception to this trend right now in the S&W revolver line is in the alloy frame "airweight" models. It is reported that S&W found it impossible to match the color of the alloy frame to the stainless steel barrel and cylinder on such models as the 642 Airweight Stainless Centennial, and so discontinued the guns due to unacceptable cosmetics. Its passing has been lamented by many, who found the combination of lightweight, corrosion resistance and snag-free hammerless design to make the 642 possibly the finest "pocket" revolver ever made.

Smith & Wesson stainless steel revolvers have "6" as the first digit in their model number. In many models, the stainless model uses the carbon steel model number with a "6" in front of it (for example, the Model 29 is a carbon steel .44 Magnum while the Model 629 is the same design in stainless).

MODEL 60: The .38 CHIEFS SPECIAL STAINLESS:

Cal-.38 S&W Special, 5-shot, 2" barrel, round butt, satin finish, checkered walnut grips, 1/10" serrated ramp front sight, w/square notch rear sight, pinned barrel, J frame, .240" service hammer, .312" smooth combat trigger, first stainless steel revolver mfd. by S&W. Numbered within the Chiefs Special series to 786544 until 1969 when an "R" serial prefix was assigned. 1965-DATE

Serial number ranges 401754-401792 and 409802-410698 are a bright polished finish with a polished hammer and trigger. Retail $431-$458.

Serial number range 475001-480000 is a bright finish with case colored hammer and trigger.

Serial number range 490001-712250 is a satin finish with flash chromed trigger and hammer. However, exceptions frequently exist!

NIB	Exc	VG	Good	Fair	Poor
360	285	250	185	150	100

Specials and variations, not cataloged:

- **Model 60 Carry Comp:** Cal-.38 Special +P rated, from the S&W Performance Center w/ported barrel, dovetail front sight, 3" full lug barrel w/adj. rear sight, round butt frame w/rosewood laminate grips or pearl inlaid synthetic grip, w/blue hard case, contoured thumbpiece. Dist by Lew Horton. Product code: 170029. 300 mfd., 1993. NIB $800.
- **Model 60 w/Saudi Arabian crest:** 1976.
- **Fairfax VA Police Commemorative:** 1932-1987. 180 mfd., 1987.
- **Product Code 102305:** 2" barrel w/round butt, adj. sights. Limited production, special 1986.

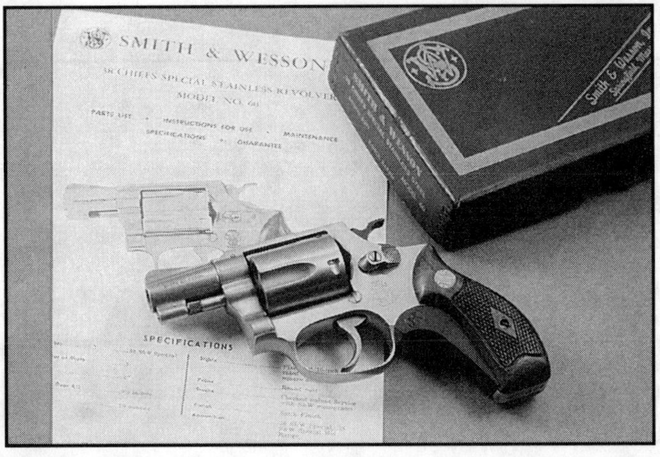

Model 60

- **Product Code 102314:** 2" barrel with double action only, synthetic grips, round butt, and bobbed hammer. 2000 mfd., 1989.
- **Product Code 102316:** 2" barrel w/round butt, unfluted cylinder, wood grips, special for Mich. Police Supply. 500 mfd., 1989.
- **Product Code 102318:** 3" barrel, double action only, synthetic grips, round butt, bobbed hammer. 2000 mfd., 1989.
- **Product Code 102320:** 3" barrel, double action only, synthetic grips, round butt, bobbed hammer. 2000 mfd., 1989.
- **Model 60-4: .38 Chiefs Special Full Lug Target:** Cal-.38 S&W special, 1990 special production w/3" full lug, pinned black front ramp sight w/black adj. rear sight, 5-shot J frame, Uncle Mike's Santoprene grips, +P rated, .375" semi-target hammer, .347" serrated trigger, became std. production in 1992. 1990-1995. Product code: 102298, 24.5 oz.

Changes:

60	1965	Introduction
	1969	Begin "R" serial prefix @ R1
60-1	1972	3" SB, heavy barrel version, limited production of 171
	1982	Delete pinned barrel
	1986	Special run of this model w/adj. sight
60-2	1987	3" barrel for N.Y.C.P.D.
60-3	1988	New yoke retention system
60-4	1990	Limited production of target Model w/full underlug
60-5	1990	DA only for N.Y.C.P.D.
60-6	1990	LadySmith version
60-7	1990	New sight width, heat treated package
60-8	1990	New sight width for N.Y.C.P.D., heat treated package
	1994	Change extractor, synthetic grips

Product Codes:

102302	2"	S RB	84-95	19 oz.
102304	3"	S HB SB	88	

MODEL 60LS: The .38 LADYSMITH STAINLESS:

Cal-.38 S&W Special, 5-shot, 2" regular or 3" heavy barrel, frosted stainless finish, grips are anatomically designed for women, round butt, wood combat grips on 3", fixed sights, serrated ramp front sight w/square notch rear, J frame, .240" service hammer, .312" smooth trigger w/beveled edge, "LADYSMITH" engraved on the frame. First production with a hard plastic case, 1992 with a softside Bob Allen case. Retail $461. 1989-DATE

NIB	Exc	VG	Good	Fair	Poor
360	285	250	185	150	100

Changes:

60-6	1992	Discontinue 3" barrel
	1994	Rosewood laminate grips
60-7	1994	Change extractor

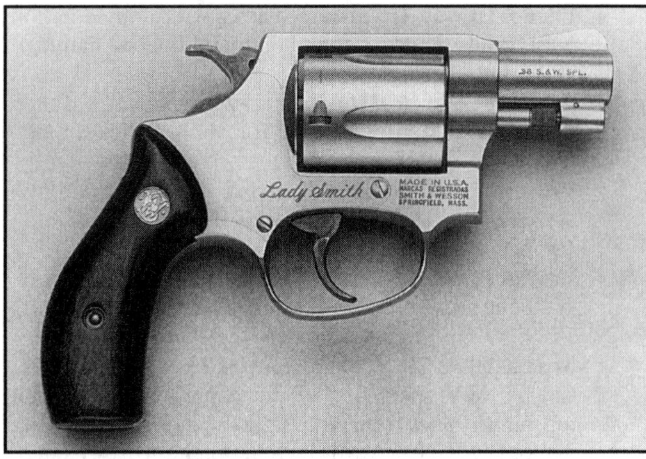

LadySmith Model 60LS

Product Codes:

102310 2"	S LS w/case	89-91	20 oz.
102309 3"	HB S LS w/case	89-91	23 oz.
102290 2"	S LS w/soft case	92-94	
102324 2"	S LS w/o case	91	
102322 3"	HB S LS w/o case	91	

MODEL 61: POCKET ESCORT:

See Autoloaders

MODEL 62:

Experimental

MODEL 63: 1977 .22/32 KIT GUN STAINLESS:

Cal-.22 Long Rifle, 4" pinned barrel, red ramp on ramp base, black stainless adj. rear sight, 6-shot, square butt with checkered walnut grips, JT frame, .312" smooth combat trigger, .375" semi-target hammer. First 100 units were a pilot lot, s/n's M101699-101798. Full production began at M103577. Retail $458-$462. 1977-DATE

NIB	Exc	VG	Good	Fair	Poor
365	285	210	175	150	100

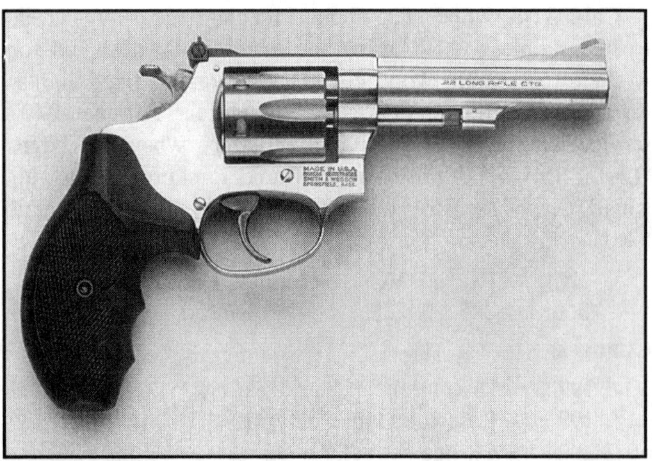

Model 63

Variations:

- 5" barrel known to exist. Worth premium.

Changes:

63	1977	Introduction of "M" serial prefix @ M99999
63-1	1982	Delete pinned barrel
63-2	1989	Special for Lew Horton 2" barrel, Hogue grips
63-3	1989	New yoke retention system/radius stud package
	1991	Introduce 2" round butt – special production, 1000 mfd.
	1992	2" barrel with round butt became std. production
	1994	Uncle Mike's grips, change extractor

Product Codes:

102402 4"	S SB RR	84-86	24.5 oz.
102404 4"	S SB RR	87-96	
102405 2"	S RB RR	89	Special 500 mfd./Lew Horton
104000 2"	S RB RR	91-96	22 oz.

MODEL 64: The .38 MILITARY & POLICE STAINLESS:

Cal-.38 S&W Special, the stainless version of the Model 10, 2" standard barrel with round butt, 3" or 4" heavy barrel with square butt, 6-shot, 1/8" serrated ramp front sight w/square notch rear, K frame, walnut service stocks, .265" service hammer, .312" smooth combat trigger. Early variations chambered in .357 Magnum to become the Model 65. Retail $415-$425. 1970-DATE

NIB	Exc	VG	Good	Fair	Poor
350	270	200	160	125	100

Variations:

- Oklahoma Highway Patrol Commemorative: Model 64-1, 750 made in 1973

Changes:

64	1970	Introduction w/tapered barrel
64-1	1972	4" heavy barrel introduction, made for Oklahoma Highway Patrol, became Model 65
64-2	1977	2" std. barrel, change gas ring from yoke to cylinder
64-3	1977	Heavy barrel gas ring change, introduce 4" barrel

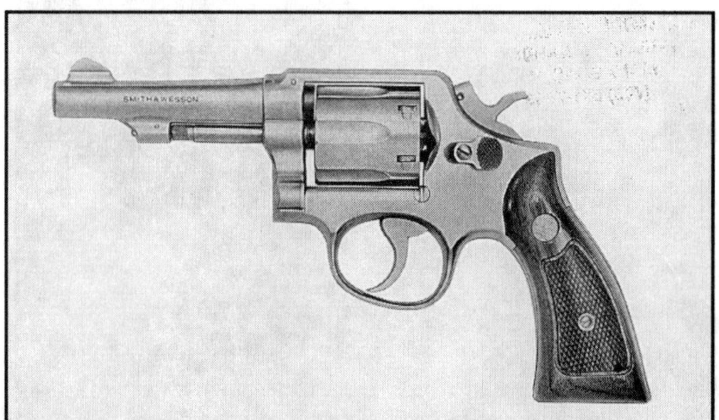

Model 64

	1982	Delete pinned barrel
64-4	1988	New yoke retention system/radius stud package
64-5	1988	New yoke retention system on heavy barrel 3" and 4"
	1991	3" heavy barrel standard
	1994	Change extractor, synthetic grips

Product Codes:

102501 2"	DA S RB	87-93 in various lots	
	Special for N.Y.C.P.D., bobbed hammer, matte finish, laser etched		
102502 2"	S RB	84-96	28 oz.
102504 3"	HB S RB	84-96	30.5 oz.
102506 4"	HB S SB	84-96	34 oz.
102602 4"	S SB	93	33.5 oz. special

MODEL 65: The .357 MILITARY & POLICE HEAVY BARREL STAINLESS:

Cal-.357 Magnum, stainless version of the Model 13 without extractor shroud, 3" heavy barrel with round butt or 4" heavy barrel with square butt, .312" combat trigger, .265" service hammer, K frame, 6-shot, counterbored cylinder, pinned barrel, 1/8" serrated ramp front w/square notch rear sight, original "D" serial prefix. Retail $427. 1972-DATE

NIB	Exc	VG	Good	Fair	Poor
350	270	210	175	150	100

Variations:

- **(Model 65) .357 Magnum "F Comp":** Cal-.357 Magnum, 3" full lug barrel w/compensator, dovetailed tritium front night sight w/dot, tuned action, round butt w/rubber grips, counterbored cylinder, contoured cylinder latch, from the S&W performance center. Dist by Lew Horton. Product code: 170024. Approx. 300 mfd., 1993. NIB $800.

Changes:

65-1	1972	Year of introduction
65-2	1977	Change gas ring from yoke to cylinder
65-3	1982	Eliminate cylinder counterbore and pinned barrel
65-4	1988	New yoke retention system - 4" square butt
65-5	1988	New yoke retention system - 3" round butt
	1994	Change extractor , synthetic grips

Product Codes:

102602 3"	HB S RB	84-96	31 oz.
102604 4"	HB S SB	84-96	34 oz.

MODEL 65LS: The .357 LADYSMITH:

Cal-.357 Magnum, K frame, round butt with rosewood laminate grips, .312" smooth combat trigger w/bevel edge, .265" service hammer, serrated ramp front sight w/square notch rear, 3" barrel with shrouded extractor rod, 6-shot, frosted stainless finish, burgundy w/silver Bob Allen softcase and cleaning kit, "LadySmith" laser engraved. Retail $427. 1992-DATE

NIB	Exc	VG	Good	Fair	Poor
360	275	210	175	150	100

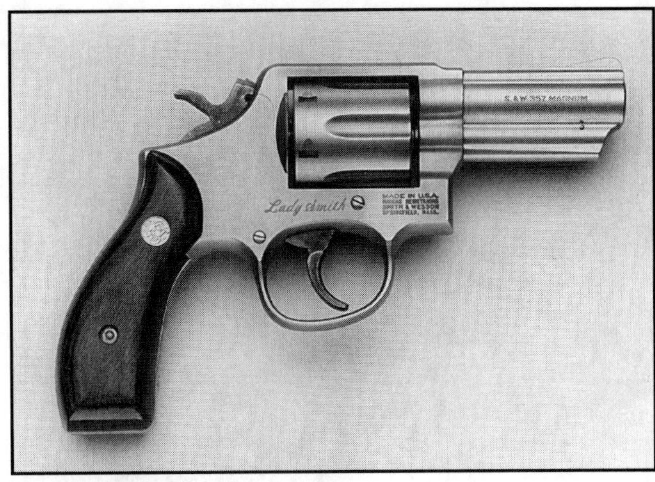

LadySmith Model 65LS

Changes:

65-5	1994	Change Extractor

Product Code:

102608 3"	S RB GB w/soft case	92-96	31 oz.

MODEL 66: The .357 COMBAT MAGNUM STAINLESS:

Cal-.357 Magnum, stainless version of the Model 19, 2-1/2" barrel with round butt, 4" or 6" barrel with square butt, adjustable white outline rear sight, first production models found with stainless rear sight, target, .400" target, .312" smooth combat or .265" service triggers, .375" semi or .500" target hammer, target stocks, 1/8" serrated red ramp front sight, counterbored cylinder, KT frame, 6-shot, shrouded extractor rod, pinned barrel with rib. Retail $466-$471. 1970-DATE

NIB	Exc	VG	Good	Fair	Poor
375	285	210	175	150	100

Variations:

- Group made in 1970s with 6-1/8" barrels (Note: The nominal 6" barrel is actually closer to 5-7/8"). Worth 20% premium.
- **Treasury Dept:** 2-1/2", stamped w/Treas. Dept. seal, special s/n.
- **Arizona Highway Patrol:** Cal-.357 Magnum, fifty-year commemorative seal on sideplate, 1931-1981. Numbered AHP xxx, 1981.
- **Bureau of Alcohol Tobacco and Firearms:** Cal-.357 Magnum, 4" barrel. 1,012 mfd.
- **Chicago Police:** Cal-.357 Magnum, 4" barrel, 125th year, presentation cased.
- **Dallas Police Department:** 1881-1981. Cal-.357 Magnum, 6", cased w/belt buckle.
- **Indiana State Police:** Cal-.357 Magnum, 4" , w/wood presentation case. 800 mfd., 1975.
- **Iowa Highway Patrol:** Cal-.357 Magnum, 66-1, 4" barrel w/wood presentation case. 250 mfd., 1982.
- **Maine Warden Commission:** Cal-.357 Magnum.
- **Missouri Highway Patrol:** Fifty years, Cal-.357 Magnum, 4" barrel, cased with Bowie knife and badge. 900 mfd., 1981. $450.

Model 65 and Model 66s

- **Minnesota State Patrol:** Cal-.357 Magnum, 4" barrel. 450 mfd.
- **Montana Highway Patrol:** Cal-.357 Magnum, 66-1, 4" barrel, belt buckle, 44 years of service. 213 mfd., 1979.
- **Montana Fish and Game:** 130 issue guns in 1975, s/n range 6K93186-93320, seal on sideplate, stamped MFG001-MFG130.
- **Naval Investigative Service:** (C&R) Cal-.357 Magnum, 4" barrel, red ramp, white outline, numbered x of 333 on frame, N.I.S. Special Agent Badge etched on the sideplate, cherrywood case, "Naval Investigative Service" in script on right barrel, sold only to N.I.S. personnel through a normal dealer channel. Special order # 8078. Product code: 102705. 333 mfd., 1988.
- **Oklahoma City Police Department Commemorative:** 782 w/4" barrel made in 1979.
- **Rhode Island State Police Issue Handgun:** Marked "RISP."
- **Shreveport Police Department Issue Handgun**: Marked "SPD."
- **South Carolina Highway Patrol:** Cal-.357 Magnum.
- **Tulsa Police:** Cal-.357 Magnum.
- **U.S. Border Patrol:** (C&R) Cal-.357 Magnum, 50th Anniversary, border patrol badge etched on the frame. "USBP" serial prefix, 3138 mfd., 1976.
- **Virginia State Police Commemorative:** 4" barrel, 1500 mfd., 1982.
- **"Critical Moment":** See Twelve Revolvers in "Commemoratives and Specials" section.

Changes:

66	1970	Introduction @ serial K949100
	1974	Introduce 2-1/2" with round butt
66-1	1977	Change of gas ring from yoke to cylinder
	1978	Introduce 6" barrel
66-2	1982	Eliminate cylinder counterbore and pinned barrel
	1985	Special production of 3" barrel for Ashland Arms, 5000 mfd., "ALU" serial prefix
66-3	1986	New yoke retention system/radius stud package
	1988	Special 3" full lug version, with full-length extractor rod
	1994	Uncle Mike's grips on 2-1/2"
66-4	1994	Change rear sight, drill and tap, Hogue grips, change extractor

Product Codes:

102702 2-1/2	S RB RR	84-93	30.5 oz.
102703 2-1/2	S RB RR WO SG	84-96	
102705 4"	S TS RR	84-93	36 oz.
102706 4"	S TS RR WO	84-96	
102707 4"	S TS TT TH RR WO	84-91	
102709 6"	S TS RR	84-96	39 oz.
102710 6"	TS RR WO	84-91	
101711 6"	TS TT TH RR WO	84-92	
102712 3"	FL RR	special 1988	

MODEL 67: The .38 COMBAT MASTERPIECE STAINLESS:

Cal-.38 S&W Special, stainless version of the Model 15, 4" barrel, stainless adj. rear sight, 6-shot, KT frame, pinned barrel with rib, red ramp front sight on ramp base, walnut stocks, non-shrouded extractor, .375" semi-target hammer, .312" smooth combat trigger. Retail $467. 1972-DATE

NIB	Exc	VG	Good	Fair	Poor
360	275	210	175	150	100

Changes:

67	1972	Introduction
67-1	1977	Change gas ring from yoke to cylinder
	1982	Delete pinned barrel
67-2	1988	New yoke retention system/radius stud package
67-3	1994	Change extractor, drill and tap, Hogue grips, change rear sight

Product Code:

102802 4"	S SB RR	84-96	32 oz.

MODEL 68: .38 CALIFORNIA HIGHWAY PATROL:

Cal-.38 S&W Special, rated +P+, 6-shot, 6" pinned and ribbed barrel, black stainless target sights, red ramp front sight, walnut grips with speedloader cutouts, KT frame, shrouded extractor rod, square butt, .275" service trigger, .375" service hammer, mfd. for the California Highway Patrol and later for the L.A.P.D. in 1983. "CHP" stamped on frame, overstamped "OHB" when sold. Produced when the Cal. Hwy. Patrol was not permitted to carry .357 Magnum sidearms. Identical in appearance to a Model 66 except the barrel is stamped ".38 Special." "K" serial prefix. 1976 and 1983

NIB	Exc	VG	Good	Fair	Poor
750	600	450	250	200	150

Variations:

- **Model 68: California Highway Patrol Commemorative:** Cal-.38 Special, a limited edition version of the CHP Model 68 offered in May 1984, engraved with the CHP "Winged Wheel" on the sideplate, with "California Highway Patrol" engraved on the barrel, with belt buckle, laser engraved walnut presentation case, 1984.

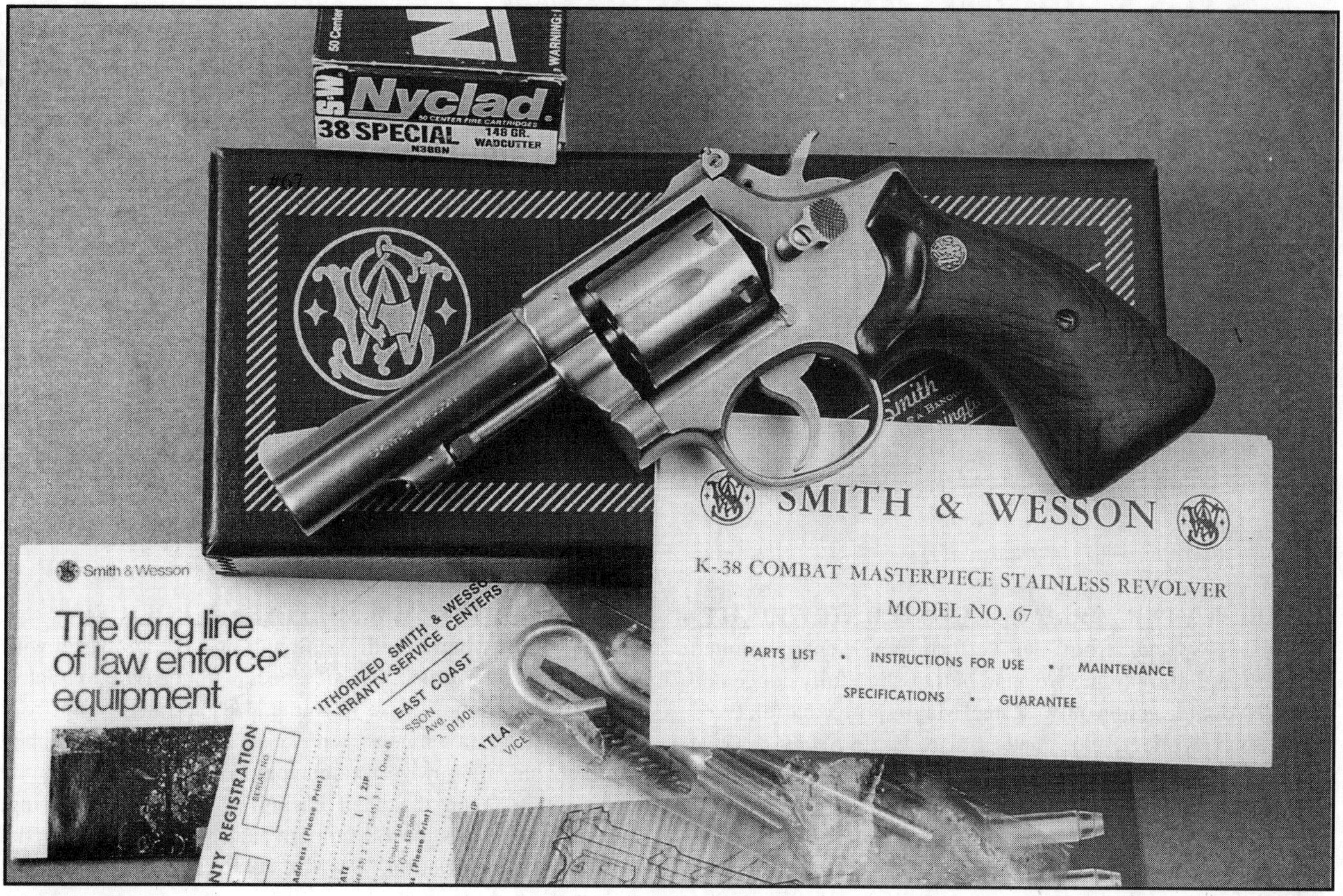

Model 67

Changes:

68-1	Example not yet found or observed
68-2	Eliminate pinned barrel, w/three-letter prefix

MODEL 69:

Experimental

MODEL 442: CENTENNIAL AIRWEIGHT:

Cal-.38 S&W Special, 5-shot, 2" barrel, concealed hammer, alloy frame, steel barrel and cylinder, double action only, Uncle Mike's grips, .312" smooth trigger, matte blue or satin nickel finish, serrated ramp front sight w/square notch rear sight, early 1993 production is "Airweight" marked on the barrel with later production markings deleted, and 1994 production is laser inscribed on the sideplate, shipped with Uncle Mike's "boot grip," successor to the Model 042. Retail $427-$442.

1993-DATE

NIB	Exc	VG	Good	Fair	Poor
365	275	210	175	150	100

Changes:

442 1994 Change extractor

Product Codes:

102810	2"	B DA SG GB RB	93-96	15.8 oz.
102812	2"	N DA SG GB RB	93-95	

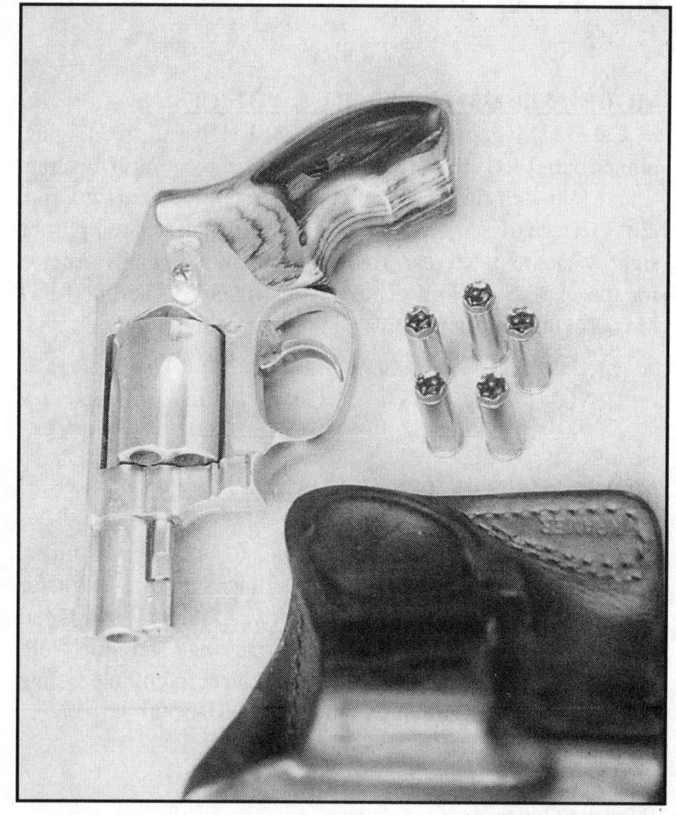

Model 442

Model 460

Model 520

MODEL 460: PERFORMANCE CENTER AIRWEIGHT:

Cal-.38 Special from the Performance Center, limited production, J alloy frame w/round butt, 5-shot, fully concealed hammer, double action only, 2" steel Magna ported barrel, fixed sight, steel cylinder, blue matte finish, Eagle Secret Service grips, .312" smooth trigger, Performance Center logo laser etched on sideplate, does not have the standard S&W trademark on the frame, shipped in a Performance Center blue plastic case, approx. Weight 15.8 oz. NIB $580.

SDE 0xxx serial prefix 450 mfd. 1994

Product Code:

170055

MODEL 520: .357 MILITARY & POLICE:

Cal-.357 Magnum, N frame, blue finish, 4" barrel, fixed sights, pinned barrel and counterbored cylinder, flat blue finish topstrap, square butt with checkered walnut grips, shrouded extractor rod, .265" service trigger, .265" service hammer, serrated ramp front sight w/square notch rear, smooth backstrap, originally ordered for the N.Y. State Police but never delivered. The only .357 Magnum mfd. on an N frame without target sights. 40 oz.

"N" serial prefix 3,000 mfd. 1980

NIB	Exc	VG	Good	Fair	Poor
400	325	230	185	160	100

MODEL 544: THE TEXAS WAGON TRAIN COMMEMORATIVE (C&R):

Cal-.44-40, N Target frame, 5" barrel, 6-shot, target hammer, target trigger, red ramp and white outline, shrouded extractor rod, top rib, smooth Goncalo Alves stocks, basswood presentation case with Texas etched markings and blue cloth lined, marked "1836 Texas 1986" on barrel to commemorate the Texas Sesquicentennial (150 years). NIB $500.

Serial number range TWT001-TWT7800

7,800 mfd. 1986

Product Code:

103195

MODEL 547: The 9 MM MILITARY & POLICE:

Cal-9mm, 3" barrel with round butt or 4" heavy barrel with square butt, blue finish, 6-shot, special finger type extractor, fixed sights, walnut grips, K frame, 1/8" serrated ramp front sight w/square notch rear, with a short throw semi-bobbed hammer, has a cartridge retainer pin on the frame above the firing pin to keep the shell casing in place during firing, non-shrouded extractor rod, smooth backstrap, successor to the Model 19 9mm variation. "9MM CTG PAT 4127955" marked on barrel's right side.

Original "6D" serial prefix 1980-1985

NIB	Exc	VG	Good	Fair	Poor
425	300	225	175	150	100

Changes:

547 1982 Begin AAF serial prefix and delete pinned barrel

Product Codes:

103202 3"	HB B RB	84-85
103204 4"	HB B SB	84-85

L Frame Revolver Background Information

The K frame .357 Magnums became immensely popular as police revolvers. However, some felt that extensive firing of full power .357 ammunition in the relatively light framed guns was wearing on both gun and shooter. There appeared to be a demand for a .357 that handled like a K frame but offered the heft and durability of an N frame. The L frame was introduced as this compromise size, and quickly established itself in the law enforcement and hunting markets. L frames also generally feature a full-

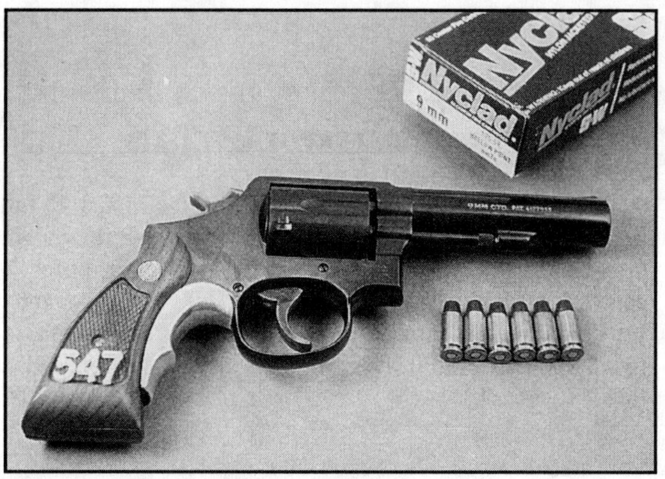

Model 547 9mm

length under-barrel lug, which adds recoil absorbing weight to the gun. The under-barrel lug has since been offered as a special feature on selected models in other frame sizes.

The L frame models are the 580s and 680s—carbon steel 581 fixed sight and 586 adjustable sight, with the stainless counterparts being the 681 and 686.

MODEL 581: The .357 DISTINGUISHED SERVICE MAGNUM:

Cal-.357 Magnum, blue or nickel finish, L frame, 6-shot, 4" full lug barrel, square butt, .312" smooth trigger, .265" service hammer, serrated ramp front sight w/square notch rear, checkered walnut stocks, smooth backstrap. 1981-1988

NIB	Exc	VG	Good	Fair	Poor
350	275	210	175	150	100

Variations:

- Model 581 chambered in .38 Special for the New York Transit Authority

Changes:

581	1981	Begin production @ AAD2120 serial prefix
581-1	1986	Radius stud package, floating hand
581-2	1987	New hammer nose and associated parts
581-M	1987	Product warning by S&W: "M" overstamped to signify a modification by the factory or warranty station for Models 581 and 581-1 to install a new hammer nose
581-3	1988	New yoke retention system

Product Codes:

103402 4"	B SB	84-86	38 oz.
103404 4"	N SB	4-86	
103405 4"	B SB	87	

MODEL 586: The .357 DISTINGUISHED COMBAT MAGNUM:

Cal-.357 Magnum, blue or nickel finish, 6-shot, L Target frame, 4", 6", or 8-3/8" full lug barrel, red ramp front sight, white outline rear sight, .375" semi-target hammer, .400" target trigger or .312" smooth trigger on 4" and 6" barrel, adjustable four-position front sight available on 6" and 8-3/8" barrel, checkered Goncalo Alves stocks on a square butt frame w/serrated backstrap. Retail $461-$466. 1981-DATE

Model 581

NIB	Exc	VG	Good	Fair	Poor
380	300	250	185	150	100

Variations:

- **Nebraska State Patrol 50th Anniversary:** Blue finish w/gold inlay, walnut case, w/patrol emblem. 364 mfd.
- **Missouri Conservation Corps:** Case and belt buckle, 250 mfd., 1987.
- **Model 586:** 2-1/2" AS, RB wood grips w/finger grooves, not cataloged.
- **Model 586 Overseas Contract:** This model w/2-1/2", 4", and 6" barrels chambered in .38 Spl is known to exist.
- **National Police Revolver Championship Commemorative:** 6" barrel, blue with gold etching, 1983.
- **Massachusetts State Police Commemorative:** Acid etched badge, s/n MSP000-MSP631, 120th commemorative year. 631 mfd., 1986.
- **Pennsylvania Game Commission Commemorative:** 2500 mfd.

Changes:

586	1981	Introduction @ AAD9030 serial prefix

Model 586

586-1	1986	Radius stud package, floating hand
586-2	1987	Change hammer nose and associated parts
586-M	1987	Product warning by S&W: "M" overstamped to signify a modification by the factory or warranty station for Models 586 and 586-1
586-3	1988	New yoke retention system
	1992	Delete 8-3/8" barrel and four-position front sight
	1992	Delete nickel finish
586-4	1994	Drill and tap, synthetic grips, change rear sight, change extractor

Product Codes:

103500 2-1/2"	B RR	93	
103502 4"	B TS RR	84-86	41 oz.
103503 4"	B TS RR WO	84-86	
103505 6"	B TS LP	84-86	46 oz.
103506 6"	B TS RR	84-86	
103507 6"	B TS HP	84-86	
103508 6"	B TS RR WO	84-86	
103509 8-3/8"	B TS TT LP	84-86	53 oz.
103510 8-3/8"	B TS TT RR WO	84-86	
103512 4"	N TS RR	84-86	
103513 4"	N TS RR WO	84-86	
103514 6"	N TS RR	84-86	
103515 6"	N TS RR WO	84-86	
103526 6"	B TS AF	86	
103528 8-3/8"	B TS TT AF	86	
103533 4"	B TS RR	87-94	
103534 4"	B TS RR WO	87-96	
103535 6"	B TS RR	87-94	
103536 6"	B TS RR WO	87-96	
103537 6"	B TS AF	87-91	
103538 8-3/8"	B TS TT RR WO	87-91	
103539 8-3/8"	B TS TT AF	87	
103540 4"	N TS RR	87-91	
103541 4"	N TS RR WO	87-91	
103542 6"	N TS RR	87-91	
103543 6"	N TS RR WO	87-91	
103544 4"	B TS RR WO Special		
103545 6"	RR WO Pach Grip		
103591 4"	SG Glass Bead, 2500 mfd., Special Production 1989		
103592 6"	SG Glass Bead, 2500 mfd., Special Production 1989		
103593 8-3/8"	Scope Mount, Glass Bead, 1000 mfd., Special 1989		

MODEL 610: 10MM STAINLESS:

Cal-10mm Auto, 5-1/2" or 6" full lug barrel with rib, combat wood grips, .400" smooth target trigger, .500" target hammer, round butt, adj. rear sights, pinned serrated black ramp, 6-shot, supplied with half moon clips, N Target frame, not cataloged.
Limited production of 5,000 1990-1991

NIB	Exc	VG	Good	Fair	Poor
575	475	400	325	250	150

Product Codes:

103578 5"	FL	90-91	42.5 oz.
103576 6-1/2"	FL	90-91	45 oz.

MODEL 617: K-22 MASTERPIECE STAINLESS FULL LUG:

Cal-.22 Long Rifle, stainless version of the Model 17 full lug. 6-shot, 4", 6", or 8-3/8" full lug ribbed barrel, straight backstrap grip, .312" smooth combat or .400" serrated trigger, combat wood grips, .375" semi-target or .500" target hammer, KT frame, pinned Patridge front sight, 4" and 6" variations also found without the full lug in limited production from 1991. Retail $ 460-$501. 1990-DATE

NIB	Exc	VG	Good	Fair	Poor
385	300	250	200	150	100

Changes:

617-1 1994 Change rear sight, drill and tap, change extractor, synthetic grips

Product Codes:

100563 4"	S CS SB CT ST	91	Special no-lug
100564 4"	S CS SB CT ST FL	90-96	42 oz.
100565 6"	S CS SB CT ST	91	41.5oz Special no-lug
100566 6"	S CS SB CT ST FL	90-94	48 oz.

Model 617

Model 617, without full lug barrel

Model 624

100567 6"	S CS SB TT TH	91	Special no-lug
100568 6"	S CS SB TH TT FL	90-96	48 oz.
100570 8-3/8"	S CS SB TH TT FL	90-96	54 oz.

Non-full lug barrels mfd. for Ashland Shooting Supplies

MODEL 624: The MODEL of 1985 .44 TARGET STAINLESS:

Cal-.44 S&W Special, 6-shot, 4" or 6-1/2" barrel, NT frame, .400" semi or .500" full target hammer, .312" smooth combat or .400" serrated trigger, pinned black ramp on ramp base w/adj. rear sight, twenty-five special editions were full factory class A engraved w/gold bead front sight and factory certificate.

NIB	Exc	VG	Good	Fair	Poor
420	350	275	200	180	150

Variations:

- 624-2 Lew Horton Special: 3" barrel with round butt, includes special fitted holster, combat grips, 7,000 mfd., 1986-1987

Changes:

624	1984	Introduction
624-1	1988	New yoke retention system/radius stud/floating hand
624-2	1990	Longer stop notch in cylinder

Product Codes:

103581 4"	84-87	41.5 oz.
103582 6-1/2"	84-87	43 oz.

MODEL 625-2: The MODEL of 1989 .45 STAINLESS:

Cal-.45 ACP, 6-shot, original introduction w/5" full lug barrel, later production w/3" and 4" barrel, round butt with Pachmayr SK/GR grips, N Target frame, pinned serrated black ramp on ramp base front sight, adj. rear sight, .400" semi-target hammer, .312" smooth combat trigger, with half moon clips, non-glare glass beaded finish. Retail $597. 1989-DATE

NIB	Exc	VG	Good	Fair	Poor
510	465	375	275	175	150

Variations:

- **Model 625-4 Springfield Armory Bicentennial Edition:** Cal-.45 ACP, special production from the Performance Center for Lew Horton Dist. A specially designed commemorative for the "Arsenal of Democracy," the Springfield Armory N.H.S., Springfield, MA. Stainless steel w/4" barrel, in mountain revolver size w/gold etched bicentennial logo on the sideplate and "Arms for the Nation" etched on the barrel. 500 mfd. w/special serial number, SAC serial prefix. Product code: 100931, 1994.

Changes:

	1988	1500 marked "Model of 1988"
	1989	1500 marked "Model of 1989"
625-2	1989	Marked "Bowling Pin 88" – 5" full lug, 2500 mfd.
625-3	1990	Longer stop notch in cylinder
625-5	1991	"625 Classic" in .45 Long Colt, 5", 1500 mfd.
	1992	Discontinue 3" and 4" barrel
625-6	1994	Change rear sight, drill and tap, change extractor, Hogue grips

Product Codes:

100921 5"	S RB FL PG GB Marked 1988 5,000 mfd.	89	45 oz.
100923 3"	S RB FL PG GB Marked 1989 4,340 mfd.	89	41 oz.
100925 4"	S RB FL PG GB Marked 1989 4,770 mfd.	89	43 oz.
100927 5"	S RB FL PG GB Marked 1989 1,500 mfd.	89	45 oz.
100927	original production which became standard	89-96	45 oz.
100930 5"	S RB FL PG GB IFS .45LC 1,500 mfd.	93	51 oz.
100931 4"	S RB FL PG GB .45ACP special: Arms for the Nation		

MODEL 627: The .357 MAGNUM STAINLESS:

Cal-.357 Magnum, special edition stainless steel version of the Model 27. Full lug 5-1/2" barrel, unfluted cylinder, 6-shot, red ramp front sight, .500" target hammer, .400" smooth target trigger, round butt with Goncalo Alves combat wood grips, finely checkered topstrap and rib, curved backstrap, "Model of 1989" marked on barrel, black stainless adj. rear sight.

BEK serial prefix 4,500 mfd. Special Edition 1989

NIB	Exc	VG	Good	Fair	Poor
500	400	300	250	180	150

Product Code:

101024 5-1/2"	FL S	50 oz.

MODEL 629: The .44 MAGNUM STAINLESS:

Cal-.44 Magnum, N Target frame, stainless version of the Model 29, pinned and ribbed barrel, counterbored cylinder, .500" target hammer, .400" smooth combat trigger, red ramp w/white outline, 100 pre-production units had a special serial number range of N629062-N629200 until May 1980 when production began @ N748564 with a 6" barrel. 5" barrels are rare. The first available production Model 629, serial N629156, was sold at auction on Feb. 10, 1979 for $80,000.00. This was extensively custom engraved and highlighted w/gold inlays. Proceeds went to the U.S. Olympic Committee. Retail $587-$606. 1978-DATE

Model 625-4, Springfield Armory Bicentennial edition (Photo courtesy Lew Horton Distributing Co.)

NIB	Exc	VG	Good	Fair	Poor
500	425	385	325	275	200

Changes:

629	1978	Introduction @ N748564
	1981	Introduce 4" and 8-3/8" barrels
629-1	1982	Eliminate cylinder counterbore and pin barrel
629-1	1986-87	8,000 mfd. with round butt and 3" barrel, distributed by Lew Horton and S&W
629-2	1988	Various internal changes, integral scope mounts available on 8-3/8" barrels
629-2E	1989	Transitional changes, hardened yoke/frame
629-3	1990	Longer stop notch, bolt block added, fixed hand
629-4	1994	Change rear sight, drill and tap, change extractor, Hogue grips

Product Codes:

103603 4"	S TS CT TH RR WO	84-96	44 oz.
103606 6"	S TS CT TH RR WO	84-96	47 oz.
103609 8-3/8"	S TS CT TH RR WO	84-96	51.5 oz.

MODEL 629: The .44 CLASSIC STAINLESS:

Cal-.44 Magnum, full lug 5", 6-1/2", or 8-3/8" barrel, 6-shot, interchangeable front sight, white outline rear sight, .500" target hammer, .400" target trigger, Hogue conversion square butt grips on a round butt frame, N Target frame,

Model 629

chamfered cylinder, drilled and tapped topstrap for scope mounting, lasersmith engraved, shipped w/red ramp front sight. Retail $62 -$650. 1990-DATE

NIB	Exc	VG	Good	Fair	Poor
525	435	400	335	275	200

Changes:

629-3 1990 Introduction
629-4 1994 Change rear sight, change extractor

Product Codes:

103636 5"	S FL SB IFS SG WO DT	91-96	51 oz.
103638 6-1/2"	S FL SB IFS SG WO DT	91-96	52 oz.
103640 8-3/8"	S FL SB IFS SG WO DT	91-96	54 oz.

MODEL 629: The .44 CLASSIC DX STAINLESS:

Cal-.44 Magnum, all of the features of the above Classic with five front sights including: black ramp, red ramp, post w/white dot, gold bead, and four black Patridge sights for 50, 100, 150 and 200 meters, w/white outline rear blade and shipped with an extra wood combat grip, 6-1/2" or 8-3/8" barrel, proof target provided with group under 1-1/2" @ 50 yds. Retail $811-$838. 1991-DATE

NIB	Exc	VG	Good	Fair	Poor
650	500	435	350	300	200

Changes:

629-3 1992 5" barrel introduced
1993 5" discontinued
629-4 1994 Change rear sight, change extractor

Product Codes:

103642 5"	S FL IFS SG WO DT	92	51 oz.
103644 6-1/2"	S FL IFS SG WO DT	91-95	52 oz.
103646 8-3/8"	S FL IFS SG WO DT	91-95	54 oz.

MODEL 629-3: The MAGNA CLASSIC STAINLESS:

Cal-.44 Magnum, also see Model 29 Magna Classic, run of 1200, .400" serrated trigger, .500" target hammer, 7-1/2" full lug barrel, "1 of 3000" marked on barrel, eight front sights included in a cherrywood case w/black leather sight box, white outline rear sight blade, fluted cylinder, N Target frame, round butt. 1990

Product Code:

103632

NIB	Exc	VG	Good	Fair	Poor
900	750	600	400	325	200

Variations:

- **Model 629-1 Stainless Combat Magnum:** 3" barrel, special run of 5,000 for Lew Horton, adj. rear and WO RR front sight, smooth combat trigger, semi-target hammer, ANCxxxx serial prefix, 1985. Product code: 103610.

NIB	Exc	VG	Good	Fair	Poor
500	400	335	300	250	200

- **Model 629-1: The .44 Magnum Classic Hunter:** Cal-.44 Magnum, NT frame, 6-shot unfluted cylinder, 6" full lug barrel, .500" target hammer, .400" smooth combat trigger, pinned black ramp front sight, white outline rear sight, Hogue soft rubber combat grips on a square butt frame (five mfd. with an adjustable front sight), AVZ serial prefix. Product Code: 103616. 5,000 mfd., 1988. NIB $535.

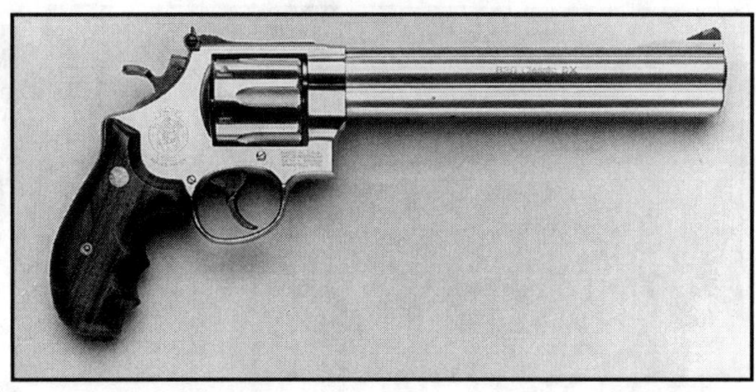

Model 629 Classic DX

- **Model 629-2 Mountain Revolver:** 4" barrel, chamfered cyl., lightweight barrel, round butt. Product Code: 103652. 4/89. NIB $550.
- **Model 629: 7-1/2" Full Lug:** Unfluted and counterbored cylinder, bolowood monogrips by Hogue, for Accusport. Product Code: 103649. 750 mfd., 6/89. NIB $650.
- **Model 629: 8-3/8" Classic Hunter:** Full lug, unfluted cylinder, Hogue grips, special production. Product Code: 103628. 2500 mfd., 8/89. NIB $525, Exc $450.
- **Model 629: 3" Classic Hunter:** Full lug, Pachmayr SKGR grip, unfluted cylinder, .500 target hammer, .400" smooth combat trigger. Product Code: 103650. 3200 mfd., 9/89. NIB $475, Exc $425.
- **Model 629-3: Classic Hunter Reintroduction:** Cal-.44 Magnum, same as above reintroduced with a production run of 2000, 1991. Product Code: 103618. NIB $500, Exc $400.
- **Model 629 w/Scope Mount:** 8-3/8" barrel, with factory barrel broaching to accommodate S&W scope mounting system, .500" target hammer, .400" serrated target trigger, red ramp front sight, w/white outline rear sight, two scope rings and two mounting bases included. Product Code: 103615. 1989. NIB -- mixed reports, $750 to $500 – more info needed.
- **Model 629 w/6" Adj. Front Sight:** Full lug, for European Arms for export. Product Code: 103596. 500 mfd., 3/90. NIB $750, Exc $675.
- **Model 629-3 Classic Hunter I**: Fluted cyl., Lew Horton. Product Code 170008. 1992. NIB $1250, Exc $1000.
- **Model 629-3: The Classic Hunter II:** From the S&W Performance Center for Lew Horton. Unfluted cylinder. Product code: 170046. 600 mfd., 1992. NIB $1250, Exc $1000.
- **Model 629-3: Magnum Carry Comp Stainless:** 3" barrel with integral compensator, dovetailed interchangeable red ramp front sight, fixed rear sight,

Model 629 Performance Center Lew Horton Quadra Port (Photo courtesy Lew Horton Distributing Co.)

beveled cylinder, .375" semi-target hammer, .312" smooth combat trigger, N frame, round butt with Goncalo Alves grips with finger grooves, contoured thumbpiece, from the S&W Performance Center for Lew Horton. 42 oz. Product code: 170012. Ltd. production, 1992. NIB $1000, Exc $925.

- **Model 629:** 3" barrel, .400" semi-target hammer, .312" smooth combat trigger, red ramp on ramp base front sight, w/white outline rear sight, Goncalo Alves smooth wood combat grips. Product code: 103610. 5,000 mfd. NIB $475, Exc $400.
- **Model 629 Magna Classic overrun:** 7-1/2", 306 mfd., 4/1992. NIB $650, Exc $610.
- **Model 629 1993 Mountain Gun:** 4" tapered barrel, chamfered cylinder, .400" semi-target hammer, .312" smooth combat trigger, Hogue rubber monogrip, drilled and tapped, round butt, lightweight barrel. Product code: 103653. 1993. NIB $500, Exc $450.
- **Model 629-3: Carry Comp II:** Cal-.44 Magnum, fully adj. rear sight, slightly different front sight, compensator system, and an unfluted Classic Hunter style cylinder, 3" barrel, w/hard case, 100 mfd. for Lew Horton, 1993. NIB $1000, Exc $925.
- **Model 629 Backpacker:** 3" barrel, N target frame w/round butt, drilled and tapped, chamfered cylinder, .400" semi-target hammer, .312" smooth combat trigger, satin stainless finish, Hogue rubber grip, red ramp on ramp base, white outline rear sight. Product Code: 130450. 4/1994. NIB $700.
- **Model 629-4: .44 Magnum Light Hunter:** From the Performance Center, 6" Magna ported slabside barrel**,** non-fluted cylinder, round butt, w/scope broaching, recessed crown, trigger stop. Product Code: 170056. Serial number range RSR3500 -RSR4000, 500 mfd. for RSR Dist., 5/1995. Two additional variations made for Lew Horton. NIB $1250.
- **Magna port Stalker:** 8-3/8", SSK rib; inverted crown; 2X Leupold scope, Magna ported, sling and swivels, through Magnum Sales, Ltd.
- **"Mountain Lion":** See Twelve Revolvers in "Commemoratives and Specials" section.

Published Product Codes of the Model 629:

103596 6"	For European Arms	90
103603 4"	Std. Production	84-94
103606 6"	Std. Production	84-94
103609 8 3/8"	Std. Production	84-94
103610 3"	Special	
103615 8 3/8"	Scope Mount	89
103616 6"	Classic Hunter	88
103618 6"	Classic Hunter	91
103628 8 3/8"	Classic Hunter	89
103632 7-1/2"	Magna Classic	90
103636 5"	Classic	91-94

103638 6		
103640 8 3/8"	Classic	91-94
103642 5"	Classic DX	92
103644 6"	Classic DX	91-94
103646 8 3/8"	Classic DX	91-94
103649 7-1/2"	Unfluted	89
103650 3"	Classic Hunter	89
103652 4"	Mountain Gun	89
103653 4"	Mountain Revolver	93
130450 3"	Backpacker	94
170012 3"	Carry Comp	92
	Carry Comp II	93
170056 6"	Hunter	95

MODEL 631: .32 MAGNUM TARGET STAINLESS:

Cal-.32 H&R Magnum, J frame, 6-shot, 2" with fixed sights, or 4" barrel with adj. sights, red ramp front sight w/white outline rear sight, narrow top rib, round butt, Goncalo Alves combat stocks, .312" smooth combat trigger .240" service hammer. 631-LS "LadySmith" version, 2" barrel with rosewood stocks, laser etched, also found in black stainless, not cataloged.

Special for 1990

NIB	Exc	VG	Good	Fair	Poor
450	350	275	175	150	100

Product Codes:

103664 2"	FS	22 oz.
103662 4"	AS	25.5 oz.
103660 2"	LadySmith marked	22 oz.

MODEL 632: .32 MAGNUM CENTENNIAL AIRWEIGHT STAINLESS:

Cal-.32 H&R Magnum, alloy frame, stainless cylinder and barrel, fully concealed hammer, 6-shot, JA frame, serrated ramp front sight w/fixed notch rear sight, 2" or 3" barrels, Uncle Mike's Santoprene grips, .312" smooth combat trigger, round butt, double action only, "Airweight" marked on barrel, S&W trademark laser etched on the sideplate and stamped on left frame side.

1991-1992

NIB	Exc	VG	Good	Fair	Poor
375	300	250	185	150	100

Model 631 Target

Model 631, black stainless

Model 637

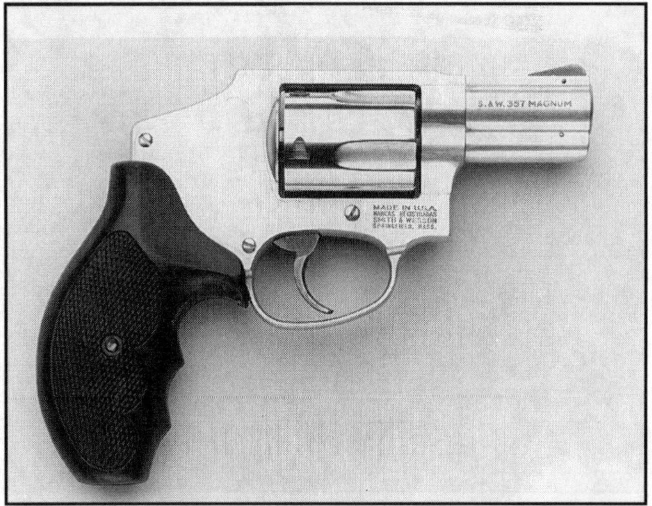

Model 640-1, new in 1995, the first J frame .357 Magnum

Changes:

1992 Discontinue 3" barrel

Product Codes:

103666 2"	S RB 91-92	15.5 oz.
103674 3"	S RB 91	17.5 oz.

MODEL 637: .38 CHIEFS SPECIAL AIRWEIGHT STAINLESS:

Cal-.38 S&W Special, 2" barrel, 5-shot, JA frame, fixed sights, clear anodized fuse alloy frame, stainless cylinder and barrel, round butt with walnut stocks, serrated front ramp, 13-1/2 oz. S&W logo laser etched on sideplate and also stamped on left side of frame, .312" smooth trigger, sideplate has a stainless steel appearance but is alloy. Not cataloged

Special production of approx. 560 Special for 1989

NIB	Exc	VG	Good	Fair	Poor
400	350	300	225	175	100

Product Code:

103790

MODEL 638: .38 BODYGUARD AIRWEIGHT STAINLESS:

Cal-.38 S&W Special, alloy frame, clear anodized fuse alloy, 2" barrel, shrouded hammer, stainless cylinder and barrel, distributed by Ellett Bros., 5-shot, JA frame, round butt, S&W trade mark laser etched on the sideplate and stamped on the frame. Special for 1989

NIB	Exc	VG	Good	Fair	Poor
375	325	285	225	175	100

Changes:

638	1989	Introduction
638-1		New 1/8" sight width on frame and barrel. ~1200 mfd.

Product Code:

103670

Model 640 Lew Horton Performance Center Carry Comp (Photo courtesy Lew Horton Distributing Co.)

Rare factory error, steel frame Model 640 w/barrel marked "Airweight"

MODEL 640: .38 CENTENNIAL STAINLESS:

Cal-.38 S&W Special, rated for +P, 2" barrel with Goncalo Alves stocks or 3" barrel with Morado wood stocks, 5-shot, J frame, round butt, fully concealed hammer, .312" smooth combat trigger, square notch rear sight with serrated ramp front sight, double action only. 1990-1995

NIB	Exc	VG	Good	Fair	Poor
360	300	250	200	150	100

Variations:

- **Model 640 Special: Carry Comp:** Cal-.38 Special +P rated, from the S&W Performance Center, mfd. for Lew Horton w/ported 2" barrel, adj. front sight, fixed rear sight, radiused hammer and trigger, 150 mfd. w/rosewood grips and 150 mfd. w/Bader mother-of-pearl inlaid finger grips. Shipped w/blue plastic case w/Performance Center logo. 23 oz. Product Code: 170042. 1993. NIB $750.
- **Model 640 Special: The Paxton Quigley:** Cal-.38 Special, 2-5/8" barrel w/integral compensator, dovetailed adj. front sight, tuned by the S&W Performance Center, laminated wood grips are stylized with mother-of-pearl inlaid heart. Boyt tapestry case and letter of authenticity from Paxton Quigley, author of "Armed & Female." Limited production of 150. Dist by Lew Horton, 1994. NIB $725.

Changes:

1993	Discontinue 3"
1994	Uncle Mike's boot grip, change extractor

Product Codes:

103796 2"	S	90-94	21 oz.
103794 3"	S	91-92	22.5 oz.
103795 3"	S		"Airweight" special

MODEL 640-1 .357 CENTENNIAL STAINLESS:

Cal-.357 Magnum, introduced in 1995, the first 5-shot .357 handgun on a small J frame. This is a slightly larger frame than a standard J with a reinforced cylinder stop, 2-1/8" barrel, round butt, concealed hammer, pinned black ramp front sight, smooth trigger, Uncle Mike's boot grip, blue plastic case, 25 oz.

NIB	Exc	VG	Good	Fair	Poor
425	385	325	250	175	100

Product Code:

103690 95-96

MODEL 642: .38 CENTENNIAL AIRWEIGHT STAINLESS:

Cal-.38 S&W Special, 2" or 3" barrel, 5-shot, fixed sight, alloy frame, stainless barrel and cylinder, Uncle Mike's grips, serrated ramp front sight w/square notch rear sight, JA frame, fully concealed hammer, .312" smooth combat trigger, round butt, double action only, logo stamped on frame and laser etched on the sideplate. 1990-1992

NIB	Exc	VG	Good	Fair	Poor
450	375	300	225	175	125

Changes:

642 1992 Discontinue 3" barrel

Product Codes:

104790 2"	S 91-92	15.8 oz.
104798 3"	S 91	17.5 oz.

MODEL 648: .22 MAGNUM RIMFIRE STAINLESS:

Cal-.22 Win. Magnum Rimfire, 6" full lug barrel, combat wood grip on a square butt, KT frame, pinned black Patridge front sight on a ramp base, 6-shot, .312" smooth combat trigger, .375" semi-target hammer, serrated backstrap, cataloged 1992. 1989-1994

NIB	Exc	VG	Good	Fair	Poor
350	300	250	175	150	100

Changes:

648-1 1994 Change rear sight, change extractor, drill and tap, Hogue grips

Product Code:

103668 6"	S FL	89-94	47 oz.

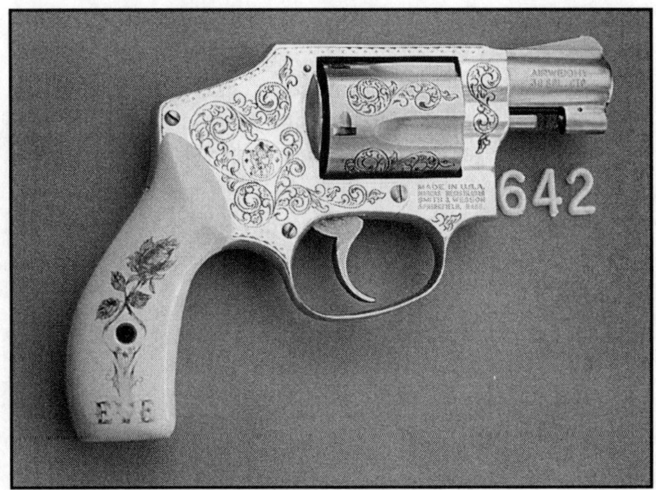

Model 642

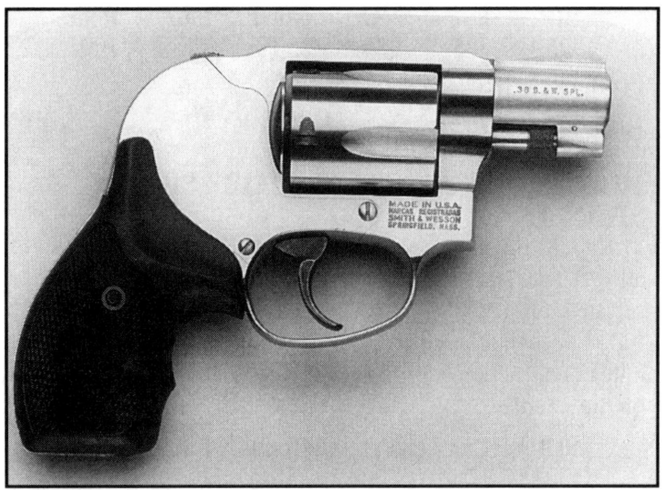

Model 649

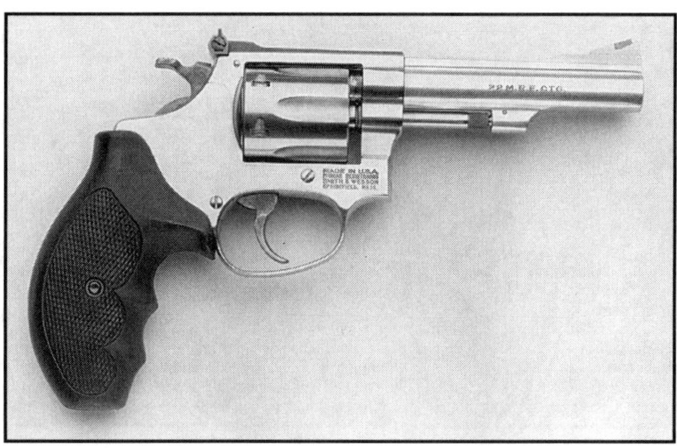

Model 651

MODEL 649: .38 BODYGUARD STAINLESS:

Cal-.38 S&W Special, stainless version of Model 49, 2" barrel, 5-shot, serrated ramp front sight w/square notch rear, shrouded hammer, .312" smooth trigger, .240" service hammer, round butt, JC frame. Retail $469. 1985-DATE

NIB	Exc	VG	Good	Fair	Poor
370	300	250	200	150	100

Variations:

- 1985: 100 marked "Model 649/1985/Limited Edition." Product code: 103750.

Changes:

649	1985	Introduction
649-1	1988	New yoke retention system/radius stud package
649-2	1990	Heat treated package, wider sight width
	1994	Change extractor, synthetic grip

Product Codes:

103750	Introductory run		
103751 2"	S RB	85-96	20 oz.

MODEL 650: .22 M.R.F. SERVICE KIT GUN STAINLESS:

Cal-.22 Win. Magnum Rimfire, 3" heavy barrel, J frame, fixed sights, 6-shot, .240" service hammer, .312" smooth combat trigger, serrated ramp front sight w/square notch rear, round butt, also found with aux. .22 LR cylinder. 1983-1987

NIB	Exc	VG	Good	Fair	Poor
425	350	250	200	150	100

Changes:

650	1983	Introduction
650-1	1988	New yoke retention system

Product Code:

103802 3"	HB S RB	84-87	23 oz.

MODEL 651: .22 M.R.F. TARGET KIT GUN STAINLESS:

Cal-.22 Win. Magnum Rimfire, 4" barrel, black adj. rear sight, w/red ramp front sight, JT frame, 6-shot, square butt, walnut service stocks, .375" semi-target hammer, .312" smooth combat trigger, also offered w/aux. .22 Long Rifle cylinder. Retail $460. 1983-1988 and 1991-DATE

NIB	Exc	VG	Good	Fair	Poor
400	350	250	200	150	100

Changes:

651	1983	Introduction
651-1	1988	New yoke retention system
	1991	Production run of 2500
	1992	Reintroduction
	1994	Change extractor, Uncle Mike's grips

Product Code:

103902 4"	S SB RR	84-96	24.5 oz.

MODEL 657: The .41 MAGNUM STAINLESS:

Cal-.41 Magnum, 6-shot, .500" target hammer, .400" smooth combat trigger, serrated black ramp on ramp base front sight, 4", 6", or 8-3/8" barrel, shrouded extractor rod, adjustable rear sight with white outline, checkered Goncalo Alves stocks, N Target frame. Retail $528. 1986-DATE

NIB	Exc	VG	Good	Fair	Poor
425	385	325	250	185	150

Variations:

- **Model 657: The .41 Magnum Classic Hunter Stainless:** Cal-.41 Magnum, 6-1/2" full lug barrel, N Target frame, Hogue grips, 6-shot unfluted cylinder, .500" target hammer, .400" smooth combat trigger, black pinned ramp on ramp base front sight, adj. rear sight w/white outline, Hogue grips on square butt, 52.5 oz. Product code: 103820. Run of 2,000, special for 1991. Dist. by Lew Horton. $500.
- **Model 657: Magnum Hunter for RSR:** Cal-.41 Magnum, 6" Magna ported barrel, w/weaver scope mount, non-fluted cylinder, .500" smooth target hammer polished and chromed, .312" smooth trigger, millet front red ramp drift adj. for windage, adj. rear sight, Hogue grips, satin finish, ball bearing lockup, chamfered charge holes, adj. trigger stop, 48 oz. Product code: 170062. Special serial number range, 500 mfd., 1995. NIB $800.

Model 657 Performance Center Classic Hunter for Lew Horton (Photo courtesy Lew Horton Distributing Co.)

- **657 Light Hunter:** 6" slabside unfluted ported w/ weaver mount. $800.

Changes:

657	1986	Introduction
	1988	Discontinue 4" barrel
657-1	1988	New yoke retention system/radius stud/floating hand
657-2	1990	Longer stop notch in cylinder
	1993	Discontinue 8-3/8" barrel
657-3	1994	Change rear sight, drill and tap, change extractor, Hogue grips

Model 657

Product Codes:

103952	4"	S TS CT TH	86-87	44.2 oz.
103953	6"	S TS CT TH	86-95	48 oz.
103954	8-3/8	S TS CT TH	86-92	52.5 oz.
170062	6"	Ported, unfluted	95	48 oz.

MODEL 681: The .357 DISTINGUISHED SERVICE MAGNUM STAINLESS:

Cal-.357 Magnum, L frame, 6-shot, 4" full lug ribbed barrel, fixed sights with serrated front ramp, square notch rear sight, .265" service hammer, .312" smooth combat trigger, square butt, stainless version of the Model 581.

Begin production @ serial AAE 3887 1981-1992

NIB	Exc	VG	Good	Fair	Poor
360	300	250	200	160	120

Changes:

681-1	1986	Radius stud package/floating hand

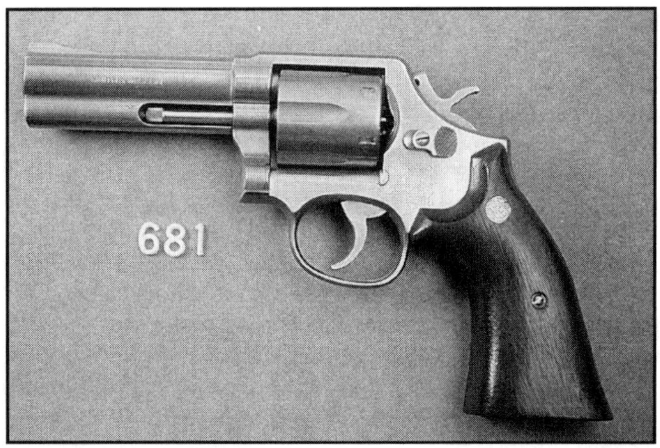

Model 681

681-M	1987	Recall by S&W and overstamped to signify a modification by the factory or warranty station, applies to 681 and 681-1 only
681-2	1987	Change hammer nose/bushing and associated parts
681-3	1988	New yoke retention system
	1992	Reintroduced

Product Codes:

104102	4"	S SB	84-86	38 oz.
104103	4"	S SB	87-92	

MODEL 686: The .357 DISTINGUISHED COMBAT MAGNUM STAINLESS:

Cal-.357 Magnum, stainless version of the Model 586, L frame, 4", 6", or 8-3/8" full lug barrel, target sights, 6-shot, square butt, .375" semi-target hammer, .312" smooth combat trigger or .400" serrated target trigger, red ramp on ramp base or four-position front sight, w/white outline rear blade, checkered Goncalo Alves grips. Retail $481-$515.

1980-DATE

NIB	Exc	VG	Good	Fair	Poor
400	325	275	225	185	125

Variations:

- Adjustable front sight worth premium.
- **Lew Horton:** 2-1/2" barrel.
- **Product Code 104228:** 3" barrel w/round butt, mfd. for U.S. Customs, pinned black front ramp; marked CS-1 above model marking, dull gray bead blast finish, 1988.
- **Product Code 104229:** 4" barrel w/round butt, mfd. for U.S. Customs, pinned black front ramp, see above, 1988.
- **Product Code 104248:** 6" barrel, finished in "Black Stainless," 2500 mfd., 1988.
- **Product Code 104249:** Classic Hunter w/unfluted cylinder, 6" barrel, .375" semi-target hammer, .312 smooth combat trigger, white outline rear sight, Hogue combat grip, 5000 mfd., 1988.
- **Product Code 104250:** 4" barrel, finished in "Black Stainless," 2500 mfd., 1988.
- **Product Code 104251:** 8-3/8" barrel broached w/scope mount, 1100 mfd., 1989.

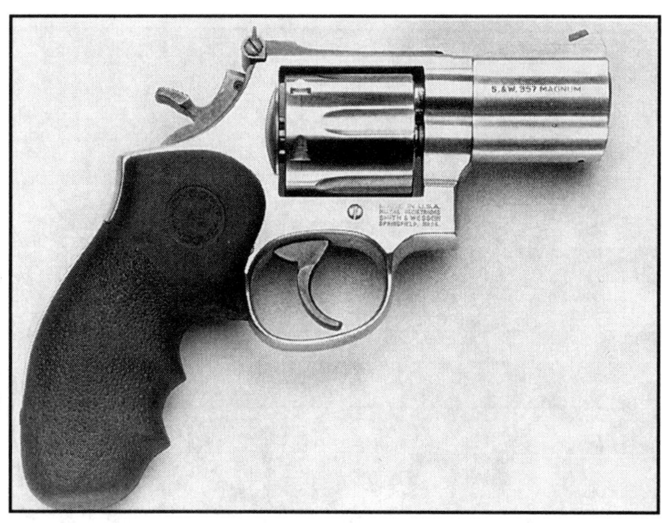

Model 686

- **Product Code 104254:** 5" barrel, mfd. for Bill Davis, dual speed loader cutouts, unfluted cylinder, 500 mfd., 1989.
- **Model 686 Mag Comp:** Cal-.357 Magnum, from the S&W Performance Center for Lew Horton Dist., integral barrel compensator, dovetailed adjustable front red ramp sight, radiused full lug barrel, white outline rear sight, radiused hammer, radiused combat trigger, Uncle Mike's grips, 3" barrel, special serial range, Performance Center logo, contoured thumbpiece, trigger over-travel stop, full-length extractor rod, 350 mfd., 1992.
- **Model 686 Carry Comp:** Cal-.357 Magnum, 4" barrel w/integral compensator, dovetailed front sight w/interchangeable post or red ramp, white outline rear sight, Uncle Mike's grips, from the Performance Center for Lew Horton Dist. NIB $1000.
- **Model 686 PPC Revolver:** Cal-.357 Magnum, 6" barrel w/custom underlug, integral barrel port, from the Performance Center.
- **Model 686 Carry Comp:** Cal-.357 Magnum, 6" barrel w/integral port, replaceable front sight, Hogue grips, .375" semi-target hammer, .312" smooth combat trigger, full underlug contour, from the Performance Center. Product codes: 170009 6" S; 170021 6" S; 170015 6" S RB.
- **Model 686 Competitor:** Cal-.357 Magnum, 6" barrel w/integral scope base and 6 ounce variable underweight, dovetailed front post, black blade rear sight, Hogue grips, fluted cylinder w/radiused charge holes, .375" semi-target hammer, .312" smooth combat trigger, from the S&W Performance Center for Lew Horton. 52-58 oz. NIB $1100.
- **Model 686 Action Revolver:** Cal-.357 Magnum, 6" match grade barrel, from the Performance Center w/barrel compensator.
- **Model 686 Hunter:** Similar to the 686 Competitor w/wood grips. 200 mfd. NIB $1150.
- **Model 686 Power Port:** Cal-.357 Magnum, 6" integral ported full lug barrel, drilled and tapped, .375" semi-target hammer, .312" smooth combat trigger, pinned

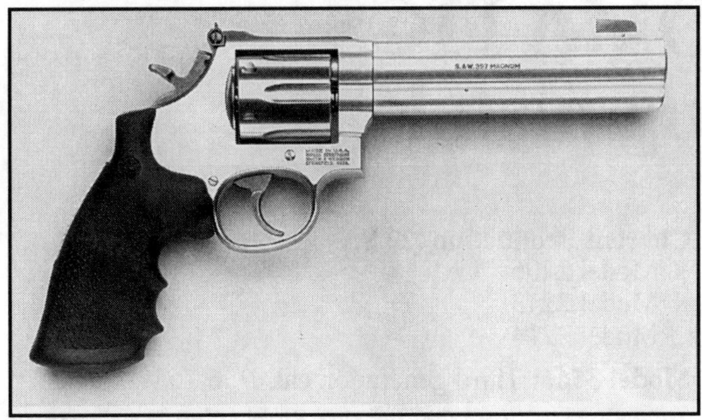

Model 686 Power Port

black Patridge front sight, black blade rear sight, 46 oz. Product code: 104272. 1994.
- **"With the Wolfhounds":** See Twelve Revolvers in "Commemoratives and Specials" section.

NOTE: As the book goes to press, S&W has just announced production of a 7-shot version of the Model 686 in .357 Magnum. As speedloaders become available, this variation should make a significant impact in the police and civilian self-defense markets.

Changes:

686	1980	Begin production @ serial AAD 4276
686-1	1986	Radius stud package/floating hand
686-M	1987	Recall by S&W and overstamped to indicate a modification by the factory or warranty station applies to the 686 and 686-1 only.
686-2	1987	Change hammer nose/bushing and associated parts
686-3	1988	New yoke retention system
	1990	2-1/2" barrel introduced
686-4	1994	Change rear sight, drill and tap, change extractor, Hogue grips
	1995	Introduce power port barrel

Product Codes:

104202	4"	S TS RR	84-86	
104203	4"	S TS RR WO	84-86	41 oz.
104215	4"	S TS AF	86	
104205	6"	S TS LP	84	46 oz.
104206	6"	S TS RR	84-86	
104207	6"	S TS HP	84	
104208	6"	S TS RR WO	84-86	
104209	8-3/8	S TS TT LP	84-86	53 oz.
104210	8-3/8	S TS TT RR WO	84-86	
104217	8-3/8	S TS TT AF	86	
104221	4"	S TS RR	87-93	
104222	4"	S TS RR WO	87-96	
104223	6"	S TS RR	87-93	
104224	6"	S TS RR WO	87-96	
104225	6"	S TS AF	87-96	
104226	8-3/8	S TS TT RR WO	87-96	
104227	8-3/8	S TS TT AF	87-91	
104231	2-1/2"	S RB CT RR	87-96	37.5 oz.
104272	6"	S SB SG CT PP PBP DT	94-95	

MODEL 940: 9MM CENTENNIAL STAINLESS:

Cal-9mm, J frame, 5-shot, 2" or 3" barrel, serrated ramp front sight w/square notch rear sight, fully concealed hammer, double action only, .312" smooth combat trigger, round butt, satin finish, Uncle Mike's Santoprene combat grips, supplied with full moon clips. Retail $474. 1991-DATE

NIB	Exc	VG	Good	Fair	Poor
370	300	250	200	160	125

Variations:

- **Model 940 Special:** Cal-.356 TSW, from the Performance Center, special for Lew Horton. Product Code: 170047. Limited production of 300, 1994. NIB $750.

Changes:

940	1993	3" discontinued
940-1	1994	Uncle Mike's boot grip, change extractor

Product Codes:

104796	2"	S RB DA	91-96	23 oz.
104260	3"	S RB DA	91-92	25 oz.

SEMIAUTOMATICS (Autoloading pistols)

Contents

6900 Series: Third Generation 9mm Compact Double Column

Model 6990
Model 6904: TDA lightweight
Model 6906: TDA lightweight stainless
Model 6924: Decocking
Model 6926: Decocking, lightweight stainless
Model 6944: DAO, lightweight
Model 6946: DAO, lightweight, stainless

SIGMA Series: Polymer frame

Model SW40F: 40 S&W
Model SW40C: 40 S&W Compact
Model SW9F: 9mm
Model SW9C: 9mm Compact
Model SW380: 380 Compact

The guns in this section are listed in order of model number.

Third Generation Action Types:

TDA: Traditional Double Action

- Safety lever decocks hammer and puts gun "on safe."
- First shot is "double action"—heavy trigger pull cocks hammer and fires gun.
- Subsequent shots are "single action"—slide action cocks hammer, light trigger pull fires gun.

Decocking

- Decocking lever decocks hammer only—does NOT act as safety.
- Otherwise operates as TDA—DA first shot, SA subsequent shots.

DAO: Double Action Only

- No safety or decocking lever.
- Every shot is "DA"—heavy trigger pull cocks hammer and fires gun.

The Smith & Wesson autoloader model numbering system: Generally, a two-digit model number is a first generation pistol, a three-digit model number is a second generation pistol, and a four-digit model number is a third generation autoloader.

Understanding Third Generation Pistol Numbers:

The first two digits indicate the caliber designator:

39 = 9mm
59 = 9mm
69 = 9mm
10 = 10mm
40 =.40 S&W
45 =.45 ACP
35 =.356 TSW

The third digit indicates the type of model:

0 = standard model
1 = compact
2 = standard with decocking lever
3 = compact with decocking lever
4 = standard with double action only
5 = compact with double action only
6 = nonstandard length barrel
7 = nonstandard length barrel with decocking lever
8 = nonstandard length barrel with double action only

The fourth digit indicates the type of material:

3 = aluminum frame with stainless slide
4 = aluminum frame with carbon slide
5 = carbon frame and slide
6 = stainless frame and slide
7 = stainless frame with carbon slide

Feature Codes for Modern Autoloaders:

Note: These codes may change from year to year in sales publications.

AA	alloy frame
AMSF	ambidextrous safety
ATS	adjustable target sights
AS	adjustable sights
B	blue finish
CB	curved backstrap grip
DA	double action only
DT	drilled and tapped
FS	fixed sights
FNS	fixed night sights
HB	heavy barrel
LS	LadySmith
MNSF	manual safety (single side)
NLMC	Novak Lo-Mount Carry fixed sight
PF	polymer frame
S	satin stainless finish
SB	straight backstrap grip
TDA	traditional double action
TS	target stocks
#SH	magazine capacity
w/	with

Note: *Published magazine capacity is stated as the firearm was manufactured. Capacity above ten rounds is for law enforcement sales only after May 1994. High capacity mags mfd. after May 1994 are so marked and not available through normal channels of trade, i.e.: non-law enforcement sales. Although stated capacity may be higher than ten rounds, only a ten-round magazine will be shipped after pre-May 1994 stock is exhausted. Therefore the collector can find a mixture of magazines (when two are supplied) in shipments 1994-95.*

Clement Design Early Pocket Semiauto Background Information

S&Ws first venture into the semiauto pistol field consisted of a design based on the Belgian-made Clement pistols. Initial production was for a S&W proprietary cartridge, the .35 S&W Auto. This was followed by a .32 ACP version. An experimental .30 caliber version was made at one time, but was not introduced as a production item. A prototype was also made in .380.

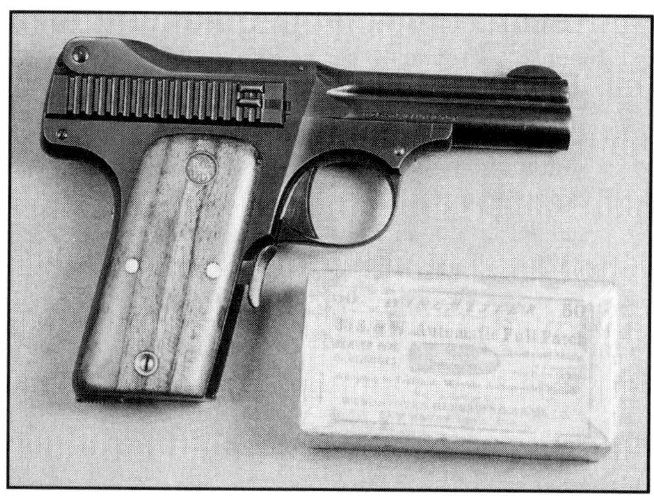

.35 Semiauto

32 SEMIAUTOMATIC PISTOL:

Cal-.32 ACP, 7-shot magazine, 3-1/2" barrel, smooth walnut grips, blue finish, improved version of the 35 automatic, barrel fixed to the frame.

Serial number range 1-957 957 mfd. 1924-1936

NIB	Exc	VG	Good	Fair	Poor
3000	2000	1500	1200	800	600

35 SEMIAUTOMATIC PISTOL (Model of 1913):

Cal-.35 S&W Auto, 7-shot magazine, 3-1/2" barrel, fixed sights, blue or nickel finish, plain walnut grips, eight variations of manufacture, grip and manual safety, no magazine disconnect safety.

Serial number range 1-8,350 8,350 mfd. 1913-1921

NIB	Exc	VG	Good	Fair	Poor
700	450	400	300	250	200

Variations:

- Add about $300 for nickel in higher condition grades
- Serial number ranges are approximate only

First Generation DA and Early .22 Model Background Information

It was nearly twenty years before S&W took another try at autoloading pistols, but when they did, they came up with a pair of classic designs.

The Model 39 is the beginning of the **First Generation** of S&W centerfire semiautos. It was the first American-made DA 9mm semiauto, and as such is the predecessor of the "Wonder-nines," which began to figure prominently in the U.S. market in the 1980s and 90s. The related Model 52 .38 Master became a prominent target pistol chambered for .38 Special wadcutters.

The .22 Target Model 41 was introduced an few years later. A totally different design than the first generation centerfires, it became the predominant American-made gun of its type.

MODEL 39: EARLY STEEL FRAME and STEEL SLIDE (C&R):

Cal- 9mm, 8-shot magazine, 4" barrel, walnut stocks, blue finish, adj. rear sight, military version becomes double action M41 without the fine finish and walnut grips. First commercial 9mm double action mfd. in the U.S.

927 mfd. 1954-1966

NIB	Exc	VG	Good	Fair	Poor
1250	950	700	600	500	300

Variations:

- **Military Purchase:** Some modified versions found without serial numbers.
- **Hush puppy:** A special version with a silencer or suppressor was used in Southeast Asia in the late 1960s. Named for one of its intended uses—silencing enemy guard dogs— it included a slide lock to fire in single-shot mode, avoiding the noise of the operating mechanism. The double column Model 59 reportedly was developed in this program.
- Add $75 for detachable dust cover.

MODEL 39-1: ALLOY FRAME and STEEL SLIDE:

Cal-9mm, double action, 8-shot mag., 4" barrel, alloy frame with steel slide, checkered walnut grips, 1/8" serrated front ramp, w/micrometer click square notch rear sight, magazine safety, 27 oz. Last M-39 shipped 2-15-83, s/n A747148. 1954-1982

NIB	Exc	VG	Good	Fair	Poor
400	350	285	250	220	150

Variations:

- **Venezuela Contract:** A small lot of M-39s were marked with the Venezuelan seal on the right slide
- **Connecticut State Police Commemorative:** 704 made in 1979, two-tone blue and nickel

Model 39 steel frame w/dust cover

Changes:

39-1	Alloy frame
39-1 1970	Begin "A" serial prefix
39-2 1971	Change extractor

MODEL 41: THE .22 RIMFIRE TARGET PISTOL:

Cal-.22 Long Rifle, match target pistol, single action, 10-shot mag., adj. rear sights, checkered walnut grips with modified thumb rest, blue finish only, 5-1/2" or 7" barrel, early version with muzzle brake on 7-3/8" barrel, 5" version may have an extended sight, early versions have a cocking indicator on the rear of the slide in the form of a small protruding pin. Patridge undercut front sight, adj. trigger stop, concealed hammer, .365" wide trigger with S&W grooving and adj. stop, action opens by swinging down the triggerguard. Accessories include: adjustable Olympic counterweights, alloy and steel weights clamped onto the barrel recess, oversize triggerguard also available. A drop-in conversion kit for .22 short was also available. At about s/n 16000 relief cuts at the rear of the triggerguard were added. At about 27500 the model number was moved from the left side of the frame to the right side. Retail $753. 1957-DATE

NIB	Exc	VG	Good	Fair	Poor
700	600	500	425	300	200

Variations:

- Premium for early guns.
- Add 15-20% for extendable front sights.

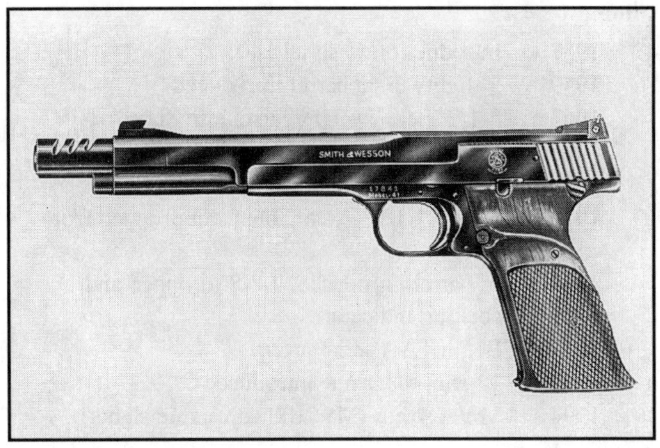

Model 41 w/muzzle brake

- Full set of steel and aluminum barrel weights worth $350-$500.
- .22 short conversion unit worth $500-$750.
- **Military Purchase:** Considered one of the world's finest target pistols and is purchased for military marksmen. Military markings have been observed. A documented military gun will bring double to 4X standard value. **Authors' note:** The "P" on the butt near the magazine well is an S&W proof, not a military mark.
- **Coast Guard:** Nineteen in 1971, s/n's in range of A130587-130623.

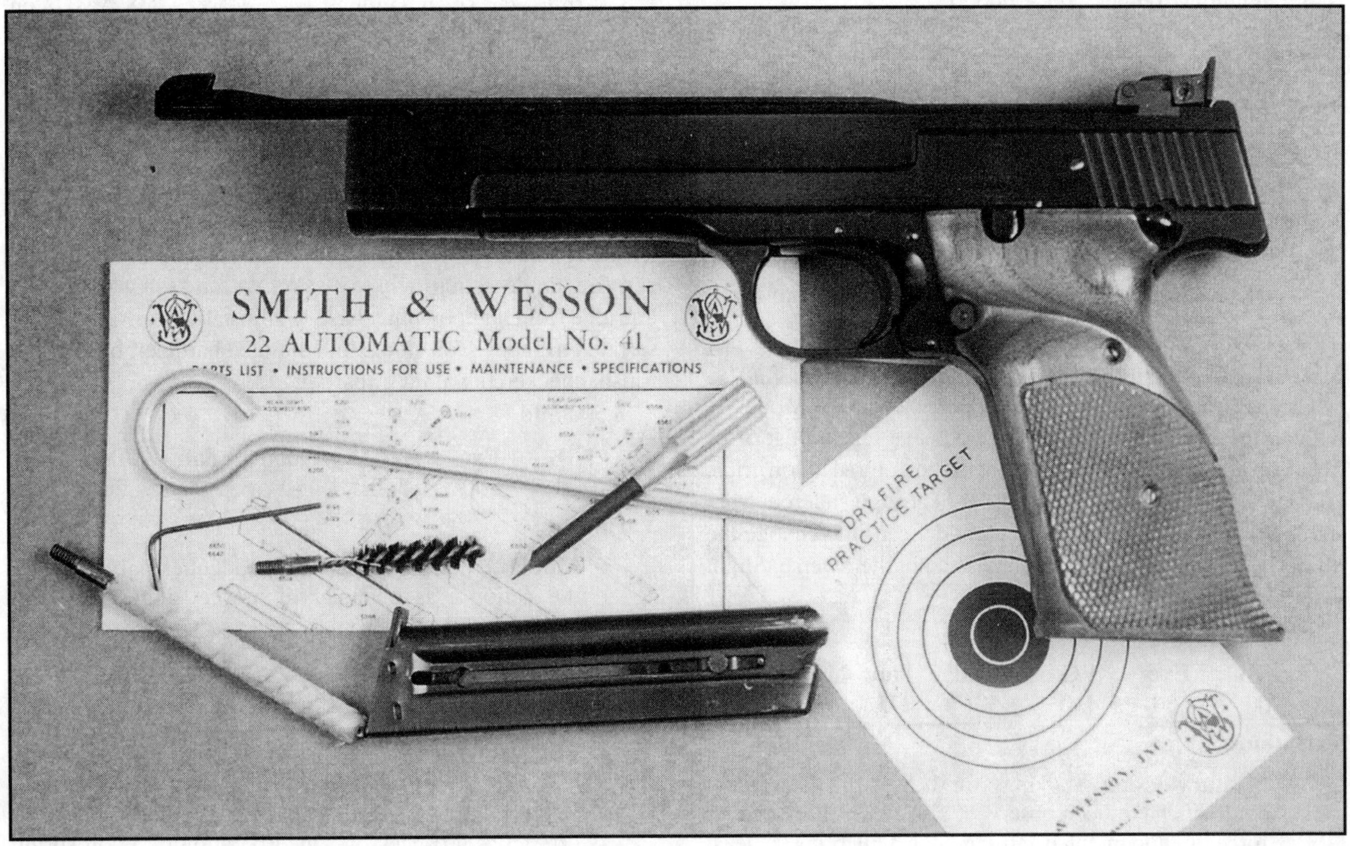

Model 41 w/extendable front sight

Changes:

41	1957	Introduction @ serial 1401
	1959	5" lightweight barrel introduced
	1963	5-1/2" heavyweight barrel introduced
	1965	5-1/2" extendable front sight introduced
	1970	Begin "A" serial prefix
	1976	5" and 5-1/2" extendable front dropped from catalog
	1978	7" barrel introduced, 7-3/8" dropped and cocking indicator
	1984	Begin TAA serial prefix
	1992	12-shot magazine introduced
	1994	Millet series (MS) 100 adjustable sights

Product Codes:

101802 5-1/2"	HB B 10SH AS	84-94	44 oz.
101804 7"	B 10SH AS	84-94	41 oz.
130500 5-1/2"	MS 12SH D&T	95-96	44 oz.
130508 7"	MS 12SH D&T	95-96	42 oz.

MODEL 41-1 (C&R):

Cal-.22 Short only, similar to the Model 41, made for international target shooting. Manufactured with a lighter spring, alloy slide, different extractor/slide stop. Five-round magazine. The "-1" model indicator is not always found with the 41 stamping. Magazine has a plug for the shorter .22 short. Guns numbered in the Model 41 s/n range. In 1986, 28 were assembled from parts on hand.

Serial number range 20000-350000

Under 1,000 mfd. 1960-1973

NIB	Exc	VG	Good	Fair	Poor
1200	1000	700	550	350	250

MODEL 44:

Cal-9mm, a single action only version of the Model 39-1. No model number stamping. Blue finish only.

10 mfd. 1958-1959

NIB	Exc	VG	Good	Fair	Poor
-----	9000	7000	5000	3000	-----

MODEL 46: .22 Rimfire target, economy model (C&R):

Cal-.22 Long Rifle, similar in appearance to the Model 41 without the fine blue finish or the extensive machining, 5" or 7" barrel, no muzzle brake or cocking indicator, red nylon grips, 10-round magazine, adj. rear sight, 1/8" Patridge undercut front sight, adjustable trigger stop. This model can interchange the Model 41 slide and barrel assembly, but not the reverse. Slight variations of this model are found.

4,000 mfd. 1959-1968

NIB	Exc	VG	Good	Fair	Poor
700	550	450	350	275	200

Variations:

- **Military Issue:** Markings for U.S. Army and Navy contracts have been observed, also was sold to the air force. A documented military gun will bring at least double standard value. **Authors' note:** As with the Model 41, the "P" on the butt near the magazine well is not a military proof mark. This is an S&W proof mark.
- 5" sport barrel, add 25%.
- 5-1/2" heavy barrel, add 25-75%.

Model 46

Changes:

46	1959	7" barrel introduced, 2500 mfd.
	1959	5" light field barrel introduced, 1000 mfd.
	1964	5-1/2" heavy barrel introduced, 500 mfd.

MODEL 52-A ("AMU") (C&R):

Cal-.38 AMU (a semi rimless .38 special ctg.). Made for the U.S. Army Marksman Training Unit. Marked "38 AMU" on the ejection port. 5" barrel, similar to the Model 39.

Serial number range 35850-35927 87 mfd. 1961-1964

NIB	Exc	VG	Good	Fair	Poor
3000	2500	2000	1200	800	500

MODEL 52: THE .38 MASTER:

Cal-.38 Special wadcutter only, similar action to the Model 39, except incorporates a set screw to lock out the double action, and fire single action only, 5" barrel with a 5-shot mag, 1/8" Patridge front sight on ramp base w/adjustable rear sight, .365" serrated trigger w/adj. stop. .260" serrated hammer, bright blue finish, checkered walnut grips.

3,500 mfd. 1961-1963

NIB	Exc	VG	Good	Fair	Poor
900	800	550	450	300	200

Variations:

- **Model 52-1:** Cal-.38 Special wadcutter only, in 1963 the action was changed to a true single action, a counterweight was now offered as an accessory, 1963-1970.

NIB	Exc	VG	Good	Fair	Poor
750	650	500	375	250	200

- **Model 52-2:** In 1971 an improved version of the Model 52, with a more efficient extractor was added. Adj. trigger stop, serrated hammer, counterweight was offered as an accessory, incorporation of a coil spring style extractor. 1971-1994.

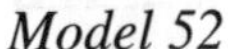

Model 52

Model 59

NIB	Exc	VG	Good	Fair	Poor
700	600	500	375	250	200

Changes:

52 1961 Introduction

Product Code:

102102 5" B 5SH AS 84-94 41.5 oz.

Model 59 Background Information

Although the Model 39 is often cited as the first American double action 9mm, the Model 59 is perhaps even more significant as possibly the first of the "Wonder-nine" breed that eventually came to play a major role in the police and defensive handgun market in the 1980s and 1990s. "Wonder-nine" is a term coined for 9mm semiauto pistols that combine the traditional double action operating method, first used on the German WWII issue Walther P-38, with the double column high capacity magazine introduced on the Browning High Power of the same era. The Model 59 was reportedly developed partly as a result of attempts to improve the Model 39 "Hush puppy" variation for Navy Seal usage. Two 13-shot stainless steel prototypes have been reported from this program.

Early Model 59s with smooth grip straps

MODEL 59:

Cal-9mm, similar to the Model 39, 14-shot mag, black nylon grips, alloy frame, w/steel slide, 100 early versions with smooth front and rear grip strap starting @ A170000, otherwise serrated front and rear grip straps, "A" serial prefix, last M-59 shipped 7/82, s/n A747407. 1971-1982

NIB	Exc	VG	Good	Fair	Poor
420	370	300	275	230	175

Variations:

- Early guns with smooth grip straps will bring double to triple standard values. Twenty believed to exist, add 150% premium.
- An experimental "Aircrewman" alloy frame 9 mm compact was reportedly made in the early 70s in a bid for an air force contract. It is unclear to the authors whether this was based on the single stack 39 or double stack 59.

MODEL 61: POCKET ESCORT:

Cal-.22 LR, 5-shot, blue or nickel finish, 2-1/8" barrel, plastic grips, semiauto, fixed ramp front sight, square notch rear, with zippered plastic case, manual safety, serial number range B1-B65438, B1-B500 and B500-B1000 were special presentation groups. 1970-1973

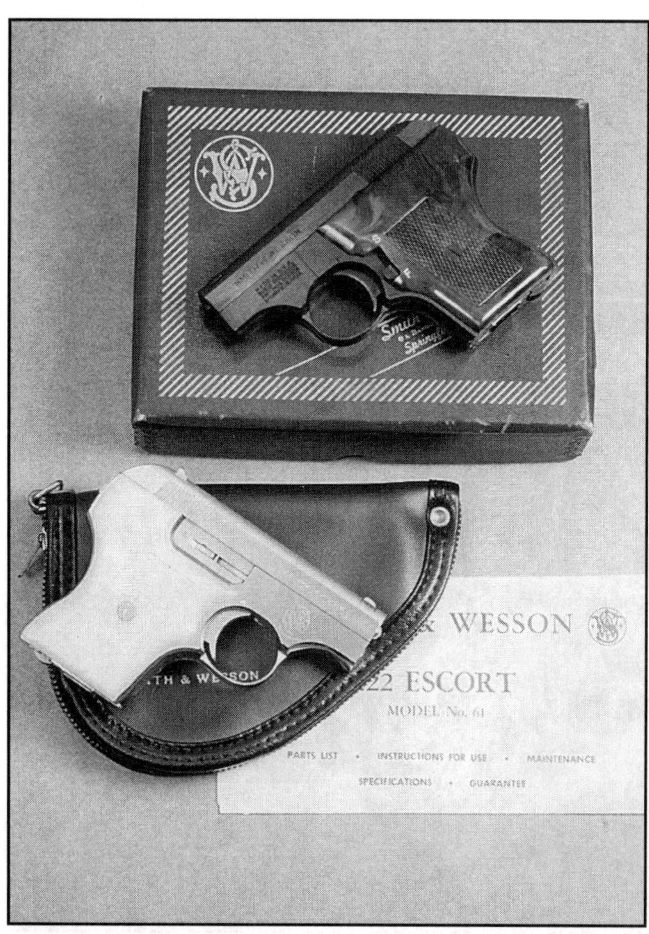

Model 61 Escorts

Model 147A

Model 411

NIB	Exc	VG	Good	Fair	Poor
250	185	140	120	80	50

Changes:

61 1970	Serial range B1001-B7800
61-1 1970	Magazine safety added, serial number range B7801-B9850
61-2 1970	Addition of barrel nut, serial number range B9851-B40000
61-3 1971	Forged aluminum frame, serial number range B40001-B65438

MODEL 147A (C&R):

Cal-9mm, 14-shot, steel frame, 4" barrel, black nylon grips, adjustable rear sight for windage only, similar to model 59. The model number stamping originally started as a model 47, and was later overstamped 147A.

112 mfd. 1979

NIB	Exc	VG	Good	Fair	Poor
1250	950	800	600	400	250

MODEL 411:

A "no-frills" third generation semiauto. Cal-.40 S&W, alloy frame, blue carbon steel slide, flat blue finish, post with white dot front sight, fixed rear sight, right hand slide mounted manual decocking lever, 4" barrel, 11-round mag., .260" serrated hammer, .304" smooth trigger, Xenoy one-piece wraparound stock with straight backstrap. Retail $525. 1992-1995

NIB	Exc	VG	Good	Fair	Poor
400	350	325	275	225	200

Product Code:

108517 4" B DL TDA 11SH FS MNSF AA 92-95 29.4 oz.

MODEL 422: .22 SINGLE ACTION FIELD:

Cal-.22 Long Rifle, single action, 4-1/2" or 6" barrel, aluminum frame with steel slide, 10-shot mag., fixed sights, black plastic grips, matte blue finish, .125" blade serrated front sight, concealed hammer, .312" serrated trigger. Serial number TAP0001 is engraved and gold inlaid, was auctioned at the SHOT Show Jan, 1987. Retail $235. 1987-DATE

NIB	Exc	VG	Good	Fair	Poor
200	175	150	125	100	60

Variations:

- Fifteen units in "First Edition" engraved by Paul Piquette, simulated ivory grips, certificate

Changes:

422	1987	Introduction w/ammo, oil and targets
	1992	12-shot magazine

Product Codes:

102821 4-1/2"	B 10SH FS AA	87-96	
102825 6"	B 10SH FS AA	87-96	
102831 4-1/2"	B FS	87-93	22 oz.
102833 6"	B FS	87-93	23 oz.

Model 422

MODEL 422: .22 SINGLE ACTION TARGET:

Cal-.22 Long Rifle, identical to 422 FIELD with adj. rear sights, checkered walnut grips, matte blue finish. Retail $290. 1987-DATE

NIB	Exc	VG	Good	Fair	Poor
225	200	175	150	120	80

Changes:

422	1987	Introduction
	1992	12-shot magazine

Product Codes:

102823 4-1/2"	B 12SH AS AA	87-96	
102827 6"	B 12SH AS AA	87-96	
102830 4-1/2"	B AS	87-93	22 oz.
102832 6"	B AS	87-93	23 oz.

Second Generation DAs, Carbon Steel or Alloy Frame

MODEL 439:

Cal-9mm, double action, 4" barrel, blue or nickel finish, alloy frame with steel slide, single column 8-shot magazine, checkered walnut grips, 1/8" serrated ramp front sight, .260" serrated hammer, .356" smooth trigger, protected adjustable rear sight for windage and elevation, fixed rear sight for windage only, with or without ambidextrous safety, 20-round mag. available. "A" serial prefix, early production models have frames w/rounded triggerguards and late models have squared triggerguards. 28.5 oz. 1979-1988

NIB	Exc	VG	Good	Fair	Poor
450	385	335	300	250	125

Changes:

1984	Change to "TAA" serial prefix from original "A" serial prefix

Model 439

Product Codes:

102902 4"	B 8SH AS	84
102903 4"	B 8SH AS AM	84-88
102904 4"	B 8SH FS	84
102905 4"	B 8SH FS AM	84-88
102907 4"	N 8SH AS	84
102908 4"	N 8SH AS AM	84-86
102909 4"	N 8SH FS	84
102910 4"	N 8SH FS AM	84-86

MODEL 449:

Cal-9mm, experimental version of Model 439, only 50 mfd. This was a factory developmental model. The Model 469 was chosen for production.

Model 459

MODEL 459:

Cal-9mm, a 14-shot double column version of the Model 439, checkered nylon stocks, second generation auto with firing pin safety, serrated ramp front sight w/adjustable rear sight for windage and elevation, fixed sight for windage only, with or without ambidextrous safety. 20-round magazine available, blue or nickel finish, .265" serrated hammer, .365" smooth trigger, early models have a rounded triggerguard, later models have a squared triggerguard. 31 oz. Original "A" serial prefix. 1979-1987

NIB	Exc	VG	Good	Fair	Poor
475	400	350	300	260	135

Variations:

- **Model 459-F.B.I. Purchase:** 803 mfd. for the F.B.I. with dull brushed blue finish and special high-impact grips.
- **Model 459-M:** Cal-9mm, a small group of Model 459s (30) were prepared for the XM-9 9mm Military Competition in 1980-81 with other manufacturers of small arms. The guns were standard commercial blue w/ambidextrous safety, nonstandard rear sight w/1-1/4" dovetail, and short extractor. The winner was the Beretta M92. About 800 were available through regular channels of trade. NIB $1000.
  * The serial numbers of the thirty trial guns are on record. One of these will command a large premium over the commercial guns.
- **Natl. Assoc. of Federally Licensed Firearms Dealers Commemorative:** 250 units mfd.

Changes:

1984 Begin "TAA" serial prefix

Product Codes:

103002 4"	B 14SH AS	84-86
103003 4"	B 14SH AS AM	84-87
103004 4"	B 14SH FS	84
103005 4"	B 14SH FS AM	84-87
103007 4"	N 14SH AS	84
103008 4"	N 14SH AS AM	84-86
103009 4"	N 14SH FS	84
103010 4"	N 14SH FS AM	84-86

MODEL 469 "MINI" and Transitional 4690:

Cal-9mm, double action, short alloy frame, 12-shot extension mag, .260" bobbed hammer, 3-1/2" barrel, sandblast blue, .365" smooth trigger, ambidextrous safety, serrated ramp with yellow bar front sight w/adjustable rear sight for windage only, three-piece pebble grain molded Delrin grip, a 20-round extension magazine was available, squared triggerguard, "A" serial prefix. 1983-1988

NIB	Exc	VG	Good	Fair	Poor
465	380	350	300	250	125

Product Codes:

103101	4690 transitional	
103102 3-1/2"	B 12SH FS	84-88
103103 3-1/2"	B 12SH FS AM	84-88
103105 3-1/2"	N 12SH FS	

MODEL 539:

Cal-9mm, double action, steel frame and steel slide version of the Model 439, 8-shot magazine, 4" barrel, blue or nickel finish, adjustable rear sight w/a short production run of a fixed sight version, short extractor, checkered walnut grips, "A" serial prefix. 1980-1983

NIB	Exc	VG	Good	Fair	Poor
400	350	300	285	200	150

MODEL 559:

Cal-9mm, double action, steel frame and steel slide version of the Model 459, 14-shot magazine, 4" barrel, blue or nickel finish, adj. rear sights, w/some production of fixed sight models, early models have short extractors, later models have long extractors. "A" serial prefix. 3,750 mfd. 1980-1983

NIB	Exc	VG	Good	Fair	Poor
465	400	350	300	250	160

Model 539

Model 559

Current Production .22s, Stainless Lightweight

MODEL 622:.22 SINGLE ACTION FIELD:

Cal-.22 Long Rifle, single action, stainless alloy finish, 4-1/2" or 6" barrel, 10-shot mag., fixed sights with black plastic grips, .250" internal hammer, .312" serrated trigger, serrated ramp w/.125" blade front sight, black colored on rear groove only, alloy frame w/stainless slide. Retail $284. 1989-DATE

NIB	Exc	VG	Good	Fair	Poor
225	200	175	150	125	80

Changes:

1992 12-shot magazine

Product Codes:

102836 4-1/2"	S 10SH FS	89-96	22 oz.
102840 6"	S 10SH FS	89-96	23 oz.

MODEL 622: .22 SINGLE ACTION TARGET:

Cal-.22 Long Rifle, identical to 622 Field except with adj. sights and checkered walnut grips. Retail $337. 1989-DATE

NIB	Exc	VG	Good	Fair	Poor
275	235	200	170	135	80

Product Codes:

102838 4-1/2"	S 10SH AS	89-96	22 oz.
102842 6"	S 10SH AS	89-96	23 oz.

Second Generation DAs, Stainless Steel

MODEL 639:

Cal-9mm, stainless steel frame and slide, 8-shot magazine, .260" serrated hammer, .365" smooth trigger, serrated ramp front sight w/fixed or adj. rear sights, 4" barrel, with or without ambidextrous safety, checkered walnut grips, "TAK" serial prefix, 20-round magazine available, rounded triggerguard on early models, squared triggerguard on later production. 36 oz. 1984-1988

NIB	Exc	VG	Good	Fair	Poor
400	350	285	220	170	135

Product Codes:

103702 4"	S 8SH AS	84
103703 4"	S 8SH AS AM	84-88
103704 4"	S 8SH FS	84
103705 4"	S 8SH FS AM	84-88

MODEL 645 and Transitional 6450:

Cal-.45 ACP, 8-shot magazine, double action, stainless steel, serrated ramp front sight w/red ramp insert w/white outline rear sight, 5" barrel, ambidextrous safety, .260" serrated hammer, .365" smooth trigger, black checkered nylon grips, first commercial production of .45 auto by S&W. Squared triggerguard, engraved pre-production model sold at auction for $67,000 for the Olympics. 37-1/2 oz.

Model 645

First production serial range TAK0001-TAK7727
1985-1988

NIB	Exc	VG	Good	Fair	Poor
500	425	380	320	275	185

Variations:

- Twenty-five "First Edition" models specially engraved

Product Codes:

103710	transitional 645 marked 6450	
103712 5"	S 8SH FS AM	85-88
103719 5"	S 8SH AS AM	

MODEL 659 and Transitional 6590:

Cal-9mm, 14-shot magazine, stainless steel frame and slide w/satin finish, fixed or adj. rear sights, 4" barrel, .260" serrated hammer, .365" smooth trigger, serrated ramp front sight, black checkered nylon grips, with or without ambidextrous safety. Twenty-round magazine available, early models have a rounded triggerguard, later models have a squared triggerguard, "A" serial prefix, 40 oz. 1982-1988

NIB	Exc	VG	Good	Fair	Poor
485	420	350	310	260	175

Changes:

1984 "TAA" serial prefix

Product Codes:

104001 4"	S 14SH FS	transitional 659 marked 6590
104002 4"	S 14SH AS	84
104003 4"	S 14SH AS AM	84-88
104004 4"	S 14SH FS	84
104005 4"	S 14SH FS AM	84-88 transitional

MODEL 669 and Transitional 6690:

Cal-9mm, smaller version of the Model 659, 3-1/2" barrel, 12-shot finger magazine or 20-round extension magazine available, stainless slide and barrel, .260" bobbed hammer, .365" smooth trigger, aluminum alloy frame, serrated ramp with red bar front sight, black pebble grain molded Delrin stocks, rear sight adjustable for windage, "TAK" serial prefix. 26 oz.
1986-1988

NIB	Exc	VG	Good	Fair	Poor
485	400	350	320	250	185

Product Codes:

104051 3-1/2"	S 12SH FS AM	86-88
104050 3-1/2"	S 12SH FS AM	

Second Generation SAs

MODEL 745: IPSC .45 SINGLE ACTION 10th ANNIVERSARY COMMEMORATIVE:

Cal-.45 ACP, single action, 5" barrel, stainless steel frame w/satin finish, with carbon steel slide, hammer and trigger in a blue finish, checkered walnut grips, 8-shot mag., serrated ramp on ramp base front sight, w/Novak Lo-Mount Carry fixed dovetailed rear sight or special adjustable rear sight, .260" serrated hammer, .365" serrated trigger w/adjustable stop, also found with and without "IPSC 10th Anniversary 1976-1986" markings on right side of the slide, 38.75 oz.

Serial number range DVC0001-DVC5000
5,000 mfd. 1986-1990

NIB	Exc	VG	Good	Fair	Poor
700	600	500	410	350	285

Variations:

- Twenty-five "First Edition" models specially engraved

Product Codes:

103712 5"	BS 8SH FS	1st Run IPSC Engraved
103715 5"	BS 8SH FS	2nd Run Non-engraved
103721 5"	BS 8SH FS	87-90
103906 5"	BS 8SH AS	Special 1990

MODEL 845 BULLSEYE:

Cal-.45 ACP, experimental full target version of the Model 745 for approx. 10 years, now from the Performance Center. Bo-Mar low profile sights, beavertail, checkered front strap, fitted barrel bushing, Hi-Impact plastic grips, 8-round magazine, extra recoil spring, serial introduction MPC 00xx, Performance Center logo. Limited Production for Lew Horton. 1995

Product Code:

170064 8SH

900 Series: Third Generation DAs, 9mm, No-Frills

MODEL 909: Full-Size Double Action:

Cal- 9mm, new for 1995, 4" barrel, blue finish, 9-shot single stack magazine, fixed sight, manual safety, alloy frame w/steel slide. Retail $443. 1995

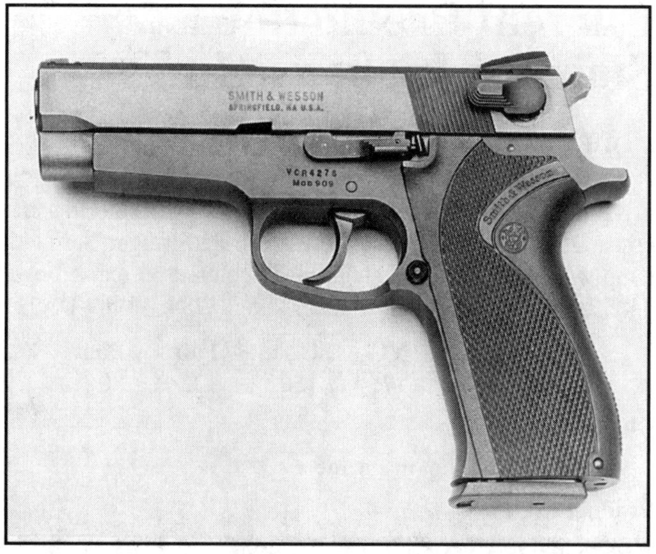

Model 909

Smith & Wesson 3rd generation semiautomatic handgun frames are found in three triggerguard designs.

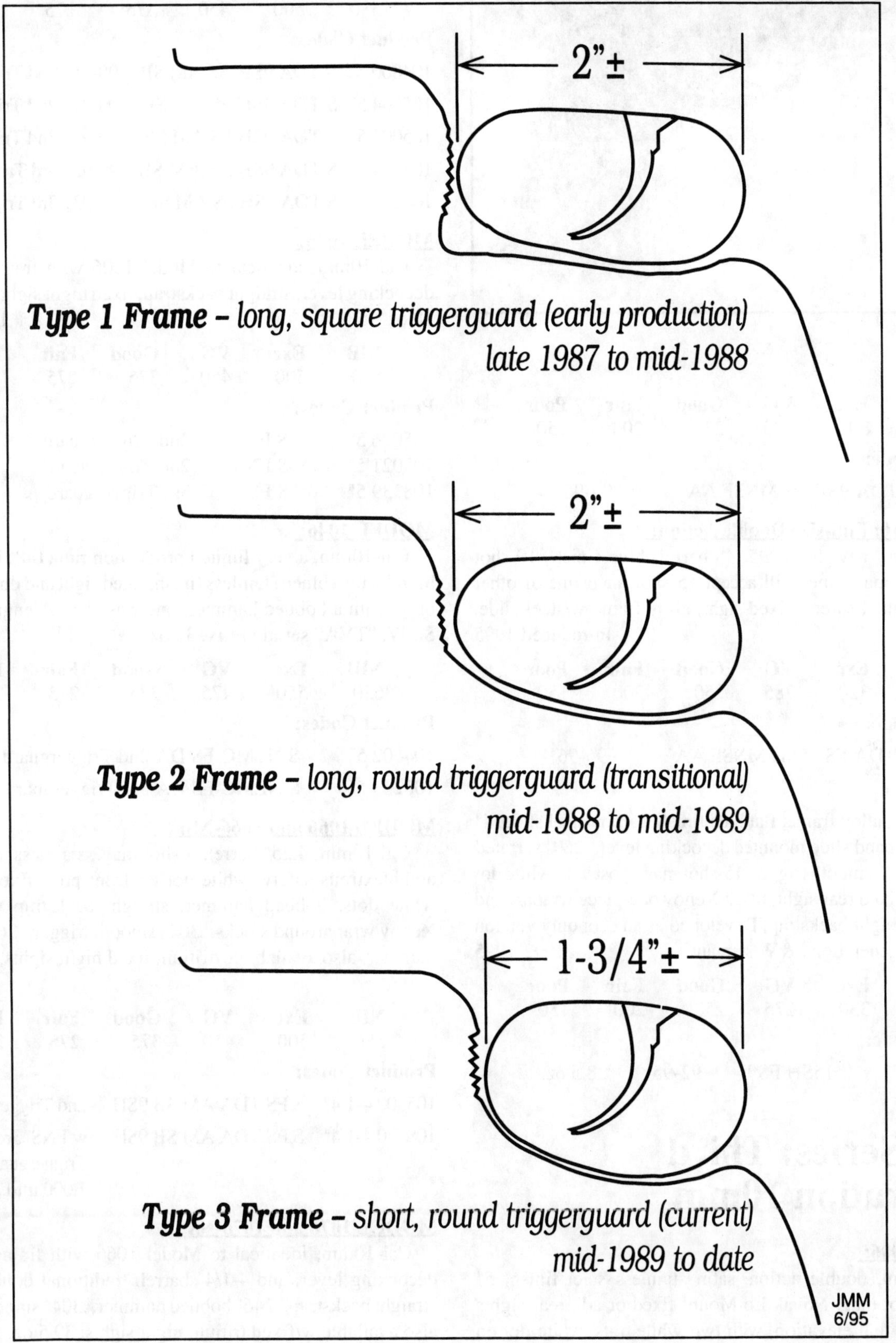

***Type 1 Frame** – long, square triggerguard (early production)*
late 1987 to mid-1988

***Type 2 Frame** – long, round triggerguard (transitional)*
mid-1988 to mid-1989

***Type 3 Frame** – short, round triggerguard (current)*
mid-1989 to date

Model 910

NIB	Exc	VG	Good	Fair	Poor
350	300	275	235	200	150

Product Code:

104760 B TDA 9SH FS MNSF AA 95-96

MODEL 910: Full-size Double Action:

Cal- 9mm, new for 1995, 4" barrel, blue finish, 10-shot doublestack magazine, will accept 15-shot magazine of other models, manual safety, fixed sight, alloy frame w/steel slide. Retail $467. Introduced 1995

NIB	Exc	VG	Good	Fair	Poor
365	320	285	250	200	150

Product Code:

104780 B TDA FS 15SH MNSF AA 95-96

MODEL 915:

Cal-9mm, alloy frame, flat blue finish, carbon steel slide, 4" barrel, right hand slide mounted decocking lever, .260" serrated hammer, .304" smooth trigger, 15-shot mag., post with white dot front sight, fixed rear sight, black Xenoy one-piece wraparound grip with straight backstrap. Developed as an economy version of the third generation S&W semiauto. 1992-1995

NIB	Exc	VG	Good	Fair	Poor
385	330	275	250	200	150

Product Code:

104792 4" 15SH FS B 92-95 28.5 oz.

1000 Series: Third Generation 10mm

MODEL 1006:

Cal-10mm, double action, satin stainless steel finish, 5" barrel, 9-shot mag, Novak Lo-Mount fixed or adj. rear sights for windage and elevation, with two white dots, white dot on front post, ambidextrous safety, one-piece black Delrin wraparound stocks with curved backstrap, .260" serrated hammer, .304" smooth trigger, slide mounted decocking lever, 38 oz. 1990-1993

NIB	Exc	VG	Good	Fair	Poor
580	500	450	375	275	200

Product Codes:

104800 5"	S TDA 9SH AS AM SB	90-91	2nd Triggerguard
105004 5"	S TDA 9SH FS AM SB	90-91	2nd Triggerguard
105005 5"	S TDA 9SH FS AM SB	90-91	2nd Triggerguard
108234 5"	S TDA 9SH AS AM SB	92-93	3rd Triggerguard
108237 5"	S TDA 9SH FS AM SB	92-93	3rd Triggerguard

MODEL 1026:

Cal-10mm, identical to Model 1006 with frame mounted decocking lever, straight backstrap, fixed night sights available, 38 oz. 1990 - 1991

NIB	Exc	VG	Good	Fair	Poor
580	500	450	375	275	200

Product Codes:

105006 5"	S FS	2nd Triggerguard
105021 5"	S FNS	2nd Triggerguard
108239 5"	S FS	3rd Triggerguard

MODEL 1046:

Cal-10mm, a very limited production run (148) in 1992. 5" barrel with a blued stainless finish, fixed sight and double action only, with a bobbed hammer, one was class A engraved from S&W, "TVA" serial prefix, 38 oz. 1990-1992

NIB	Exc	VG	Good	Fair	Poor
650	550	475	375	275	200

Product Codes:

104602 5"	S NLMC-FS DA 2nd Triggerguard
108233 5"	S NLMC-FS DA 3rd Triggerguard

MODEL 1066 and 1066-NS:

Cal-10mm, 4.25" barrel, 9-shot mag., stainless steel finish, ambidextrous safety, white dot on front post, fixed rear two white dots, bobbed hammer, straight backstrap with black Xenoy wraparound stocks, .304" smooth trigger, .260" bobbed hammer, also available w/tritium fixed night sights, 39.5 oz. 1990-1992

NIB	Exc	VG	Good	Fair	Poor
580	500	450	375	275	200

Product Codes:

105500 4-1/4"	S FS TDA AM SB 9SH	2nd Triggerguard
108270 4-1/4"	S FS TDA AM SB 9SH	w/FNS, 3rd Triggerguard, special 1,000 mfd., 1990

MODEL 1076 and 1076-NS:

Cal-10mm, identical to Model 1066 with frame mounted decocking lever, and 4-1/4" barrel, traditional double action, straight backstrap, .246" bobbed hammer, .304" smooth trigger, also available w/fixed tritium night sights, 39.5 oz. 1990-1993

NIB	Exc	VG	Good	Fair	Poor
580	500	450	375	275	200

Variations:

- **Model 1076-FBI version:** Cal-10mm, built without a magazine disconnector, two-dot modified sight and a special trigger group. 11- and 15-shot magazines supplied extra but never available outside the F.B.I. contract. An original order for 10,000 was placed, but early samples were rejected by the F.B.I. and sent to S&W for rework and the contract was reaccepted in 1993. Approx. 2,400 finally delivered, 1990.

Product Codes:

Note: All have 3rd Triggerguard

105900	Early Product Code	
105901	FBI Purchase	
105018	FBI Purchase	
108248 4-1/4"	9SH FS DL S SB	91-93
108259	FBI Purchase	
108260 4-1/4"	9SH w/FNS DL S	1991

MODEL 1086:

Cal-10mm, identical to Model 1066, with double action only, .260" semi-bobbed hammer, .304" smooth trigger, stainless finish, 38 oz. 1991-1992

NIB	Exc	VG	Good	Fair	Poor
580	500	450	375	275	200

Product Codes:

106004 4 1/4"	DAO 9SH FS S SB	2nd Triggerguard
108251 4-1/4"	DAO 9SH FS S SB	3rd Triggerguard

Current Production .22 SAs

MODEL 2206: .22 SINGLE ACTION /TARGET RIMFIRE PISTOL:

Cal-.22 Long Rifle, all stainless steel, 4-1/2" or 6" barrel, 10-shot magazine, Patridge undercut front sight, fixed or adj. micrometer click rear sights, black plastic grips, internal hammer, .312" serrated trigger w/adjustable stop, a small pin on the butt will protrude when cocked (this is an extension of the spring arm, not a cocking indicator.) Retail $385-$327. 1990-DATE

NIB	Exc	VG	Good	Fair	Poor
250	200	175	150	120	80

Variations:

- Add $40 for adjustable sights
- Add $100 for target model

Changes:

1992	12-shot magazine
1993	Discontinue 4-1/2" barrel
1994	2206 Target: production w/Millet 100 series sight, drilled and tapped for scope mount, Herrett walnut grips

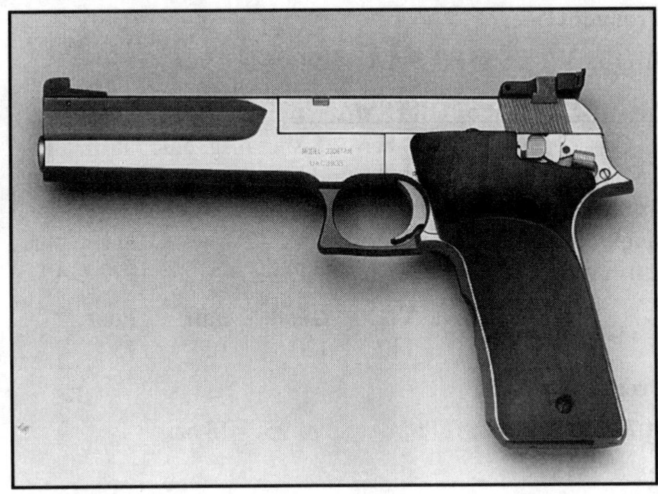

Model 2206

Product Codes:

107000 4-1/2"	S FS	90-93	35 oz.
107002 4-1/2"	S AS	90-93	
107004 6"	S FS	90-95	39 oz.
107006 6"	S AS	90-96	
107010 6"	TGT MS SM DT	94-96	42 oz.

MODEL 2213: "SPORTSMAN" STAINLESS SPECIAL:

Cal-.22 Long Rifle, stainless steel frosted finish, 8-shot magazine, 3" barrel, cocking indicator on butt like the 2206, black neoprene grips, .312" serrated trigger, two white dot fixed .131" rear sight, dovetail Patridge with white dot front sight, supplied with detachable holster and zippered case as a first promotional issue of 1500. Retail $314. 1991-DATE

NIB	Exc	VG	Good	Fair	Poor
235	180	160	135	100	75

Changes:

1992	Standard production

Model 2213

Product Code:

107198 3" S 8SH FS AA 91-96 18 oz.

MODEL 2214: "SPORTSMAN":

Cal-.22 Long Rifle, 3" barrel, 8-shot mag, blue finish, alloy frame w/steel slide, dovetail Patridge with white dot front sight, fixed .131" notch two white dot rear sight, black plastic grips, single action, .250" internal hammer, .312" serrated trigger, blue finish version of the 2213. Retail $269. 1990-DATE

NIB	Exc	VG	Good	Fair	Poor
210	170	140	120	100	75

Product Code:

107200 3" B 8SH FS AA 90-96 18 oz.

Third Generation Caliber .356 TSW

MODEL 3566:

Cal-.356 TSW, a new caliber initially developed for the S&W shooting team. A 9 X 21.5mm cartridge developed for Team Smith & Wesson, (TSW) this frame has a titanium barrel bushing on a stainless frame, with a combination matte blue and hand rubbed stainless finish, with oversize frame rails and match grade barrels. About 200 mfd. in a 3-1/2" compact version with a 12-shot magazine, dist. by Lew Horton. A longer 5" version is the .356 TSW Limited, a competitive version w/15-round clip, adjustable trigger, fitted slide and barrel, Bomar adjustable sights, checkered front strap and extended magazine well. The 3566 TSW series' most distinctive feature is the high polish stainless and black contrasting finish. This was a combined effort from Federal Cartridge and S&W. "TSW" serial prefix. Distributed by Lew Horton. 1993

Product Codes:

170027 3-1/2"	7SH AS	"Shorty"	93	NIB $1000
170032 5"	15SH AS	"Limited"	93	NIB $1350
170052 4-1/4"	12SH AS	"Compact"	94 35 oz.	NIB $1000
		"Tactical"		$1200

3900 Series: Third Generation Single Column Compact 9mm

MODEL 3904:

Cal-9mm, double action, aluminum alloy frame with steel slide, 4" barrel with fixed barrel bushing, 8-shot magazine, ambidextrous safety, beveled magazine well, Delrin one-piece wraparound grips, available with fixed or adj. rear sights with two white dots, white dot front sight, blue finish, serrated hammer, smooth trigger. 1988-1990

NIB	Exc	VG	Good	Fair	Poor
475	400	350	300	225	175

Product Codes:

102911 4"	B 8SH AS AM	28.5 oz.	1st Triggerguard
102913 4"	B 8SH FS AM	28 oz.	1st Triggerguard
102918 4"	B 8SH FS AM	28 oz.	1st Triggerguard

MODEL 3906:

Cal-9mm, stainless steel version of the Model 3904, later production w/Novak Lo-Mount sights. 1988-1990

NIB	Exc	VG	Good	Fair	Poor
500	425	375	300	250	200

Product Codes:

103706 4"	S 8SH AS AM	35.5 oz.	1st Triggerguard
103708 4"	S 8SH FS AM	35.5 oz.	1st Triggerguard
103737 4"	S 8SH NLMC AM		1st Triggerguard

MODEL 3913:

Cal-9mm, 8-shot magazine, 3-1/2" barrel, bobbed hammer, no half cock position, Novak Lo-Mount fixed sights, w/white dot post front sight, two-dot fixed rear sight adj. for windage only, frosted stainless steel finish, .304" smooth trigger, stainless steel slide, alloy frame, one-piece Xenoy wraparound grip with straight backstrap, ambidextrous safety, traditional double action, slide mounted decocking lever, 25 oz. Retail $622. 1989-DATE

NIB	Exc	VG	Good	Fair	Poor
525	450	385	300	250	200

Variations:

- 1989 Prototypes: 451 guns lacking a milling cut in the triggerguard area, s/n TDF0000-0450

Product Code:

103730 3-1/2" S FS TDA 8SH AM AA SB 91-96 3rd Triggerguard

Model 3913

Model 3913 LadySmith

Model 3914

MODEL 3913LS LADYSMITH:

Cal-9mm, identical to the Model 3913 NL with laser etched "LADYSMITH" on frame side. Specially designed for women. Bobbed hammer, .304" smooth trigger w/rounded edges, frosted stainless finish, Novak Lo-Mount sights, right hand manual safety, alloy frame w/stainless slide, angled profile frame rather than a straight cut, 3-1/2" barrel, TDA, gray one-piece Delrin wraparound grip, straight backstrap, with carry case, 3rd Triggerguard style, 25 oz. Retail $640. 1990-DATE

NIB	Exc	VG	Good	Fair	Poor
535	450	385	300	250	200

Product Codes:

103918 3-1/2" S TDA 8SH FS MNSF AA SB LS w/hard case 90-91

108290 3-1/2" S TDA 8SH FS MNSF AA SB LS w/soft case 92-96

MODEL 3913 NL:

Cal-9mm, Model 3913 with an angled profile frame and slide rather than the straight cut. Identical to 3913LS without the LadySmith markings, double action, Novak Lo-Mount sights, 3rd Triggerguard, 25 oz. 1991-DATE

NIB	Exc	VG	Good	Fair	Poor
525	450	385	300	250	200

Product Code:

103913 3-1/2" S FS TDA 8SH MNSF AA SB 91-94

MODEL 3914:

Cal-9mm, blue finish version of Model 3913 NL, Novak Lo-Mount sights, 3rd Triggerguard, 25 oz. Retail $562. 1990-DATE

NIB	Exc	VG	Good	Fair	Poor
460	400	365	300	250	200

Variations:

- 1989 Prototypes: 472 guns w/ difference in triggerguard area, s/n TDF0501-0972

Product Code:

102914 3-1/2" B FS TDA 8SH AM AA SB 91-94

MODEL 3914LS LADYSMITH:

Cal-9mm, identical to Model 3914 NL with laser etched "LADYSMITH" on frame side, bobbed hammer, .304" smooth trigger, black grips, slide mounted right hand safety, alloy frame w/steel slide, specially designed for women, blue finish, with hard carry case, traditional double action, Novak Lo-Mount sights, 3rd Triggerguard, 25 oz. 1990-1991

NIB	Exc	VG	Good	Fair	Poor
470	400	365	300	250	200

Product Code:

103920 3-1/2" B 8SH MNSF FS AA SB 90-91

MODEL 3914 NL:

Cal-9mm, blue finish version of Model 3913 NL, Novak Lo-Mount sights, 3rd Triggerguard, 25 oz. 1991

NIB	Exc	VG	Good	Fair	Poor
460	400	365	300	250	200

Product Code:

103915 3-1/2" B FS TDA 8SH MNSF AA SB

MODEL 3953:

Cal-9mm, 8-shot magazine, double action only version of Model 3913, .260" semi-bobbed hammer, .304" smooth trigger, post w/white dot front sight, Novak Lo-Mount sights w/two white dots rear sight drift adj. for windage only, alloy frame w/stainless slide, 3rd Triggerguard, 25.5 oz. Retail $622. 1991-DATE

NIB	Exc	VG	Good	Fair	Poor
525	450	385	300	250	200

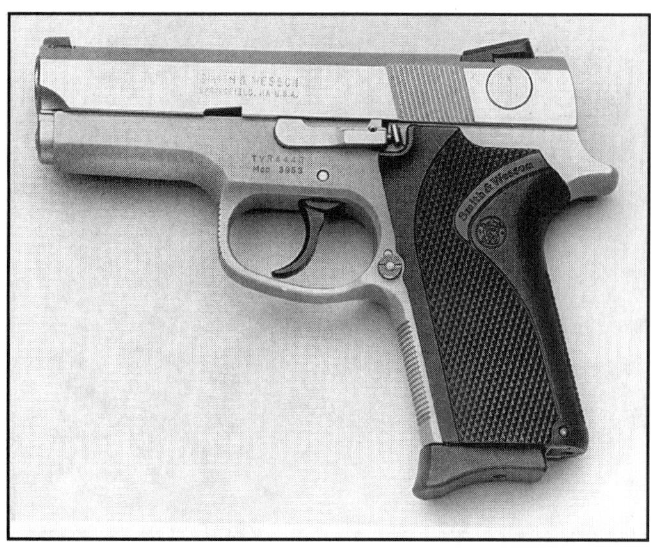

Model 3953

Product Code:

108502 3-1/2" S DA 8SH FS AA SB 91-96

MODEL 3954:

Cal-9mm, double action only version of Model 3914, 8-shot mag., .260 semi-bobbed hammer, .304" smooth trigger, post w/white dot front sight, Novak Lo-Mount fixed sights w/two-dot rear sight drift adj. for windage only, black one-piece wraparound grip, alloy frame w/blued carbon steel slide, 3rd Triggerguard, 25 oz. 1991-1992

NIB	Exc	VG	Good	Fair	Poor
460	400	365	300	250	200

Product Code:

108510 3-1/2" B DA 8SH FS AA SB 91-92

4000 Series: Third Generation .40 S&W Background Information

The 1980s saw a movement in choice of police sidearms away from the traditional revolver to the semiauto pistol. A debate raged between advocates of double stack high capacity 9mms and .45 ACPs, with advocates of the latter claiming greater "stopping power" for the larger diameter bullet. However, the .45 was considered too fat for a comfortable grip double stack magazine at the time. The 10mm cartridge was an initial attempt at a compromise, but proved too long for a comfortable grip when a double stack high capacity magazine was used. Furthermore, like the .41 Magnum in revolvers, some authorities thought the 10mm had too much velocity and penetration for most effective and safe police usage.

When the F.B.I. adopted the 10mm in a S&W, the law enforcement market took note. The F.B.I. specified a 10mm cartridge loaded to less than full power for its sidearm. S&W came up with a shorter cartridge that could be adapted to a comfortable grip double column design and was loaded to the lower power levels of the 10mm F.B.I. load. Both the 10mm and the .40 S&W took the same diameter bullet.

Early scoffers nicknamed the round the "40 Short & Weak." However, ballistic tests and street results soon proved the .40 S&W to be nearly ideal as a police round, and it has since become the choice of many departments and civilian shooters. The government ban on manufacture of new magazines with greater than 10-round capacity for civilian sale is expected to further move the civilian handgun market toward .40 and .45 caliber semiautos.

S&W "SHORTY FORTY":

Cal-.40 S&W, 3-1/2" Bar-Sto barrel with spherical bushing, bobbed hammer, Novak Lo-Mount sights, 9-round magazine, alloy frame, grips and frame stamped with the logo from the S&W Performance Center. Beveled trigger, windage adjustable front dovetail sight, double stack magazine, oversize slide rails, special production from the S&W Performance center, distributed by Lew Horton, 27 oz.

500 mfd. 3 production runs: 1992, 1993, and 1995

NIB	Exc	VG	Good	Fair	Poor
950	700	600	400	325	250

Variations:

- **S&W "Tactical Forty":** Cal-.40 S&W, a full-size companion to the "Shorty Forty" offered by Lew Horton, 5" barrel. Product Code: 170020. Limited production, 1993. NIB $1500.
- **S&W "Compensated Forty":** Cal-.40 S&W, this model was again offered by Lew Horton, with a compensator mounted on a ported barrel that extended from the front of the slide. Limited Production. NIB $1700.
- **Shorty Forty MK III:** Third variation made in 1995.

Product Code:

170011

MODEL 4003:

Cal-.40 S&W, stainless and alloy version of Model 4006, 11-round mag., 4" barrel, .260 serrated hammer, .304" smooth trigger, post w/white dot front sight, Novak Lo-Mount w/two white dots rear sight, black one-piece wraparound grip, traditional double action, 3rd Triggerguard, 28 oz. 1991-1992

NIB	Exc	VG	Good	Fair	Poor
550	475	425	350	300	225

Product Code:

108512 4" S TDA 11SH FS AM AA SB 91-93

MODEL 4004:

Cal-.40 S&W, blued alloy version of Model 4003, traditional double action, Novak Lo-Mount fixed sights, 3rd Triggerguard, 28 oz. 1991-1992

Shorty Forty (Photo courtesy Lew Horton Distributing Co.)

NIB	Exc	VG	Good	Fair	Poor
535	460	420	350	300	225

Product Code:

108522 4" B TDA 11SH FS AM AA SB

MODEL 4006 and 4006-NS:

Cal-.40 S&W, 11-shot mag, 4" barrel, Novak Lo-Mount fixed sights, drift adj. for windage w/two white dot, stainless steel slide and frame, double action, straight backstrap with one piece Delrin wraparound grip, slide mounted ambidextrous safety, .260" serrated hammer, .304" smooth trigger, also available with fixed tritium night sights on a Novak Lo-Mount, 3rd Triggerguard, 39 oz. Retail $745-$855. 1990-DATE

NIB	Exc	VG	Good	Fair	Poor
625	525	450	375	300	225

Variations:

- Night sights, add $100

Product Codes:

102940	4"	11SH AS w/bobbed hammer	
102944	4"	TDA 11SH FS AM S SB	
102946	4"	TDA 11SH AS AM S SB	
104400	4"	TDA 11SH AS AM S SB	90-92, 94
104402	4"	TDA 11SH FS AM S SB	90-92, 94
104403	1st Issue 4"	S TDA 11SH FNS AM SB	92/94
104404	2nd Issue 4"	S TDA 11SH FNS AM SB	92/94

MODEL 4013:

Cal-.40 S&W, 3-1/2" barrel, 8-shot magazine, Novak Lo-Mount fixed rear sight with two white dots w/white dot front post, stainless slide with alloy frame, slide mounted ambidextrous safety, bobbed hammer, .304" smooth trigger, wraparound black Xenoy stock with straight backstrap, traditional double action, 3rd Triggerguard, 27 oz. Retail $722. 1991-1992

NIB	Exc	VG	Good	Fair	Poor
625	525	450	375	300	225

Product Code:

108524 3-1/2" S TDA 8SH FS AM AA 91-96

MODEL 4014:

Cal-.40 S&W, blue steel slide and blue alloy frame version of the Model 4013, Novak Lo-Mount fixed sights, 3rd Triggerguard, 27 oz. 1991-1993

NIB	Exc	VG	Good	Fair	Poor
585	500	400	325	275	200

Product Code:

108526 3-1/2" B TDA 8SH FS AM AA 91-93

MODEL 4026:

Cal-.40 S&W, traditional double action with frame mounted decocking lever, .246" bobbed hammer, .304" smooth trigger, 11-round magazine, curved backstrap with black Xenoy wraparound grip, Novak Lo-Mount w/two white dot rear sight, 4" barrel, 3rd Triggerguard. 1991-1993

NIB	Exc	VG	Good	Fair	Poor
600	500	400	325	275	200

Product Code:

102950 4" S TDA/DL 11SH FS S CB 92-93

MODEL 4043:

Cal-.40 S&W, double action only, stainless steel slide, 4" barrel, alloy frame, .260" serrated semi-bobbed hammer, .304" smooth trigger, 11-shot mag., post w/white dot front sight, Novak Lo-Mount w/two white dot rear sight, straight backstrap w/black one-piece Xenoy wraparound grip, satin stainless finish, 3rd Triggerguard, 28 oz. Retail $727. 1991-DATE

NIB	Exc	VG	Good	Fair	Poor
600	525	450	375	300	225

Product Code:

108528 4" S DA 11SH FS AA SB 91-94

MODEL 4044:

Cal-.40 S&W, double action only, blue finish, alloy frame with steel slide, 4" barrel, 11-shot mag., fixed Novak Lo-Mount w/two white dot rear sight, post w/white dot front sight, .260" serrated semi-bobbed hammer, black Xenoy one-piece wraparound grip with straight backstrap, 3rd Triggerguard, 30 oz. 1991-1993

NIB	Exc	VG	Good	Fair	Poor
575	500	425	350	275	210

Product Code:

108532 4" B DA 11SH FS AA SB 91-93

MODEL 4046 and 4046-NS:

Cal-.40 S&W, double action only version of Model 4006, .260" semi-bobbed hammer, .304" smooth trigger, Novak Lo-Mount fixed sights, no decocking lever, Xenoy one-piece wraparound grip, straight backstrap, 3rd Triggerguard, also offered with fixed tritium night sights, 38.5 oz. Retail $745-$855. 1991-DATE

NIB	Exc	VG	Good	Fair	Poor
600	525	450	375	300	225

Variations:

- Add $100 for night sights

Product Codes:

102952 4" S DA 11SH FS SB 93-95

102953 4" S DA 11SH FS SB

102955 4" S DA 11SH w/FNS SB 92-95

108597 4" S DA 11SH w/FNS Special

Model 4053

MODEL 4053:

Cal-.40 S&W, double action only version of Model 4013, semi-bobbed hammer, Novak Lo-Mount sights, 3rd Triggerguard, 28 oz. Retail $722. 1991-DATE

NIB	Exc	VG	Good	Fair	Poor
600	525	450	375	300	225

Product Codes:

108538 3-1/2" S DA 8SH FS AA 91-96

108539 3-1/2" LS

MODEL 4054:

Cal-.40 S&W, double action only version of Model 4014, blue finish, steel slide and alloy frame, Novak Lo-Mount sights, 3rd Triggerguard, 28 oz. Only 154 mfd. 1991-1992

NIB	Exc	VG	Good	Fair	Poor
575	485	385	310	275	210

Product Code:

108534 3-1/2" B DA 8SH FS AA 91-92

4500 Series: Third Generation .45 ACP

MODEL 4505:

Cal-.45 ACP, blued finish, 5" barrel, 8-shot magazine, ambidextrous safety, Novak Lo-Mount fixed sights, limited production of adjustable sights, 3rd Triggerguard, 41 oz. 1991

NIB	Exc	VG	Good	Fair	Poor
600	525	450	375	300	225

Product Codes:

108316 FS B AM 8SH

108318 AS B AM 8SH

MODEL 4506 and 4506-1:

Cal-.45 ACP, 5" barrel, 8-shot magazine, stainless steel finish, Novak Lo-Mount fixed sights or drift adj. rear sights with two white dots, straight backstrap, Xenoy one-piece wrap-around grips, .260" serrated hammer, .304" smooth trigger, slide mounted ambidextrous safety, 41 oz. Retail $774-$806.

1988-DATE

NIB	Exc	VG	Good	Fair	Poor
625	535	450	375	300	225

Variations:

- Less than 200 known with 4506 features, but marked Model 645. Boxes marked "Special."

Product Codes:

103710 5"	S 8SH FS AM	89	1st Triggerguard
103722 5"	S 8SH FS AM	89	1st Triggerguard
103723 5"	S 8SH AS AM	89	1st Triggerguard
103781 5"	S 8SH FS AM	91	1st Triggerguard
108143 5"	S TDA 8SH AS AM SB	92-96	3rd Triggerguard (4506-1)
108163 5"	S TDA 8SH FS AM SB	92-96	3rd Triggerguard (4506-1)

MODEL 4516:

Cal-.45 ACP, compact version of Model 4506, stainless steel frame and slide, w/stainless finish, 3-3/4" barrel, 7-shot mag., .365" smooth trigger, .260" bobbed hammer with no half cock notch, Novak Lo-Mount fixed rear sight w/two white dots, drift adjustable for windage only, post w/white dot front sight, one-piece black Xenoy wraparound grips with straight backstrap, 34.5 oz. Retail $774.

1991-DATE

NIB	Exc	VG	Good	Fair	Poor
650	550	450	375	300	225

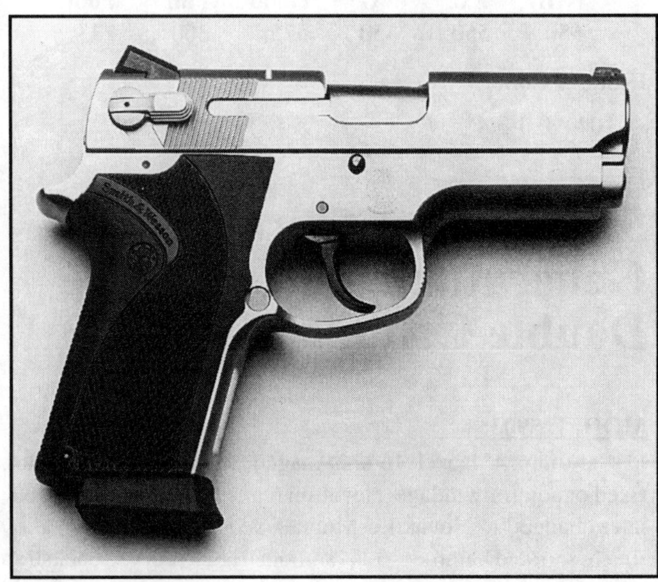

Model 4516

Variations:

- **Model 4516-1: U.S. Marshall Bicentennial Edition:** Cal-.45 ACP, w/display case and certificate, 1993. NIB $750.

Changes:

4516-1		3rd Triggerguard
4516-1	1991-92	Does not have extensive frame and slide milling as the slightly heavier 4516
4516-2	1994	

Product Codes:

103729 3-3/4"	S TDA 7SH FS AM	91-92 (4516)
108548 3-3/4"	TDA 7SH	95-96 (4516-2)

MODEL 4526:

Cal-.45 ACP, identical to the Model 4506 with frame mounted manual decocking lever, stainless frame and slide, stainless finish, .246" bobbed hammer, .304" smooth trigger, straight backstrap, Novak Lo-Mount fixed sights, 41 oz. 1991

NIB	Exc	VG	Good	Fair	Poor
625	535	450	375	300	225

Product Codes:

103774 5"	S FS DL 8SH	1st Triggerguard
108160 5"	S FS DL 8SH	3rd Triggerguard

MODEL 4536:

Cal-.45 ACP, compact version of Model 4516 with frame mounted manual decocking lever, .246" bobbed hammer, .304" smooth trigger, 3-3/4" barrel, 7-shot magazine, Novak Lo-Mount sights, 3rd Triggerguard, 41 oz. 1991

NIB	Exc	VG	Good	Fair	Poor
625	535	450	375	300	225

Product Code:

103748 3-3/4" S FS DL 7SH

MODEL 4546:

Cal-.45 ACP, double action only version of Model 4506, .260" semi-bobbed hammer, .304" smooth trigger, stainless frame and slide, stainless finish, Novak Lo-Mount sights. 1991

NIB	Exc	VG	Good	Fair	Poor
600	535	450	400	325	225

Product Codes:

103776 5"	S FS DA 8SH	1st Triggerguard
108162 5"	S FS DA 8SH	3rd Triggerguard

MODEL 4556:

Cal-.45 ACP, double action only version of Model 4516, Novak Lo-Mount sights, 3rd Triggerguard. 1991

NIB	Exc	VG	Good	Fair	Poor
600	535	450	400	325	225

Product Code:

108550 3-3/4" S FS DA

Model 4566

MODEL 4566:

Cal-.45 ACP, 4-1/4" barrel version of Model 4506, Novak Lo-Mount fixed sights, stainless steel finish, bobbed hammer, slide mounted decocking lever, .304" smooth trigger, 38.5 oz. Retail $774. 1991-DATE

NIB	Exc	VG	Good	Fair	Poor
625	535	450	375	300	225

Product Codes:

104406 4-1/4" S FS TDA 8SH AM SB 91-92 1st Triggerguard

108225 4-1/4" S FS TDA 8SH AM SB 93-96 3rd Triggerguard

MODEL 4567-NS:

Cal-.45 ACP, blue slide with stainless frame, black post w/tritium insert front sight, Novak Lo-Mount w/two tritium dot rear sight, .260" bobbed hammer, .304" smooth trigger, deep blue Xenoy one-piece wraparound grip on a straight backstrap, 4-1/4" barrel, 8-round mag., 39.4 oz.

Limited production of 2,500 1991

NIB	Exc	VG	Good	Fair	Poor
675	575	475	400	325	225

Product Code:

108304 4-1/4" w/FNS TDA 3rd Triggerguard

MODEL 4576:

Cal-.45 ACP, frame mounted manual decocking lever version of Model 4566, .304" smooth trigger, .246" semi-bobbed hammer, stainless frame and slide, stainless finish, Novak Lo-Mount sights, 39 oz. 1991-1992

NIB	Exc	VG	Good	Fair	Poor
600	535	450	400	325	225

Product Codes:

104426 4-1/4" S FS TDA/DA 8SH SB 1st Triggerguard

108226 4-1/4" S FS TDA/DL 8SH SB 3rd Triggerguard

Model 4586

MODEL 4586:

Cal-.45 ACP, double action only version of Model 4566, .260" semi-bobbed hammer, .304" smooth trigger, stainless frame and slide, straight backstrap, Novak Lo-Mount fixed sights, 39 oz. Retail $774. 1991-DATE

NIB	Exc	VG	Good	Fair	Poor
625	535	450	375	300	225

Product Codes:

104408 4-1/4" S DA 8SH FS SB 91 2nd Triggerguard

108231 4-1/4" S DA 8SH FS SB 91-96 3rd Triggerguard

108232 4-1/4" Special 3rd Triggerguard

MODEL 4596:

Cal-.45 ACP, 4506-1 frame with 4516-1 slide , special for Lew Horton, Novak Lo-Mount fixed sights, 1st Triggerguard.

~500 mfd. 1990

NIB	Exc	VG	Good	Fair	Poor
650	550	450	375	300	225

Product Code:

104490 3-3/4"

5900 Series: Third Generation 9mm Full-Size Double Column

MODEL 5903:

Cal-9mm, 4" barrel, 15-shot mag., front post with white dot, fixed or adj. for windage, elevation rear sight w/two white dots, later changed to Novak Lo-Mount fixed sights, stainless alloy finish, serrated hammer, .304" smooth trigger, curved backstrap with Xenoy one-piece wraparound stocks, slide mounted ambidextrous safety, 29 oz. Retail $694. 1990-DATE

NIB	Exc	VG	Good	Fair	Poor
600	510	450	375	300	200

Product Codes:

104010 4"	S TDA 15SH AS Georgia Hwy. Patrol		1st Triggerguard
104042 4"	S TDA 15SH AS	90-91	1st Triggerguard
104018 4"	S TDA 15SH FS	90-91	3rd Triggerguard
108194 4"	S TDA 15SH AS AM AA	92	3rd Triggerguard
108179 4"	S TDA 15SH FS AM AA	92-96	3rd Triggerguard

MODEL 5903-SSV:

Cal-9mm, 3-1/2" barrel, short slide variation, bobbed blue hammer, .304" smooth blue trigger, post with white dot front sight, Novak Lo-Mount fixed two dot rear sight, straight backstrap with Delrin wraparound grip, stainless alloy finish with blue steel slide.

Special production of 1,500 1990

NIB	Exc	VG	Good	Fair	Poor
625	550	450	400	325	285

Product Code:

104100 3-1/2" FS FNS 90 1st Triggerguard

MODEL 5904:

Cal-9mm, carbon blue steel slide with alloy frame, blue version of Model 5903, later production w/Novak Lo-Mount fixed sights. Also found with 9 x 21 chamber for Italian commercial market. Retail $642. 1988-DATE

NIB	Exc	VG	Good	Fair	Poor
585	510	425	375	300	200

Product Codes:

103001 4"	B FS 14 SH	88	1st Triggerguard
103016 4"	B FS 14 SH	89	1st Triggerguard
103015 4"	B AS 14SH AM	89-91	1st Triggerguard
103017 4"	B FS 14SH AM TDA	89	Some mfd. for XM-10 test program
103027 4"	B FS 14SH AM TDA	91	1st Triggerguard
108110 4"	B AS 15SH AM TDA AA	92-93	3rd Triggerguard
108117 4"	B FS 15SH AM TDA AA	92-96	3rd Triggerguard

MODEL 5905:

Cal-9mm, 4" barrel, blue steel, Novak Lo-Mount fixed sights, 3rd Triggerguard. Special for 1991

NIB	Exc	VG	Good	Fair	Poor
600	535	450	400	325	200

Product Codes:

108303 4"	FS B
108302 4"	AS B
179000	rework

Model 5906

MODEL 5906-5906 NS

Cal-9mm, stainless steel frame and slide version of Model 5903, also found with 9 x 21 chamber for Italian commercial, some found with Model 659 stamping as a transition model, Novak Lo-Mount fixed sights on later production, fixed tritium night sights available, 38 oz. Retail $707-$817. 1989-DATE

NIB	Exc	VG	Good	Fair	Poor
600	535	450	400	325	200

Variations:

- Add $100 for night sights
- **Model 5906 "PC-9":** Cal-9mm, from the Performance Center, 3-1/2" titanium barrel with spherical bushing, 15-shot magazine, blue slide with stainless satin frame, smooth .300" trigger, bobbed hammer, Novak Lo-Mount fixed rear sight, dovetail front sight, 27 oz. Limited Production for Lew Horton Inc.

Product Codes:

104001 4"	S 14SH	89	1st Triggerguard
104006 4"	S 14SH AS AM	89	1st Triggerguard
104008 4"	S 14SH FS AM	89	
104012 4"	S 14SH	89	Special test finish and rd edges, 1st Triggerguard
104014 4"	S 14SH FS AM	91	1st Triggerguard
108170 4"	S 15SH AS AM TDA	92-96	3rd Triggerguard
108176 4"	S 15SH FS AM TDA	92-96	3rd Triggerguard
108255 4"		93	High polish finish w/wood grain Xenoy grips, stocking dealer special
108559 4"	S 15SH CB w/FNS	93-96	

MODEL 5924:

Cal-9mm, blued steel version of Model 5903 with manual frame mounted decocking lever, Novak Lo-Mount fixed sights,

.246" bobbed hammer, .304" smooth trigger, alloy frame, steel slide, curved backstrap, 38 oz. 1990-1991

NIB	Exc	VG	Good	Fair	Poor
585	510	450	375	300	200

Product Codes:

103029 4" B FS DL 15SH 1st Triggerguard

108119 4" B FS DL 15SH 3rd Triggerguard

MODEL 5926:

Cal-9mm, 4" barrel, decocking lever version of Model 5906, .304" smooth trigger, black Xenoy one-piece wraparound grip with curved backstrap, .246" bobbed hammer, stainless frame and slide, Novak Lo-Mount fixed sights, 28.5 oz. 1990-1993

NIB	Exc	VG	Good	Fair	Poor
600	535	450	400	325	200

Product Codes:

104034 4" S FS DL 90 1st and 2nd Triggerguard

108189 4" S FS DL 91-93 3rd Triggerguard

MODEL 5943:

Cal-9mm, double action only version of Model 5903 with alloy frame and stainless slide, Novak Lo-Mount fixed sights, 37.5 oz. 1991

NIB	Exc	VG	Good	Fair	Poor
600	535	450	400	325	200

Product Code:

108560 4" S FS DA 91 3rd Triggerguard

MODEL 5943-SSV:

Cal-9mm, short slide variation of 5943, .260" semi-bobbed hammer, .304" smooth trigger, black post with tritium night sight inserts on front sight, Novak Lo-Mount fixed rear sight with two tritium night sight inserts, black curved backstrap, stainless finish frame with blue slide, double action only, 38 oz. 1991

NIB	Exc	VG	Good	Fair	Poor
600	535	450	400	325	200

Product Code:

108308 3-1/2" w/FNS DA 1st Triggerguard

MODEL 5944:

Cal-9mm, blued version of Model 5904, double action only, carbon steel slide and alloy frame, .260" semi-bobbed hammer, .304" smooth trigger, curved backstrap, Novak Lo-Mount fixed sights, 38 oz. 1991-1992

NIB	Exc	VG	Good	Fair	Poor
575	500	425	375	300	200

Product Codes:

103021 4" B FS Special run 3rd Triggerguard

103022 4" B FS DA 15SH 91 1st Triggerguard

108116 4" B FS DA 15SH 3rd Triggerguard

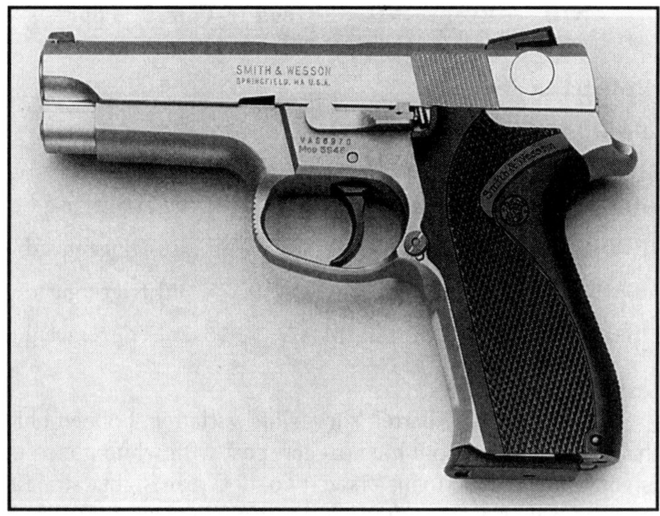

Model 5946

MODEL 5946:

Cal-9mm, double action only version of Model 5906, .260" semi-bobbed hammer, .304" smooth trigger, curved backstrap, Novak Lo-Mount fixed sights, 3rd Triggerguard, 28.5 oz. Retail $707. 1991-DATE

NIB	Exc	VG	Good	Fair	Poor
600	535	450	400	325	200

Product Codes:

104025 Special run

104026 4" S FS DA 15SH 91

108186 4" S FS DA 15SH 91-96

MODEL 5967:

Cal-9mm, 5906 frame with 3914 slide, special for Lew Horton, stainless steel frame with blue carbon steel slide. Novak Lo-Mount fixed sights. Special 1990

NIB	Exc	VG	Good	Fair	Poor
600	535	450	400	325	200

Product Code:

103048 4" 1st Triggerguard

6900 Series: Third Generation 9mm Compact Double Column

MODEL 6990

Possible pilot gun marked 669, 1992.

MODEL 6904:

Cal-9mm, 3-1/2" barrel, blue finish, alloy frame with steel slide, 12-shot mag, rear sights fixed with two white dots, front post with white dot, bobbed hammer, black Xenoy one-piece wraparound grip w/curved backstrap, .304" smooth trigger, 26.5 oz. Retail $614. 1988-DATE

NIB	Exc	VG	Good	Fair	Poor
485	420	375	325	250	180

Variations:

- Possibly less than 200 guns shipped with Mod. 6904 features, but marked Model 469, boxes marked "Special"

Product Codes:

103101	3-1/2" B 12SH FS AM TDA AA 88	1st Triggerguard
103106	3-1/2" B 12SH FS AM TDA AA 88-92	1st Triggerguard
103108	3-1/2" B 12SH FS AM TDA AA	
108130	3-1/2" B 12SH FS AM TDA AA 93-96	3rd Triggerguard

MODEL 6906-6906 NS:

Cal-9mm, stainless slide and alloy frame version of Model 6904, satin finish, Novak Lo-Mount fixed tritium night sights available, 26.5 oz. Retail $677-$788. 1988-DATE

NIB	Exc	VG	Good	Fair	Poor
535	425	385	335	285	180

Product Codes:

104008	3-1/2"	S 12SH		1st Triggerguard
104052	3-1/2"	S 12SH		1st Triggerguard
104054	3-1/2"	S 12SH FS AMSF	89-92	1st Triggerguard
104071	3-1/2"	S 12SH FS		1st Triggerguard
108211	3-1/2"	S 12SH FS AMSF	93-96	3rd Triggerguard
108611	3 -1/2"	S 12SH w/fixed night sight	92-96	3rd Triggerguard

MODEL 6924:

Cal. 9mm, manual decocking version of Model 6904 with fixed tritium night sights, 3rd Triggerguard. Limited production. 1992

Product Code:

108131

MODEL 6926:

Cal-9mm, manual decocking version of Model 6906, Novak Lo-Mount fixed sights. 1991

NIB	Exc	VG	Good	Fair	Poor
535	425	385	335	285	180

Product Codes:

104064	3-1/2"	S FS DL	1st Triggerguard
108207	3-1/2"	S FS DL	3rd Triggerguard

MODEL 6944:

Cal-9mm, double action only version of Model 6904, Novak Lo-Mount fixed sights, 1991.

NIB	Exc	VG	Good	Fair	Poor
535	425	385	335	285	180

Product Codes:

103124	3-1/2"	B FS DA 12SH	1st Triggerguard
108138	3-1/2"	B FS DA 12SH Special	3rd Triggerguard

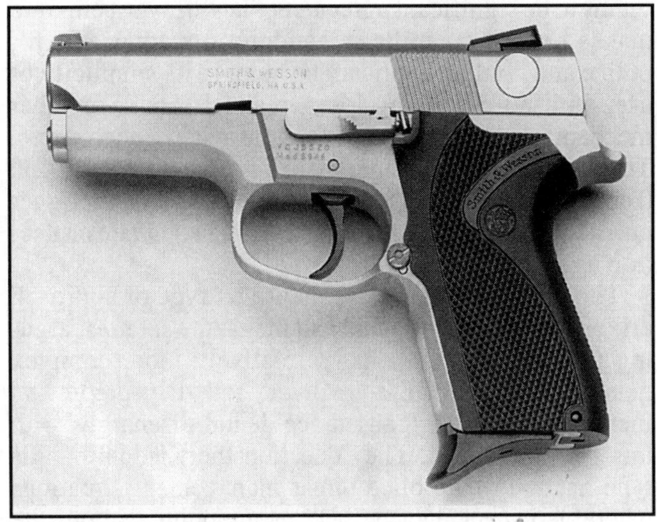

Model 6946

MODEL 6946:

Cal-9mm, double action only version of Model 6906, stainless finish, .260" semi-bobbed hammer, .304" smooth trigger, alloy frame, stainless slide, curved backstrap, Novak Lo-Mount fixed sights, 26.5 oz. Retail $677. 1991-DATE

NIB	Exc	VG	Good	Fair	Poor
535	425	385	335	285	180

Product Codes:

104065 3-1/2"	Special run night sights	3rd Triggerguard
104066	Early Product Code	3rd Triggerguard
108209 3-1/2"	S FS DA 12SH AA 91-96	3rd Triggerguard

Sigma Series: Polymer Frame Background Information

It is no secret that the Sigma line was launched by S&W at least partly in response to the inroads that the polymer framed Glock was making into police and civilian handgun markets. Like the Glock, the Sigma is a polymer framed high capacity double column semiautomatic with no external manual safety and no magazine disconnect safety (i.e., if there is a round in the chamber, the gun can be fired even if the magazine has been removed). However, S&W added their own improvements to the concept with no fewer than twelve patent applications submitted. Glock has filed suit, and there has been no resolution on the matter as of this writing.

The trigger system is unlike other TDA or SA systems on other semiautos. In use, it comes closest to a DAO type system, with a consistent eight- to ten-pound trigger pull required for each shot.

As with any new handgun design, the Sigma/Glock type pistol has both advocates and detractors. There seems to be significant agreement that this type semiauto makes sense as a military handgun. Its advocates for police and civilian applications point to its simplicity of use, with no decocking lever, manual safety, or other mechanical devices to worry about when under stress. They claim such a system makes for an easy transition from the police revolver and the relatively heavy trigger pull and internal safety devices provide adequate protection against accidental discharge.

Those who are skeptical about this type of approach criticize the lack of manual and magazine safeties, arguing that any semiauto has a relatively more complex manual of arms than a revolver, and they predict an increase in operator-caused accidental discharges with this type of system. They question the wisdom of this type handgun for police threat management situations where a suspect may be held at gunpoint without the weapon being fired.

Be that as it may, the Sigma has met with a strong initial market reception. Like the Glock, shooters seem to love it or hate it, with little middle ground.

As with any other recently introduced model, the authors will confess that they may be guilty of blowing smoke in the reader's ear by listing "good, fair, and poor" values. These guns have been around for such a short period of time that they will seldom be found in less than "very good" condition.

Sigma SW40F

MODEL SW40F:

Cal-.40 S&W, Smith & Wesson's entry in the marketplace with a polymer frame w/steel slide autoloader. Fifteen-round double stack magazine w/initial production, later a ten-round mag. was produced, 4-1/2" barrel, double action only, slide very easily removable for cleaning. Three white dot sight system, blue plastic carry case, instruction manual, one extra mag. Fixed tritium night sights available. Serial number 0001 sold at auction for $10,250 in July 1994. Retail $593 to $697. 1994-DATE

Sigma case; typical of new packaging for all S&Ws

NIB	Exc	VG	Good	Fair	Poor
475	420	375	325	275	200

Product Codes:

120002 4-1/2"	DA B 15SH PF FS	94-96	26 oz.
120010 4-1/2"	DA B 15SH PF w/FNS	94-96	26 oz.

MODEL SW40C:

Cal-.40 S&W, a compact version of the SW40F, introduced in 1995,w/14-round double stack magazine, 4" barrel, double action only, blue finish, fixed sights, night sights available, polymer frame. Not released by publication—should be priced similar to full-size. 1995

Product Codes:

120004 4"	B DA 14SH PF FS	95-96	24.4 oz.
120012 4"	B DA 14SH PF w/FNS	95	24.4 oz.

MODEL SW9F:

Cal-9mm, as with the model SW40F this model is also a polymer frame with a steel slide and barrel assembly, initial production as of August 1994 was shipped w/17-round magazine, three white dot sight system, shipped w/extra magazine in a blue plastic carry case, instruction manual, double action only, 4-1/2" barrel, "PAC" serial prefix on initial production. Fixed tritium night sights available. Later limited to one 17-round magazine and a certificate for another 10-round magazine when available. 1994-DATE

NIB	Exc	VG	Good	Fair	Poor
475	420	375	325	275	200

Product Codes:

120006 4-1/2"	DA B 17SH PF FS	94-96	26 oz.
120014 4-1/2"	DA B 17SH PF w/FNS	94-96	26 oz.

MODEL SW9C:

Cal-9mm, a compact version of the Model SW9F, introduced in 1995, w/16-round double stack magazine, 4" barrel, double action only, blue finish, polymer frame, fixed sights, night sights available. Not released at publication date; should be priced similar to full-size. 1995

Product Codes:

120008 4"	B PF 16SH DA FS	95-96	24.7 oz.
120016 4"	B PF 16SH DA w/FNS	95	24.7 oz.

MODEL SW380:

Cal-.380 ACP, S&W first entry in the .380 market, introduced in 1995, a very compact polymer frame autoloader, 6-shot magazine, double action only, fixed sights, 3" barrel, blue finish. 1995

NIB	Exc	VG	Good	Fair	Poor
325	285	235	185	150	125

Product Code:

120100 3"	B DA 6SH FS PF	95-96	14 oz.

Baby Sigma, Model SW380

LONG GUNS

MODEL 320 REVOLVING RIFLE:

Cal-.320 S&W Rifle, 6-shot fluted cylinder with a two-piece barrel that is non-separable but slightly noticeable just forward of the cylinder, detachable shoulder stock, blue or nickel finish, top-break action with auto shell extraction, red mottled hard rubber forearm, hand grip with S&W monogram open, peep, or globe sights, with leather carry case, single action, with triggerguard. The extension stock is Circassian walnut with a black rubber butt plate. The cartridge case is noticeably counter sunk in the shell case in appearance and is scarce to find. Three are known to have been factory engraved. See Neal and Jinks for specific serial numbers. 840 sold in the U.S., 137 exported.

Serial number range 1-977 977 mfd. 1879-1887
(16" barrel 239 mfd.)
(18" barrel 514 mfd.)
(20" barrel 224 mfd.)

Exc	Fine	VG	Good	Fair	Poor
8000	6000	5000	4000	3500	2500

Variations:

- 10% premium for 16" or 20" barrel
- 20-40% premium for nickel
- Original case worth $2000 -$3500

MODEL OF 1940 LIGHT RIFLE MARK I (C&R):

Cal-9mm Luger, produced for the British government during WWII. Fluted 9-3/4" barrel, blue finish, 20-round magazine, black molded plastic stock, fixed front sight is a blade type, rear sight is micrometer adjustable type, semiautomatic fire only from an open bolt, weight 8 lbs. 4 oz. Most were destroyed by the British government with few (130) remaining in the U.S. Removed as an NFA weapon due to short barrel length but reclassified as a curio and relic by the Bureau of Alcohol, Tobacco, and Firearms.

Serial number range 1-2200 inclusive w/Mark II
1,010 mfd. 1940

Either light rifle in Exc to VG will bring $2500-$3000.

MODEL OF 1940 LIGHT RIFLE MARK II (C&R):

Cal-9mm Luger, a modified and improved version of the Mark I with a new style barrel sleeve on the frame, forward of the triggerguard. Most were destroyed by the British government with few (80) remaining in the U.S.

Serial number range 1-2200 inclusive w/Mark I
200 mfd. 1941

Sporting Rifles

(Imported from Sweden and Manufactured by Husqvarna)

MODEL A: BOLT ACTION REPEATING RIFLE:

Cal-.22-250 Rem., .243 Win., .270 Win., .308 Win., .30-06 Spfld., 7mm Rem., or 300 Win. Mag., .270, .30-06, .308, and 7mm calibers have four lands and grooves, all others have six lands and grooves with a 23-3/4" barrel, adjustable folding rear leaf sight, hooded front sight with German silver bead. Receiver drilled and tapped for most scope mounts. Checkered Monte Carlo style stock with rosewood forend tip and pistol grip cap. 7 lbs. 1969-1972

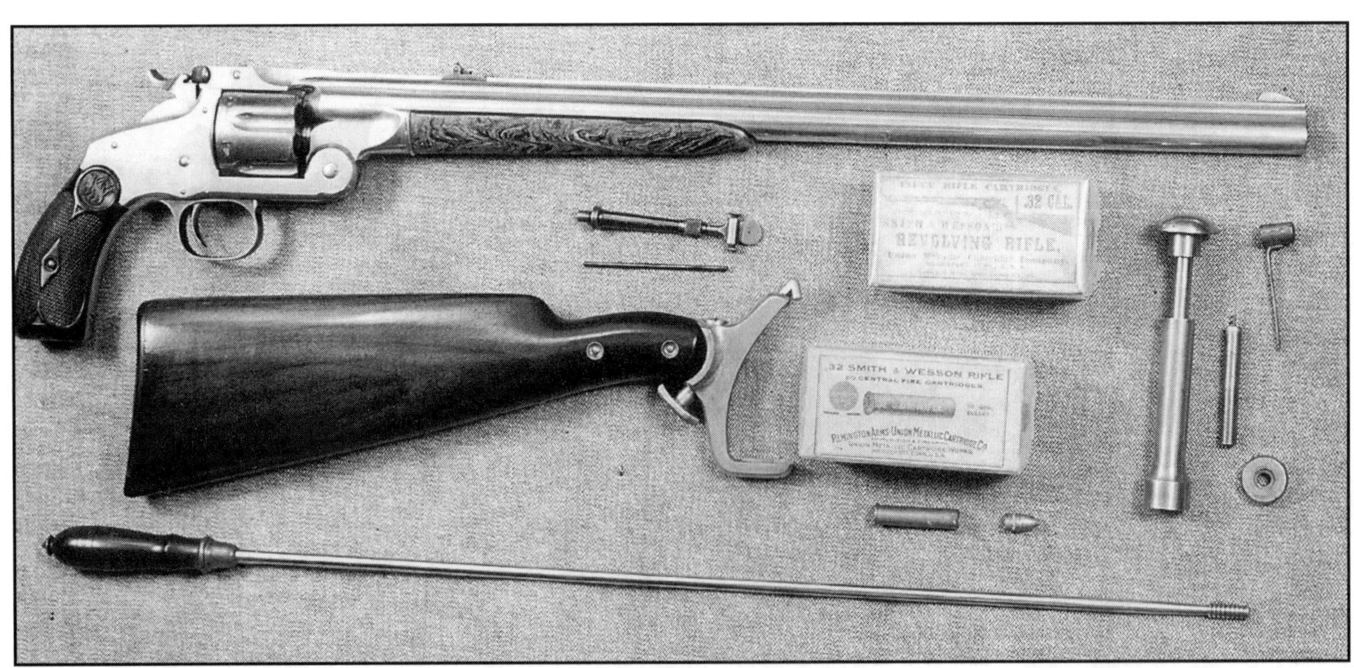

320 Revolving Rifle w/stock detached

NIB	Exc	VG	Good	Fair	Poor
400	350	300	220	185	150

MODEL B: BOLT ACTION LIGHT REPEATING RIFLE:

Cal.-.243 Win., .270 Win., .30-06 Spflg., .308 Win., 20-3/4" barrel with four lands and grooves, .243 Win has six lands and grooves, European walnut Monte Carlo stock w/built-in cheek rest and Schnabel type forend, folding rear sight and hooded front sight w/German silver bead, drilled and tapped for scope mount, similar to the Model A, 6.6 lbs.

NIB	Exc	VG	Good	Fair	Poor
400	350	300	220	185	150

MODEL C: BOLT ACTION LIGHT REPEATING RIFLE:

Cal- .270 Win., .30-06 Spfld., .308 Win., .243 Win., 20-3/4" barrel w/four lands and grooves, .243 has six lands and grooves, similar to the Model B without the Monte Carlo style stock. Drilled and tapped for scope mount. 6.6 lbs.

NIB	Exc	VG	Good	Fair	Poor
400	350	300	220	185	150

MODEL D: BOLT ACTION REPEATING RIFLE:

Cal-.270 Win, .30-06 Spfld., .308 Win., .243 Win., similar to the Model C. Full-length Mannlicher style stock of two-piece construction extending to the tip of the barrel. Also drilled and tapped for scope mount. 6.6 lbs.

NIB	Exc	VG	Good	Fair	Poor
550	450	385	275	225	175

MODEL E: BOLT ACTION REPEATING RIFLE:

Cal-.270 Win., .30-06 Spfld., .308 Win., .243 Win., similar to the Model D. Full-length Mannlicher style Monte Carlo stock with two-piece construction extending to the tip of the barrel, with a built-in cheek rest. Also drilled and tapped for scope mount. 6.6 lbs.

NIB	Exc	VG	Good	Fair	Poor
550	450	385	275	225	175

Model 1500 Series Imported From Japan 1981-1985

(Manufactured by Howa)

MODEL 1500 STANDARD:

Cal-.222 Rem., .223 Rem., .243 Win., .25-06 Rem., .270 Win., .30-06, .308 Win., 22-250. Repeating bolt action, twin locking lugs, 22" barrel, 5-shot mag., (.222 and .223 are a 6-shot mag.,) American walnut stock and forend, swivel posts, drilled and tapped for scope mount, safety locks trigger but allows bolt to be opened for inspection and unloading. Hooded ramp front sight with gold bead and fully adjustable rear sight. Length 42.5", 7 lbs. 10 oz. 1981-1985

NIB	Exc	VG	Good	Fair	Poor
375	320	260	200	175	130

MODEL 1500 DELUXE W/RECOIL PAD:

Cal-7mm and 300 Win. similar to the Model 1500 with a recoil pad with 24" barrel, weight 7 lbs. 12 oz.

NIB	Exc	VG	Good	Fair	Poor
425	360	320	230	185	150

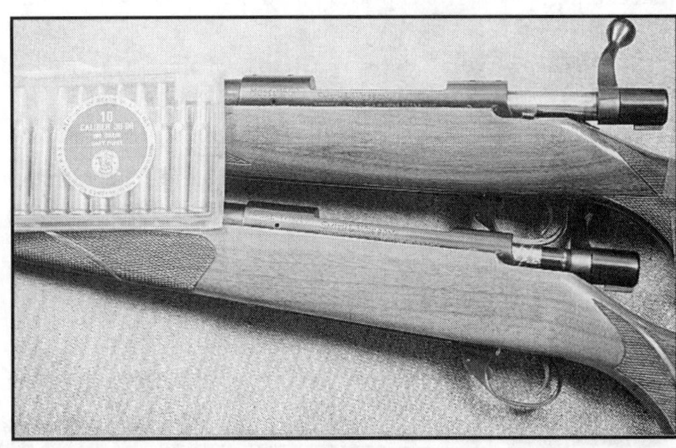

Above and below: Model 1500 (top), Model 1700 (bottom)

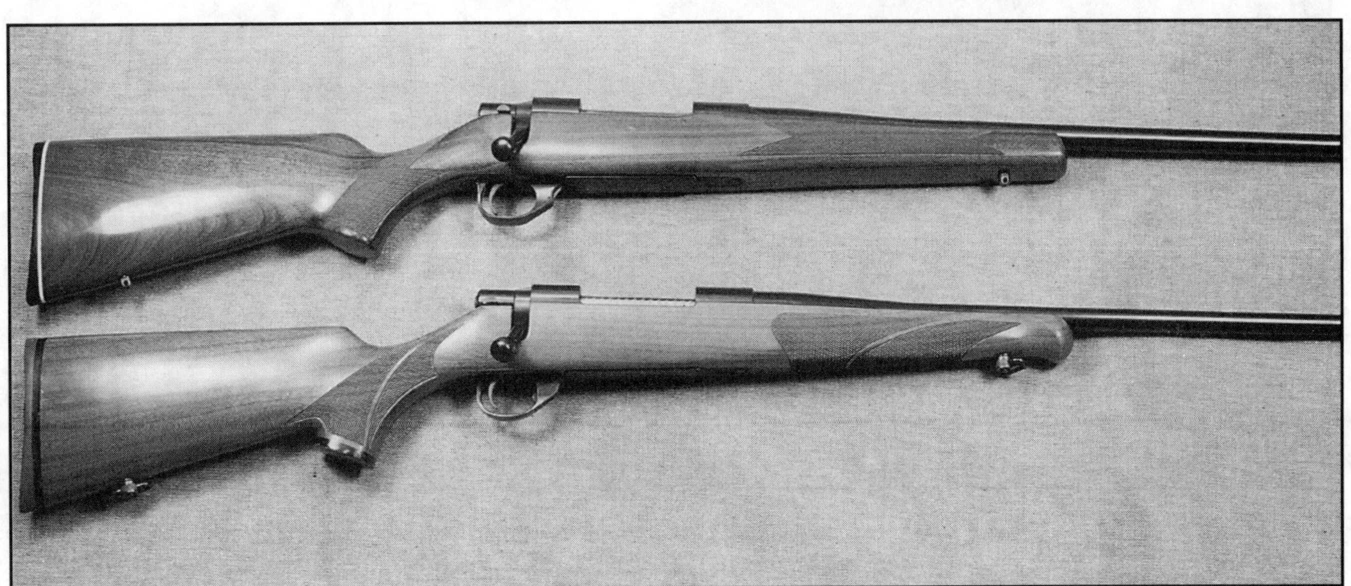

MODEL 1500 MOUNTAINEER:

Cal-.223 Rem., .243 Win., .270 Win., 30/06, 22" barrel, similar to the Model 1500 with 18 line hand checkering and whiteline spacer. 7 lbs. 8 oz.

NIB	Exc	VG	Good	Fair	Poor
400	350	300	220	185	150

MODEL 1500 MOUNTAINEER: W/RECOIL PAD:

Cal-7mm Rem. Mag., similar to 1500 with 24" barrel, 4-shot mag. Length 44.5", weight 7 lbs. 10 oz.

NIB	Exc	VG	Good	Fair	Poor
425	370	320	230	185	150

MODEL 1600 DELUXE:

Cal-same availability as the 1500 with Monte Carlo comb and cheekpiece, skip-line checkering, pistol grip cap with inlaid S&W seal, grade walnut, without sights, 22" barrel, 7 lbs. 10 oz. 1981

NIB	Exc	VG	Good	Fair	Poor
400	350	300	220	185	150

MODEL 1600 DELUXE HEAVY BARREL VARMINT:

Cal-.222 Rem., .22-250,.223 Rem., 24" barrel, skip-line checkering, pistol grip cap with inlaid S&W seal, 9 lbs. 5 oz. 1981

NIB	Exc	VG	Good	Fair	Poor
400	350	300	220	185	150

MODEL 1700 LS "CLASSIC HUNTER":

Cal-.243 Win., .270 Win., .30-06, 22" barrel, 5-shot mag., solid recoil pad, without sights, Schnabel forend, finely checkered, 7 lbs.

NIB	Exc	VG	Good	Fair	Poor
475	385	320	220	185	150

Shotguns

WESSON FIREARMS CO. DOUBLE BARREL SHOTGUN:

Although a product of the Wesson Firearms Co., this arm is well within the scope of this catalog to Smith & Wesson collectors. 12-gauge, 30" double barrel w/double triggers, straight buttstock, steel butt plate and checkered butt. Mfd. about 1868-1870, total quantity about 100 to 200. S/n 1 has a different style frame; s/n's of other known examples are between 100 and 220. Marked: "WESSON FIRE ARMS CO. SPRINGFIELD MASS." Serial number on the triggerguard strap. A few are found engraved by the shop of Gustave Young. Some examples are found without serial numbers or address markings.

If marked, will bring as much as $5000 in excellent condition to $1000 in good condition. Unmarked specimens will bring less than half this amount.

Shotguns Imported from Japan

(Manufactured by Howa Machinery Ltd. for Smith & Wesson)

MODEL 916 SLIDE ACTION SHOTGUN W/FIXED BARREL:

Gauge-12 or 20, chambered for 2-3/4" and 3" magnum shells, fixed barrels are 18", 20", 26", 28", or 30" in length with various chokes: full, modified, improved cylinder, cylinder, plain pistol grip. This model is found with a plain barrel or with ventilated rib, 7-1/4 lbs. 1972

Top: Model 916; Bottom: Model 3000 Police w/folding stock and Mighty Midget gas grenade launcher attached. Also pistol grip, synthetic stock, and extension magazine, all S&W marked.

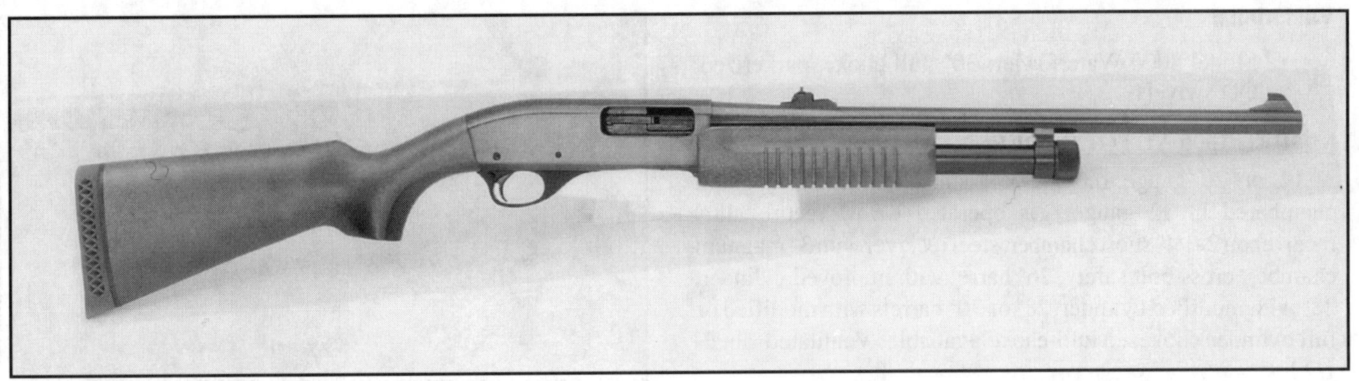

Model 3000 Police, slug sights, wooden stock

NIB	Exc	VG	Good	Fair	Poor
225	185	150	125	100	75

MODEL 916T W/INTERCHANGEABLE BARRELS:

Similar to the 916, but with interchangeable barrels that do not require any prior fitting.

NIB	Exc	VG	Good	Fair	Poor
250	220	170	140	125	75

MODEL 96 SLIDE ACTION:

Various gauges.

NIB	Exc	VG	Good	Fair	Poor
200	150	125	100	85	60

MODEL 1000 P SLIDE ACTION:

Essentially the same gun as the Model 3000. Not to be confused with the Model 1000 autoloader.

MODEL 3000 SLIDE ACTION:

12 or 20 gauge only, pump action with dual bars, chambered for 2-3/4" and 3" magnum shells, barrels interchangeable without fitting, steel receiver, single front bead sight, vented recoil pad, multi-choke available. 1983

Detail, folding stock marking on Model 3000 Police

NIB	Exc	VG	Good	Fair	Poor
300	275	225	175	125	75

MODEL 3000 POLICE:

12 gauge only, blue or parkerized finish, 18" or 20" barrel.

NIB	Exc	VG	Good	Fair	Poor
325	300	250	185	135	75

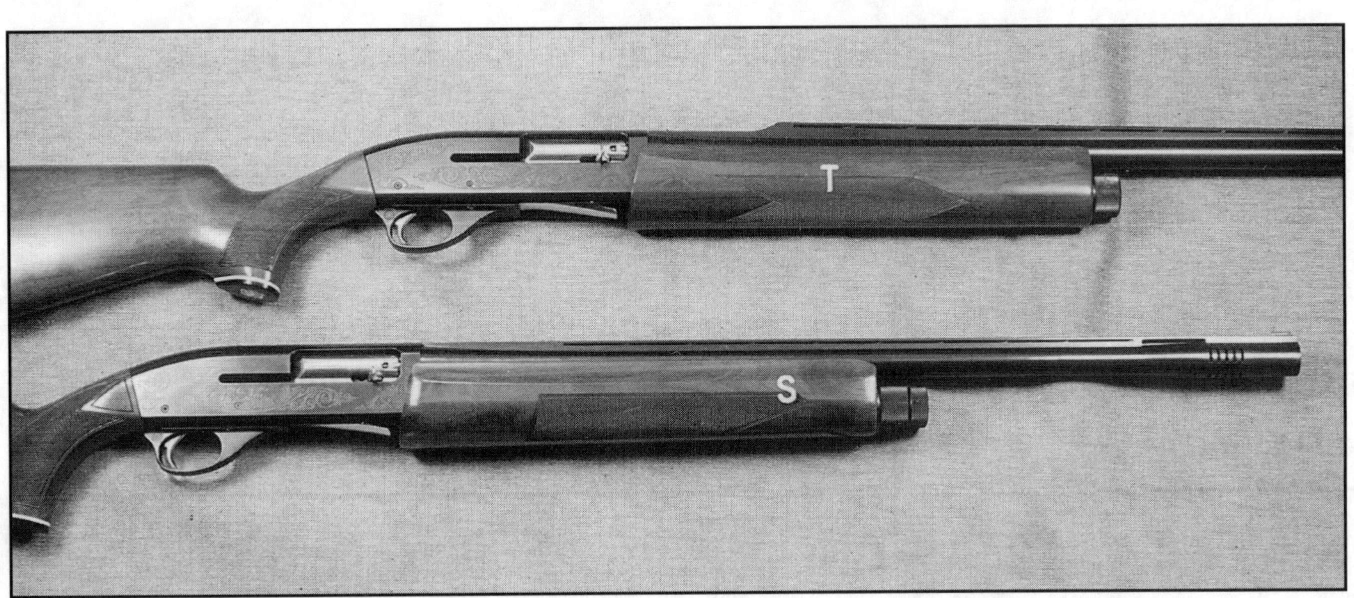

Model 1000 Trap (top) and 1000 Skeet

Variations:

- Model 3000 Waterfowler: 30", full choke, parkerized, QD swivels

MODEL 1000 AUTOLOADER:

12 or 20 gauge only, 2-3/4" chamber or 3" magnum chambered in 12 gauge, gas operated w/low recoil, alloy receiver on 2-3/4" short chamber, steel receiver with 3" magnum chamber, cross bolt safety, 26" barrel with improved cylinder, 28" with modified cylinder, 28" or 30" barrels with modified or full cylinder chokes. Multi-choke available. Ventilated rib, 7-1/2 lbs.

NIB	Exc	VG	Good	Fair	Poor
375	325	275	225	175	100

Variations:

- Model 1000 Waterfowler: 30", full choke, parkerized, QD swivels
- Model 1000 Trap
- Model 1000 Super 12: Handle any load, 12 ga., 1984

MODEL 1000 S SUPER SKEET 12:

12 gauge only, 2-3/4" chamber, steel receiver with scroll engraving on both sides, pistol grip cap w/inset S&W seal, 25" barrel with wide center tract ventilated rib, midpoint sighting bead and "bright point" light gathering fluorescent red bead front sight. Special recessed choke. Cross bolt safety, length 45.7", 8-1/4 lbs.

NIB	Exc	VG	Good	Fair	Poor
550	425	350	285	225	150

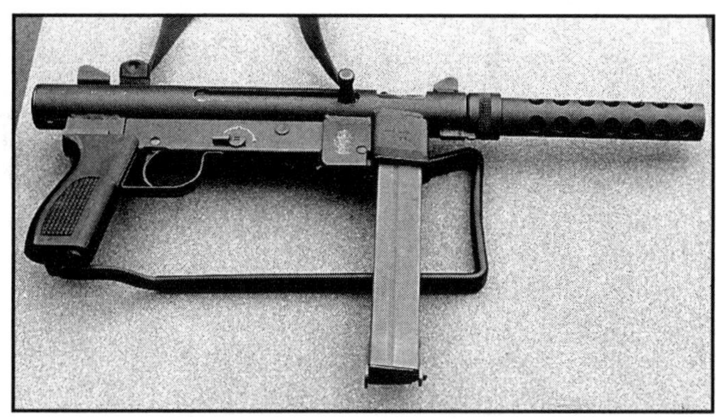

Model 76 Machine Pistol

The Machine Pistol

THE MODEL 76 MACHINE PISTOL:

Cal-9mm, capable of semi or full automatic fire, 36-round clip, folding stock, detachable barrel and barrel shroud, fires from an open bolt, approx. 720 round/min. firing rate, parkerized finish, consisting of 12 major components for ease in field striping, black plastic grip, fixed sights, "U" serial prefix. A caseless Ammo version was developed and tested but never put in production due to problems with dampness with the ammo. Classified as a curio and relic by the Bureau of Alcohol, Tobacco, and Firearms with all N.F.A. rules in effect. Full automatic arms must be registered and taxed, and may be purchased only through a Class III federally licensed dealer.

Serial number range U100-U6200 6,100 mfd. 1968-1974

COMMEMORATIVES AND SPECIALS

Club guns; zero or zero prefix serial number

Club Guns – Zero s/n

"Club guns" are those whose serial number begins in zero. They were assembled by S&W for presentations or for gifts. Many went to shooting clubs for prizes in shooting matches, hence the "club gun" name. It has been speculated that some club guns may have been assembled from remaining parts in inventory some time after a particular gun had been discontinued. It is believed about fifty club guns were made over the years for the Wesson family, with the serial number of each being the single digit "0." Production of around seven hundred other club guns has been estimated, and each of these would have a multiple digit serial number beginning with "0."

Commemoratives

The following is a partial list of commemoratives. These are decorated collector guns and should not be confused with the carry issue gun of the departments commemorated. More details may be found under the model number listed for the particular commemorative. Due to the limited numbers made, and the sometimes restricted initial distribution, detailed pricing information is not available on many of these. Additional information would be most appreciated. In trying to determine a price, a buyer or seller should assess the number made, the extent of decoration, the issue price, and the regional demand. To bring the full value, commemoratives should be unfired and preferably unturned with all original packaging material.

Arizona Highway Patrol 50th – Model 66
California Highway Patrol – Model 19 and 68
Chicago Police – Model 66
Connecticut State Police – Model 39
Dallas Police Department 100th – Model 66
Fairfax County, Virginia, Police – Model 19
Fraternal Order of Police – Model 19
F.B.I. Commemorative – Model 27
Indiana State Police – Model 66
Iowa Highway Patrol – Model 66
IPSC 10th – Model 745
Elmer Keith – Model 29
Kentucky State Police – Model 19
City of Los Angeles 200th – Model 19
Maine Warden Commission – Model 66
Maine State Police 120th – Model 586
Maryland State Police – Model 19
Minnesota State Police – Model 66
Missouri Conservation Corps – Model 586
Missouri Highway Patrol 50th – Model 66
Montana Centennial – Model 25
Montana Highway Patrol 44th – Model 66
National Assoc. Federally Licensed Firearms Dealers – Model 459
National Police Revolver Championship – Model 586
Nebraska State Police 50th – Model 586
New Mexico State Police – Model 19
North Carolina Highway Patrol – Model 29
Oklahoma City Police Dept. – Model 66
Oregon State Police – Model 19
General Patton – Model 27
Pennsylvania State Police – Model 19
Prince William County Police Dept. – Model 19

125th Anniversary Model 25

S&W 125th – Model 25
S&W Collectors Assoc. 25th – Model 29
South Carolina Highway Patrol – Model 66
Springfield Armory Bicentennial – Model 625
Tennessee Highway Patrol – Model 19
Texas Dept. of Public Safety – Model 27
Texas Ranger 150th – Model 19
Texas Wagon Train Commemoratives – Model 544
Tulsa Police Dept. – Model 66
U.S. Border Patrol – Model 66
U.S. Custom Dept. – Model 19
U.S. Marshall Bicentennial – Model 4516-1
Virginia State Police – Model 66
Washington State Police – Model 28
Washington State Penitentiary – Model 19
West Virginian State Police – Model 19

First Editions

During the 1980s there was a practice of giving special factory serial numbers to new models being introduced. A limited number of the first production of a new model would be specially engraved with authenticity certificates.

Limited Edition Model 24: fifty done in nickel
Model 624: twenty-five made
Model 645: twenty-five made
Model 745: unknown quantity
Model 639: unknown quantity
Model 669: unknown quantity
Model 649: one hundred(?) made
Model 422: fifteen made

The "Twelve Revolvers"

Manufactured in 1990 by S&W for Ellett Bros. of Chapin, South Carolina, this series of twelve different guns was sold by subscription, with a different gun offered each month. The firearms each have an action scene engraved on the sideplate and were sequentially numbered from one to five hundred. Each was created with a special theme based on the early S&W advertising paintings. Each set of twelve revolvers was delivered with a special calendar book that featured color artwork of each revolver for that month. However, this series was never fully completed by S&W due to a parting of the business relationship. The author does not have further details on the number of full sets completed. The Twelve Revolvers are found in full and broken sets.

THE "TWELVE REVOLVERS" INCLUDE:

January Edition:

Model 29 with a 8-3/8" barrel w/blue finish, .500" target hammer, .400" serrated target trigger, checkered target stocks, red ramp front sight w/white outline rear, with a scene from "Hostiles" and so lettered.

February Edition:

Model 686 with a 6" barrel w/stainless finish, .375" semi-target hammer, .312" smooth combat trigger, smooth target stocks, black pinned ramp front sight w/black blade rear, with a scene from "With the Wolfhounds" and so lettered.

March Edition:

Model 629 with a 4" barrel w/stainless finish, .400" semi-target hammer, .312" smooth combat trigger, black pinned ramp front sight w/black blade rear, round butt, smooth combat stocks, with a scene from "Mountain Lion" and so lettered.

April Edition:

Model 66 with a 6" barrel w/stainless finish, .500" target hammer, .400" serrated trigger, smooth target stocks, red ramp front sight w/white outline rear, with a scene from "Critical Moment" and so lettered.

May Edition:

Model 57 with a 6" barrel w/blue finish, .500" target hammer, .400" serrated trigger, red ramp front sight w/white outline rear, target stocks, with a scene from "Last Cartridge" and so lettered.

June Edition:

Model 17 with a 6" full lug barrel w/nickel finish with .500" target hammer, .400" serrated trigger, red post pinned front sight w/black blade rear, target stocks, with a scene from "The Revolver" and so lettered.

July Edition:

Model 24 with a 6-1/2" barrel w/blue finish, .375" semi-target hammer, .265" serrated service trigger, serrated black ramp front sight w/black blade rear, checkered target stocks, with a scene from "Through the Line" and so lettered.

August Edition:

Model 14 with a 8-3/8" barrel w/nickel finish, .500" target hammer, .400" serrated trigger, red post Patridge front sight w/black blade rear, with a scene from "Last Stand" and so lettered.

September Edition:

Model 27 with a 7" barrel w/blue finish, a counterbored cylinder, gold bead Patridge front sight w/black blade rear, .375" semi-target hammer, .265" serrated service trigger, with a scene from "Outnumbered" and so lettered. P.C. 100999.

October Edition:

Model 29 with a 7-1/2" full lug barrel w/blue finish, .500" target hammer, .400" serrated target trigger, red ramp front sight w/white outline rear notch, smooth combat stocks, with a scene from "The Attack" and so lettered.

November Edition:

Model 25-5 with a 8-3/8" barrel w/blue finish in .45 Colt caliber, .500" target hammer, .400" serrated trigger, checkered target stocks, red ramp front sight w/white outline rear, with a scene from "The Horse Thief" and so lettered.

Twelve Revolvers

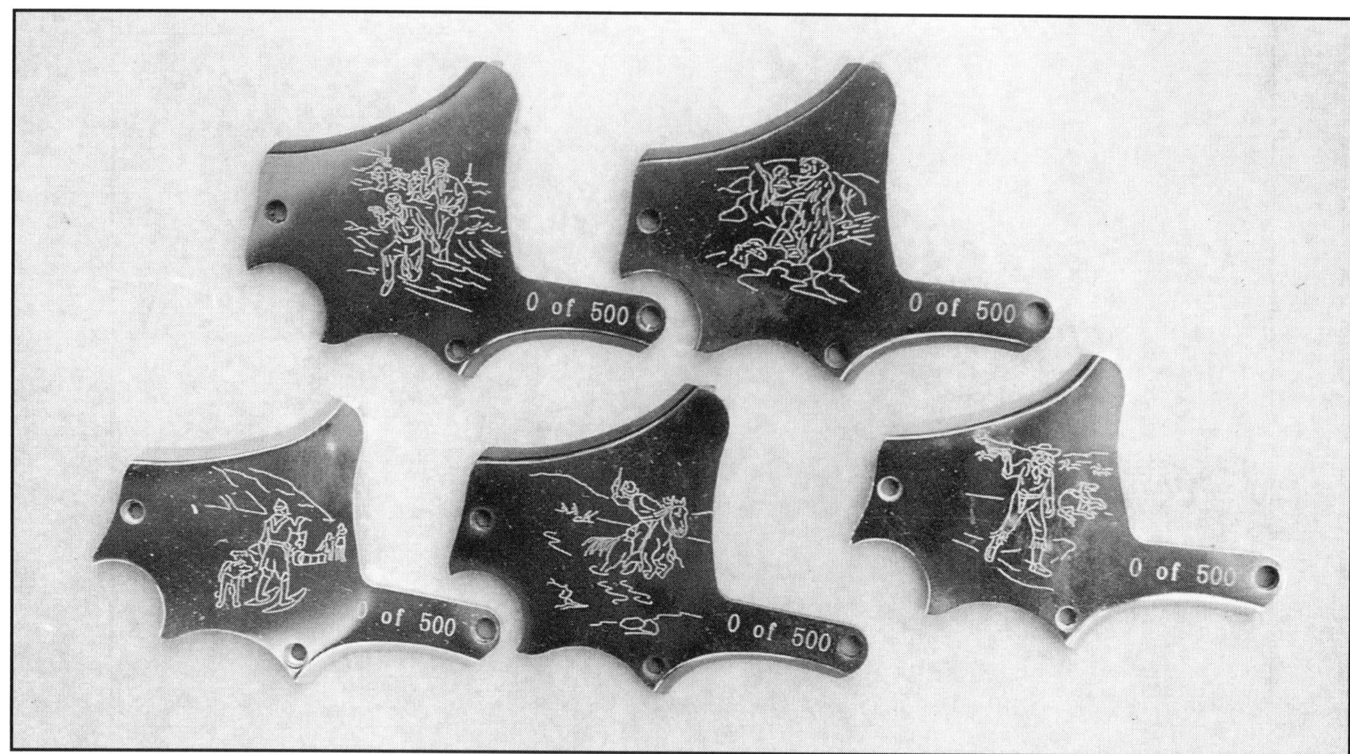

Detail, Twelve Revolvers lasersmith sideplate engraving

December Edition:

Model 19 with a 6" barrel w/nickel finish, .375" semi-target hammer, .265" serrated service trigger, black post front sight w/black blade rear, with a scene from "Hands Off" and so lettered. P.C. 100730.

Twelve Revolver Set:

NIB, $6000. Individual revolvers may bring a slight premium over what a standard model would bring, either for their collectibility, or for their unusual combination of features.

Lew Horton Specials

Specials made for Lew Horton Dist. by Smith & Wesson. Most are listed in detail in the main catalog section, but are accumulated here for easy reference.

- Model PC-13 .357: 400 mfd., 1995.
- Model 19: 75 mfd., 1995. Product Code: 100701.
- Model 24-3: 5,000 mfd., 1983-1984.
- Model 29: Cal-.44 Magnum, 1984. Product Code: 101224.
- Model 29-3 The Classic Hunter: Run of 5,000, 1987. Product Code: 101230.
- Model 60: Carry Comp: 300 mfd., 1993. Product Code: 170029.
- Model 63: 500 mfd., 1989. Product Code: 102405.
- Model .357 "F Comp": 300 mfd., 1993. Product Code: 170024.
- Model 624-2 Lew Horton Special: 37,000 mfd., 1986-87.
- Model 625-4 Springfield Armory Bicentennial: 1994. Product Code: 100931.
- Model 629-3: The Classic Hunter II: 600 mfd., 1992.
- Model 629-1: Stainless Combat Magnum: 1985. Product Code: 103610.
- Model 629-3: Magnum Carry Comp Stainless: 1992. Product Code: 170012.
- Model 629-3: Carry Comp II: 100 mfd. for Lew Horton, 1993.
- Model 640 Special: The Paxton Quigley: 150 dist. by Lew Horton, 1994.
- Model 640 Special: Carry Comp: 23 oz., 150 mfd., 1993. Product Code: 170042.
- Model 657: The .41 Magnum Classic Hunter Stainless: 2,000 mfd., 1991. Product Code: 103820.
- Model 686 Magnum Comp: 350 mfd., 1992.
- Model 686 Carry Comp: 1994.
- Model 686 Competitor: 1994.
- Model 940 Special: 300 mfd., 1994. Product Code: 170047.
- Model 3566:170027 3-1/2"7SH AS "Shorty" 93
  170032 5" 15SH AS"Limited" 93
  170052 4-1/4"12SH AS"Compact"94 35 oz.
- S&W "Shorty Forty": 500 mfd., three production runs: 1992, 1993, and 1995 (1995 called "Mark III"). Product Code: 170011.
- S&W "Tactical Forty": Limited production, 1993. Product Code: 170020.
- S&W "Compensated Forty": Limited production of 150, 1992.
- Model 5906: "PC-9."
- Model 5967: 1990. Product Code: 103048.
- Model 4596: ~500 mfd., 1990. Product Code: 104490.

MISCELLANEOUS S&W ITEMS

Contents:

Air Guns and Projectile Launchers

CO_2 and Air Rifles and Pistols:

MODEL 80 CO_2 BB RIFLE:

Cal-BB .177, a semiautomatic BB rifle powered with a CO_2 cartridge. Monte Carlo style stock of high impact molded polymer, fixed post front sight with fully adjustable rear sight, automatic safety. 39" long, 3-1/4 lbs., velocity of 300 fps.

MODEL 77A AIR RIFLE:

Cal-.22 Pellet, a lever action single-shot pump rifle, blue finish, automatic safety, fixed front post sight w/fully adjustable rear sight, rifled steel barrel w/ten lands, right hand twist, Monte Carlo style stock w/walnut finish. 40" long, 6 lbs. 8 oz., velocity of 420 fps up to 575 fps.

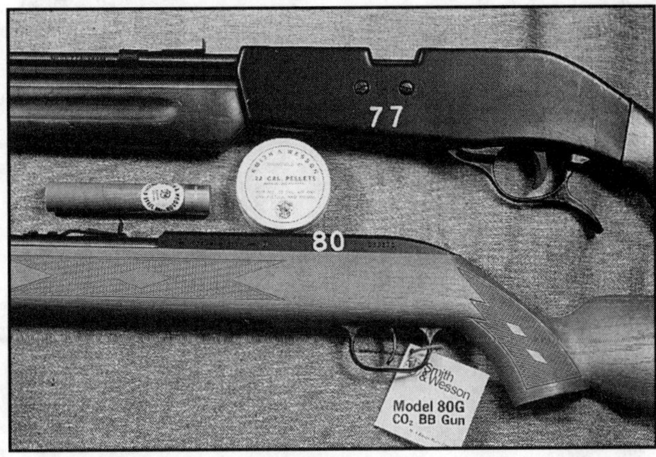

Models 77 and 80 Air Rifles

Model 78G Air Pistol

MODEL 78G CO_2 PELLET PISTOL:

Cal-.22 Pellet, single-shot w/pull bolt, similar in appearance to the Model 41 .22 Long Rifle Target Pistol, w/Patridge front sight, fully adjustable rear sight, positive cross-bolt safety, 8-1/2" barrel of rifled steel w/ten lands in right hand twist, blue finish, has high-low power adjustment, stocks are of simulated checkered walnut, marked "Smith & Wesson Air Gun Div." 42 oz., max. velocity of 420 fps using a standard 12.5 gram CO_2 cartridge.

MODEL 79G CO_2 PELLET PISTOL:

Cal-.177 Pellet, identical to the Model 78G except for caliber.

Gas, Line-Throwing, and Flare Guns:

MODEL 209/277 GAS PISTOL:

Cal-1-1.2" (37mm), built on the modified N frame w/a top-break barrel, pistol grip w/standard stocks, 7-1/2" barrel w/self extractor, single or double action. Service trigger and service hammer. Has no thumbpiece. Parkerized finish, brass bead front sight. Built by Smith & Wesson Chemical Co. in Rock Creek, Ohio. Exc. to NIB $400-$500.

MODEL 209/276 SHOULDER FIRED GAS GUN:

Similar to above, w/long barrel and wooden stock. Exc. to NIB $500-$600.

OTHER CHEMICAL PRODUCTS:

A wide variety of gas grenades, training projectiles, other projectiles, and miscellaneous related items were offered for the above two gas guns, along with other products ranging from large foggers to individual chemical mace sprays and gas masks.

Shoulder and hand gas guns

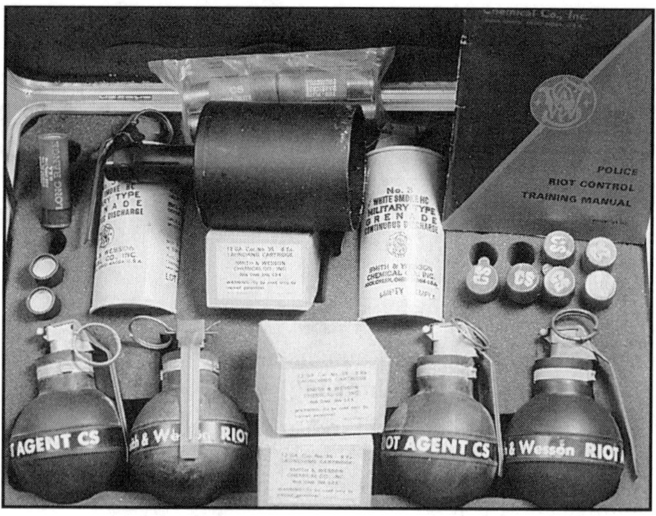

Riot control chemical kit

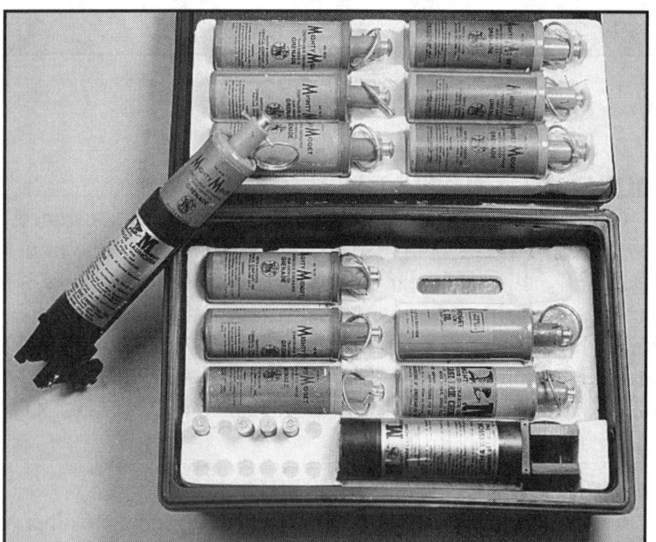

Mighty Midget barrel mounted gas grenade launching kit

MIGHTY MIDGET GAS GRENADE SYSTEM:

A grenade launching device designed to be mounted on the muzzle of a revolver or shotgun for launching small gas grenades and other projectiles.

MODEL 210 PYROTEX LINE-THROWING GUN:

Similar to the Model 209 series of gas guns, pistol configuration w/long barrel w/attached handle, designed to launch a large wooden-tipped line projectile bearing a line between ships, or other applications. Exc. to NIB $500-$650.

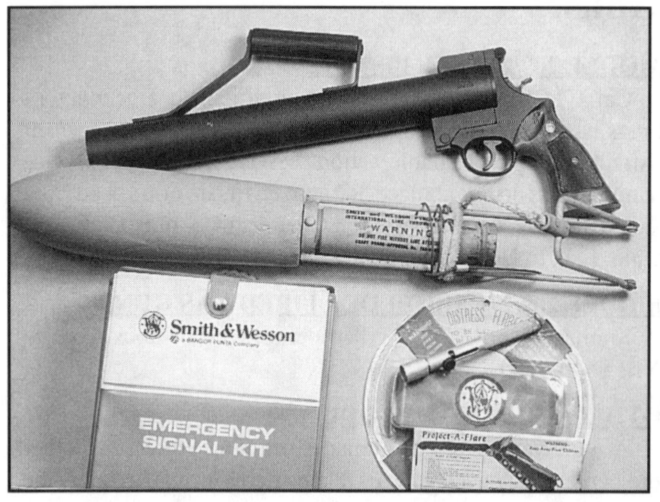

Line Throwing gun, Emergency Signal Kit, Project-a-flare

Chemical agent instruction flip chart

Chemical agent equipment chart, along w/S&W police equipment, airguns, long guns, etc.

MERCOX DART PROJECTILE GUN:

Based on a K-22 frame, this handgun type device could be used to deliver hypodermic dart syringes, or such diverse materials as teargas, dye, or explosive or crowd control projectiles. Very few made—possibly experimental only. Twenty-five manufactured.

PROJECT-A-FLARE:

Miniature fountain pen size reusable emergency flare launcher.

S&W riot shield and helmet

Miscellaneous Police and Firearm-Related Items

Since they began selling gutta-percha cases and "Number One" .22 rimfire cartridges for the Model One 1st Issue, S&W has sold various gun-related items as part of their product line. Many of these were made by other firms and sold through S&W with the prestigious Smith & Wesson name on them. More recently, the Bangor Punta era at S&W saw expansion into a wide range of police products. There is collector interest in any product that has been made or authorized by S&W, although the market is generally much narrower than for S&W handguns.

RELOADING TOOLS:

Among the earliest S&W accessories were tool kits for the reloading of metallic cartridges. A set of reloading tools might consist of a mallet, primer punch, shell holder, bullet seater, and so on, with the primary piece being the bullet mould, which was the only piece marked "Smith & Wesson." Three styles of moulds are known:

Duck bill, w/a piece at the end of the handles to hold them together during casting, 1876-1879

Iron handle, similar to above but lacking the duck bill, 1880-1889

Wood handle, 1889-1912.

Calibers offered included .44 American, .44 Russian, .32 S&W, .38 S&W, .320 Rifle, .32-44, .38-44, .32 S&W Long, and .38 M&P. Sets were unmarked. More information can be found in an early *S&W Journal* article by Roy Jinks, which is reprinted on page thirty-eight of the 25th Anniversary compilation.

HOLSTERS:

S&W reportedly sold a line of holsters and gun belts from 1861 to 1915. However, it is not believed that these were marked in any way that would identify them as S&W products. During the Bangor Punta era, a line of S&W leather and cordura nylon ("Scout") holsters were sold. Even more recently, Bianchi holsters have been offered through S&W. All of these recent holsters tend to sell at their utility value, priced in similar ranges to their other brand commercial counterparts.

AMMUNITION:

During the Bangor Punta years, S&W offered an extensive handgun ammunition line, including .22LR, .25ACP, .32ACP, .32 S&W (very scarce) .357, .38 Special, .380ACP, 9mm, .44 Magnum and .45ACP, often with several loadings in each caliber, plus "indoor" and "outdoor" blanks. Shotgun shells included .410 (very scarce), 20, 16, and 12 ga. Rifle ammunition was offered in .243, .270, .30-30, .308, and .30-06. The S&W line of reloading components included bullets and Alcan made primers.

S&W ammunition

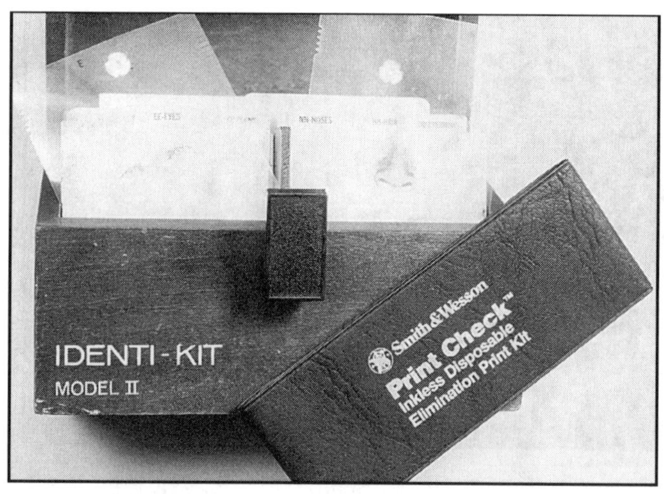

Indenti-Kit and Print Check

Of special interest to collectors are unusual loads such as the .38 Special "Chiefs Special" load, shotgun slugs, and the nylon cased "Nyclad" line of ammunition. Currently, S&W brand ammunition can often be picked up at the same price as comparable current production commercial ammunition, but collector interest is increasing somewhat, and may affect pricing in the future.

An older type of ammunition of special interest to S&W collectors used the S&W patented "self-lubricating" bullet. This projectile was designed to pump lubrication onto the bearing surface of the bullet when the cartridge was fired.

IDENTI-KIT:

Still offered, and found in police departments throughout the country, the Identi-Kit features files of various facial features printed on transparencies that can be used by police to help a witness develop a portrait of a suspect.

HANDCUFFS:

S&W first began to make handcuffs in the 1920s, but they were sold under the "Peerless" brand name through about 1940. Production under the S&W brand began in 1952 and continues through today.

Early model designations and year of introduction:

Model 44 - maximum security hinged model cuffs (introduced 1969)

Model 90 - dull blue or nickel standard model steel cuffs (intro 1952)

Model 91 - bright blue or nickel cuffs (1952)

Model 800 and 810 - belly chain (1965)

Model 820 and 830 - lead chain (1965)

Model 925 - lightweight aluminum nickel cuffs (1958)

Model 926 - lightweight aluminum polished bright cuffs (1958)

Model 936 - stainless steel polished bright cuffs (1961)

Model 938 - stainless steel cuffs, standard finish (1961)

Current model designations:

Model 100 - carbon steel cuffs, blue or nickel

Model 103 - stainless cuffs

Current model designations:

Model 104 - high security keyed carbon steel cuffs, nickel
Model 110 - large sized carbon steel cuffs, blue or nickel
Model 300 - hinged carbon steel cuffs, blue or nickel
Model 1800 - belly chain
Model 1900 - leg irons

OTHER POLICE PRODUCTS:

Other products offered during the Bangor Punta era include riot shields, riot helmets, body armor, dress uniform hats w/protective crown inserts, and Print Check inkless fingerprint kit.

Knives

Information in this section is based on conversations with Clarence E. Rinke and on information in his book, *The Knives of Smith & Wesson.*

In about 1972, S&W began a series of commemorative knives. Production continued through the early 1980s, when S&W sold their knife operations to Vermont Knife Co. In late 1993 or early 1994, S&W again began marketing knives.

The following listed knives are from the earlier production. Prices are for knives in new condition:

Blackie Collins Designs

TEXAS RANGER:

5-1/2" blade, 8,000 sold w/commemorative Model 19s; an additional 12,000 sold individually. 1972, $250.

- "One Riot, One Ranger" etched blade scene Texas Ranger Bowie, $650.

BOWIE:

Model 6010; 15,000 made, $200.

- Missouri Highway Patrol Bowie: 750 sold w/revolver; knife alone, $250.

OUTDOORSMAN:

Model 6020; 13,000 made, 5-1/2" blade, hollow handle, $200.

SURVIVAL:

Model 6030; 17,500 made. 5-1/2" blade, hollow handle, $200.

SKINNER:

Model 6070; 15,500 made, 3-1/2" drop point blade, $175.

FOLDING HUNTER:

Model 6060; 35,000 made, 3-1/2" blade folder, $140.

- Police Marksman Association Folding Hunter: $250.
- 125th Anniversary Folding Hunter w/ H. Smith and D. Wesson: Not authorized by S&W, 131 made, $425.

S&W Collectors Series (Bowie, Outdoorsman, Survival, and Skinner) in case; "One Riot, One Ranger" Texas Ranger Bowie; commemorative Folding Hunter; Deer scene Maverick; Kit Knife; Elephant Blade

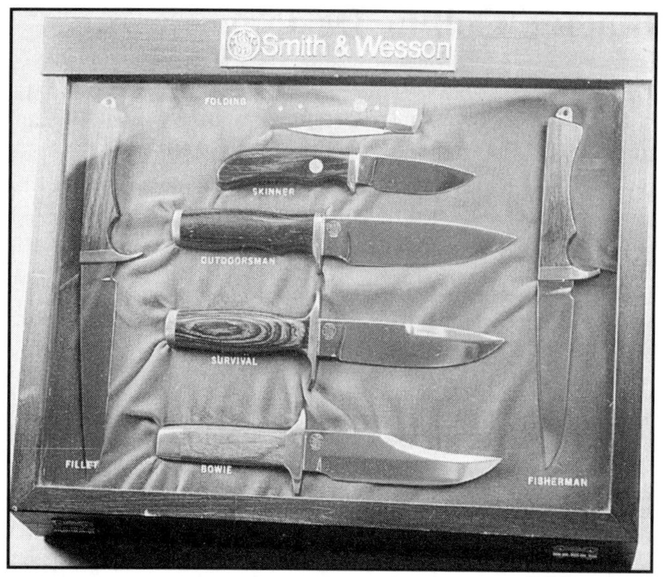

In dealer display case, Folding, Skinner, Outdoorsman, Survival, Bowie, Filet, and Fisherman

FILLET:

Model 6040; 4,500 made, 6-1/2" blade, $225.

FISHERMAN:

Model 6050; 4,500 made, 5-1/2" blade, $225.
Dealer display cases for above knives:
Five knife display case, $175
Seven knife display case, $225

COLLECTOR SERIES:

Four-knife Blackie Collins set, each highly decorated (Bowie-eagle, Outdoorsman-deer, Survival-bear and Skinner-ram), est. 800 completed sets made, total 3,752 knives made. Wood case, $1700 for complete set, individual knives around $350 each.

COLLECTOR SERIES FOLDERS:

Never officially approved by S&W, only a few knives of each design exist (wolverine, beaver, raccoon, bear, and quail designs), valued at $1200 to $2000 each.

KIT KNIFE:

To be finished and assembled by owner, serrated spine, never authorized for sale by S&W, $200.

ELEPHANT BLADE:

Similar to survival knife blade w/elephant scene, 100 made, $700.

Maverick variations, top to bottom, left to right: 1983 Limited Edition, The Hostiles, Gathering Strays; Folding Hunter; commemorative Swing Blade; Ultra Thin variations including World Skeet and 1983 Limited Editions; Desert Storm Swing Blade

Later Designs

MAVERICK:

General purpose folder, rosewood inset panels, "Smith & Wesson" marked large on blade, available with clip or drop point, 1980, $65.

Maverick variations:

- Safelight Windshields, Lear Seigler: 200 made, est. $250
- Deer scene: $200 standard, $300 gold filled
- Gary Hawk "Gathering Strays": 237 made, est. $700

ULTRA THIN:

Small all stainless folder, 1/4" thick, 3" long when closed, $35.

Ultra Thin variations:

- NRA Competition Division: 24 made, est. $500
- Cartech: 72 made, est. $200
- Gun Owners Action League: 200 made, est. $200
- 1983 World Skeet Championships: 12 made, est. $400

AMERICAN SERIES:

Posi-grip rubber handle, available in four blade styles: Large Upsweep, Small Upsweep, Light Duty, and Heavy Duty. 1981, $30 each.

SWING BLADE:

Offered in single edge Sportsman or double edge Boot, 4-3/4" when closed, $55.

Swing Blade variations:

- Etched Swing Blade sporter: 35 made for salesman samples, $400

SHOOTERS KNIFE:

Folder w/screwdriver and knife blade, $45.

Shooters Knife variations:

- S&W Collectors Association Shooters knife: 196 made, $100

BOOT KNIFE:

4-1/2" double edge blade, rubber posi-grip handle, $150 stainless, $175 blue.

LYLE:

S&W marked Folding Hunters, various exotic scale materials, 30 made, $700.

Sets

1983 LIMITED EDITION:

Set of six knives (three ultra thins, a shooters knife, a Maverick, and an American), each with a game scene and "1983," $400 for a matching set or $50 each for individual knives.

1983 LIMITED EDITION KNIFE AND BUCKLE SETS:

Ultra thin with three designs (eagle, duck, and trout from 1983 ltd. edition), each gold filled with matching buckle in a case, $100 for cased knife and buckle.

THE HOSTILES:

Highly decorated Maverick, with matching poster and buckle, 1500 made, $700.

FIRST MATCHED SET:

Consisting of Model 586 Revolver, Model 1500 Deluxe bolt action rifle, and shooters knife w/S&W factory etched on blade, all three with same serial number, 200 sets made, $2000 for set.

Catalogs and Posters

S&W Catalogs

by Don Mundell

The following are some of the different catalogs S&W produced between 1876 and 1952. Although this list is not complete, it will be of help to all collectors.

Date published: April 1, 1878

Name of catalog: None - first catalog S&W released
Cover: Gray w/black letters. The words "Smith & Wesson" in the center, with "Price List" arched above. "Manufacturers of Superior Revolvers, Springfield Mass. April 1, 1878" arched below.
Size: 6 x 7 Number of pages: 16
Price: Seldom encountered. Will bring upwards of $1000.
Comments: Announced new rebounding lock, preventing accidental discharge; prepared to produce 125 revolvers a day; "We put rubber stocks on the nickel-plated pistols only."

Date published: 1892

Name of catalog: None - safety hammerless cover
Cover: Ivory. An embossed full-size 3rd Model .38 Safety Hammerless on the cover. Green inside the scalloping of the cover.
Size: 9-7/8 x 7-3/16 Number of pages: 48
Price: Seldom seen, starting price $500.
Comments: Introduces safety hammerless; includes single-shot, combination 1891 sets, self lubricating bullets, special sights and brass handled screwdriver, repeating (revolving) rifle.

Date published: 1900

Name of catalog: None
Cover: Gray cover, S&W logo on right side in black under which appears the date 1900.
Size: 4-1/8 x 5-3/8 Number of pages: 72
Price: Scarce, will bring $100+.
Comments: Includes revolvers and parts, along with a telegraph code that retailers would use to order specific items from the catalog.

Date published: 1901

Name of catalog: None
Cover: Same as 1900, except for date 1901
Price: Mint condition $150+.
Comments: Same as 1900 catalog

S&W catalogs and literature

S&W catalogs and literature

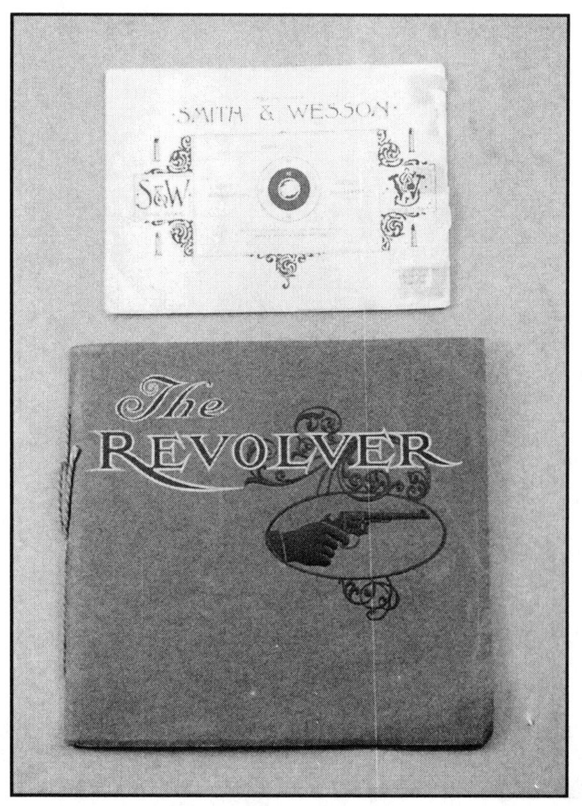

S&W catalogs and literature

Date published: 1905-1906

Name of catalog: "The Revolver"

Cover: Black cover with a picture of a hand holding Model 1905. "The Revolver" outlined in gold. Held together with black string.

Size: 6-3/8 x 6-1/8 Number of pages: 48

Price: Scarce, mint will bring $100 and up.

Comments: Includes short history of the development of the handgun w/S&W commissioned paintings; reasons why their revolver is superior to all others. Discusses finish, pearl stocks (cautions against inferior aftermarket stocks), engraving, target shooting. Found with pink supplement pages consisting of Mar. 1, 1909, price list and introduction of .44 HE and .38 Perfected.

Date published: 1907-1908

Name of catalog: "The Revolver"

Cover: Green w/black lettering, otherwise same as above.

Price: $100

Comments: Similar to above, except includes Perfected and .44 HE.

Date published: 1911

Name of catalog: "Police Models"

Cover: Medium blue, double-line border 7/16" all around outside edge. Printed in dark blue "Police Models" (at top), S&W logo in circle (center), and "Smith & Wesson" (bottom).

Size: 6-5/8 x 6-1/2 Number of pages: 12

Price: Scarce, mint will bring $100+.

Comments: Includes .35 auto.

Date published: 1909-1912

Name of catalog: "The Revolver"

Cover: Same color green as 1907-1908. "The Revolver" in red outlined w/silver. Held together w/green string.

Size: 6-1/2 x 6 Number of pages: 44

Price: Seldom seen, mint will bring $150.

Comments: No longer lists .38 single actions and spare single-shot target barrel. Adds .22 single-shot Perfected (3rd Model). May include price list insert, pink, Nov. 10, 1911.

Date published: 1913

Name of catalog: "Plunders, Old and New" (called "Three Pirates" by collectors)

Cover: Lithographed picture of three pirates, by Philip Lyford. "Smith & Wesson" at bottom in silver, white background.

Size: 7 x 10 Number of pages: 30

Price: Mint $250+.

Comments: May include October 1, 1914 price list insert.

Date published: 1915

Name of catalog: Catalog "S"

Cover: "Mountain Lion," same as Catalog D, except in Spanish—"Revolveres."

Size: 7 x 10 Number of pages: 32

Price: Rare, prices should start at $100.

Comments: Spanish language catalog. Includes end labels of boxes for each pistol, which can help the collector identify period of boxes.

Date published: 1917-1919

Name of catalog: Catalog "D"

Cover: "Mountain Lion" painting by Philip Lyford, full color of cliff climbing photographer with an S&W preparing to fend off an irate cougar.

Size: 4-11/16 x 6 Number of pages: 16

Price: Scarce, $100+.

Comments: Four-page foldout on "Regulation Police" and price list dated March 1, 1917 included inside original envelope.

Date published: August 1, 1919

Name of catalog: Catalog "D-1"

Cover: "Revolvers and Pistols," red border all around the cover, gray background shows a hand holding a .45 S&W revolver with "The Gun That Won" at bottom left—obvious reference to WWI victory in Europe.

Size: 4-1/2 x 6 Number of pages: 16

Price: $45+

Comments: Refers to S&Ws effort in winning the war in Europe and their desire to produce all of their models as soon as possible (S&W was taken over by the government during WWI). They refer to producing future catalogs as their line is expanded. Includes rather extensive notice warning against foreign copies.

Date published: 1921

Name of catalog: Catalog "D-2"

Cover: Light blue border; "Catalog D-2, top; S&W logo inside blue circle surrounded by red, "The Seal of Quality" under logo; pale yellow background; "Smith & Wesson Springfield Mass., U.S.A." at bottom.

Size: 4-1/2 x 6 Number of pages: 16

Price: $50+

Comments: Notes that they are only making certain models "for some time to come," and supplements will be published when their complete line is available. Notes that they have stopped placing the monogram (medallion) on the stock and instead are marking the trademark on the frame.

Date published: 1923

Name of catalog: Catalog "D-3"

Cover: Same as D-2, except on dull brown background.

Size: 4-1/2 x 6 Number of pages: 20

Price: Mint $50+.

Comments: Notes that they can only furnish models shown in this catalog, and that until large first quality shells become available, pearl stocks cannot be furnished. Announces new service sight on M&P square butt.

Date published: February 1925

Name of catalog: Catalog "D-4"

Cover, size and number of pages: Same as D-3, except marked D-4.

Price: Mint $45.

Comments: Notes "we are developing an entirely new model of .22 calibre target pistol which will be fully illustrated and described in the next edition of this catalog."

Date published: 1925

Name of catalog: None

Cover: Brown, 1-1/8" down from top is a black banner w/orange trim; inside banner in orange is "Smith & Wesson, Manufacturers of Superior Revolvers."

Size: 4-1/2 x 6 Number of pages: 44 (40 in some variations)

Price: Fairly common, $40.

Comments: Several variations exist, all in $35-$45 price range. They include:

- Page 11 showing picture of Patridge front sight
- Page 11 devoted mostly to trigger pull
- As above, but include four-page unnumbered insert between pp. 22 and 23
- Large 7-3/8 x 9-1/2 format
- Large format as above, but w/notice about too light trigger pulls and changed ballistics

Date published: 1926

Name of catalog: "Pocket catalog of Smith and Wesson Revolvers"

Cover: Ivory w/ black letters

Size: 4-2/8 x 5-7/8 Number of pages: 20

Price: Uncommon, $50.

Date published: Printed "Marzo 1923"; possibly revised and reprinted "Enero 1929".

Name of catalog: None - Spanish catalog

Cover: S&W trademark in black, "Smith and Wesson, Inc." in brown, "Springfield Mass, U.S.A., Revolveres / Para precios y pomenores dirijase a la casa distribuidora"

Size: 8 x 16 unfolded; 8 x 5-1/2 folded Number of pages: 6

Price: Seldom encountered, starts at $50.

"Anniversary Catalogs"

In 1931, when S&W published the 75th anniversary catalog, they were using 1856 as the starting date for the formation of the company. In 1938 they used 1854. Sometime between 1941 and 1952, they used 1852 as the start-up date, apparently referring to the first Smith & Wesson partnership that produced the "Volcanic" type lever action pistols. Without the above information, it is very difficult to date these catalogs. Dating a catalog may be attempted by noting the inclusion or exclusion of new models, new finishes, grip medallions, target sights, and so on.

Date published: 1931

Name of catalog: 75th Anniversary Catalog

Cover: Blue banner w/ "Smith & Wesson / Manufacturers of / Superior Revolvers" in blue; "75th Anniversary Catalog" on bottom; S&W logo in circle inside border that goes around front cover.

Size: 4-1/2 x 6 Number of pages: 48

Price: $35

Comments: "Special Notice" that they are engraving "Made in the USA" on products, starting 1924; includes .38/44 Super Police (Heavy Duty). At least two variations:

- Pg. 10 shows target sights in one version, standard sights in the other
- One includes call bead front sight on page 12, other doesn't
- Pg. 24, one calls it ".38/44 Super Police"; the other ".38/44 Heavy Duty"
- Only one has ".38/44 S&W Special" on ballistics chart

Date published: 1936

Name of catalog: 80th Anniversary Catalog

Cover, size and no. pages: Same as 75th, except notes 80th.

Price: $35

Comments: Page 48 introduces .357 Magnum revolver. At least two versions: one has information on the .357 on pages 33 and 34; the other has the Straight Line on these pages.

Date published: 1936

Name of catalog: "85th Anniversary Catalog"

Cover: Same as other previous anniversary catalogs, except "85th"

Size: 4 ? x 6 Number of pages: 52

Price: $40-$45

Comments: Introduces the "red luminous" front sight (beginning of the red ramp), white outline rear sight, grip adapter, Magna stock, and .357 ballistics. Versions found with or without the humpback hammer on page 52. A variation is identical, except shows date of January 1937 on page 1.

Date published: 1930

Name of catalog: None - Spanish foldout catalog.

Cover: Gray w/double line red border, black S&W logo, "Smith & Wesson, Inc." in red, "Revolveres" inside red border.

Size: 5-1/2 x 8, unfolds to 5-1/2 x 16-1/4 Number of pages: 1

Price: Uncommon, $30 mint.

Comments: Spanish language flyer.

Date published: 1939

Name of catalog: Smith & Wesson

Cover: Overall dark brown; silver line from top right to bottom left; "Smith & Wesson" and logo in silver.

Size: 5-9/16 x 6-15/16Number of pages: 50 numbers w/2 at end not numbered

Price: Seldom encountered, $50.

Comments: Similar to anniversary catalog series.

Date published: 1940

Name of catalog: Smith & Wesson

Cover: Overall blue. Picture of Target, S&W logo in ten ring; "Smith and Wesson" curled outside of seven ring; "Superior revolvers since 1854" at bottom; all print in silver.

Size: 5-1/2 x 7 Number of pages: 34 numbered w/2 at end not numbered

Comments: An uncommon variation of this catalog, valued at $50, included the following (not included in the more common version):

- Page 17 lists the .38/22 as The Terrier.
- Page 23 includes new K-22 Masterpiece.
- Does not offer the "Burning Powder" booklet.

Ten-Ring Tips
DO'S
DONT'S
The Perfect Hold
Be Careful
14 Famous Features
that make Smith & Wesson Revolvers the most reliable sidearms ever built
SMITH & WESSON

SHOOTING RANGE INSTRUCTION CHART
SAFETY RULES
10 RING TIPS
14 Famous Features
— that make Smith & Wesson Revolvers the most reliable firearms ever built!
14 Famous Models
— of the many modern Revolvers made possible by 100 years of experience!
SMITH & WESSON
SPRINGFIELD, MASSACHUSETTS, U.S.A.

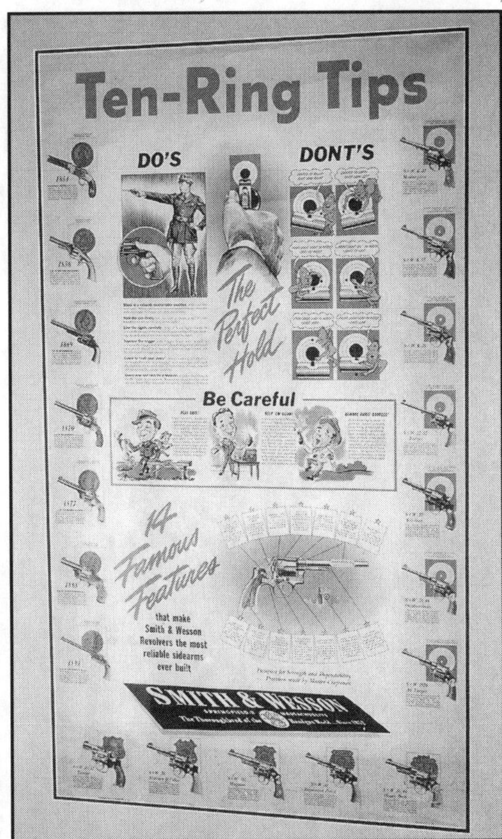

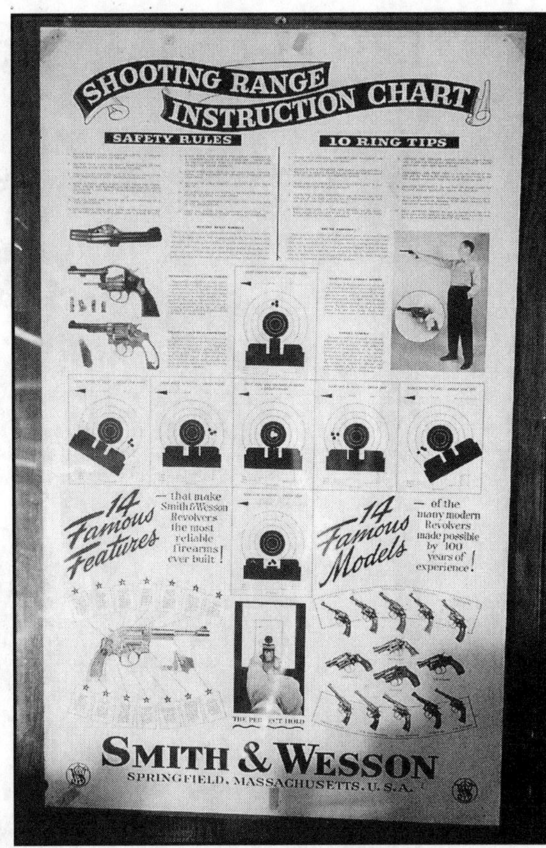

S&W posters

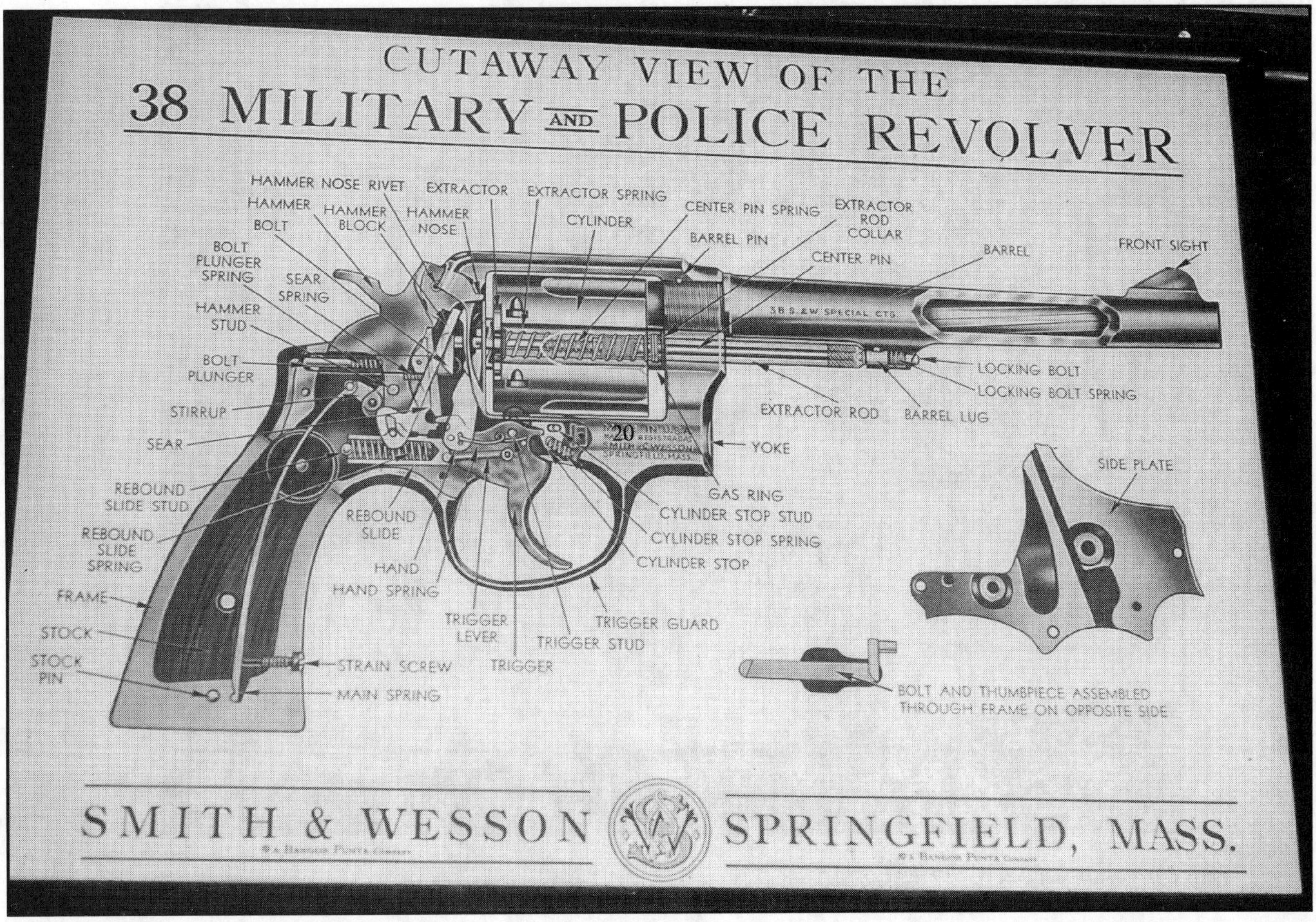

CUTAWAY VIEW OF THE
38 MILITARY AND POLICE REVOLVER
HAMMER NOSE RIVET
EXTRACTOR
EXTRACTOR SPRING
HAMMER
HAMMER BLOCK
HAMMER NOSE
BOLT
CYLINDER
CENTER PIN SPRING
EXTRACTOR ROD COLLAR
BARREL PIN
CENTER PIN
BARREL
FRONT SIGHT
BOLT PLUNGER SPRING
SEAR SPRING
HAMMER STUD
BOLT PLUNGER
STIRRUP
SEAR
REBOUND SLIDE STUD
REBOUND SLIDE SPRING
FRAME
STOCK
STOCK PIN
38 S.&W. SPECIAL CTG.
LOCKING BOLT
LOCKING BOLT SPRING
EXTRACTOR ROD
BARREL LUG
YOKE
GAS RING
CYLINDER STOP STUD
CYLINDER STOP SPRING
CYLINDER STOP
REBOUND SLIDE
HAND
HAND SPRING
TRIGGER LEVER
TRIGGER STUD
TRIGGER GUARD
TRIGGER
STRAIN SCREW
MAIN SPRING
SIDE PLATE
BOLT AND THUMBPIECE ASSEMBLED THROUGH FRAME ON OPPOSITE SIDE
SMITH & WESSON
SPRINGFIELD, MASS.

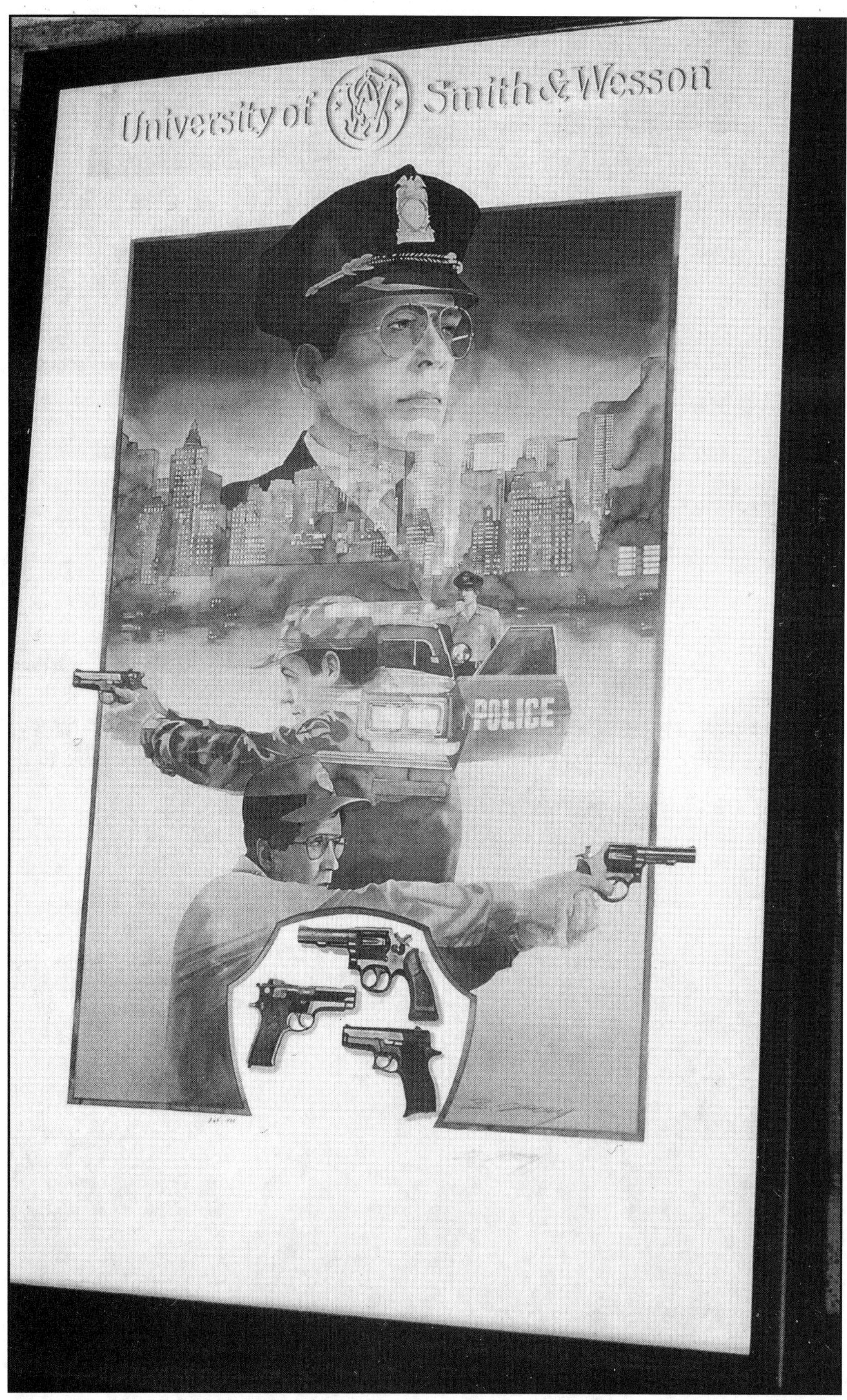

University of S&W Series poster

Date published: 1941
Name of catalog: Smith & Wesson
Cover, size, and number of pages: Same "target" cover as 1940, except color is purple.
Price: Uncommon, $50.
Comments: Contents similar to 1940, drops .32 safety.

Date published: 1952
Name of catalog: Centennial Catalog
Cover: Blue cover w/ black letters, red S&W logo in ten ring of target. "Centennial Catalog" top.
Size: 6 x 8-15/16 Number of pages: 62
Price: Common, $25.
Comments: Includes preface by S&W President Carl Hellstrom, aerial view of new factory. A rare printer's error variation has pages 46 and 47 where pages 18 and 19 should be and vice versa; may be worth $100.

Parts List Catalogs

Along with the standard catalogs, S&W released catalogs known as parts lists.

Date published: 1904
Name of catalog: Smith & Wesson Revolvers/ Price List of Parts/ Nineteen Hundred and Four
Cover: Dark green with black letters
Size: 6-1/2 x 9-1/2 Number of pages: 32
Price: Scarce, $75

Date published: 1909
Name of catalog: Smith & Wesson Revolver/ Price List of Parts
Cover: Brown w/raised black letters; held together w/two brass rivets.
Size: 6-15/16 x 9-15/16 Number of pages: 32
Price: $100

Date published: 1917
Name of catalog: Smith & Wesson Revolvers/ Price List of Parts/ Catalogue P
Cover: Blue w/black letters
Size: 6 x 9 Number of pages: 4
Price: Scarce, $75

Date published: January 1922
Name of catalog: As above, except "Catalogue P-1"
Cover: Mustard yellow w/blue letters
Size: 6 x 9 Number of pages: 36
Price: Fairly common, $60
Comments: A scarce variation has 40 pages, will bring $80.

Date published: 1927
Name of catalog: As above, except "Catalogue P-2"
Cover: Light brown w/black letters
Size: 6 x 9 Number of pages: 40
Price: Fairly common, $50
Comments: A couple variations of the last page are known.

Date published: 1938
Name of catalog: As above, except "1938" and "Catalogue P-3"
Cover: Brown w/black letters
Size: 6 x 9 Number of pages: 40
Price: Common, $45

Date published: 1941
Name of catalog: As above, except "1941" and "Catalogue P-4"
Cover: Light blue w/black letters
Size: 6 x 9 Number of pages: 40
Price: Scarce $60

S&W Posters

THE TWELVE:

In 1902 and 1903, S&W commissioned a series of twelve posters by famous artists. These are the images represented on "The Twelve Revolvers" series (listed in the "Commemoratives and Specials" section), with the sole exception that a painting called "At Close Quarters" was omitted in favor of a later image, "The Mountain Lion." Illustrations of the original twelve paintings can be found in the Neal and Jinks book, or in Roy Jinks' book, *Twelve Revolvers.*

Prices for an original poster from 1902-1903 probably start at $500 and go up. Some of the more popular images have been reprinted. For example, "The Hostiles," probably the best known, was originally released in March of 1903. It was reprinted for S&W's 75th anniversary, and again for their Centennial in 1952. The Centennial reprint will bring around $200. It was reprinted yet again, along with "The Last Cartridge," during the Bangor Punta years, and these reprints will bring around $25 to $35 a copy.

MORE RECENT POSTERS:

There seems to be no end to the variations in S&W paperwork that will be of interest to collectors. The authors lack the expertise to begin to catalog them all, but submit the following limited examples as illustrations of the market:

- **Ten Ring Tips:** Color, exc. $300.
- **Shooting Range Instruction Chart:** B&W, exc. $150-$200.
- **University of S&W Series:** Three different designs, color, exc. $150 each.
- **Cutaway View of .38 M&P:** Large S&W Inc. version, $75; smaller Bangor Punta version, $25.

Gimcracks and Geegaws

There is an endless variety of S&W memorabilia, whatsits, and just plain neat stuff, all of which will be scarfed up by collectors at the right price. One of the authors will admit to treasuring a S&W marked sugar packet from the factory cafeteria. Now that the reader has some inkling of the radical forms this disease can take, the following general categories are submitted for your temptation or puzzlement:

Blade saver case

Diversification

Some unexpected S&W products show up as results of various attempts to diversify the product line. This is especially true of the era following WWI, when S&W sought to establish an presence outside of the firearms market. The results:

Dishwashers and washing machines
Flush valves (for toilets)
Blade savers: Devices for holding safety razor blades so that they can be sharpened like straight razors. Three types made. Will bring a C note from a collector who is hard up for a S&W fix. At least that's what I was told when I bought the one that is languishing unsold on my shelf.
Gutta-percha light socket fixtures, reportedly S&W marked

Promotional Items

This section includes S&W logo marked products that are offered for sale to the public through Smith & Wesson or by licensing agreement. The accompanying photos will give the reader some idea of what is available. A partial list would include the following:

Tie tacs, lapel pins or hat tacs: There are rare ones that bring a couple hundred dollars. On the other hand, there are ones that were given away by the bucketful at the most recent promotional event.
Jewelry: Tie clasps, cuff links, key chains, necklaces, bracelets, etc.
Lighters, measuring tapes, playing cards
Neckties (eight patterns reported at last count)
Pens
Small promotional knives
Belts and belt buckles
Clothing: Jackets, shirts, caps, and so on—lots introduced recently
Cast iron toys (tapping two collector groups at once—pretty smart!)
Electric train set
Christmas tree ornaments
Gun shop counter mat
Patches, decals
Shotgun shell caddies
Gun rugs, cases, grips, sights
Mugs, glasses, coasters
Letter openers
Pistol grip bookends
Ladies scarves
Billfold and money clips
Blazer buttons
Desk sets (six different) made from gun parts
Tote and duffel bags

S&W factory guard badge

S&W jewelry and key chains

S&W toys

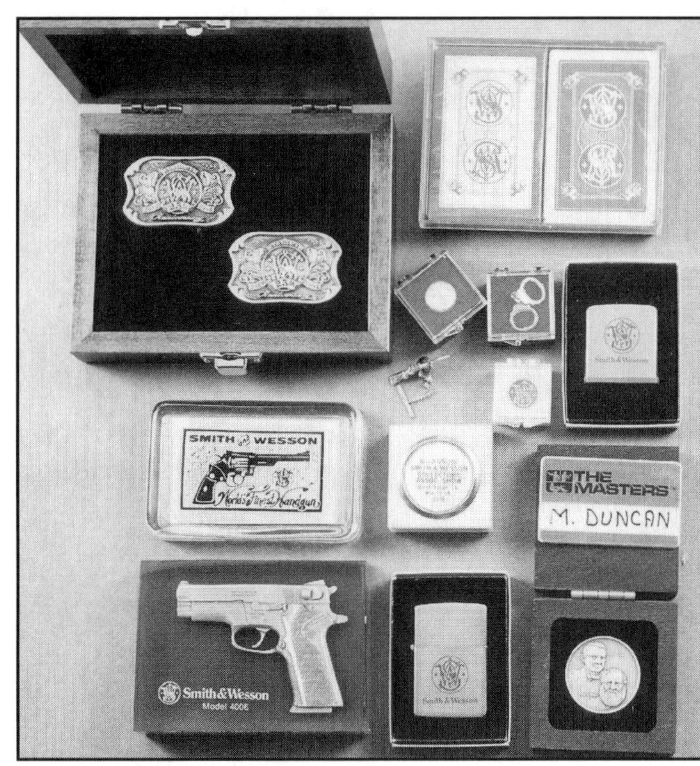

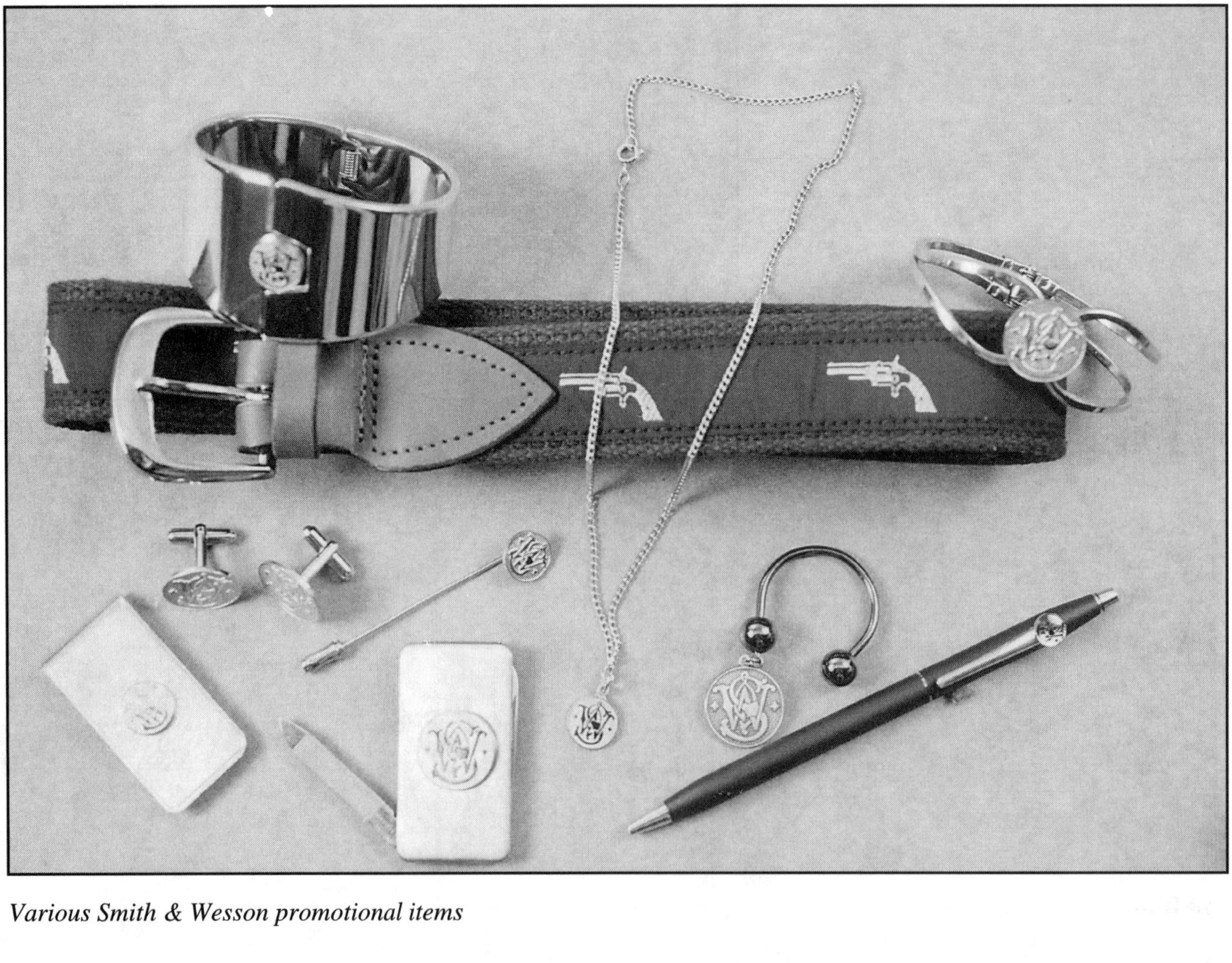

Various Smith & Wesson promotional items

***A note on unauthorized promotional items:** The S&W logo or references to Smith & Wesson will not infrequently appear on items not authorized by the company, despite that such usage may be illegal. Generally, such items do not interest collectors as much as those that have official blessings. Locally produced "Insured by Smith & Wesson" bumper stickers may be a hot item at a buck a pop at the neighborhood novelty shop, but they won't generally bring a premium from a collector ten years from now.*

Factory Stuff

This would include items that were made for internal use by S&W, or used as promotional items focused at a narrower audience than the general public—for example, promotional pieces made for S&W distributors.

Such items are always popular among hard-core collectors, and value tends to increase based on the uniqueness of the object, how closely it was associated with the factory, age, and general coolness. Original obsolete factory tooling or objects provable as having been owned by D. B. Wesson would be quite desirable. Promotional displays distributed to hundreds of S&W stocking dealers within the past ten years would be less so.

Items will turn up in this genre that might be surprising. Decades ago, S&W had a company baseball team. S&W baseball uniforms exist (for that matter, so do uniforms from the recently disbanded Team S&W shooting team). We have recently seen a curved glass display case with the S&W logo in stained glass on the ends that reportedly was made for a turn of the century exposition. Promotional items or prototypes that were discarded when the company changed direction or ownership will sometimes find their way into the collector network where, if it says S&W, it will find a loving home.

APPENDIX 1
S&W Historic Milestones

1808 - Horace Smith born
1825 - D. B. Wesson born
1853 - First S&W partnership formed to make Volcanic style lever action repeating pistols
1854 - Patented .22 rimfire cartridge
1855 - Rollin White patented bored-through cylinder
Volcanic lever action production turned over to Oliver Winchester & Co.
1858 - Second S&W partnership manufactures the first S&W revolver: Model 1, .22 rimfire
1860 - Move to new factory in Stockbridge
1861 - Model 2 introduced in new .32 rimfire cartridge
Civil War begins
1867 - Begin marketing efforts in Europe
1870 - Model 3 introduced; S&Ws first top-break, first .44 caliber, and first centerfire
1871 - First Russian military contract
1873 - Smith retires; D. B. Wesson president
1876 - .38 S&W cartridge introduced in "Baby Russian"
1878 - .32 S&W cartridge introduced in .32 single action revolver
1880 - S&Ws first double action: .38 DA
1886 - S&Ws first safety hammerless: .38 Safety
1893 - Horace Smith dies
1896 - S&Ws first hand ejector revolver: .32 HE 1st, first I-frame
1899 - .38 Special cartridge introduced in the first K frame: .38 M&P
1905 - "5th screw" added to hand ejector frames
1906 - D. B. Wesson dies; Walter Wesson president
1908 - .44 Special cartridge introduced in the first N frame: .44 HE
1915 - Joe Wesson president
1918-19 - Army takes over management of plant for WWI production
1920 - Harold Wesson president
1935 - .357 Magnum cartridge introduced in first .357 Mag. handgun: the Registered Magnum
1946 - C. R. Hellstrom president
1949 - Move to new plant
1950 - First J frame: Chiefs Special
1952 - First alloy frame airweights
1955 - Model 39 introduced: first American 9mm DA
End 5-screw hand ejectors; begin 4-screw hand ejectors
1957 - Model numbers introduced for all models
1961 - End 4-screw hand ejectors; begin 3-screw hand ejectors
1963 - William Gunn president
1965 - S&W sold to Bangor Punta
First stainless steel handgun: Model 60
1971 - Model 59: the first "wonder-nine"
1973 - James Oberg president
1981 - L frame revolvers introduced
1982 - Second generation semiauto DAs introduced
Pinned barrel eliminated on hand ejectors
Counterbored cylinder eliminated on magnum hand ejectors
1984 - Lear Siegler purchases S&W
1987 - Tompkins p.l.c. of London purchases S&W
1988 - Third generation semiauto DAs introduced
1990 - .40 S&W cartridge introduced
1992 - Ed Schultz president
1994 - Sigma series of polymer frame semiautos introduced
1995- Seven-shot .357 Magnum introduced
Don Hinmon president
1996- Ten-shot Model 17 introduced

APPENDIX 2
Serial Number Ranges by Years

A note about serial number ranges:

The Smith & Wesson collector will quickly realize that S&W has made many firearms with the same serial letter prefix that applied to many different models and calibers. Sorting out serial numbers and ranges for the purpose of establishing a manufacturing date can be difficult. The authors have provided a compilation of serial ranges to assist in this task. As an example of this mixing of models and calibers, consider the history of the letter "K" serial prefix.

The letter "K" serial prefix covers eleven models made from 1946 to 1983 in six calibers. The first was the Model 17, followed by the Model 14, 16, 15, 18, 19, 48, 53, 66, 67 and 68, all over a time span of about thirty-seven years that covers approximately 3.1 million firearms. The listed serial dates are considered accurate to within plus-one year, but some frames were stamped with a serial number and did not leave the factory for some time.

Actual ship dates may be confirmed by the factory historian at Smith & Wesson, Mr. Roy G. Jinks.

Smith & Wesson initiated their design changes by a date, not by a specific serial number, nor were handguns assembled in an exact chronological order. For these reasons, the collector will always find exceptions to this serial number data.

Due to the 1968 Gun Control Act, which prohibited any two firearms of the same caliber and manufacturer from having the same serial number, 1969 was a year of serial number revisions by S&W. This prompted the introduction of the single letter serial prefix on all S&Ws.

About 1980, space for numbers was running out and S&W had to again revise the serial number scheme. This was done with a three-letter serial prefix followed by a four-digit number on all firearms. This system is the one presently in use, and would theoretically allow over 175 million serial numbers without duplication.

Serial Number Ranges Quick Reference

Listed in order of caliber:

Model 1s

1857-1860	1st	1-11671
1860-1868	2nd	11672-126361
1868-1881	3rd	1-131163

Single-Shot Pistols

1893-1905	1st	1-28107
1905-1909	2nd	1-4615
1909-1923	3rd	4618-11641
1925-1936	4th	1-1870

.22 HE LadySmith

1902-1906	1st	1-4575
1906-1910	2nd	4576-13950
1910-1921	3rd	13951-26154

.22/32 Hand Ejector Series

1911-1941	160000-536684
1923	384xxx

K-22 Outdoorsman

1931-1940	632132-682419

K-22 Masterpiece

1940-1941	682420-696952

Model 1-1/2 (Rimfire Tip-Up)

1865-1868	1st	1-26300
1868-1875	2nd	26301-127100

Model 1-1/2 (Centerfire Top-Break)

1878-1892	1-97574

Model 2 ("Old Army" .32 Rimfire)

1861-1874	1-77155

Model 320 Revolving Rifle

1879-1887	1-977

.32 Double Action

1880	1st	1-30
1880-1882	2nd	30-22172
1882-1883	3rd	22173-43405
1883-1909	4th	43406-282999
1909-1919	5th	283000-327641

.32 Safety Hammerless

1888-1902	1st	1-91417
1902-1909	2nd	91418-170000
1909-1937	3rd	170000-242981

.32 Hand Ejector Series and Models 30,31

1896-1903	1st model	1-19712
1903-1904	2nd model	1-19425
1904-1906	1st change	19426-51126
1906-1909	2nd	51127-95500
1909-1910	3rd	95501-96125
1910	4th	96126-102500
1910-1917	5th	102501-263000
1911-1942	3rd model	263001-536684
1946-1960	postwar	536685-712953
1961-1970	model 30,31	712954-826977

.32-20 Winchester

1899-1902	1st model	1-5311
1902-1905	2nd model	5312-9811
1903-1905	1st change	9812-18125
1905-1906	model of 1905	18126-22426
1906-1907	1905 1st	22427-33500
1906-1907	1905 2nd	33501-45200
1909-1915	1905 3rd	45201-65700
1915-1940	1905 4th	65701-144684

.38 Single Action

1876-1877	1st	1-25548
1877-1891	2nd	1-108255
1891-1911	3rd	1-28107

.38 Double Action

1880	1st	1-4000
1880-1884	2nd	4001-119000
1884-1895	3rd	119001-322700
1895-1909	4th	322701-539000
1909-1911	5th	539001-554077

.38 Perfected

1909-1920	1-59400

.38 Safety Hammerless

1887	1st	1-5250
1887-1890	2nd	5251-42483
1890-1898	3rd	42484-116002
1898-1907	4th	116003-220000
1907-1940	5th	220000-261495

.38 Special Hand Ejector M&P

1899-1902	1-20975
1902-1903	20976-33803
1903-1904	33804-62449
1905-1906	62450-73250
1906-1909	73251-146899
1909-1915	146900-241703
1915-1942	241704-700000
1940-1945	700000-1000000

.38/200 and .38 Special Victory Models:

1942-1945	V1-V811119 And SV prefix

.38 Special M&P Postwar and Models 10,11,12,45, and Aircrewman

1945-1948	S811120-S999999
1948-1967	C1-C999999

.38 Regulation Police and Models 32,33

1917-1940	1-54474
1949-1969	54474-122678

Model 3s (All Calibers)

1870-1872	1st Model American	1-8000
1872-1874	2nd Model American (and 1st Russian)	8000-32800
1871-1878	Russian Model s/n ranges complicated - see text or Neal and Jinks	
1875	1st Schofield	1-3035
1876-1877	2nd Schofield	3036-8969
1878-1912	New Model #3	1-35796
	Estimated ranges only:	
	1878-1885	1-14000
	1883-1890	14000-20000
	1887-1898	20000-30000
	1896-1907	30000-35796
1887-1910	N.M. #3 Target	1-4333
1879-1883	N.M. #3 Turkish	1-5461
1885-1908	N.M. #3 Frontier	1-2072
1900-1907	N.M. #3 .38 Winchester	1-74
1881-1913	44 D.A. 1st	1-54668
1882-1883	Wesson Favorite	some of 8900-10100
1886-1913	D.A. Frontier	1-15340
1900-1907	D.A. .38 Winchester	1-276

.44 Hand Ejectors: 1st Model, 2nd Model, 3rd Model, sorted by year and serial starts

1908	1	1926	25000
1909	2050	1927	28500
1910	5000	1928	29500
1911	7050	1929	30000
1912	9100	1930	34000
1913	11150	1931	36000
1914	13200	1932	38375
1915	15250	1933	41200
1916	15500	1934	43350
1917	16000	1935	45500
1918-1919	no production	1936	47200
1920	16200 (after 12-6-20)	1937	48700
1921	16300	1938	52000
1922	18400	1939	57200
1923	19600	1940	59000
1924	20800	1941	62350
1925	22000	1942-1945	no production

1917 U.S. Service Model/.45 DA Army .45 ACP

1917-1946	1-209791
1946-1950	209792-210782

.455 Hand Ejectors

1914-1915	1st	1-5000
1915-1917	2nd	5001-74755

"S" Serial Prefix: N Frames Postwar

Models: 20, 21, 22, 23, 24, 25, 26, 27, 28, 29, 57, 58 and their pre-model number variations

1946-1947	S62489-S67999
1947-1948	S68000-S71999
1948-1949	S72000-S72499
1949-1950	S72500-S74999
1950-1951	S75000-S80499
1951-1952	S80500-S85999

1952-1953	S86000-S94999
1953-1954	S95000-S102999
1954-1955	S103000-S139999
1955-1956	S140000-S149999
1956-1957	S150000-S175999
1957-1958	S176000-S181999
1958-1959	S182000-S194499
1959-1960	S194500-S206999
1960-1961	S207000-S219999
1961-1962	S220000-S227999
1962-1963	S228000-S231999
1963-1964	S232000-S235999
1964-1965	S236000-S257999
1965-1966	S258000-S261999
1966-1967	S262000-S289999
1967-1968	S290000-S304999
1968-1969	S305000-S329999
1969-1970	S330000-S333454

"N" Serial Prefix: N Frames

Models: 25, 27, 28, 29, 57, 58, 520, 629 approximate dates

1970-1972	N1-N60000
1972-1974	N60001-N190000
1975-1977	N190001-N430000
1978	N430001-N550000
1979	N550001-N580000
1980	N580000-N700000
1980	N700001-N790000
1980-1981	N790001-N820000
1981	N820001-N932100
1983	N932101-N932xxx

"K" Serial Prefix by Year, Postwar

Models: 14, 15, 16, 17, 18, 19, 48, 53, 66, 67, 68 and their pre-model versions

1946	K101-K614	Introduction of pre M-17
1947	K615-K18731	Introduction of pre M-14 and pre M-16
1948	K18732-K73121	Introduction of pre M-15 and pre M-18
1949	K73122-K84149	
1950	K84150-K104047	
1951	K104048-K136690	
1952	K136691-K175637	
1953	K175638-K210095	
1954	K210096-K231255	
1955	K231256-K266164	Introduction of pre M-19
1956	K266165-K288988	
1957	K288989-K317822	
1957	Began Model Number stamping	
1958	K317823-K350547	
1959	K350548-K386804	Introduction of M-48
1960	K386805-K429894	
1961	K429895-K468098	Introduction of M-53
1962	K468099-K515478	Introduction of M-56
1963	K515479-K553999	
1964	K555000-K605877	
1965	K605878-K658986	
1966	K658987-K715996	
1967	K715997-K779162	
1968	K779163-K848781	
1969	K848782-K946391	
1970	K946392-K999999	Introduction of M-66
	1K1-1K39500	
	2K1-2K22037	
1971	1K39501-1K99999	
	2K22038-2K55996	
	3K1-3K31279	
1972	2K55997-2K99999	Introduction of M-67
	3K31280-5K6616	
	4K1-4K1627	
1973	4K1628-4K54104	
	5K6617-5K73962	
1974	4K54105-4K99999	
	5K73963-6K58917	
	7K1-7K26043	
1975	7K26044-7K70577	
	6K58918-8K20763	
	8K20764-9K1	
	8K20000-9K100000	
1976	9K10001-9K99999	Introduction of M-68
1977	10K0001-24K9999	
1978-1979	25K0001-56K9999	
1980	57K0001-91K6800	
1981	91K6801-124K000	
1982	125K000-269K999	Oct. 1982: Begin three-letter serial prefix
1983	270K000-311K273	For all models

"R" Serial Prefix:

Models: 60, 651

1969	R001-R30000
1970-1973	R30001-R99999
1974-1977	R100000-R190000
1977-1978	R190001-R220000
1979-1980	R220001-R280000
1980-1981	R280001-R300800
1982	R300801-R329000
1983	R329001

"H" Serial Prefix

Models: 30, 31, 32

1969-1970	H00001-H30001
1971-1972	H30002-H60000
1972-1976	H60001-H99999
1975-1980	H100001-H139900
1981	H139901-H160000
1982	H161001-H161200
1983	H161201-Hxxxx

Early "J" Frame Serial Range:

Models: 36, 37, 38, 49, 50 and their pre-model versions

1950-1969 1-786544 (no prefix)

Approximate mfd. dates:

1950	1
1952	7369-21342
1953	28916
1955	55050-75000
1957	117770-125000

1962	295000
1969	786544

"J" Serial Prefix:

Models: 36, 37, 38, 49, 50

1969-1970	J1-J99999
1971-1972	1J1-999J99
1973-1974	J100000-J250000
1975-1976	J250001-J370000
1976-1977	J370001-J610000
1977-1978	J610001-J670000
1979-1980	J670001-J760000
1981	J760001-J915400
1982	J915401-1J18600
1983	1J18601-1Jxxxx

Postwar "S" Serial Range: (K Frame)

Premodels: 10, 11, 45

1945-1948 S 811120 to S 999999

"C" Serial Prefix: approximate mfd. dates

Models: 10, 11, 12, 45, Aircrewman, and their pre-model versions

1948	C1
1952	C223999
1953	C236004-C261483
1954	C277555-C314031
1957	C402924-C405018
1960	C429741
1961	C474149
1963	C622700
1966	C810533
1967	last # C999999

"D" Serial Prefix:

Models: 10, 12, 13, 14, 45

1968	D1-D90000
1969-1970	D90001-D330000
1971-1972	D330001-D420000
1972-1973	D420001-D510000
1973-1974	D510001-D659901
1974-1975	D659902-D750000
1975-1976	D750001-D870000
1976-1977	D870001-D999999

"1D" Serial Prefix:

Models: 64, 65

1976-1977	1D1-1D30000
1978-1979	1D30001-1D45000
1979-1980	1D45001-1D99999

"2D-17D" Serial Prefix:

Models: 10, 12, 13, 45, 64, 65, 547

1977	2D00001-2D80000
1978	2D80001-2D99999
1979	4D00001-6D10000
1980	6D10001-7D10000
1981	7D10001-9D44500
1982	9D44501-17D8900
1983	17D8901-21D0883

Approx last # 30D9291

1953 .22/32 Kit Gun:

Models: 34, 35, 43, 51 and their pre-model versions

1953-1969 101-135465

Approximate dates:

1953	101
1954	5000
1955	11000
1959	52673-62316
1960	70000
1965	108087
1969	135464

"M" Serial Prefix:

Models: 34, 35, 43, 51, 63

1969-1971	M1-M30000
1971-1973	M30001-M60000
1973-1977	M60001-M99999
1978-1979	M100000-M130000
1980-1981	M130001-M160000
1981	M160001-M193000
1982	M193101-M219800
1983	M219801-Mxxxx

All Other Revolver Models Beginning in the Transition Years 1980-1983 with a Three-Letter Serial Prefix and Four-Digit Number:

(Approx serial starts)

	1980	AAA 0000
	1981	AAD 2120
Oct	1982	AAF 9000
Dec	1982	ABL 3999
Jan	1983	ABL 4000
Oct	1983	ADE 6700
Dec	1983	ADT 2999
Jan	1984	ADT 3000
Jan	1985	AHA 0667
Jan	1986	AHC 1687
Jul	1987	AVB 8654
Jul	1987	AWW 7874
Dec	1987	AYW 9023
Jan	1988	AYY 1139
Oct	1988	BBT 2293
Jul	1990	BFL 1101-BFL 1535
Aug	1990	BFN 4343-BFN 4668
Jan	1991	BFW 3337-BFY 8122
Jul	1991	BHJ 8613-BHJ 9628
Aug	1991	BKN 5330-BKN 6905
Jan	1992	BHT 6706-BHT 7337
Feb	1992	BKZ 1014-BKZ 2310
Sep	1992	BFV xxxx
Feb	1993	BMB xxxx
Mar	1993	BNW xxxx
Oct	1993	BPD xxxx
Nov	1993	BPE xxxx

Dec	1993	BPK xxxx
Aug	1994	BRF xxxx

Modern Autoloading Pistols Serial Number Ranges:

Serial number range beginning 1954 starts @ 1001 and continues to 115000 in 1970. Applies to Models 39, 41, 44, 46, and 52. Serial number range beginning in 1970 starts with an "A" serial prefix @ A115001 and continues to about A880000. "A" serial prefix - semiautomatic pistols. Certain models may have an "A" serial suffix as well as an "A" prefix due to some rare serial duplications.

Models: 39, 41, 46, 52, 59, 422, 439, 449, 459, 469, 539, 559, 639, 645, 659, 669, and 745

1970-1971	A115001-A156801
1972-1973	A145801-A174999
1973-1974	A175001-A235000
1974-1975	A235001-A265000
1975-1976	A265001-A295000
1976-1977	A295001-A385000
1977-1978	A385001-A475000
1978-1979	A475001-A565000
1979-1980	A565001-A655000
1981	A655001-A745000
1982	A745001-A806933
1983	A806936-A874999
1984	A875000-Axxxx

March 1984 Begin three-letter serial prefix for all products including autoloaders. It appears that autoloaders now begin with the "TAA" three-letter serial prefix. Certain prefixes were already reserved for future production.

1984	TAA1985-TAD9549
1986	TAK7879
1987	TAT2512
1987	TBC3155-TBL7954
1988	TBL7955-TCB4082
1989-1990	TFJ1141-TFP0372
1991	THA1016-TVC7046
1994	VAMxxxx

APPENDIX 3
Listing by Caliber and Year of Introduction - Early Models

Early Models: Introduction by Caliber and Year, 1857-1955

Only primary caliber listed if model was offered in more than one caliber.

.22 Rimfire:

1857 Model #1
1860 Model #1 2nd Issue
1868 Model #1 3rd Issue
1893 1st Model Single-Shot
1902 LadySmith Hand Ejector 1st Issue
1905 2nd Model Single-Shot
1906 LadySmith 2nd Issue
1909 3rd Model Single-Shot
1910 LadySmith 3rd Issue
1911 .22/32 Hand Ejector
1925 4th Model Single-Shot
1931 K-22 Outdoorsman
1935 .22/32 Kit Gun
1940 K-22 Masterpiece
1946 K-22 Postwar
1948 22 M&P M-45
1949 K-22 Combat Masterpiece
1953 Model of 1953 .22/32 Kit Gun
1953 Model of 1953 .22/32 Target
1955 22/32 Kit Gun Airweight

.32 Rimfire:

1861 #2 Army
1865 Model 1-1/2 1st Issue
1868 Model 1-1/2 2nd Issue

.32-44 S&W:

1887 New Model #3 Target Model

.320 Revolving Rifle:

1879 .320 Revolving Rifle

.32 S&W Centerfire: Top-Breaks in .32 S&W; Hand Ejectors in .32 S&W Long:

1878 Model 1-1/2 Single Action
1879 320 Revolving Rifle
1880 .32 Double Action 1st Model
.32 Double Action 2nd Model
1882 .32 Double Action 3rd Model
1883 .32 Double Action 4th Model
1888 .32 Safety 1st Model
1896 .32 Hand Ejector 1st Model
1902 .32 Safety 2nd Model
1903 .32 Hand Ejector
1904 .32 Hand Ejector 1st Change
1906 .32 Hand Ejector 2nd Change
1909 .32 Double Action 5th Change
.32 Safety 3rd Change
.32 Hand Ejector 3rd Change
1910 .32 Hand Ejector 4th Change
.32 Hand ejector 5th Change
1911 .32 Hand Ejector 3rd Model
1917 .32 Regulation Police Target
1936 K-32 1st Model
1948 .32 M&P
1947 K-32 Masterpiece
1949 .32 Regulation Police Postwar

.32 ACP:

1924 Model .32 ACP Auto Pistol

.32-20 Winchester:

1899 .32-20 Hand Ejector 1st Model
1902 .32-20 Hand Ejector 2nd Model
1903 .32-20 Model of 1902 1st Change
1905 1905 Model
1906 1905 Model 1st Change
1907 1905 Model 2nd Change
1909 1905 Model 3rd Change
1915 1905 Model 4th Change

.35 S&W:

1913 Model 35 Auto Pistol

.357 Magnum:

1935 .357 Magnum Factory Registered
1938 .357 Magnum Prewar
1949 .357 Magnum Postwar
1954 The Highway Patrolman
1955 The Combat Magnum

.38 S&W:

1876 .38 Single Action 1st Model
1877 .38 Single Action 2nd Model
1880 .38 Double Action 1st Model
.38 Double Action 2nd Model
1884 .38 Double Action 3rd Model
1887 .38 Safety Double Action
.38 Safety Double Action 2nd Model
1890 .38 Safety Double Action 3rd Model
1891 .38 Single Action 3rd Model
.38 Single Action Mexican

1895	.38 Double Action 4th Model
1898	.38 Safety Double Action 4th Model
1907	.38 Safety Double Action 5th Model
1909	.38 Double Action 5th Model
	.38 Double Action Perfected
1917	.38 Regulation Police
1936	.38/32 Terrier
1938	.38 Regulation Police Post Office
1940	.38/200 British Service Model
1949	.38 Regulation Police Postwar

.38 Special:

1899	.38 Hand Ejector M&P 1st Model
1900	.38 U.S. Navy Model
	.38 Winchester Double Action
1901	U.S. Army Model
1902	.38 Hand Ejector M&P 2nd Model
	U.S. Navy Model
1903	.38 Hand Ejector M&P of 1902 1st Change
1905	.38 Hand Ejector M&P of 1905
1906	.38 Hand Ejector M&P of 1905 1st Change
	.38 Hand Ejector M&P of 1905 2nd Change
1915	.38 Hand Ejector M&P of 1905 4th Change
1930	.38/44 Heavy Duty
1931	.38/44 Outdoorsman
1942	.38 Victory Model
1945	Military & Police
1946	.38/44 Heavy Duty Postwar
	.38/44 Outdoorsman Postwar
1947	K-38 Masterpiece
1949	K-38 Combat Masterpiece
1950	.38/44 Outdoorsman Model of 1950
	Chiefs Special
	Chiefs Special Target
1952	Chiefs Special Airweight
	Military & Police Airweight
	Aircrewman
	Centennial Airweight
1953	Centennial
1955	Bodyguard Airweight

.38/44 S&W Target:

(not to be confused with .38/44 version of .38 Special)

1887	New Model #3 Target Model

.38 Winchester (.38-40):

1900	New Model #3 .38 Winchester
	DA .38 Winchester

9mm:

1953	The Model 39

.44 American:

1870	1st Model American
1872	2nd Model American

.44 S&W Russian:

1871	1st Model Russian
1873	2nd Model Russian
1874	3rd Model Russian
1878	New Model #3
1881	.44 Double Action 1st Model
1882	Model .44 Double Action Wesson Favorite

.44 Rimfire:

1870	Some American model variations
1879	New Model #3 Turkish

.44 Winchester (.44-40):

1885	New Model #3 Frontier Single Action
1886	Model .44 Frontier Double Action

.44 Special:

1907	.44 Hand Ejector 1st Model
1915	.44 Hand Ejector 2nd Model
1926	.44 Hand Ejector 3rd Model
1950	Model 1950 .44 Military
	Model 1950 .44 Target

.44 Magnum:

1955	The .44 Magnum

.45 S&W (.45 U.S.):

1875	1st Model Schofield
1876	2nd Model Schofield

.455:

1914	.455 Mark II Hand Ejector 1st Model
1915	.455 Mark II Hand Ejector 2nd Model

.45 ACP:

1917	U.S. Service Model of 1917
1950	1950 Target Model - light barrel
1951	.45 Hand Ejector of 1950 - Military
1955	1955 Target Model - heavy barrel

APPENDIX 4
Numbered Models - Year of Introduction

Model Introduction Sorted by Year (all numbered models and those that had pre-model number versions)

Year		Model
1917	pre Model 33	
1936	pre Model 32	
1938	pre Model 11	
1946	pre Model 17	
	pre Model 20	
1947	pre Model 14	
	pre Model 16	
1948	pre Model 10	
	pre Model 45	
1949	pre Model 15	
	pre Model 18	
	pre Model 27	
	pre Model 30	
	pre Model 31	
1950	pre Model 24	
	pre Model 26	
	pre Model 36	
1951	pre Model 21	
	pre Model 22	
1952	pre Model 12	
	pre Model 37	
	Aircrewman	
	pre Model 40	
	pre Model 42	
1953	pre Model 34	
	pre Model 35	
1954	pre Model 28	
	pre Model 39	
1955	Model	19
		25
		29
		38
		43
		50
1957	Model	41
1958	Model	44
1959	Model	48
		49
		46
1960	Model	51
		41-1
1961	Model	53
		52-A
		52
1962	Model	56
1963	Model	52-1
1964	Model	57
		58
1965	Model	60
1970	Model	64
		61
1971	Model	66
		52-2
		59
1972	Model	67
1974	Model	13
		65
1976	Model	68
1977	Model	63
1979	Model	629
		147-A
		439
		459
1980	Model	520
		547
		581
		681
		586
		686
		539
		559
1982	Model	659
1983	Model	29 Silhouette
		650
		651
		469
1985	Model	624
		649
1986	Model	544
		657
		639
		645
		669
1987	Model	422
		622
		745
1989	Model	625-2
		638
		3904
		3906
		4506
		4516
		5904
		5906
		6904
		6906
1990	Model	36LS
		60LS
		610
		617
		632
		637
		640
		642
		648
		1006
		2206
		4006
		4596
		5903
1991	Model	631
		940
		1026
		1066
		1066-NS
		1076

Year		Models
1991 (cont.)		1086 2213 2214 3913 3913-NL 3914 3914-NL 3913-LS 3914-LS 3953 3954 4003 4004 4013 4014 4046 4053 4054 4526
1991 (cont.)		4536 4546 4556 4566 4567 4576 4586 5924 5943 5944 5946 5967 6926 6944 6946
1992	Model	411 915 032 042 65-LS
1993	Model	442 3356TSW
1994	Model	Sigma SW40F Sigma SW9F 2206 GT 460
1995	Model	Sigma SW9C Sigma SW40C Sigma SW380 640-1 686+ 7-shot
1996	Model	908 909 410 457 622 VR 17 10-shot 642LS

APPENDIX 5
Modern Revolvers by Caliber

Modern Production Revolvers Sorted by Caliber, 1957-1994

.22 Long Rifle:

Models: 17, 18, 34, 35, 43, 45, 63, 617, 650

.22 Winchester Magnum:

Models: 48, 51, 648, 651

.22 Magnum Centerfire Jet:

Model: 53

.32 S&W:

Models: 16, 30, 31

.32 H&R Magnum:

Models: 16-4, 631, 632, 032

.38 S&W:

Model: 11

.38 Special:

Models: 10, 12, M13-USAF, 14, 15, 20, 23, 32, 33, 36, 36LS, 37, 38, 40, 42, 042, 442, 49, 50, 460, 56, 60, 60LS, 64, 67, 68, 637, 638, 640, 642, 649,

.357 Magnum:

Models: 10-6, 13, 19, 27, 28, 65, 65LS, 66, 520, 581, 586, 681, 686, 640-1

.41 Magnum:

Models: 57, 58, 657

.44-40 Caliber:

Model: 544

.44 Special:

Models: 21, 24, 624

.44 Magnum:

Models: 29, 629 (all variations)

.45 Long Colt:

Models: 25-3-4-5-7-9

.45 ACP:

Models: 22, 25-1-2-6-8, 26, 625-2

9mm:

Models: 547, 940, 19-2

10mm:

Model: 610

.356 TSW:

Model: 940

APPENDIX 6
Identification Characteristics

The following features should be considered when identifying an S&W handgun, as each one will have many of the following features:

Action: Single action, double action, single-shot, traditional double action (applies to autoloaders), top-break, bottom-break, hand ejector

Accessories: Muzzle brakes, barrel weights, and so on

Barrel length and availability: A factory barrel?

Barrel broaching for scope mount

Barrel pin: Pre 1982

Backstrap (also called tang): Smooth or serrated on revolvers, curved or straight on autoloaders

Butt shape: Round or square butt revolvers

Caliber: Single or dual capability, i.e. .357 and .38

Cylinder: Number of flutes or non-fluted

Cylinder chamfer: Yes or no

Cylinder counterbore: All magnums until 1982 and most .22s

Engraved by hand: A, B, or C class

Engraving by laser: Lasersmith

Extractor rod: Shrouded or non-shrouded extractor

Finish: Blue, nickel, stainless, parkerized, combination, matte, black stainless, brush blue, bright blue, and so on

Frame size: I, improved I, J, K, L, M, N, H frame revolvers; compact or full-size autos

Frame material: Alloy, carbon steel, stainless steel, polymer, brass

Frame screws: 3, 4, 5, or 6 (with bug screw)

Front sight styles: Patridge, 1/10", 1/8", Paine, red ramp, ramp on ramp base, serrated, post, gold bead, plain, McGivern, Baughman, king, call, marbles, round blade, adjustable four-position, white dot on post, dovetail, interchangeable, high profile, low profile

Factory errors: These do occur and are easily counterfeited

Grips or stock material: Walnut, hard rubber (black, green, brown), rosewood, mottled red rubber, checkered, diamond walnut, smooth walnut, Goncalo Alves, mother-of-pearl, service, Magna, roper, extension stocks, ivory, stag horn, O.E.M., i.e. Uncle Mike's, Hogue, Eagle

Hammer style: Target, service, humpback, bobbed, concealed, or shrouded, and width of hammer

Lanyard ring: Present or not

Logo markings of S&W: On right sideplate, left side of frame, or both

Rear sight style: Adjustable, fixed, white outline, narrow, target, micrometer, night sights, dovetail, Novak Lo-Mount Carry, two-dot

Rear sight leaf: Serrated or non-serrated (M-56 and M-28)

Refinishing markings: By factory on the butt or under the grips

Slide material: Alloy, carbon steel, stainless

Shot capacity: 4, 5, 6, 7, single-shot, or the magazine capacity

Serial number and serial number location: Yoke cut, butt, cylinder face, inside the topstrap, barrel, top latch, right grip, inside the crane, behind the star extractor, inside the barrel shroud

Serial prefix: One-letter or three-letter

Serial suffix: May occur with a duplication of serial numbers

Thumbpiece: Flat latch (early, late and current production). The flat latch appeared about 1950 and continued to about 1966 on J frames and I frames and early 6-shot airweights. Three distinct flat latch styles have been observed. Contoured thumbpiece on more modern production.

Trigger style: Smooth, target, narrow, service, serrated spur, and width of trigger

Triggerguards: Present or not

Scope mounting: Broaching or drilled for scope

Top rib: Narrow, wide, or no rib

Weight in ounces

APPENDIX 7
New Products for 1996

MODEL 17: REINTRODUCTION FOR 1996:
Cal-.22 Long Rifle, 6" full lug barrel, blue finish, K Target frame, **now with a 10-shot cylinder**, target hammer, target trigger, drilled and tapped for scope mount, square butt w/synthetic grips.

Product Code:
104522 42 oz.

MODEL 60 CHIEFS SPECIAL STAINLESS:
Cal-.357 Magnum, **new for 1996 chambered in .357 Magnum**. Available with 3" full underlug barrel and adjustable sights or 2-1/8" barrel and fixed sights, both w/stainless finish. .240" service hammer, .312" smooth trigger, 5-shot. Also available in a LadySmith version with smooth wood grips early in 1996.

Product Codes:

102420	2-1/8"	23 oz.
not assigned	3"	Full lug w/target sights available April-May24.5 oz.
102414	2-1/8"	LadySmith version

MODEL 410: FULL-SIZE .40 S&W:
Cal-.40 S&W, traditional double action, 10-shot magazine, 4" barrel, .260" serrated hammer, single side safety, straight backstrap, fixed sights. **Replaces the 411 in the "Value Series."**

Product Code:
104740 29.4 oz.

MODEL 457: COMPACT .45:
Cal-.45 ACP, carbon steel slide, alloy frame w/blue finish, traditional double action, 7-shot magazine, 3-3/4" barrel, .260" bobbed hammer, single side safety, straight backstrap, fixed sight. **Part of S&W's new "Value Series."**

Product Code:
104804 29 oz.

MODEL 622 VR:
Cal-.22 Long Rifle, restyled for 1996 with the same features as the 622 but now with a **ventilated rib barrel** in 6" configuration.

Product Code:
102846 23 oz.

MODEL 629 CLASSIC POWER PORT:
Cal-.44 Magnum, 6-1/2" barrel, .500" target hammer, .400" smooth combat trigger, Patridge front sight set back from the Power Port at the barrel's very end. Hogue grips.

Product Code:
103624 52 oz.

MODEL 637: CHIEFS SPECIAL AIRWEIGHT STAINLESS:
Cal-.38 Special, originally produced on a limited basis, now **reintroduced for 1996**. Alloy frame, stainless cylinder and barrel, stainless finish with clear coat.

Product Code:
103050 13.5 oz.

MODEL 642 AND 642LS:
Cal-.38 Special, **reintroduced in 1996** again as a hammerless Centennial with alloy frame and stainless cylinder and barrel. Clear coat finish, .312" smooth trigger, 5-shot, LadySmith version also available with hardwood grips.

Product Codes:

103810	15.8 oz.
103808	LadySmith

MODEL 686 PLUS:
Cal-.357 Magnum, now available in the still fabulous L frame, with a **7-shot cylinder**. Available in three barrel lengths.

Product Codes:

104192	2-1/2" barrel	34.5 oz.
104194	4" barrel	40.0 oz.
104198	6" barrel	45.0 oz.

MODEL 908 COMPACT 9MM:
Cal-9mm, traditional double action, 8-shot magazine, 3-1/2" barrel, .260" bobbed hammer, single side safety, straight backstrap, fixed sights. **Replaces the Model 3914 as part of the "Value Series."**

Product Code:
103882 26.0 oz.

ILLUSTRATED GLOSSARY AND INDEX

(Abbreviations in parentheses, page numbers in italics)

ACTION: The operational and trigger system of a firearm. Types include single action (SA) or double action (DA) on revolvers; on semiautos, in addition to SA and DA (sometimes called traditional double action or TDA), options include TDA w/decocking lever and double action only (DAO). *153*

ADJUSTABLE SIGHTS (AS): Sights that can be adjusted, usually by a screw, sometimes by drifting, for elevation and windage; sometimes called target sights. *19-21*

AIR GUNS: *187*

AIRCREWMAN: Airweight revolvers developed for the U.S. Air Force. Early versions had alloy cylinders as well as alloy frames, and were deemed inadequate for the .38 Special cartridge. Most government purchase guns were destroyed. The K frame version was called the M13 by the air force. *95, 96, 100, 158*

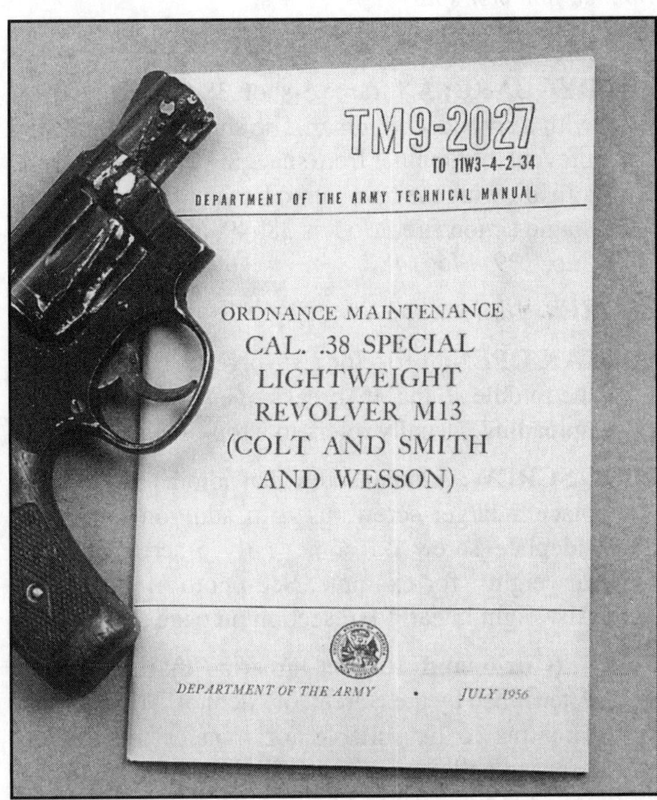

Aircrewman, destroyed by government

AIRWEIGHT: S&Ws term for lightweight revolvers with alloy frames.

ALLOY FRAME: Lightweight aluminum alloy (AA) frame.

AMBIDEXTROUS SAFETY (AM): A manually operated slide-mounted safety on semiautos that has operation levers on both sides of the slide so as to be easily reached by either right- or left-handed shooters.

AMERICAN: The first version of the S&W Model 3 Single Action. *55-60*

ANTIQUE: A firearm made in or before 1898. Generally exempt from federal paperwork and recordkeeping requirements; may be subject to state or local regulation.

ASSEMBLY NUMBER: A number stamped on various parts of a gun to keep parts fitted to a specific gun with that gun. Not the serial number. Assembly numbers of various parts should match. *15*

AUSTRALIAN COLONIAL POLICE: New Model #3s purchased by the Australian government for police usage, most with a detachable shoulder stock. *68*

AUTOLOADERS: Semiautomatic firearms. The terms "auto-pistol" and "automatic" are technically incorrect. However, they are so commonly used that protesting this terminology is best left to serious gun cranks with not much else to worry about. *152-177*

BABY AIRCREWMAN: Small 5-shot J frame aircrewman. Surviving examples are very rare. *100*

BABY RUSSIAN: Nickname for .38 Single Action Model 2, 1st Model, 5-shot spurtrigger top-break .38 S&W. *47, 48*

BABY SIGMA: Small polymer frame semiauto introduced in 1995; the first S&W chambered for .380ACP round. *177*

BACKSTRAP: The rear portion of the grip part of the frame of a handgun. Also called the "tang." Will be found smooth or serrated on revolvers and curved or straight on semiautos.

BALTIMORE POLICE: Baby Russians purchased by this department and marked "Balto City Police." *47*

BANGOR PUNTA: The parent company of S&W, approx. 1965-1987. Expanded into many police market items in addition to handguns.

BARREL WEIGHTS: Aluminum or steel weights attached to the barrel of a target gun to adjust its feel and dampen felt recoil. See photo of Model 41. *155*

BAUGHMAN FRONT SIGHT: Ramp front sight. *20*

BAUMANIZE: A custom gunsmithing procedure that converts a Model 27 N frame .357 Magnum into a 7-shot .357 that can be loaded via full-moon clips.

Baumanize seven-shot conversion w/full moon clips

BEKEART: An early twentieth century California S&W distributor, Phillip Bekeart ordered the first .22/32 hand ejectors, which have come to be called "Bekeart Models" by collectors. A "True Bekeart" is one of the original guns actually order by Bekeart before they became a standard S&W model. *79, 80*

BICYCLE GUN: A Safety Hammerless ("lemon squeezer') with a two-inch barrel; the short barrel necessitated special marking procedures. Scarce. *46-47*

BIRDSHEAD GRIPS: A term sometimes used for the grip configuration of early spurtrigger S&Ws; rounded on the back and coming to something of a point at the bottom.

BISLEY: A famous shooting range in England; location of many late nineteenth century handgun target shooting contests.

BLACK POWDER: The first propellant used in cartridges up to around the turn of the century, when it began to be replaced by "smokeless powder." Black powder is noted for the corrosive fouling it leaves in a barrel. It is unsafe to shoot modern ammunition in guns originally made for black powder cartridges.

BLADESAVER: A metal device for holding a safety razor blade so that it could be sharpened on a strop like a straight razor. Manufactured by S&W as "Wesson Products" in the 1920s. *202*

BLUE (B): Dark firearms finish; sometimes appears closer to black than blue. Less resistant to corrosion and wear than nickel or stainless finishes.

BOBBED: Cut off; usually refers to removing the hammer spur to "snag-proof" a handgun. However, may also refer to an after-factory shortened barrel or the removal of the triggerguard spur from a Russian type revolver.

Bobbed hammer spur

BODYGUARD: A J frame 5-shot .38 Special revolver with a shrouded hammer. The shroud is intended to prevent the hammer from snagging on clothing while still allowing the revolver to be manually cocked for single action fire. Models 38, 49, and 649. *99, 100, 126, 129, 146, 148*

BOXES: *18, 19*

BREAK OPEN: Term for a revolver that is hinged in the middle so that it "breaks open" for loading and unloading. Usually refers to a top-break.

BUG SCREW: A small screw that adjoins and locks in place a larger screw; used in addition to the top sideplate screw on some early 5-screw J frame airweights, for example. See photo of Centennial Airweight in early HE section on page 100.

C&R (Curio and Relic): Firearms that have been determined by the Bureau of Alcohol, Tobacco, and Firearms to be suitable for transfer to federally licensed collectors. Generally, it includes guns that are over fifty years old, are certified by a qualified museum curator, or "derive a substantial part of their value from the fact they are novel, rare, bizarre, or because of their association with some historical figure, period, or event." C&R at a gun listing in this book indicates it is on the BATF list. This is significant to licensed collectors only. For all other non-licensed individuals, a C&R gun is treated as any other modern firearm.

CALL: A call front sight consists of a flat gold or ivory bead on a post. *20*

CARBON STEEL: Common type of metal used for firearms, usually finished in blue or nickel; term used to distinguish from stainless steel or aluminum alloy construction.

CATALOGS: *193-201*

CENTENNIAL: A "hammerless" (actually concealed hammer) J-frame hand ejector. The version made 1952-1974 included a grip safety similar to the earlier top-break lemon squeezers. The 1990s reintroduction did not include the grip safety. Models 40, 42, 442, 632, 640, 642, and 940. Recently introduced in .357 Magnum as the Model 640-1. *99-101, 108, 123, 127, 132, 137, 145, 147, 151*

CENTERFIRE: A cartridge with the primer mounted in the center of the case head. First introduced on S&Ws in 1870 with the .44 American cartridge. All modern handgun cartridges except the .22 rimfires are centerfire. An advantage is that the brass case can be "reloaded" in most cases.

CHAMFERED: Refers to a right angle edge that has been intentionally rounded or clipped to reduce the sharpness of the edge, as in a chamfered cylinder.

CHEMICAL AGENTS: *187-189*

CHIEFS SPECIAL: The first S&W 5-shot J frame .38 Special; the classic "snub nosed revolver" configuration. Models 36, 37, 50, 60, and 637. *77, 99, 124-126, 129, 132, 133, 146*

CLIP: The only S&Ws that use "clips" are the revolvers chambered for rimless cartridges, such as the Model 1917 in .45ACP. Those gizmos that hold ammunition in semiautos are called "magazines." The authors may be willing to sit quietly grinding their teeth when a semiauto is referred to as an "auto," but they can become downright abusive to the doofus who calls a magazine a "clip."

CLUB GUN: A gun with "0" as the first digit of the serial number. *183*

COMBAT: "Combat" in a S&W model designation generally indicates an adjustable sight gun made for military or police usage, usually with a four-inch barrel. This term is opposed to "service," which suggests a fixed sight model or "target" with an adjustable sight revolver and a longer barrel.

COMBAT GRIPS (CG) or COMBAT STOCKS (CS): Smooth wood grips with finger grooves. *17*

COMBAT HAMMER: Narrow spurred hammer.

COMBAT MAGNUM: Term used for the K frame .357 introduced in 1955; predecessor of the Model 19. *91, 115, 135, 139, 143, 150*

COMBAT MASTERPIECE: "Combat" version of the Target Masterpiece, i.e., a target sighted gun with a four-inch service length barrel. *113, 114, 136*

COMBAT TRIGGER: On current production, a mid-sized .312-inch wide smooth trigger with no grooves or serrations.

COMMEMORATIVE: A limited edition gun with special decoration commemorating a particular organization or event. These should not be confused with specially marked guns that are purchased by a government agency for issue sidearms. A commemorative must be unfired, and preferably unturned, in the original box to bring full collector value. Once fired, their value diminishes toward that of an undecorated specimen. *183-186*

COMPACT: A gun smaller than the standard service size. Often preferred for concealed carry or other applications where a full-size gun might be awkward.

CONDITION: *30-32*

COUNTERBORED CYLINDER: See "recessed" in this glossary.

CYRILLIC: Letters of the Russian alphabet; "Cyrillic" marked Russian Model 3s are those intended for sale to the Russian government. *61, 62, 72, 73*

DIAMOND GRIPS: Wooden grips for hand ejectors with a single diamond of wood left uncheckered around the screw and escutcheon. See page 102 for examples.

DISTINGUISHED: In a gun model name this indicates an L frame .357 Magnum. *139, 149*

DOUBLE ACTION (DA): A gun that can be fired either by first cocking the hammer and then pulling the trigger (resulting in a relatively light trigger pull), or by pulling the trigger without first cocking the hammer (resulting in a relatively heavy trigger pull). While it is sometimes thought that the "double" action means there are two different ways of firing the gun, perhaps it would be more appropriate to think of the trigger pull as having a "double" mechanical action—it both cocks the hammer and releases it. Guns that can be operated ONLY in this mode are called "double action only" (DAO). *153*

DOUBLE ACTION MODELS: .32 caliber: *43-45*; .38 caliber: *49, 50*; .44 caliber: *70, 71*

DOUBLE ACTION ONLY (DAO): *Note: sometimes abbreviated "DA" in recent S&W catalogs.* A gun in which pulling the trigger both cocks the hammer and releases it, and in which the hammer cannot be cocked manually (see "double action" above). The lemon squeezers and Centennial "hammerless" revolvers can be thought of as DAO. Some police departments also order various other hand ejectors modified to be DAO. However, it is most often thought of as applying to those third generation semiautos that are designed to be fired DAO. These are sometimes called "slick side" or "slick slide" autos since they do not have a safety or decocking lever in the usual location on the rear of the slide. Third generation DAOs may be identified from the model number, which will have a "4," "5," or "8" as the third of four digits. *153*

DOUBLE STACK (Double column): A high-capacity magazine in which the cartridges inside the magazine stack in a double row rather than one on top of the other as they would in a single column magazine. For example, in a full-size 9 mm, a single column magazine will hold eight rounds and have a thinner grip, whereas a double column magazine design will generally hold fifteen rounds, requiring a fatter grip.

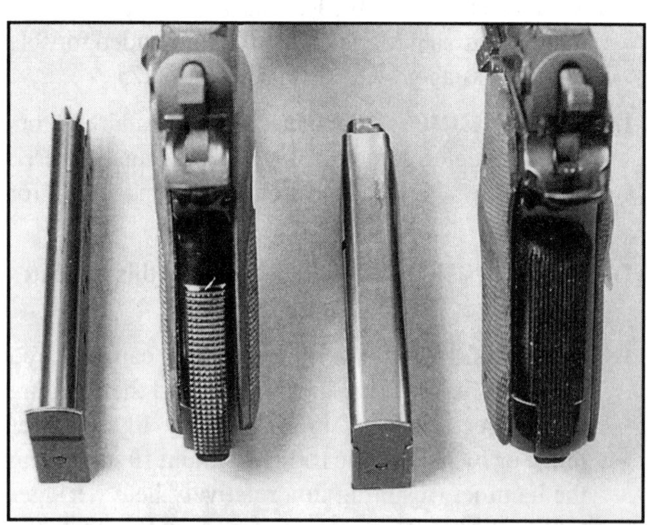

Double column (right) and single column (left) magazines and semiautos

DUST COVER: A sheet metal shield that fits over the ejection port (see photo of Model 39). *154*

EJECTOR: The mechanism for removing a cartridge or empty case from a chamber. In the case of S&W revolvers, the star configuration device on the rear of the cylinder.

EJECTOR HOUSING: On top-break revolvers, the part of the barrel that is below the bore and extends in front of the hinge, housing the ejector mechanism. As the top-break design evolved during the 1870s, the ejector housing got progressively shorter until it was essentially a stub on models produced after about 1878.

EJECTOR ROD: The piece that extends from the front of a HE revolver when the cylinder is opened and is pushed to eject shells. May be shrouded or non-shrouded.

EJECTOR SHROUD: On hand ejectors, the part of the barrel below the bore that shelters the ejector rod when the cylinder is closed. Not present on all HE models.

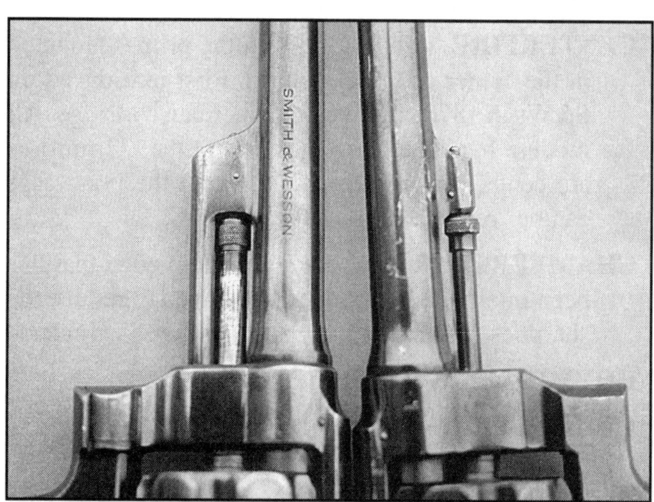

Shrouded (left) and unshrouded ejector rods

ELECTROLESS: A durable non-glare matte nickel finish.

END LABEL: The label on the end of a cardboard gun box. Information on the label should match the gun it contains for the combination of box and gun to bring full premium price.

ESCORT: A small .22 "pocket" semiauto, the Model 61, made by S&W in the 1970s. *158*

ESCUTCHEON: The knurled nut in the right grip that receives the grip screw.

EXTRACTOR ROD: See ejector rod above.

Flat latch (top two) and later style (bottom) centennials

FACTORY LETTER: A letter from the S&W factory historian on a particular gun, indicating what factory records show as that gun's original configuration, shipping date, and destination. *33*

FACTORY REFINISH: A gun that has been reblued or renickeled at the S&W factory, often marked with a star or other indication. *14, 30-32*

FACTORY REWORK STAR: A star by the serial number on the butt indicating a return to the factory for some rework or refinish. *14*

FIRST EDITIONS: *184*

FIRST FIRST: Shorthand for Model One, 1st Issue. The first revolver made by S&W, this was a tiny 7-shot .22 tip-up spurtrigger. There are six variations, and these may be added to the shorthand, such as "First first third." *37*

FIRST MODEL AMERICAN: The first eight thousand or so Model 3 American .44 caliber large frame revolvers, characterized by a straight line on the bottom of the frame and non-interlocking hammer and latch. *56-58*

FIRST MODEL RUSSIAN: The first Model 3 chambered for the Russian cartridge; essentially identical to the American model, except for the chambering. *55, 60*

FIRST MODEL SCHOFIELD: The first three thousand or so Model 3 Schofields. *64, 65*

FIVE-SCREW: From about 1906 to about 1955, most hand ejectors were made with "five-screw" frames—four on the sideplate (the bottom screw is sometimes covered by the grip) and one on the front of the triggerguard. *12*

FIXED SIGHTS (FS): Non-adjustable sights; may be integral to gun's frame and barrel. *19-21*

FLAT LATCH: Thumb latch configuration used on I and J frames and airweight K frames from about 1950 to 1966. Three types known.

FLORAL GRIPS: (Also called peacock or turkey grips.) An unusual pattern hard rubber grip with a floral pattern where the checkering usually is found, and small wild turkeys, peacocks, or some type of bird in the pattern. Found only on Second Model .32 DAs.

Floral grips

FLUSH VALVE: S&W manufactured flush valves for toilets at one time. Quite collectible if you can persuade the owner to do without.

FLUTED (NON-FLUTED) CYLINDER: Fluted cylinders have metal removed on their exterior between chambers. Non-fluted cylinders are perfectly round. Early tip-ups were all non-fluted, with cylinder flutes added to the new designs of the

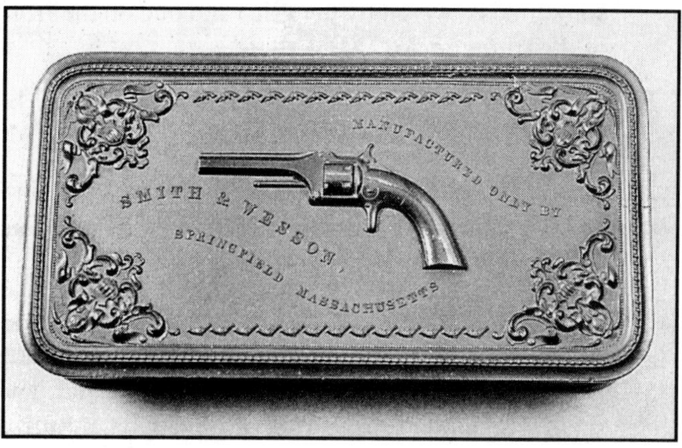

Gutta-percha case

Model 1 3rd Issue and Model 1-1/2 New Model. All top-breaks had fluted cylinders. Hand ejectors all had fluted cylinders until recently, when unfluted cylinders have made a comeback on some special production variations because a) they add recoil-moderating weight, b) they appear to increase the strength of the cylinder, or c) they look pretty cool.

FOUR-SCREW: From about 1955 to 1961, most hand ejectors were made with "four-screw" frames, with the "fifth" screw—the top sideplate screw—eliminated about 1955 on most models. Some early hand ejectors between 1899 and 1910 also have four-screw frames since the triggerguard screw was not added until about 1905. *13*

FRAME SIZES: *11-13*

FRONTIER: A top-break revolver chambered for the .44-40 (.44 Winchester) cartridge. *69-71*

FULL LUG: Part of the barrel consisting of a solid cylinder of metal underneath and parallel to the full-length of the barrel; adds recoil absorbing weight and the heavy muzzle feel preferred by some shooters. Ejector rod fits into the rear of the lug. First offered as standard on the L frame, and since offered on a number of special production runs and some standard models. For examples, see page 140.

FULL MOON CLIP: See "half moon clip" below. Photo at "baumanize" in this glossary.

GAS GUNS: *187, 188*

GONCALO ALVES: A type of South American wood used to make most S&W wooden target grips on recent production guns. *17*

GUN OF THE WEEK: A term humorously used to refer to the 1989-1991 era at S&W, which saw a huge increase in the number of new models and variations introduced, attributable mainly to the profusion of variations of third generation semiautos. Actually, nearly literally true for 1991, with around forty models and variations introduced that year. *214, 215*

GUTTA-PERCHA: An early forerunner of plastic used to make cases for the Model One at mid-nineteenth century. *18-38*

HALF MOON CLIP: A device that holds three .45ACP rounds for use in a 1917 Model or Model 25 revolver; made of sheet metal and developed at S&W when the government wanted .45ACP revolvers for WWI military usage due to lack of adequate production of 1911 type semiautos. Later made in "full moon" six-shot configuration (or five-shot for the Model 940 9mm revolver), or two-shot "one-third moon" configuration. See photo of 1917 Model .45 HE or Model 625 Springfield Armory Commemorative for examples. *104*

HALF PLATE: Part plated and part blue finish, usually referring to a tip-up with a blue barrel and cylinder and a nickel or silver plated frame.

HAMMERLESS: A revolver with the hammer concealed entirely within the frame; cannot be fired single action. Primary examples are the top-break Safety Hammerless, or "lemon squeezer," models and the hand ejector Centennials.

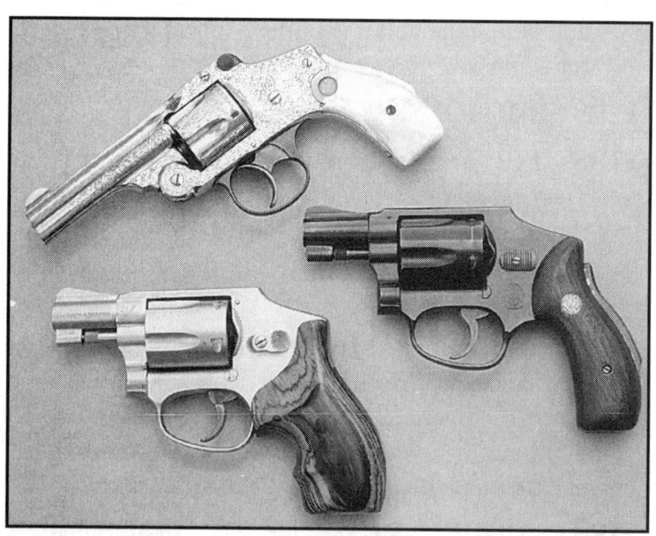

Hammerless revolvers

HANDCUFFS: *190*

HAND EJECTOR (HE): A revolver of the modern style in which the cylinder swings out to the left side of the frame for loading and unloading, and the cases are ejected from the cylinder by hand by pushing on the end of the ejector rod. *8, 77, 78*

HARD RUBBER (HR): A molded material that looks and feels somewhat like plastic and was used for grips for top-break and early hand ejector revolvers. *17*

HEAVY BARREL (HB): A barrel that does not taper, or is thicker than standard.

HEAVY DUTY: The first N frame .38 Special revolver, designed to fire a heavy loaded version of that cartridge, called the .38-44. *97, 98, 116*

HIGH HORN: Type of grips used on Centennials and Bodyguards where the wood extends higher than usual up the backstrap.

HIGH PROFILE FRONT SIGHT: Just what it says, abbreviated (HP).

HIGHWAY PATROLMAN: An N frame .357 Magnum with a plain utilitarian finish; became the Model 28, an "economy" version of the Model 27. *91, 119*

HOSTILES (The): One of several turn of the century advertising posters commissioned by S&W, this one shows a mounted rider crossing a river turning in the saddle to fire a revolver at pursuing hostile Indians. "The Hostiles" and "The Last Cartridge" are the two best known of these posters, and these images have been used in various commemorative and collectible items. *120, 184, 193, 201*

HOGUE MONOGRIPS: One-piece pebble-textured, finger-grooved synthetic grips provided with some current and recent S&W revolvers. See photo of Model 586 for example. *139*

HUMPBACK HAMMER: An optional special order hammer offered by S&W beginning in the 1930s; has a humpbacked appearance between the spur and the face of the hammer.

I FRAME: The first size hand ejector frame introduced, primarily used for 6-shot .32s, but also some .22s and 5-shot .38 S&Ws, eventually replaced by the J frame, which was slightly larger to accommodate 5-shot .38 Specials. *12*

IDENTI-KIT: *190*

IMPROVED I FRAME: Slightly larger than I frame. The opening for the cylinder is 1.5 inches long in a standard I frame; 1.515 inches long in an improved I frame; and 1.645 inches long in their successor, the J frame. *13*

INTERCHANGEABLE FRONT SIGHTS (IFS): Front sight blades that can be easily switched for another height or configuration; standard on Classic and Classic DX .44 Magnums.

IVORY GRIPS: These were available on custom order, and also from non-factory sources.

J FRAME: Smallest revolver frame size currently manufactured; 5-shot .38 Chiefs Special size. Replaced the slightly smaller I frame. Currently made in .22, .32, and .38, and recently introduced in .357 Magnum as the Model 640-1. Other J frames include the Models 30, 31, 32, 33, 34, 35, 36, 37,38, 40, 41, 42, 43, 50, 51, 60, 63, 442, 460, 632, 637, 638, 640, 642, 649, 650, 651, 940. See page 12.

JAPANESE NAVY (NEW MODEL NUMBER THREE JAPANESE GOVERNMENT CONTRACT GUNS): *67,68*

JET: Refers to the Model 53 and the high-power .22 centerfire cartridge designed expressly for it. *114, 130*

JINKS: Collector's shorthand for *The History of Smith & Wesson* by factory historian Roy Jinks. *34*

K FRAME: S&Ws medium frame hand ejector revolver frame, introduced in 1899 as a 6-shot .38 Military & Police revolver, and in continuous production ever since. Currently offered as a basis for .22, .32, .38, and .357 Magnum revolvers. Models 10, 11, 12, 13, 14, 15, 16, 17, 18, 19, 45, 48, 53,64, 65, 66, 67, 520, 547, 617, 631, and 648. See page 12.

KELTON SAFETY: Large thumb-operated safety device installed on a very few Schofield and New Model #3 revolvers. Very rare.

KING: Custom gunsmith famous for modifying target shooters' handguns.

KIT GUN: Compact .22 J frame, 4-inch or shorter barrel, usually round butt, originally marketed as ideal take-along companion in a fishing or camping kit. Models 34, 51, 63, 650, and 651.

King conversion

"K" marked in yoke cut on King conversion

KNIVES: *191-193*

KNUCKLE: The bump at the top of the backstrap of the grip frame where the web of the thumb rests, first introduced on the Second Model Russian. Also called the "prawl."

KORNBRATH: Noted engraver. *29*

L FRAME: Medium-large frame introduced in 1981 to provide a more compact .357 Magnum than the N frame with more heft and durability than the K frame. Models 581, 586, 681, and 686. See page 12.

LADYSMITH: Originally, tiny M frame 7-shot .22 hand ejectors, made 1902-1921. The "LadySmith" name was resurrected in recent years, and applied to several models that were given special design and appearance changes to address the women's market. Models 36LS, 60LS, 65LS revolvers. The semiauto LadySmiths, Models 3913LS and 3914LS, were popular enough with both genders that they were introduced in a variation without the markings (no "LadySmith" logo) as the 3913NL and 3914NL for guys who liked the design but couldn't take the locker room teasing for packing a LadySmith. *12, 77-79, 124, 125, 133, 135, 145, 153, 167*

LANYARD RING: Metal ring installed on the butt of a revolver for attachment of a military style lanyard (sort of like when your mom put your mittens on a string so you wouldn't lose them). Example page 104.

LASERSMITH: A method of "engraving" introduced in the late 1980s utilizing computer controlled lasers programmed to cut the desired image into the metal. *29, 186*

LAST CARTRIDGE (The): One of a series of turn of the century advertising posters commissioned by S&W, this one depicts a revolver-wielding man locked in combative embrace with a bear. Along with "The Hostiles," probably the best known of the posters, and the image has been used on various promotional and commemorative items. *184, 186, 201*

LEMON SQUEEZER: Nickname for the "Safety Hammerless" or "New Departure" models; from the grip safety on the backstrap that must be squeezed by the gripping action of the shooting hand to render the gun shootable. *46, 47, 51, 52*

LEW HORTON: A major firearms distributor, Lew Horton has ordered many special runs of guns with unique features produced exclusively for them through the S&W Performance Center. *186*

LIGHT RIFLE: *178*

LINE-THROWING GUNS: *187*

LONG TOPSTRAP (or Long Cylinder): On New Model #3s and related models and .44 DAs, refers to a cylinder 1-9/16 inches long, which replaced the older 1-7/16-inch cylinder late in production. The change was due to the decision to chamber these models for the longer .44-40 and .38-40 Winchester cartridges, and the desire to make only one frame and cylinder size for all large frame top-break models. *66, 69, 70*

LUDWIG LOEWE: German arms company that manufactured Third Model Russian pattern revolvers for the Russian government and for commercial sale. *62, 73*

M FRAME: The tiny frame size of the original .22 LadySmith revolvers of the early twentieth century. *12, 78, 79*

M&P: "Military & Police," generally refers to a service revolver with integral rear notch fixed sights, most often a K frame, although the N framed Model 58 is known as an M&P.

MWR: See "Robinson, MW."

MACHINE PISTOL: *182*

MAGAZINE SAFETY or "Magazine Disconnect Safety": A safety device intended to render a semiautomatic firearm inoperable when the magazine is removed. This is a feature of some, but not all, S&W semiautomatics.

MAGNA GRIPS: Introduced in the 1930s; wood grips that came higher along the backstrap, up to the knuckle, to provide a broader recoil absorbing surface at the web of the thumb. *17*

MAGNA PORT: A proprietary process of cutting vents or "ports" in the top of the muzzle end of the barrel to reduce felt recoil.

MAGNA TRIGGER SAFETY: Non-S&W custom gunsmithing procedure applied to hand ejectors to modify them so they cannot be fired unless the shooter is wearing a special magnet ring.

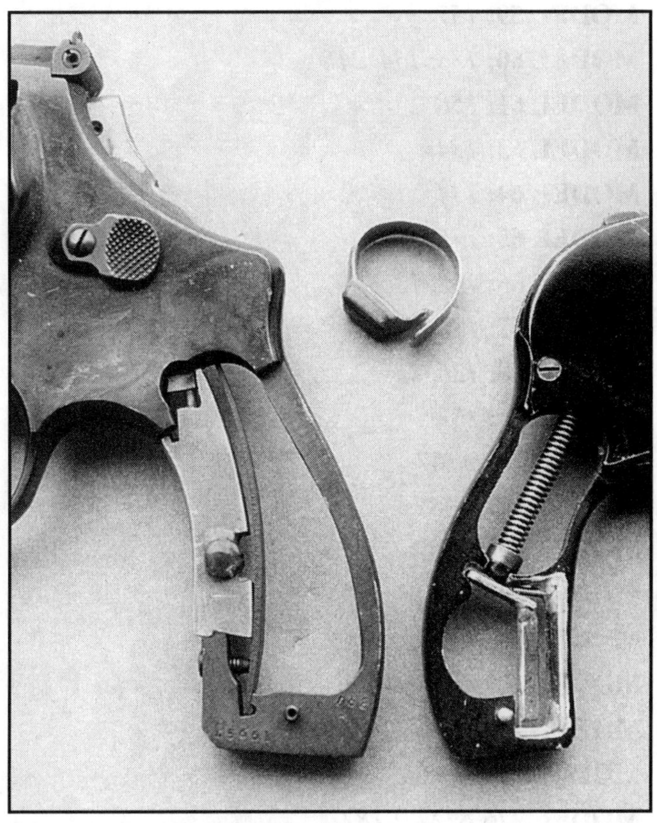

Magna trigger safety and ring

MAGNUM: A term first applied to firearms and cartridges by S&W; in general usage, designates a cartridge of higher power than previous loadings of that caliber, or the firearms intended to fire such cartridges. Several handgun magnum cartridges have been designed by lengthening an existing cartridge (so that it cannot be fired in older guns not designed to withstand the increased pressure), starting with the .357 Magnum, which is a lengthened .38 Special. Similarly, the .44 Magnum is a lengthened .44 Special (which in turn is a lengthened .44 Russian), and the .32 Magnum is a lengthened .32 S&W Long. The standard "parent" loadings can be fired in the magnum handguns, but NOT vice versa. The .41 Magnum and .22 Magnum do not have "parent" cartridges in current production.

MARTIAL: Term used to describe handguns that have been officially purchased by a branch of the military service. Often, but not always, have military markings such as "U.S.," ordnance department "flaming bomb," etc.

MASTERPIECE: Hand ejector K frame design with adjustable sights, introduced about 1940, including micrometer click adjustable sights, short fast action, and built-in anti-backlash trigger. *82, 83, 87, 88, 96, 101, 112-114, 128, 136, 140, 198*

MATCHING (Serial Numbers or Assembly Numbers): Various parts of different guns are marked with numbers that identify them to that specific gun (see comments in introductory chapters). A collector asking, "Is it all matching?" is asking if all the parts are correctly numbered to the original gun. *15, 16*

MATTE FINISH: A dull finish, sometimes preferred for its non-reflective nature or adopted as an economy measure since it requires less polishing.

McGIVERN: Famous exhibition shooter; the McGivern sight, consisting of a hemisphere gold bead in a black post, was named for him. *20*

MEDALLION GRIPS: Grips with a S&W logo inset into the upper portion. Medallions were added to S&W produced pearl and ivory grips in the late nineteenth century to differentiate them from non-factory aftermarket fancy grips. Collectors refer to these as "medallion pearls," etc. *16*

MERCOX: An experimental syringe dart gun based on a S&W K frame. *189*

MEXICAN MODEL: Model of 1891, .38 Single Action, 3rd Model, which has a spur trigger rather than the standard round triggerguard of this model. A scarce variation, with fakes not uncommon. *47*

MICROMETER CLICK SIGHTS: Adjustable rear sights introduced in 1940, and standard still today, which provide positive "click" screwdriver adjustment for windage and elevation. *20*

MINI-GUN: Term used for compact semiautos, especially the double stack 9mms such as the 469, 669, 6904, and 6906.

MODEL 1 TIP-UP: *37, 38*

MODEL 1-1/2 TIP-UP RIMFIRE: *39*

MODEL 1-1/2 TOP-BREAK .32 CENTERFIRE: *43-46*

MODEL 2 OLD ARMY .32 RIMFIRE: *40*

MODEL 2 TOP-BREAK .38 CENTERFIRE: *47-52*

for .41, .44, and .45 caliber revolvers, has also been used for .38 and .357 Magnum. Models 20, 21, 22, 23, 24, 25, 26, 27, 28, 29, 57, 58, 610, 624, 625, 627, and 629. See page 12.

NASHVILLE POLICE: A group of thirty-two First Model American revolvers with non-standard length 6-inch barrels purchased by the Nashville Police and so marked on the backstrap. *56*

NEAL and JINKS: Collector's shorthand for *Smith & Wesson, 1857 to 1945* by Robert Neal and Roy Jinks. Regional usage examples: Southern - "Hey Bubba, yew gotcher Nayll and Jainks? Ah need the sayrial number rainge fer them Nashville Po-lice." Northeastern - "You sumbitch, that Nashville Palice ya sold me idn't listed in NealanJinks." Mid-western - "Yup, the handle of that old six-shooter was all scratched up, but I draw-filed it sos you caint even tell." *34*

NEW CENTURY: First model .44 hand ejector Triple Lock. *101*

NEW DEPARTURE: Nickname for Safety Hammerless or "lemon squeezer" top-break revolvers. *46, 47, 51, 52*

NEW MODEL NUMBER THREE: Final configuration of the large frame top-break single action, quickly distinguished by stubby ejector housing. *41, 63, 65-70*

NEW MODEL RUSSIAN: Model 3 Russian, 3rd Model; distinctive large knuckle in backstrap, triggerguard spur, and large thumbscrew in topstrap to retain cylinder. *60-62*

NEW MODEL 1-1/2: Five-shot .32 rimfire tip-up with birdshead butt, fluted cylinder, and round barrel. *39, 40*

NEW YORK STYLE ENGRAVING: Profuse, professionally done scroll engraving dating from the late nineteenth or possibly early twentieth century. Nearly synonymous with "Nimschke-style," but sounds a little less as if you're trying to pass off the gun as actually done by Nimschke. *21-29*

NICKEL: Bright shiny metal plating, more resistant to corrosion than bluing. *13*

NIGHT SIGHTS: Sights with glow-in-the-dark tritium inserts, allowing for usage in semi-darkness.

NIMSCHKE: L. D. Nimschke is probably the most famous nineteenth century firearms engraver, best known for his masterful profuse floral engraving. Since he greatly influenced engraving styles of the era, and like most engravers, seldom signed his work, it is very difficult to identify exactly which guns are his work. Unless a specific rubbing can be identified in his pattern book (which has been published as *L. D. Nimschke, Firearms Engraver* by R. L. Wilson), or otherwise proven to be actually done by Nimschke, it's best to consider such engraving "in the style of Nimschke." *23, 24*

NOVAK SIGHTS: A snag-free, "melted" low profile sight design introduced on third generation semiautomatics.

NYCLAD: Type of ammunition made by S&W with a nylon coated lead bullet. Touted both for reduction on airborne lead pollution on indoor ranges and its tendency to expand at relatively low velocities. *190*

OLD ARMY: Nickname for the Model 2 tip-up 6-shot .32 rimfire. *39, 40*

OLD MODEL RUSSIAN: Model 3 Russian, 2nd Model, identified by extreme backstrap knuckle, triggerguard spur, and small screw in topstrap retaining cylinder. *60, 61*

OLD OLD MODEL RUSSIAN: Model 3 Russian, 1st Model, externally identical to the American Model, except for the chambering. *55, 60*

OUTDOORSMAN: Term used for the first K frame target .22 (pre-micrometer click sights), and the N frame adjustable sight version of the .38-44 Heavy Duty. *81, 98, 117*

PACHMAYR GRIPS: Brand name of popular rubber grips, standard on many current models. Also often found replacing original wood grips on police handguns. See photo of Model 617 on page 140. *18*

PAINE: Ira Anson Paine, famous champion nineteenth century target shooter and designer of the Paine front target sight first used on New Model #3s. The sight consists of a long round bead running the full-length of the top of a thin square blade. *20, 66, 70, 74, 79*

PARKERIZING: A phosphate process finish used on military arms, WWII era, with a flat textured gray or greenish-gray appearance.

PATRIDGE: Type of front sight, appears as a thin rectangle to the shooter, with a vertical or undercut rear blade face to reduce light glare off the sight blade. *20*

PERFECTED: Refers to the .38 DA Perfected, the Third Model Single-Shot, based on the same frame, or the Third Model LadySmith. *50, 74-76, 79*

Perfected models

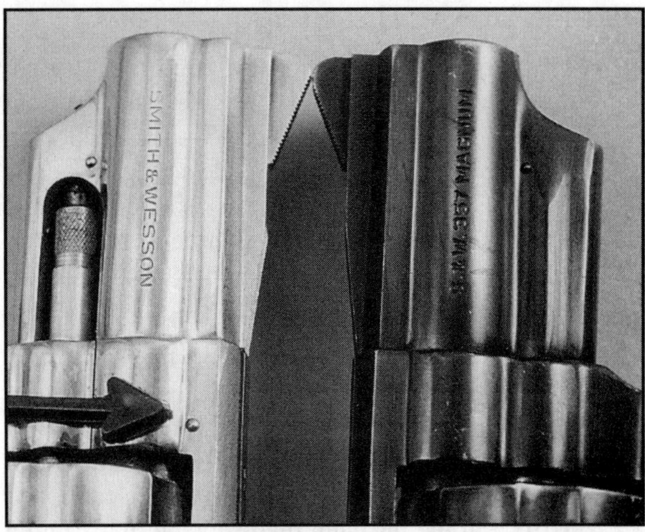

Pinned and non-pinned barrels

PERFORMANCE CENTER (PC): S&Ws in-house custom gunsmithing shop; performs special order custom work or develops special limited issue guns.

PIQUETTE: Paul Piquette, current S&W master engraver. *25-29*

PINNED: Usually refers to the method of attaching hand ejector barrels by pinning them to the frame, introduced about 1899 and discontinued about 1982 (pre-82 hand ejectors are often noted as "pinned and recessed," for this feature and recessed chamber heads). Also can refer to the method of attaching the front sight; in top-breaks, sometimes models will be differentiated by whether the front sight blade is pinned to the barrel or forged as an integral part of the barrel.

POCKET PISTOL: Term used for any small handgun that could be carried in a pocket. This terminology notwithstanding, it is an unsafe practice to carry a handgun loose in a pocket. There are pocket holsters made for this purpose that will enclose the triggerguard and position the gun properly in the pocket.

POCKET ROCKET: Slang for the Model 940 Centennial in caliber .356 TSW. *151*

POLICE ITEMS: *189, 190*

POLYMER: A high durability plastic type substance used for the frames of Sigma series semiautos. *175-177*

PORTED: Having vents cut in the top of the muzzle end of a barrel to reduce felt recoil.

POSTERS: *199-201*

POWER PORT: Type of barrel porting used by S&W Performance Center to reduce felt recoil.

PRAWL: Knuckle or bump in the top of the grip backstrap where the web of the thumb rests.

PRE-MODEL: Term used to identify a gun made before 1957 model numbers were introduced, but of a model continued as a numbered model. For example, an early .44 Magnum with no model designation in the yoke cut might be called a "Pre-model 29."

PREWAR/POSTWAR: Made before or after World War II (1940-1945). A key design change occurring during the war was the incorporation of a type of internal hammer block safety device designed to prevent accidental discharge of the gun if dropped on a hard surface. Most postwar guns will include this safety improvement.

PROMOTIONAL ITEMS: *202-204*

RAMP: A type of front sight that appears as a right triangle when viewed from the side, with the front face of the sight vertical and the rear face sloping down from muzzle end to provide a snag-free draw from holsters. The sight appears as a tall rectangle to the shooter and the face is usually serrated to reduce glare. The most common type of sight on modern S&Ws. *20*

RECESSED: Cylinder chambers where the rear portion has been counterbored to allow the entire cartridge, including the rim, to sit flush with the rear face of the cylinder. Originally used on both magnum and rimfire hand ejectors, the practice was discontinued in 1982 on the magnum revolvers, but is still used on rimfires.

Recessed and non-recessed cylinders

RECURVE TRIGGERGUARD: Seen on early models of the DA top-breaks; a triggerguard with a fairly vertical rear portion that curves forward toward the trigger.

RED RAMP (RR): A ramp front sight with a red rectangle insert. *20*

REGISTERED MAGNUM: The first .357 Magnum, introduced 1935, with such a wide range of buyer options that it was essentially a custom made gun. S&W would "register" the gun to the original purchaser, if desired, and issue a registration certificate. *89, 90*

REGULATION POLICE: An I (or later J) frame revolver, either a 6-shot .32 or 5-shot .38 S&W, with a square butt. *85-87, 96, 97, 122, 123, 197*

RELOADING TOOLS: *178, 189*

REVENUE CUTTER SERVICE (COAST GUARD NEW MODEL NUMBER THREE): *68*

REVOLVING RIFLE: *178*

RIB: A flat portion of the barrel above the bore. Presence or absence of a rib, and whether the rib is narrow or wide, can be a key to identifying certain early hand ejectors.

RIFLES: *178-180*

RIMFIRE: A cartridge with priming compound spun into the rim of the case head and detonated by the firing pin striking the rim. Still common in .22 cartridges only, early Model 3s were sometimes chambered for the old .44 Henry rimfire cartridge.

ROBINSON, MW: S&Ws largest distributor during the 1800s, New York based, and a common destination for revolvers of that era both for domestic sale and foreign export, including some government purchases. *18, 38*

ROLLIN WHITE: See "White."

ROUND BUTT (RB): Describes a grip frame with a slightly rounded bottom contour when viewed from the side; tends to be of a more consistent width for the entire length of the grip than "square butt" grip frames, which widen noticeably near the bottom.

RUSSIAN: Refers to the 1870s era large frame single action top-break revolvers that incorporated designs requested by the Russian government in their large military orders; or to the .44 Russian cartridge that was initially developed for the same Russian contract, but came to be the cartridge of choice for S&W big bore revolvers up to the turn of the century. The .44 Russian cartridge was noted for exceptional accuracy, and was lengthened to develop the .44 Special cartridge.

SAFETY HAMMERLESS: The .32 and .38 Safety top-break revolvers, featuring a "hammerless" (actually enclosed hammer) design and a grip safety; aka "New Departure" or "lemon squeezer." *42, 46, 47, 51, 52, 193*

SAN FRANCISCO POLICE (SCHOFIELD VARIATION): *64*

SCHOFIELD: .45 caliber single action Model 3 top-break designed for and used by the U.S. Army in the 1870s; the only large frame top-break with the latch mounted on the frame rather than on the barrel. *41, 43, 62-66*

SCOPE MOUNT (SM): A device for attaching a scope to a firearm.

SCREWDRIVERS: *19*

SECOND QUALITY: S&W found slight cosmetic casting flaws in the frames of some of their early tip-up revolvers. Combining typical Yankee thriftiness and commitment to quality rather than wasting these frames, the firm made them into revolvers, but marked the end product "2D QUAL'TY." Originally sold at a discount, today these scarce variations bring a premium from collectors. *38-40*

SELF LUBRICATING BULLET: Unusual late nineteenth century S&W ammunition in which firing the cartridge forced lubrication from inside the loaded round to the external surface of the bullet. *190*

SEMI-TARGET HAMMER (ST): Checkered hammer spur .375 inches wide, between the narrower standard hammer and the wider target hammer.

SERIAL NUMBER (S/N): The unique number identifying a specific individual gun. On S&W revolvers, usually found on the butt of the grip frame. On semiautos, usually found on the side of the frame. *15*

SERVICE: In a model name, usually designates a fixed sight model.

SERVICE TRIGGER: On modern revolvers, a narrow .265-inch wide trigger, usually serrated or grooved.

SHORTY FORTY: A compact version of the third generation .40 S&W semiautos, currently produced by the Performance Center for distribution through Lew Horton. *168, 186*

SHOTGUNS: *180-182*

SHROUDED EJECTOR: See "ejector shroud" above.

SHROUDED HAMMER (SH): The sides of the frame extend up, "shrouding" all but the tip of the hammer spur, to prevent snagging on clothing, but still allow the hammer to be manually cocked for single action fire. Used on the Bodyguard models.

SIDEPLATE: The removable plate on the side of a revolver that provides access to the inner mechanical workings. With its tight press fit, the sideplate should NEVER be pried loose. Instead, remove the screws and smartly tap the grip frame. The sideplate will pop loose. The sideplate is on the left side of all tip-ups and top-breaks, except the .38 Perfected, and on the right side of all hand ejectors and the .38 Perfected.

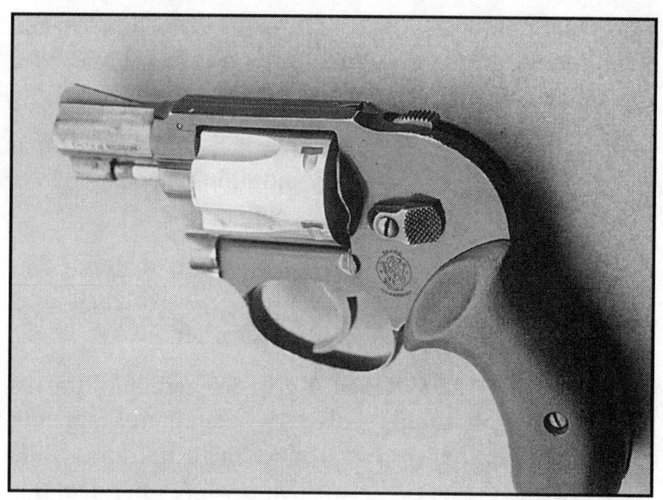

Shrouded hammer on Bodyguard model

SIDEPLATE, SQUARE or STRAIGHT EDGE or STRAIGHT CUT: Early configuration for DA revolver sideplate where the front and rear edge of the sideplate are relatively straight compared to later curved edges. Key to identifying .38 DA First Model, and very rare and desirable .32 DA First Model. See photo of .38 DA First Model. *49*

SIGMA: New line of polymer framed semiauto pistols; hinged trigger performs safety function, DAO type action, no external manually operated safety lever, no magazine disconnect safety. *7, 13, 175-177*

SINGLE ACTION (SA): A firearm in which the hammer must be cocked manually or, in the case of a semiauto, by the action of the slide, before it can be fired. Pulling the trigger performs only the "single action" of dropping the hammer (firing the gun). Pulling the trigger does not perform the "double action" of cocking the hammer and then dropping it.

SINGLE-SHOT: One shot. The gun does not have any device for holding additional ammunition and must be manually reloaded between shots. *74-76*

SKU (Stock Keeping Unit): The "product code" used by S&W to identify a particular variation of a particular model.

SLICK SLIDE (or slick side): A DAO semiauto with no safety or decocking levers on the slide.

SMOKELESS POWDER: Introduced around the turn of the century, smokeless powder was an improvement over black powder in that it produced less fouling and less smoke, and could produce high pressure, resulting in higher velocity and thus more power in any given cartridge case. Modern ammunition is loaded with smokeless powder and should never be fired in guns originally made for black powder cartridges.

SPEEDLOADER: An ammunition holding device that allows the user to quickly and simultaneously reload all chambers in a revolver cylinder.

SPEEDLOADER CUTS: Area where material has been removed from the top of a revolver's grip (stock) to allow use of a speedloader.

SPEGEL BOOT GRIPS: A grip design that improves handling of small revolvers without increasing bulk by filling the space in front of the grip frame while leaving the rear grip strap exposed. A version of this design produced in rubber by Uncle Mike's is currently used by S&W on many of their J frames. See photo of Model 442 page 137.

SPORTSMAN: Current production short barrel .22 semiautos. *165, 193*

SPUR TRIGGER: A revolver on which the trigger appears to project directly from the bottom of the frame as a spur, with no encircling triggerguard. Typical of all S&Ws earliest tip-up revolvers and most of their early single action medium (.38) and small (.32) frame top-breaks.

SQUARE BUTT (SB): A grip frame that becomes significantly wider near the bottom, with relatively sharp corners at the front and rear of the butt.

STAINLESS STEEL (SS, or sometimes "Stainless," abbreviated "S"): An alloy steel that is highly resistant to rusting and corrosion and requires no external finish (such as nickel plating or bluing) on a handgun. All stainless steel S&W revolvers have a model number beginning with "6," except for the Model 940 Centennial 9mm Stainless. Stainless steel is similar in weight to carbon steel, and either may be used as slide material in conjunction with an aluminum alloy frame to produce a lighter weight gun.

STRAIGHT LINE: The 4th Model Single-Shot, so called because both the trigger pull and the hammer fall are in a straight line parallel to the bore, as opposed to the arcing motion on the earlier revolver frame based single-shots. The Straight Line has an appearance more similar to a semiauto. 75, *76, 198*

STAR: When stamped next to serial number on butt, indicates factory rework.

SWCA (SMITH & WESSON COLLECTORS ASSOCIATION): *33*

SWING-OUT CYLINDER: Standard modern revolver configuration; a hand ejector with a cylinder that swings out of the frame for loading and unloading.

SYNTHETIC GRIPS (SG): Non-wood grips, usually made of rubber or plastic-like material.

TAKATA: The distributor through which S&W sold many revolvers to the Japanese military in the late 1800s. *67, 68*

TARGET HAMMER (TH): A hammer with a wide .5-inch spur. Usually slightly more turned down than a service hammer.

TARGET GRIPS (TG) or TARGET STOCKS (TS): Large oversized wood grips. Usually made of Goncalo Alves, except for walnut target stocks (WTS). *17*

TARGET MASTERPIECE: A post-1940 K frame revolver with the Masterpiece enhancements (see "Masterpiece"), and a barrel longer than four inches (usually six inches); usually square butt. *83, 96*

TARGET MODEL: Always implies adjustable sights, and may include other target options, usually with a six-inch barrel.

TARGET SIGHTS: Adjustable sights. *20*

TARGET TRIGGER (TT): A fat .400-inch wide serrated trigger.

TEAM S&W (TSW): A professional competitive shooting team briefly sponsored by the S&W factory in the late 1980s/early 1990s. Team members included Brian Enos, Jerry Miculek, J. Michael Plaxco, and Judy Woolley. Also refers to a cartridge, the .356 TSW, developed to allow sufficient energy to "make major" in IPSC style shooting while still allowing the maximum magazine capacity.

TEN RING TIPS: An old poster by S&W with shooting advice. *199, 201*

THREE PIRATES: An early S&W catalog, so called for the cover illustration. *195, 197*

THREE SCREW: The hand ejector frame configuration after about 1961 when the triggerguard screw was eliminated, leaving just the three sideplate screws (the rear of which is often hidden by the grips). *13*

THREE T'S: Shorthand for target hammer, target trigger, and target stocks.

.38/44: A .38 caliber revolver on a .44 sized frame. Also the name of two very different S&W cartridges—the relatively mild .38/44 target round for the top-break New Model #3 Target Model and the hot-

Lew Horton Specials in cal. .356 TSW from S&W Performance Center: Model 940, .356 Shorty, and .356 Limited

loaded .38/44 Super Police version of the .38 Special for the heavy framed .38/44 Heavy Duty and Outdoorsman hand ejectors. *69, 97, 98*

.38/32: A .38 caliber revolver on a .32 sized frame (Terrier and Regulation Police). *97*

.32/44: The .32 caliber New Model #3 Target Model, made on the .44 top-break frame, and the cartridge it chambered. *69*

THUMBPIECE: Located on the left rear of a revolver's frame, the thumbpiece is a latch that opens the cylinder. See also flat latch.

TIP-UP: A revolver with a hinge at the top rear of the barrel so that the barrel tips up in front of the cylinder for removal and loading/unloading. **Note:** While this is the most common usage among S&W collectors, some will refer to the revolvers we've called "top-break" as "tip-up." Forget you ever heard that usage, and we'll get along just fine. *36-40*

TOP-BREAK: A revolver with a hinge at the bottom rear of the barrel so that the revolver breaks open at the top and the barrel tips down. All S&W top-break revolvers automatically eject the shells when opened unless a lever near the bottom of the hinge is pressed while opening. *41-73*

TRADITIONAL DOUBLE ACTION (TDA): Semi-auto mode where the first shot is double action (a long heavy trigger pull cocks and drops the hammer) and subsequent shots are single action, with the hammer being cocked by the action of the slide after a shot is fired.

TRANSITIONAL: S&W doesn't waste parts. Never has. Never will. (Well, except for those pencil holders made out of cylinders ….) Accordingly, there often is not a clean break between model variations, and there are sometimes guns produced with some features of both old and new models. These are called Transitionals, and are often sought after by collectors due to their relative scarcity. Examples would include the Transitional Model American, with the straight bottom frame line of the First American and the interlocking hammer and latch of the Second American, or the Model 1-1/2 Transitional tip-up with the octagonal barrel and unfluted cylinder of the Old Model 1-1/2 and the birdshead butt of the New Model 1-1/2.

TRIPLE LOCK: The .44 Hand Ejector, 1st Model, so called because the cylinder locked up at three points rather than the usual two. *101, 102*

TRIGGERGUARD SPUR: A finger rest of dubious utility added to the rear of Second and Third Model Russian triggerguards, and available by special order on the New Model #3. Cowboys, being sensible, often chopped 'em off. See photos on pages 60 and 69.

TRITIUM: Slightly radioactive glow-in-the-dark material used for most night sight inserts.

TURKISH MODELS (RIMFIRE MODEL THREES MADE FOR TURKEY): *61, 62, 69*

TWELVE REVOLVERS: Special set of twelve hand ejectors, each with a unique configuration and a scene from a different turn of the century S&W poster, issued one a month through Ellett Brothers distributors. *184-186*

UNFLUTED CYLINDER: See "fluted cylinder."

U.S. AMERICAN: A group of one thousand First Model Americans purchased by the U.S. government in 1871. The first cartridge revolver adopted by the U.S. military. *56-59*

VICTORY MODEL: .38 M&P K frames produced during WWII, mostly for military usage, with a V (for Victory), VS, or SV serial number prefix. *93, 94*

VOLCANIC: A lever action tubular magazine handgun and rifle produced by the first S&W partnership in the early 1850s. Predecessor of the Winchester lever action rifles. *37, 198*

WELLS FARGO: This colorful Old West express company purchased a number of cut barrel Schofields to arm their messengers, and these guns show Wells Fargo markings on the ejector housings. *63, 64*

WESSON FAVORITE: A rare variation of the .44 DA featuring patent markings on the cylinder instead of the top of the barrel, a groove down the barrel rib, and lightening cuts on the frame below the cylinder. *71*

WHITE OUTLINE (WO): A white outline on three sides of the rear sight blade, preferred by some shooters to enhance the visibility of the sight.

WHITE, ROLLIN, PATENT: 1854 patent for a cylinder bored through end to end, necessary for an effective metallic cartridge revolver. S&W purchased the rights to use the patent, and thus gained a virtual monopoly of the cartridge revolver market through 1872. *37, 42*

WINANS: Walter Winans was a world champion target shooter of the late 1800s, and a front sight of his design with a bead notched into a semi-circular blade bears his name. *20, 66, 70*

WIPERS: Cleaning rods packaged with S&W handguns. *19*

WONDER-NINE: A high capacity double action semiauto.

XENOY: Synthetic material used for third generation semiauto grips.

YOKE: The piece that connects the cylinder of a hand ejector to the frame.

YOKE CUT: The cutout in the frame where the yoke rests when the cylinder is closed. The model number of modern hand ejectors is stamped in the yoke cut.

YOUNG: Gustav Young and his sons, Oscar and Eugene, were some of the greatest engravers of the 19th century. S&W hired Gustav away from Colt to be their head factory engraver, and his sons succeeded him in this role. *22, 25-27, 29, 180*

Z BAR: The type of latch, pushed sideways to open, used on the First Model .38 Safety. *51-52*

Z bar release

The following firms and organizations have graciously assisted the authors in compiling information for this book:

M/Sgt. C.H. Benjamin USAF Ret.
1023 Ridgewood Avenue
Holly Hill, FL 32117

Ernie Lyles, Manager
Gilbert - Small Arms Range, Inc.
8195-M Backlick Road
Lorton, VA 22079

Clark Brothers Guns
Route 5, Box 100
Warrenton, VA 22186

The Blue Ridge Arsenal
Chantilly, VA

Professional Armaments, Inc.
4555 S. 300 W., Suite 200
Murray, UT 84107

Terry Clokey
The Treasure Island Armory
Fairfax, VA

William R. Powell
Firearms Consultant and Appraiser
P.O. Box 186
Roanoak, TX 76262

Mr. Bob Coyle
Lew Horton Distributing Co., Inc.
15 Walkup Drive, P.O. Box 5023
Westboro, MA 01581

Mr. Ken Jorgenson
Smith & Wesson
Springfield, MA

The authors welcome comments. If submitting a correction or addition, please include documentation.

Richard Nahas
SMX Systems
PO Box 66
Manassas, VA 20110

Jim Supica
Old Town Station, Ltd.
PO Box 15351
Lenexa, KS 66285
Phone 913-492-3000
Fax 913-492-3022
E-mail "OldTownSta@aol.com"